WBI DEVELOPMENT STUDIES

The Right to Tell

The Role of Mass Media in Economic Development

The World Bank
Washington, D.C.

Contents

PART II: WHAT ENABLES THE MEDIA

PART III. WHAT THE MEDIA SAY ABOUT THE MEDIA

Foreword

Over 1.2 billion people live on less than a dollar a day. And many of these poor people not only suffer from physical and human deprivation but also lack voice in decisions that affect their lives. Moreover, corruption and weak governance corrode aid effectiveness. Undoubtedly, there has been progress on these challenges, but development is a complex issue involving actions on several fronts. A key ingredient of an effective development strategy is knowledge transmission and enhanced transparency. To reduce poverty, we must liberate access to information and improve the quality of information. People with more information are empowered to make better choices.

For these reasons, I have long argued that a free press is not a luxury. It is at the core of equitable development. The media can expose corruption. They can keep a check on public policy by throwing a spotlight on government action. They let people voice diverse opinions on governance and reform, and help build public consensus to bring about change. Such media help markets work better—from small-scale vegetable trading in Indonesia to global foreign currency and capital markets in London and New York. They can facilitate trade, transmitting ideas, and innovation across boundaries. We have also seen that the media are important for human development, bringing health and education information to remote villages in countries from Uganda to Nicaragua.

But as experience has shown, the independence of the media can be fragile and easily compromised. All too often governments shackle the media. Sometimes control by powerful private interests restricts reporting. Low levels of literacy, human capital, and technology can also limit the positive role the media can play. And we have seen the impact of irresponsible reporting and manipulation—witness the devastating effects of war propaganda in Rwanda. It is clear that to support development, media need the right environment—in terms of freedoms, capacities, and checks and balances.

The World Development Report 2002 *Building Institutions for Markets* devoted a chapter to the role of the media in development. This volume is an extension of that work. It is an important contribution to our understanding of how the media affect development outcomes under different circumstances and it presents evidence on what policy environment is needed to enable the media to support economic and political markets and provide a voice for the disenfranchised. To this end, it draws together the views of academics as well as perspectives from those on the front line—journalists themselves. The book will be of interest to policymakers, nongovernmental organizations, journalists, researchers, and students.

This publication supports the work that the World Bank is doing on transparency and governance, and it complements the ongoing efforts of the World Bank Institute, which provides training for journalists in investigative reporting in over 50 countries. It also supports the work of our External Affairs Department, which cooperates with governments to shape effective development communication.

Looking forward, this book is one of a series of steps that the World Bank, together with its partners, will take toward building a more transparent world and accountable government.

JAMES D. WOLFENSOHN

PRESIDENT
THE WORLD BANK GROUP

About the Contributors

This book is a continuation of the work carried out for the *World Development Report 2002: Building Institutions for Markets*. It was prepared by a team led by Roumeen Islam and comprising Simeon Djankov and Caralee McLeish. Alice Faintich was responsible for copyediting and John Didier for oversight of the publishing process.

Mahfuz Anam is the editor in chief of the *Daily Star*, a Bangladeshi newspaper.

Timothy Besley is a professor of economics at the London School of Economics and director of the Suntory and Toyota International Centres for Economics and Related Disciplines.

Robin Burgess is a lecturer in economics at the London School of Economics and the director of the Programme for the Study of Economic Organisation and Public Policy at the Suntory and Toyota International Centres for Economics and Related Disciplines.

Tim Carrington is a senior public information officer at the World Bank Institute in Washington, D.C.

Mark Chavunduka is a former editor with *The Standard*, Zimbabwe's leading independent newspaper.

Kavi Chongkittavorn is executive editor of *The Nation*, the leading English-language newspaper in Thailand.

Simeon Djankov is a senior economist with the Private Sector Advisory Services of the World Bank.

Alexander Dyck is an associate professor of business and government at the Harvard Business School.

Gabriel García Márquez is a journalist and writer and the winner of the Nobel Prize for Literature for 1982.

Edward Herman is Professor Emeritus of finance at the Wharton School of the University of Pennsylvania.

Roumeen Islam is manager of the Poverty Reduction and Economic Management Unit at the World Bank Institute.

Hisham Kassem is editor of the *Cairo Times*, an English-language news magazine in Egypt.

Peter Krug is a professor of communications law at the University of Oklahoma, College of Law.

Caralee McLiesh is an economist with the Private Sector Advisory Services of the World Bank.

Adam Michnik is the editor-in-chief of *Gazeta Wyborcza*, Poland's leading daily newspaper.

Victor Muchnik is editor-in-chief of the television station TV2 in Tomsk, Russia.

Yulia Muchnik is a journalist with the television station TV2 in Tomsk, Russia.

Mark Nelson is a program manager for the World Bank Institute's operations in Paris.

Tatiana Nenova is a financial economist at the Private Sector Advisory Services of the World Bank.

Bruce Owen is president of Economists Incorporated, a consulting firm specializing in microeconomic analysis.

Andrea Prat is a lecturer in economics at the London School of Economics and a member of the editorial board of the *Review of Economic Studies*.

Monroe Price is the founder and co-director of the Programme in Comparative Media Law and Policy at Oxford University, United Kingdom, as well as the Joseph and Sadie Danciger Professor of Law at the Benjamin N. Cardozo School of Law at Yeshiva University, New York.

Robert Shiller is the Stanley B. Resor Professor of Economics at Yale University.

Andrei Shleifer is the Whipple V. N. Jones Professor of Economics at Harvard University and the winner of the 1999 John Bates Clarke Award.

Joseph Stiglitz is a professor of finance and economics at the Graduate School of Business, the School of International and Public Affairs, and the Economics Department at Columbia University and winner of the Nobel Prize for Economics for 2001.

David Strömberg is a research fellow at the Institute for International Economic Studies, Stockholm, Sweden.

Ruth Walden is a professor and director of graduate studies at the School of Journalism and Mass Communication, University of North Carolina at Chapel Hill.

Luigi Zingales is the Robert C. McCormack Professor of Entrepreneurship and Finance at the University of Chicago, Graduate School of Business.

1

Into the Looking Glass:
What the Media Tell and Why—An Overview

Roumeen Islam

The media industry, whether public or private, plays an important role in any economy by garnering support or opposition for those who govern, by highlighting or failing to do so the views and/or sins of industry, by providing a voice for the people or not doing so, and by simply spreading economic information. For their ultimate survival the media depend on the state that regulates them, on the firms that pay to advertise through them, and on the consumers they serve. Balancing these different interest groups is a difficult task. How the media industry does so determines not just its ability to survive, but its effect on economic performance. This book is about the factors that determine whether and how the media industry can support economic progress.

Clearly as important providers of information, the media are more likely to promote better economic performance when they are more likely to satisfy three conditions: the media are independent, provide good-quality information, and have a broad reach. That is, when they reduce the natural asymmetry of information, as Joseph Stiglitz puts it in chapter 2, between those who govern and those whom they are supposed to serve, and when they reduce information asymmetries between private agents. Such a media industry can increase the accountability of both businesses and government through monitoring and reputational penalties while also allowing consumers to make more informed decisions.

This book cites many examples that demonstrate the value of information provided by the media. Alexander Dyck and Luigi Zingales (chapter 7) discuss how the media can pressure corporate managers and directors to behave in ways that are socially acceptable, thereby avoiding actions that will result in censure and consumer boycotts. They also report that in Malaysia, a recent survey of institutional investors and equity analysts asked which factors were most important to them in considering corporate governance and the decision to invest in publicly listed corporations. Those surveyed gave more importance to the frequency and nature of public and press comments about companies than to a host of other factors considered key in the academic debate. However, the dissemination of credible information in a timely manner depends critically on how the media business is managed and regulated. The chapters in this book document evidence on media performance and regulations in countries around the world and highlight what type of public policies and economic conditions might hinder the media in supporting economic development in poor countries.

Before discussing the three criteria for effective media—independence, quality, and reach—I would like to draw attention to two general issues pertinent to the themes of the chapters in this volume. The first is the relationship between free media and democracy. It seems obvious that generally, more democratic countries also have a freer press, as figure 1.1 shows, but do free media promote greater democracy or does a functioning democracy promote free media? Undoubtedly the effect can work both ways, and there are degrees of media freedom and democracy. Even among democratic countries, the level of freedom of the media varies between countries, and even relatively undemocratic states may differ in their tolerance of media freedom. For example, two democracies, Russia and the United States, have quite different

Figure 1.1. Freedom of the Press and Democracy

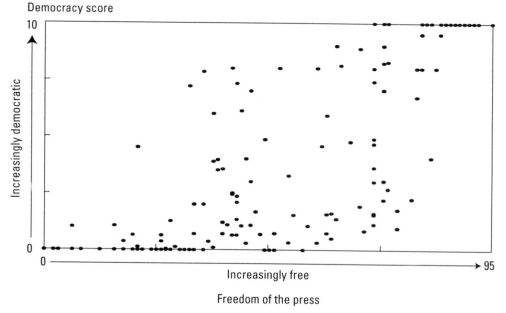

Source: Freedom House (n.d.).

attitudes toward the media and the concept of media freedom. In addition, within the same democracy certain types of news coverage may be unregulated while other types may be regulated, for example, economic news may be less regulated than purely political news. Freedom of the press is also correlated with income: richer countries seem to value information more, but there is variation. Colombia, Portugal, and Ukraine have similar measures of democracy but quite different measures of press freedom.

The second issue I would like to address concerns the general relevance of laws and formal regulations for the independence, quality, and reach of the media. In many circumstances laws affecting the media sector have only limited relevance. In addition, adopting a law is no guarantee that it will be implemented or effective. This is partly because implementing a law is much more difficult that simply adopting it. Also informal codes of conduct may be in conflict with laws and dilute their effectiveness. In most countries the freedom and independence of the media are guaranteed not solely by laws, but by the culture or accepted mores of society. Thus while the United Kingdom has had a rather restrictive Official Secrets Act (until 1989 even the type of biscuit served to the prime minister was a secret), the British media rank highly on any measure of freedom: Freedom House gives the United Kingdom a score of 80 out of 100 on its index of press freedom.

Changes in media freedom are affected by changes in culture and expectations, just as culture and expectations can be changed through information provided by the media. In countries where the media have had a long tradition of independence and are well-established businesses, legal restrictions mandated by arbitrary governments are hard to maintain over time. Nascent media face the greatest challenge. In countries where information has always been scarce or kept secret, several effects work against the media, namely: (a) the potential value of more information is underestimated or not well understood; (b) the public perceives that information alone will not help, because coalitions strong enough to make use of the available information do not exist; and (c) the weak financial state of the media and their shaky consumer base make the industry vulnerable. Nevertheless, each of these elements can be expected to improve slowly over time.

The evidence suggests that legal systems are important. Governments have manipulated laws and legal systems to legitimize their actions against the media, but also to safeguard the rights of the media. Journalists have used laws to protect their right to know and tell. Sometimes a law is important because even though governments may not deliberately withhold information, it is not readily available because it is not required to be in an accessible format. Laws promoting greater freedom of expression and information can be useful even when all parties are not convinced of their relevance. Merely the act of adopting a law can limit certain abuses and can build expectations of what is permissible and what is not, particularly if the judiciary is effective and independent. Adopting laws brings freedom of information issues to the forefront of public discussion, and can result in genuine change. As Kavi Chongkittavorn explains in chapter 14, Thailand's adoption of the Freedom of Information Act has encouraged people to ask the government for information, in essence changing expectations and behavior. In contrast, as Mark Chavunduka discusses in chapter 17, Zimbabwe's government has adopted several laws with the intention of silencing the press. According to Hisham Kassem in chapter 16, however, innovative media entrepreneurs often find ways to operate around the laws that bind them.

In the remainder of the overview I have organized the discussion around the three main factors affecting media performance mentioned earlier: independence, quality, and reach.[1]

Independence and Quality

Independence refers to the media industry's ability to report information it receives without undue fear of being penalized. It also refers to a media industry that is not controlled by any interest group, but still has access to necessary data. No media outlet can be completely independent: even when the government does not directly penalize unfavorable news, it can refuse to provide information about good stories. Stiglitz notes the mutual dependence of those who leak information to the media and the media. Leaks are important, because they get otherwise secret information into the public domain, but they also allow public officials to shape news coverage in ways that advance their own interests and causes.

The quality of the media is a difficult thing to assess, or even to describe. Here high-quality media are defined as those with access to and the capacity to report (more or less) objectively on basic economic, social, and political information; those that can express a diversity of views and are accountable for the information they publish; and those that have the capacity to analyze the information obtained for its news value and "truth." In chapter 13 Gabriel García Márquez defines the "best" news as that which is not always the news that is obtained first, "but very often the news that is best presented." Edward Herman's definition of objectivity (chapter 4)—a key element of quality—is "first . . . presenting a variety of sides to a story, searching out facts without political constraint, and presenting those fairly and impartially; and second, deciding what is newsworthy on the basis of consistently applied news values, unaffected by a political agenda or biased by ideological premises or compromised by strategic or profitability considerations."

Independent media may nonetheless take sides on an issue or be unable to produce credible reports. Given their potential to affect the behavior of a large number of people or of a few key players, the media can raise or diminish issues in the public

---

1. Some of the material is also discussed in World Bank (2001).

eye, and therefore affect the distribution of benefits in society. Influence of this type needs to be subject to checks and balances, as discussed later. High-quality media have greater power to influence consumers of information: Dyck and Zingales report that in the Republic of Korea it was the *Financial Times'* reporting of insider dealings at SK Telecom that lent credibility to the story, because it is more reputable than the local newspapers.

Several factors determine the independence of the media, namely:

- The ownership structure of the media
- The economic structure of industry, economic conditions, and the availability of financing
- The laws regulating access to information, production of information, entry into the media industry, and content
- The policies regarding industries related to the media.

Notions of quality and independence are linked, for example, quality can be compromised by media dependent on concentrated sources of financing. For this reason they are discussed together. Two additional factors are relevant for quality:

- The training and capability of journalists and of those who manage the media business
- The checks and balances on journalists and people in the media industry.

Ownership

Ownership of the media confers control over the nature of the information disseminated. Proponents of public ownership of the media argue that because information is a public good—that is, once it has been supplied to some consumers it is hard to keep it away from others who have not paid for it—private owners tend to provide less information than would be socially desirable. They also argue that with private ownership the media industry runs the risk of representing the views of only a narrow group in society,[2] and state ownership of the media is necessary to expose the public to desirable cultural or educational themes or values and to ensure that broadcasts of locally produced content in local languages are available.[3]

---

2. Because of the large, potential nonfinancial benefits of owning media outlets, both public and private owners have incentives to control media firms through concentrated ownership in the media industry.

3. In the Netherlands a 1998 act requires that public service programming be at least 25 percent news, 20 percent culture, and 5 percent education. Italy requires that 50 percent of broadcasting be of European origin. Most of the benefits attributed to public ownership can also be achieved with private ownership and public regulation.

Opponents of public ownership argue that government control of the media can be used to manipulate people and distort the information supplied in the incumbent government's favor. Moreover, experience shows that government-owned enterprises (and presumably media enterprises are like other enterprises in this regard) are less likely to be responsive to consumer demand. Finally, government-owned media are not subject to competition, thus giving rise to the danger of both poor-quality production and inefficiencies. A recent article on the British Broadcasting Corporation (BBC) (*Economist* 2002a) claims that government ownership makes it harder than it would otherwise be for other media companies to grow. The article claims that the large amounts of tax revenue that are given to the BBC gives it an advantage relative to private companies. It also contends that as a private company, the BBC would be more dynamic, and therefore better able to compete with global media firms.

There are problems with both sides of the argument when faced with realities in developing countries, but the problems inherent in managing public enterprises effectively may bias the scales in favor of private ownership. In many countries, even "autonomous" public agencies have a difficult time remaining truly autonomous and operating on a level playing field. This is particularly so in developing countries. Private media firms that have close links with business or government are also in danger of distorting information. Moreover, if they do not face competition they may be as guilty as government owners of ignoring consumer preferences. In Italy for example, control over the media by a few families has been the subject of significant discussion and controversy. Herman claims that where the mainstream media are privately owned and are funded almost entirely by commercial advertisers as in the United States, they align with the corporate community, in particular the larger players, who are hostile to antibusiness messages. While agreeing that the news media may bias public policy, in chapter 6 David Strömberg claims that increasing returns to scale in news production undermine the political power of special interest groups and minorities and enhance the political power of large groups. News production by private profit-oriented producers should therefore favor large groups.

Recent research by Simeon Djankov, Caralee McLiesh, Tatiana Nanova, and Andrei Shleifer, reported in chapter 8, indicates that ownership of media firms tends to be highly concentrated. Firms are mostly owned by the state or families, and widely dispersed ownership structures are infrequent. Moreover, the percentage of total firms controlled by the state is high, especially in developing countries. On average, the state controls about 30 percent of the top five newspapers and 60 percent of the top five television stations in these countries. The television audience for privately-owned television stations in Belgium, France, and Japan accounts for 56 to 60 percent of the total market. In Australia 83 percent of the audience watches privately-owned television stations, and in Canada 66 percent of the audience does so. In the industrial countries newspapers are mostly privately owned. In many poor countries such as China, Egypt, and Malawi the state controls all television. Poorer countries and countries with more autocratic governments are more likely to have high state own-ership of the media. Djankov and others find that high levels of state ownership reduce the effectiveness of the media in providing checks and balances on public sector behavior and are negatively correlated with economic and social outcomes.

To encourage independent reporting many countries, such as the Netherlands and the United Kingdom, have created independent or autonomous state media agen-cies that are charged with providing public interest programs that the private sector might not offer, but are allowed to operate without political interference. For ex-ample, the BBC is state owned, and its board of governors, appointed by govern-ment officials, is accountable to the government. However, the BBC's charter establishes it as an independent corporation and guarantees it freedom from govern-ment interference in the content and timing of its broadcasts and in the management of its internal affairs.

In theory, a system of checks and balances could be built into the design of au-tonomous state media agencies to insulate them from undue influence by either the government or business, but the issue of whether private agencies would face "un-fair" competition still remains, that is, whether the public agency would receive pref-erential treatment such as subsidies. Another issue is that the independence of such agencies can be eroded over time in countries where a well-developed system of checks and balances on the state does not exist. In 1981 the Zimbabwean government established the publicly-owned but politically independent Mass Media Trust to manage Zimpapers, the only national newspaper chain. Yet the government has twice dismissed the entire board in retaliation for unfavorable media coverage, and it now regularly intervenes in decisions regarding content.

Where the state does not dominate the market, but accounts for only a relatively small share, it is less likely to stifle private media. Defining the relevant market, however, is not always simple. If newspapers and broadcast and electronic media all serve the same audience but the state is only dominant in one area, competition from private sources in the market for news may be sufficient. If the market is segmented according to the type of media considered (newspapers, television, radio, electronic) and the population's income group or education levels, then dominance in one area is more likely to have negative effects, irrespective of whether the dominance is by publicly-owned or privately-owned media. People who cannot read will not buy newspapers and will only get their information from the radio; however, if their neighbors or relatives can read and transmit information, this factor is mitigated.

Privatization, with all its flaws, is a potential solution for assuring arms-length (from government) reporting. In Mexico, for example, the privatization of broadcast-ing in 1989 substantially increased the coverage of government corruption scandals. This greater coverage contributed to a 20 percent increase in the private station's market share, forcing the government-owned station to cover these issues as well. The privatization of state-owned media in transition countries supported by broader market liberalization and knowledge transfers from foreign owners with experience in journalism has generated dramatic increases in the coverage of economic and financial news (Nelson 1999). In chapter 9 Bruce Owen contends that in general, the privatization and deregulation of electronic mass media has increased competition and reduced concentration.

What does this say for the choice between privatizing and creating autonomous public agencies? Privatization can wrest control of information flows from the government, but privatization and subsequent regulation need to be approached carefully to avoid monopoly control of information. The case for creating autonomous state agencies is weakened if one considers that autonomy may be easily eroded and that regulation and public financing allocated on a competitive basis for "socially desirable" programs could achieve similar results. In any case, a dominant role for the state is hard to justify.

Economic Structure and Financing

How nonmedia industries are structured and the government's overall economic policies have significant effects on the media's independence and performance. The harassment of Russia's private media, which are critical of the government, by Gazprom, a gas company in which the state has significant ownership stakes and influence, is a case in point. Where state-owned firms dominate the economy even private media can have difficulty surviving without state support. In describing the history of the Bangladeshi media sector, Mahfuz Anam (chapter 15) mentions that even privatizing the media industry will not solve the problems of bias if the only advertisers, and thus the financiers, are state-owned enterprises, or even a select group of private firms. In some countries the choice may be about choosing the lesser of two evils.

As Bruce Owen (chapter 9) and Tim Carrington and Mark Nelson (chapter 12) point out, the survival of the media as a business—often under adverse economic conditions—takes priority. If the business does not survive, then quality is not an issue. In many fledgling economies new, small firms can provide a sufficient source of financing for the media, as evidenced by the case of TV2 in Tomsk, described by Victor and Yulia Muchnik in chapter 19. Overall economic policies will determine the entry and survival of such firms. Connections and networks can be important too. In the case of TV2, the start-up costs were financed with the help of a loan from a domestic bank. These entrepreneurs had access to credit because their loan was guaranteed by the chairman of the Tomsk city council, a friend.

Carrington and Nelson point to the importance of foreign investment in helping new media companies stand on their feet in developing countries. Under a new regime in 1991, the government newspaper *Rzeczpospolita* in Poland was deprived of public funds, told to be independent, and thrust into a failing economy. Its survival was ensured by foreign investment: the French Hersant newspaper group bought 49 percent of the company and helped upgrade its technology and printing plants. Similarly, in the Slovak Republic the Media Development Loan Fund backed a private newspaper, and in addition a strong private sector had emerged to support the media industry.

A competitive market structure (as well as sources of financing) promotes diversity and provides checks on quality. According to Stiglitz, the most important check against abuses by the press is the presence of a competitive press that reflects a variety of interests. Owen points out that the content that best serves those media owners whose goal is power and influence is not, in general, the same content required for commercial success, and perhaps therefore for survival in a competitive market environment. This might be interpreted as meaning that a more competitive environment can limit the abuse of power by media owners.

Licensing media enterprises can be an effective way to control content and limit competition.[4] Licensing restrictions may be explicit, prohibiting certain kinds of broadcasts, or implicit, as when the government might not renew licenses unless it perceives the broadcasting content as favorable. For the newspaper industry, unlike for television and radio broadcasting, licensing is not needed for technical reasons. The primary purpose of licenses for newspapers is to allow governments to influence information flows by limiting entry.[5] In the case of Korea, soon after licensing regulations were liberalized the number of daily newspapers in Seoul alone grew from 6 to 17, and dozens more were launched in other parts of the country. Moreover, a diversity of voices found expression, with opposition, progovernment, business, sports, and church papers competing with one another (Heo, Uhm, and Chang 2000; Webster 1992). In some countries, such as Ethiopia, newspapers renew newspapers' licenses annually following payment of a renewal fee. Licensing is contingent on proof of solvency, which requires all current and prospective newspapers to maintain a bank balance of Br 10,000 (US$1,250) as collateral against any offenses their journalists might commit. Publications that fail to prove solvency at the start of every year or whenever requested to do so by the Ministry of Information and Culture lose their license (Committee to Protect Journalists n.d.).

---

4. For television some form of licensing broadcasters is needed to define property rights for the limited broadcasting frequencies; however, many governments extend licensing systems beyond what is required for technical reasons, including imposing restrictions on the content of broadcasts.

5. Some argue that licensing serves the public interest by encouraging responsibility and standards in reporting. Opponents counter that licenses allow regulators to prevent the employment of journalists who might cover the government unfavorably. International courts have supported the latter argument. In 1985, in a landmark case concerning an uncertified journalist in Costa Rica, the Inter-American Court of Human Rights found that licensing journalists contravened the American Convention on Human Rights.

Entry restrictions come in other forms too. As Kassem reports, extensive registration requirements with uncertain delays led journalists in Egypt to set up their offices offshore. Furthermore, journalists were not allowed to become union members, and therefore to receive certain health benefits, unless they worked for a government newspaper. More than a third of Latin American countries regulate journalists through licensing or accreditation procedures (see the Inter-American Press Association database at http://www.sipiapa.org).

Aside from the regulatory structure, the media business confronts forces that favor monopolies on the one hand, and other forces that favor producer diversity on the other, as described by Owen. First, the production of mass media content is characterized by enormous economies of scale, which tends to favor large firms. Second, advertising to large circulations is more efficient than advertising to small ones. However, a third basic characteristic is that output is heterogeneous: firms compete by differentiating their output, because different people have different tastes. This means that smaller companies can differentiate their content and find a niche. New, small firms seeking a niche may be more likely to diversify than larger, older ones.[6] For example, local newspapers may specialize by having more local content (which also means that they often cannot effectively compete in other localities). Owen cites the example of Ulaanbaator in Mongolia, which could probably not have supported 18 principal newspapers in 1994 if these had not been sharply differentiated along political and other lines.

Technology, infrastructure, and geography also limit the scale of newspapers and affect the nature of market competition, because they affect transport costs and delivery delays. These barriers are more easily breached by broadcast media, hence even the United States had national radio and television networks long before it had national newspapers. In Africa, where the state of technology is less developed and literacy is low, private radio stations seem to be booming (*Economist* 2002b). In Uganda, for example, those villages that in 1985 had 10 community broadcasting stations now have 300 or more.

One disadvantage that developing country governments face is their limited ability to enforce competition policy where such safeguards are needed. Some countries, both industrial and developing, prohibit or limit the cross-ownership of competing media in an effort to ensure greater diversity of sources of news and opinion. As Owen states, media concentration raises concerns if it results in monopoly or facilitates collusion leading to increased prices and reduced output. Aside from competition and diversity in content, concentration among media outlets in a given city might raise economic competition issues with respect to certain advertisers even if

---

6. Owen argues that large quasi-monopolies also pay attention to diversity to ensure their survival.

numerous other vehicles, such as television, the press, magazines, and online ser-vices, are available for the expression of ideas, including political dissent. Assessing anticompetitive behavior is always a difficult task, and the appropriate agencies in developing countries often lack the necessary skills and resources.

Legal Structure

Two types of legal institutions are critical to the performance of the media, namely, (a) those that determine access to information, and (b) those that constrain how the media use the information they obtain. The media industry's ability to report is con-strained by the amount and type of information—on public and private agencies and on general economic conditions—to which it has access through either formal or informal channels. As Dyck and Zingales point out, information disclosure that is mandated by the government is the most reliable, because it is not affected by selec-tivity, and is not provided in exchange for something. Informal or unregulated ways of obtaining information include interviewing contacts or getting information from those who want to present a particular point of view to the public. Here I will restrict my comments to the formal process of obtaining information.

Information flow is regulated by a variety of laws that may give wide or preferen-tial access to critical data. Laws regulating disclosure of company accounts or access to individuals' credit history determine how frequently and easily the media can obtain "formal" information about such matters. Laws regulating information dis-semination to the private sector are generally established to enable markets to work smoothly and to improve the enforcement of various other legislation, but market responses also depend critically on information mainly available in the public sector. Stiglitz argues that the information gathered by public officials at public expense is owned by the public, and that using that intellectual property for private use is just as serious an offense against the public as any other appropriation of public property for private purposes.

Starting with the constitution, several legal arrangements determine the condi-tions under which private individuals and private or public agencies obtain access to "public" information. In many countries their constitution broadly delineates the basic rights of individuals to freedom of speech and sometimes to access to informa-tion. Supporting laws may come under a variety of names, depending on the coun-try. Yet even with these basic rights outlined, actually getting information in a timely manner (in an interval short enough to be useful to those who demand it) is difficult, because laws have to be implemented, people have to be trained and given the incen-tives to respond swiftly, and the information has to be available in a readily acces-sible and understandable format.

Many countries have adopted freedom of information laws and others are in the process of doing so. The objective of such laws is to provide a framework that defines the degree of access to public information and the rights of individuals and organizations to obtain such information. The adoption of a freedom of information law can signal the government's commitment to transparency. It can also encourage private agents to ask for more information, as explained by Chongkittavorn in the case of Thailand. Currently about 46 countries have freedom of information laws, and the numbers are increasing daily; however, few poor countries have such a law, and surprisingly, only about 54 percent of high-income countries do (Islam forthcoming).[7] Table 1.1 shows some simple correlations between a freedom of the press indicator and an indicator of journalist abuse with the existence of a freedom of information law. The existence of a freedom of information law is negatively correlated with high state ownership of the media abuse of journalists and significantly positively correlated with press freedom.[8]

While adoption of a freedom of information law is an important initiative, a critical question is how does a country implement it? One option is setting up a separate agency whose sole concern is to deal with requests for various types of information, or alternatively each government department or agency may be provided with specific guidelines relating to the provision of information. Once the agency and personnel are identified, institutions need to be designed so that requests for information are attended to promptly. Additional considerations are designing the format in which the information is distributed and the associated fees required for access.

In Portugal, the Commission for Access to Administrative Documents is responsible for deciding whether to grant requests for information involving certain official documents, as well as deciding what documents may be shared among the branches of government, hearing appeals, establishing a system of document classification, and monitoring the proper application of the Access to Administrative Documents Law and other similar legislation (see http://www.infocid.pt/infocid/2092%5F1.asp). In Latvia each government agency or public institution is required to publish a summary of all generally available information in the public register. No single independent agency oversees the implementation of the Freedom of Information Law, and the process of access to information is governed by separate legislation that describes the procedures for reviewing proposals, complaints, and submissions. Appeals for denial of access are possible, and must initially be made to the director of the respondent institution (see http://www.delna.lv/english/legal_norms/ln2.htm).

However, the public sector produces a great deal of information that can readily be made available without a freedom of information law. All countries produce some information on basic economic outcomes; however, it may vary in terms of quantity,

---

7. I am using the World Bank definition of high-income countries, where high per capita income is defined as US$9,266 or more.

8. Note that correlation does not prove causality. Perhaps those countries where the press is initially free are more likely to adopt freedom of information laws to validate that freedom.

Table 1.1. Correlation of Freedom of Media Variables

Category	Freedom of press	State ownership of press	Freedom of information act	Journalist abuse
Freedom of press	1			
State ownership of press[a]	−0.64 (0)	1		
Freedom of information act	0.36 (0)	−0.49 (0)	1	
Journalist abuse[b]	−0.5 (0)	0.157 (0.163)	−0.2 (0.03)	1

Note: Numbers in parentheses are p-values for the correlation coefficients (the lower the p-value, the stronger the association between the two variables).
a. This variable is an average of the ownership variables constructed by Djankov and others (2001).
b. Weighted index of journalists killed or pressured media.
Source: Freedom of the press: Freedom House (n.d.); freedom of information act dummy: compiled by the author from various sources; state ownership of the press: Djankov and others (2001); journalist abuse: Reporters Sans Frontiéres (2000).

quality, frequency, and ease of access.[9] Cameroon provides even basic data such as gross domestic product (GDP), foreign trade statistics, foreign direct investment, and government finances with a lag of several years. By contrast Armenia, also a low-income country, provides up-to-date information, with reasonable frequency, on most major economic or financial statistics, suggesting that collecting and disseminating such information is not necessarily a function of income. Of more than 200 countries around the world, the central banks of around 100 countries have web sites that publish information, though their quality and timeliness vary significantly.

Other laws restrict the use of information obtained. The purpose of defamation and insult laws, discussed by Peter Krug and Monroe Price in chapter 10 and Ruth Walden in chapter 11, is generally to protect individuals from abuse by the media. While some form of these laws is needed to protect the reputations of individuals and ensure the accuracy of reported news, they can also be used to harass journalists, thereby encouraging self-censorship by the media (Walden 2000).

With respect to the design of such laws three main issues stand out: (a) when libel is a criminal rather than a civil offense, journalists lean toward self-censorship;

9. Such data are available in the International Monetary Fund's *International Financial Statistics*, government web sites, government publications, or the World Bank's *World Development Indicators*. Note that these sources are not considered easily available to those without access to these documents who cannot purchase or borrow these publications or do not have access to the web sites.

(b) when truth is not a defense for libel, journalists have incentives to limit their investigations; and (c) when laws provide protection against libelous statements about matters of public interest and require individuals to show that defamatory statements are knowingly or recklessly false and made with malicious intent, these favor journalistic freedom. Governments may also censor information through legal requirements for prepublication or prebroadcast reviews by government agencies. The natural incentive for journalists under these circumstances is to engage in self-censorship as a way of avoiding suspension.

Policies Governing Industries Related to the Media

Industries with direct links to the media include the paper and distribution industries. Even with free and independent media, if distribution is strictly regulated by the government, then the independence of the media can suffer. The government can also use price controls and taxes on inputs to disrupt operations, and the regulatory structure and condition of infrastructure can restrict media operations. For example, the Internet often provides a source of competition for domestic media and allows easy access to global media; however, in many countries Internet connections are difficult to maintain and expensive because the telecommunications sector is not developed. Moreover, although cybercafes are becoming more popular, in many countries access to computers is still limited.

Training and Capacity of Media Personnel

In many developing countries media personnel lack technical expertise, thereby hampering economic and political reporting. This includes both the skills of those directly involved in researching, analyzing, organizing, and writing or broadcasting the news and the managerial skills necessary to sustain the enterprise as a profitable business. As in other businesses, managerial skills may be learned over time, but training can help, particularly by exposing managers to decisionmaking and production techniques used in other countries. As Muchnik and Muchnik report, in the case of the Tomsk TV station, the appearance of foreign consultants in Russia in the early 1990s was extremely helpful, and foreign advice on managing advertising and production were critical to the station's success. Similarly in Poland, foreign investment helped bridge the management and skills gap.

What is arguably more difficult is reporting on economic and financial issues. Some sort of training can significantly enhance analysis of these issues by journalists. Poor analysis will fail to capture the more discerning readers and may misguide the less discerning ones. But hiring media personnel with the appropriate skills, even when possible, may not be a profitable undertaking unless a large enough audience of the discerning type exists. Exposing corruption or wrongdoing, however, does not necessarily require much understanding of the details of the relevant transactions. For example, bribe taking by government officials can be exposed without understanding how it may have affected economic outcomes. Marquez argues that people who are self-taught tend to be avid and quick learners and that any kind of education for journalists should focus on three key areas: determining aptitude and vocation, establishing that all journalism must be research oriented, and stressing the importance of ethical standards.

Checks and Balances

While an independent media sector is a desirable outcome, every agency or organization needs some checks and balances. Many in the media business see the role of the media as defenders of the truth and a voice for the people. Márquez (chapter 13) and Adam Michnik (chapter 18) both discuss the glory of the journalism profession, but also the need for journalists to be incorruptible, honest, and unprejudiced. Unfortunately, human nature being what it is, we sometimes fail to maintain the high standards that we aspire to attain. Without checks and balances to ensure accountability and a sense of responsibility, the media can abuse their power. As Muchnik and Muchnik point out, the abuse of power may come about from an unclear understanding of what journalism is about. They discuss how they freely participated in politics, taking sides, until they realized the difference between being dedicated to ideas and forming political alliances with specific individuals, and that good-quality journalism means maintaining a certain distance from politicians.

As Robert Shiller (chapter 5) and Timothy Besley, Robin Burgess, and Andrea Prat (chapter 3) point out, the media not only disseminate information, but can also manipulate public opinion and raise issues to unprecedented levels of importance or "salience" in the public eye. They can accelerate the rate at which news is transmitted, influence to whom it is transmitted, and affect the type of action taken in a given situation. They may not report all sides of an issue. Sometimes media actions can support greater transparency, but there is no guarantee that they will automatically do so. The desire to bring in new and exciting news can overwhelm the desire to "tell it as it is." Unfortunately, the bias toward sensationalism exists in all types of news media, including the more reputable ones, though one could argue that these tendencies are more muted the more reputable the source. One automatic check to abuse of power is the loss of influence over time if abuse is sustained.

An appropriate legal system attempts to balance free speech against abuse by the media. Another institutional solution is the establishment of self-regulation councils. Self-regulatory bodies are well established in some industrial countries, but they are only beginning to emerge in developing countries. Among the latter, Guyana and Tanzania are establishing self-regulatory press councils that will determine codes for honesty, fairness, respect for privacy, and general standards of taste. Councils use such codes to guide their decisions on complaints against the media. In many cases the councils replace traditional court processes. In Australia, for example, complainants are required to sign a declaration that they will not take their complaint to court if they are dissatisfied with the council's decision..

Certain factors determine the success of these councils. First, the decision to set up such councils needs to originate with the press itself and be desired by members of the press. Governments, nongovernmental organizations, or other interested parties can encourage the establishment of such councils. Governments might do so by promising lighter regulation in exchange for their creation. Supporting institutions, such as civil society organizations for media freedom and responsibility, can reinforce the work of councils. Second, press councils need to carry sufficient weight with the individual media organizations that media firms feel obliged to comply with their decisions (International Center against Censorship 1993, Article 19). This may be achieved in many ways, for example, council members may publicly ostracize those who do not abide by the council's decisions. Third, such councils require leadership and a genuine desire among the media profession to improve on their work. Fourth, designing ethical guidelines that balance media freedom and responsibility is critical. Fifth, to maintain legitimacy, standards have to be applied consistently..

Effective and independent judicial systems and other mechanisms that penalize undesirable behavior can complement the role of the media in improving governance, though an independent judiciary is insufficient to restrain arbitrary actions by the state. An independent judiciary can help protect journalists' rights, can help ensure that action is taken on matters exposed by the media, and can protect individuals from abuse by the media. In Zimbabwe, for example, the courts have had some success in protecting journalists' rights as discussed by Chavunduka. In the Philippines the media's exposure of toxic waste dumped by foreign military forces led to a congressional investigation, then to an official government investigation, and eventually to government enforcement of orders to discontinue the dumping.

Reach

Reach refers to the audience: how much access do people have to the print, electronic, or broadcast media? Media with reach have relevance for and bring news to most of the population. The effect that the media have on society depends to a large extent on whom they reach. The reach of newspapers, television, and radio varies a great deal across countries, with income being closely correlated with media penetration. Dyck and Zingales argue that newspaper readership numbers capture both the diffusion of newspapers and some measure of their overall credibility. That is, if newspapers were not credible, they would not be read. They find that ownership concentration has a negative and statistically significant effect on diffusion of the press and on the private sector's responsiveness to information disseminated by the media. Table 1.2 shows the diversity of penetration and circulation rates among countries at different income levels. While the high-income countries of Denmark, Japan, and the United States all have high levels of media penetration, Chad, Ethiopia, and Zambia, all low-income countries, vary widely in terms of media penetration. Botswana and Thailand have similar levels of GNP per capita, but differ markedly in the distribution of television sets.

On average, residents of industrial countries are more than 25 times more likely to receive a daily newspaper than residents in African countries; however, according to the World Association of Newspapers (2001), in many African countries , the average newspaper is read by as many as a dozen people. In villages in Bangladesh and Nepal newspapers are read out loud so that many others benefit in addition to the subscriber. While literacy does play a role in the disparity in measured circulation between countries, it is just one of the factors affecting the spread of the press. Both GNP per capita and literacy are lower in Ecuador than in Panama or Paraguay, but newspaper circulation is greater in Ecuador. Tradition or culture may also affect how people perceive different media: some cultures may be less television bound than others or less print bound than others at similar levels of GDP per capita. The state of infrastructure may also account for the differences.

Table 1.2. Media Penetration Diversity, Selected Countries

Country	Number of televisions/ 1,000 people, 1999	Newspaper circulation/ 1,000 people, 1996	GNP per capita, average 1994–98 (US$ thousands)
Bolivia	118	55	2,143
Botswana	21	27	5,486
Chad	1	1	898
China	292	42	2,644
Denmark	772	311	21,376
Ethiopia	6	2	573
Germany	580	311	19,536
India	75	27	1,882
Japan	719	580	20,952
Korea, Republic of	361	394	12,333
Malawi	3	3	614
South Africa	128	30	7,943
Syrian Arab Republic	67	20	3,041
Thailand	279	65	5,541
United States	854	212	28,567
Zambia	145	14	659

Source: Newspaper circulation: UNESCO (1999); television numbers: International Telecommunications Union database (http://www.itu.int/ITU-D/ict/publications/world/world.html) and "World Telecommunications Development Report" (http://www.itu.int/ITU-D/ict/publications/wtdr_02/index.html); GNP: World Bank (2002).

Table 1.3. Regressions on Newspaper Circulation

Category	1	2	3	4
GNP per capita, averaged over 1991–95	1.12*** (13.6)	.80*** (8.24)	.76*** (7.58)	.64*** (6.89)
Illiteracy rate, averaged over 1991–95		−.03*** (−6.89)	−.03*** (−6.15)	−.02*** (−5.7)
Ethnic diversity	−.88** (−2.88)		−.50* (−1.70)	.19 (.75)
Africa				−.94*** (−5.05)
Constant	−5.17*** (−6.73)	−2.11** (−2.46)	−1.57* (−1.77)	−.70 (−.89)
R^2	.78	.80	.81	.84
Number of observations	96	79	76	76

* Significant at the 10 percent level.
** Significant at the 5 percent level.
*** Significant at the 1 percent level.
Source: GNP: compiled from World Bank databases; illiteracy rate: UNESCO (1999); ethnic diversity fractionalization index: Taylor and Hudson (1972); state ownership of newspapers: Djankov and others (2001).

Formal regression analysis indicates (table 1.3) that newspaper circulation is negatively related to illiteracy and income. This relationship is statistically significant. The Africa region has significantly lower circulation than other regions even after accounting for income and literacy differences. Illiteracy does not seem to affect television penetration rates in the same way as ethnic diversity does, though one might expect that in a multilingual context, there may be less demand for certain media if they cater to the main language. European countries and countries of the Organisation for Economic Co-operation and Development have higher television penetration rates than other countries even after accounting for income and ethnic differences (table 1.4). Dyck and Zingales find that a country's cultural tradition affects diffusion of the press.

Television viewers do not have to be literate, but they do need costly equipment, technology, and electricity. This puts television beyond the reach of many people in developing countries, with one caveat. If just one person in a community or village has a television, many others will have access to it. Radio broadcasting is cheaper, does not require electricity, and can be transmitted to remote areas to people who do not know how to read. Not surprisingly, radio receiver penetration is higher than other media penetration in all regions, and radio is the primary medium for reaching citizens in many developing countries. According to Strömberg in chapter 6, the radio

Table 1.4. Regressions on the Television Penetration Rate

Category	1	2	3	4
GNP per capita, averaged over 1994–98	.07*** (5.43)	.13*** (12.41)	.09*** (6.12)	.08*** (5.66)
Illiteracy rate, averaged over 1994–98	−.002*** (−3.12)		−.0003 (−.58)	−.0001 (−.29)
Ethnic diversity		−.08** (−2.46)	−.08** (−2.29)	−.06* (−1.87)
Europe[a]				.09** (2.24)
Constant	−.56*** (−4.10)	−.85*** (−9.06)	−.56*** (−4.1)	−.53*** (−3.88)
R^2	.58	.69	.58	.61
Number of observations	98	135	98	98

* Significant at the 10 percent level.
** Significant at the 5 percent level.
*** Significant at the 1 percent level.
a. Dummy variable.
Source: GNP: compiled from World Bank databases; illiteracy rate: UNESCO (1999); television penetration: International Telecommunications database (http://www.itu.int/ITU-D/ict/publications/world/world.html) and "World Telecommunications Development Report" (http://www.itu.int/ITU-D/ict/publications/wtdr_02/index.html).

broke rural isolation in the United States and increased the political power of rural counties. Strömberg finds that radio and television changed the political strength of different groups by affecting who was informed. In particular, minorities and those with little education gained from the introduction of television in the 1950s.

The difference between the reach of radio and of other media is far greater in developing than in industrial countries, with income and literacy affecting both supply and demand. To overcome demand constraints related to income, in the Democratic Republic of Congo and Nigeria, newspaper vendors charge people a fraction of the sales price to read the newspaper at the stand. International donors can play an important role in this context, and have supported telecenters that provide public access to a range of media and communications facilities in remote areas.

Higher media penetration does promote greater responsiveness by public and private agents as demonstrated by Dyck and Zingales and Besley, Burgess, and Prat. The latter look at media access in different states in India, within country comparisons having the advantage of adjusting for different political and economic systems in different countries. and find that government allocations of relief spending and public food distribution during natural disasters have been greater in states with higher newspaper circulation. The greater local presence of media allowed citizens to develop a collective voice, and the effect was greater for newspapers in local languages (Besley and Burgess 2000).

Even in countries with relatively low penetration rates, media actions can have significant consequences for a large number of people. For example, in Kenya, despite a low newspaper penetration rate of 9 per 1,000 people, the local press instigated a corruption investigation that led to a minister's resignation. In addition, by reaching influential coalitions that can affect financial or macroeconomic policies the media can affect the lives of the general population.

Government policies can also improve media access. Removing barriers to entry for new media enterprises, such as licensing requirements, would be a first step. Innovations by community groups and nonprofit organizations have also succeeded in increasing media penetration in poorer countries. Nonprofit foundations have significantly increased access to community radio in developing countries through wind-up radios and satellite technology. These services have proved especially important in delivering information about health and education issues. They have also provided a channel for residents of remote communities to voice their concerns and share information with other communities. Finally, investment in infrastructure and appropriate regulation that ensures access to infrastructure can go a long way toward increasing the reach of the media.

Foreign News Media

In an increasingly globalizing world the foreign media may also affect domestic outcomes. They may do so through two channels: (a) by influencing domestic opinions and coalitions; and (b) by influencing foreign opinions and coalitions, which then pressure their governments or international organizations to undertake actions that affect the country in question. Allowing the entry of foreign news media into domestic markets can immediately begin to ease the monopoly on news that characterizes some economies. For example, the state-owned *Herald Online* reported that Tanzania's recent elections were peaceful, free, and fair. By contrast, the Associated Press reported that ruling party representatives chased voters away from polling stations.

While foreign media reporting within a host country may seem more independent, over time their independence is usually eroded in conditions where the domestic media are severely curtailed. While foreign media may be subject to similar restrictions and harassment, in some cases they can complement the domestic media. For instance, harassment of foreign journalists attracts a great deal of unpleasant attention from the international community. Foreign journalists from high-income countries may also be better trained, be less vulnerable to domestic volatility (for example, if the parent company can tide them through bad times), have better management (see chapters 12 and 19), and be good competition for domestic media. Knowledge transfers from foreign owners with experience in journalism can generate dramatic increases in the coverage and quality of news. Finally, foreign or global media enable access to information on issues not reported by local media, as evidenced by countless examples of citizens first receiving news of domestic political crises through the foreign media.

Surprisingly, local news produced for the local market by foreign media is limited, and a World Bank (2001) project showed that foreign ownership is still relatively low. Across 97 countries studied, although most permit foreign ownership of the media, only 10 percent of the top five newspapers and 14 percent of the top five television stations are controlled by foreigners in these countries (chapter 8). The reasons for this low share could be either low profitability resulting from a small market share and few advertising revenues, or in some cases from government restrictions.

On the negative side, many feel that global media conglomerates may create unfair competition and take over the media market in developing countries. Like multinationals in other fields these firms, by virtue of their sheer size and superior financial condition, easily become dominant players in some markets. This can indeed stifle competition and the government may need to employ such regulations as restricting market share. Many also feel that an influx of foreign media tends to destroy the local culture. As Owen points out, in a competitive world the economics of mass media do not favor the survival of languages or cultures that are not supported by large populations or substantial specialized economic demand. This simply reflects the superior ability of such media to deliver consumer satisfaction at an attractive price rather than cultural imperialism. Regardless of the reasons for the success of global media, concerns that local culture important to long-term social welfare may be eroded can be dealt with by requiring cultural programming some of the time; however, these concerns need to be weighed against what the people in the market demand.

Conclusion

As has been aptly demonstrated around the world, the media influence economic, political, and social outcomes. By doing so, whether or not the outcomes support economic development depends on a variety of factors, many of which are discussed in this volume. The information industry, in which the media play a key role, tends to develop faster in democratic societies that generally foster freer information flows. However, the media industry can also promote greater degrees of freedom and stronger democracies over time. While each affects the other, the important question for those who are involved in designing policy is what types of discreet steps might be taken to establish and maintain free and independent media. This is a concern for all countries, rich and poor. Arbitrary actions by government are always to be feared. If there is to be a bias in the quantity of information that is released, then erring on the side of more freedom rather than less would appear to cause less harm.

Even nascent media in countries with nondemocratic and arbitrary governments stand a chance. Progress may occur in small steps, and may even be reversed temporarily, but if the people fight for a free press, there is hope. At some point the media reach and sustain what one might call a critical or threshold level of freedom when the people have become accustomed to this freedom, and constraints on this freedom are no longer possible.

In looking to shape policy so that it enables and supports the media to give voice to the people, the importance of research, study, and data gathering, common to work in other fields, has usually been underestimated. The development history of the media in countries with independent media gives clues as to what types of legal arrangements and coalitions have succeeded in bringing about change in countries. It is undeniable that laws advancing free speech matter: adopting a law in itself changes behavior. Yet how formal laws are enforced in different countries depends partly on the culture in which they are entrenched, that is, people's expectations and norms. Because of the limitations of legalistic approaches, the emphasis must be on creating a culture of openness where the presumption is that the public should know about and participate in all decisions that affect their lives.

While the legal framework defines certain rights, so does the ownership structure. Evidence indicates that the ownership structure of media firms and the nature of the owner, whether business or state, can clearly affect how and what information is disseminated. Economic conditions and overall industry structure also determine how the media perform.

A government wishing to truly expand the reach of the media can further this objective by enhancing competition, reducing restrictions on entry, and encouraging and participating in innovative ways to reach people. Establishing journalism schools or engaging with outside agencies to help train journalists is another avenue. Finally, there is no substitute for the voice of the people. If the people want and work for a more transparent and efficient economy, then they must fight for the freedom of those who disseminate information. They must fight for the right to know and the right to tell it like it is.

References

Besley, Timothy, and Robin Burgess. 2000. "The Political Economy of Government Responsiveness: Theory and Evidence from India." Working Paper. London School of Economics, Department of Economics, London.

Committee to Protect Journalists. n.d. Available on: http://www.cpj.org/attacks00/africa00/Ethiopia.html.

Djankov, Simeon, C. McLiesh, T. Nenova, and A. Shleifer. 2001. "Who Owns the Media." Working paper. National Bureau of Economic Research, Cambridge, Massachusetts.

Economist. 2002a. "Free TV—Britain's Media Bill." May 11.

———. 2002b. "Media Freedom in Africa—Watch What You Say." May 11.

Freedom House. n.d. Freedom of Press Index. http://www.freedomehouse.org/research/pressurvey.htm.

Heo, Chul, Ki-Yul Uhm, and Jeong-Heon Chang. 2000. "South Korea." In Shelton A. Gunaratne, ed., *Handbook of the Media in Asia.* New Delhi: Sage Publications.

International Center against Censorship. 1993. "Article 19." In *Press Law and Practice: A comparative Study of Press Freedom in European and Other Democracies.* London: United Nations Educational, Scientific, and Cultural Organization.

Islam, Roumeen. Forthcoming. "Do More Transparent Governments Govern Better?"

Nelson, Mark. 1999. "After the Fall: Business Reporting in Eastern Europe." *Media Studies Journal* 13(5): 150–57.

Reporters Sans Frontiéres. 2000. *Annual Report 2000.* Available online: http://www.rsf.fr.

Taylor, Charles Lewis, and Michael C. Hudson, with the collaboration of Katherine H. Dolan and others. 1972. *World Handbook of Political and Social Indicators.* New Haven, Connecticut: Yale University Press.

UNESCO (United Nations Educational, Scientific, and Cultural Organization). 1999. *Statistical Yearbook.* Paris.

Walden, Ruth. 2000. "Insult Laws: An Insult to Press Freedom." World Press Freedom Committee, Reston, Virginia.

Webster, David. 1992. "Building Free and Independent Media." Freedom Paper no. 1. United States Information Agency, Washington, D.C.

World Association of Newspapers. 2001. *World Press Trends 2001.* Paris: Zenith Media.

World Bank. 2001. *World Development Report 2002: Building Institutions for Markets.* New York: Oxford University Press.

———. 2002. *World Development Indicators 2000.* Washington, D.C.

Part I

HOW THE MEDIA SUPPORT MARKETS

2

Transparency in Government

Joseph Stiglitz

Government is supposed to act in the interests of citizens. When alternative policies will affect different groups differently, it is supposed to identify the tradeoffs, that is, who benefits and who loses from these alternative programs. Government is not supposed to use its enormous powers to benefit its leaders or special interests at the expense of the general public.

Should voters know that the government had violated this trust, they would typically vote them out of office, yet often governments clearly do not act in the general interest, no matter how loosely we define that. To be sure, often specious arguments are put forward for why what reflects special interests is really in the general interest, and frequently the public will accept those arguments. Economic issues, in particular, are complex, and given the disagreements that exist among economists, no wonder that others may find that distinguishing among various arguments is difficult. However, many government officials go even further and try to keep what they do secret, that is, away from the glare of public scrutiny.

There is a natural asymmetry of information between those who govern and those whom they are suppose to serve, much akin to the asymmetry of information that exists between company managers and shareholders. The 2001 Nobel Prize was awarded to George Akerlof, Michael Spence, and me for our work that explored the economic implications of asymmetries of information, but such asymmetries of information also arise in connection with political processes and have important consequences in that realm. Just as such asymmetries give managers the discretion to

This paper draws on Stiglitz (1999). I am greatly indebted to David Ellerman for his insights, and especially his knowledge of the historical debates concerning secrecy, and to Roumeen Islam for suggestions concerning the links between the media and transparency. Financial support from the Rockefeller Foundation, the Ford Foundation, the MacArthur Foundation, and the Swedish Agency for Development Cooperation are gratefully acknowledged.

pursue policies that are more in their own interests than in the interests of shareholders, so they allow government officials the discretion to pursue policies that are more in their interests than in the interests of the citizenry. Improvements in information and the rules governing its dissemination can reduce the scope for these abuses in both markets and in political processes. In markets analysts and auditors play an important role in providing information. In the United States Securities and Exchange Commission regulations require the disclosure of certain types of information.[1] This chapter discusses information imperfections and asymmetries in political processes and the role of the media, especially in promoting transparency in the public sphere. It also argues that an appropriate legal framework should be in place that enables the media to obtain information and insulates it from undue harassment. To understand the role of the media, however, we must first understand public officials' incentives for secrecy.

While one can view free speech and a free press as ends in themselves—an inalienable right that governments cannot strip away from the citizenry—this chapter approaches these issues from an instrumentalist perspective, that is, as a means to achieving other equally fundamental goals. Free speech and a free press not only make abuses of governmental powers less likely, they also enhance the likelihood that people's basic social needs will be met. Sen (1980), for instance, has argued that countries with a free press do not experience famines, because the free press draws attention to the problem, and people will view a government's failure to act in such situations as intolerable. These examples highlight the role of information as part of governance processes. Similarly, work at the World Bank and elsewhere has shown, for instance, how pollution disclosure requirements can be an effective mechanism for curbing pollution levels (for an overview see World Bank 1998). Public opinion can force governments, especially democratically elected governments, to take some actions and circumscribe them from taking other actions.

An important insight of modern information theory is that in many respects information is a public good. Whatever relevance the knowledge of, say, the balance of payments has for the actions of various participants in the economy, the use of that information has a zero marginal cost. As in the case of other public goods, government has an important role in the provision of information. In a modern, complex economy, contrary to the standard theories of conventional (pre-information theory) economics, prices do not convey all the relevant information. Firms and households may care a great deal about information on the growth of the economy, the unemployment rate, or the inflation rate. Each month they eagerly await the release of the new data, which governments typically collect.

---

1. That is, there is the belief, based both on historical experience and economic theory, that market participants may not willingly disclose all the relevant information. Edlin and Stiglitz (1995) showed that managers had an incentive—and the means by which—to increase the asymmetries of information that existed between themselves and outsiders.

This information not only affects the decisions of private agents, for instance, with respect to production or investment, but also affects people's judgments about the government. If data suggest that unemployment is soaring, they will be concerned that the government is mismanaging macroeconomic policy. If data suggest that inequality is increasing, then their concerns about distribution policies and whether the government is doing enough to help the poor will be heightened. Thus the government sometimes has an incentive to distort or limit information. Sometimes the beneficiaries of distorted information may not be the government directly, but particular groups in whose interest it works. For instance, if retirees' social security benefits depend on measured increases in living costs or if wages increase with measured increases in living costs, measurements that exaggerate those increases in living costs benefit retirees or workers. In recognition of the incentives for providing distorted information, governments need to, and in some cases have already, set up institutional structures that limit the potential for abuse. Thus it may be important that statistical data be collected by independent statistical agencies rather than by agencies with close connections to particular interest groups.

An old expression maintains that what gets measured gets attention. A huge number of variables exist that could be monitored in principle, but monitoring is costly and the scope for attention is limited. Thus government has an incentive to choose to monitor variables that reflect its agenda or the agenda of the special interests that it might be serving, and not to monitor variables that are adversely affected by that agenda. For example, in the United States the Reagan administration attempted to suppress the collection of statistics related to inequality and poverty, and currently some quarters are resisting the construction of a green gross domestic product accounting system, which would take into account the deterioration of the environment and the depletion of natural resources.

While the analysis of information asymmetries has shed new light on the relationship between those governing and those governed, the basic insights have long been part of the thinking about democratic processes. In democratic societies citizens have a basic right to know, to speak out, and to be informed about what the government is doing and why and to debate it. Democratic societies have a strong presumption in favor of transparency and openness in government. But there has also long been recognition that on their own, governments and their leaders do not have the incentive to disclose, let alone to disseminate, information that is contrary to their interests. More than 200 years ago Sweden enacted what was probably the first set of laws enhancing transparency in the public domain.

The Rationale for Openness

Francis Bacon pointed out that knowledge itself is power. Secrecy gives those in government exclusive control over certain areas of knowledge, and thereby increases their power. It is thus not surprising that the issue of secrecy in matters of public affairs has long been a source of public concern (see Bok 1982 for a comprehensive overview). The arguments against secrecy cohabit with the arguments against censorship and in favor of free speech (see Emerson 1967, 1970 for a survey). James Madison, the architect of the First Amendment of the U.S. Constitution guaranteeing the right of free speech, captured the crux of the argument: "A people who mean to be their own governors must arm themselves with the power that knowledge gives. A popular government without popular information or the means of acquiring it is but a prologue to a farce or a tragedy or perhaps both" (letter from James Madison to W. T. Barry, August 4, 1822, cited in Padover 1953 and also quoted in Carpenter 1995).

Jeremy Bentham based his constitutional system on the motive of "personal interest corrected by the widest publicity"(1838–43, vol. iv, p. 317) and took publicity as the principal check against misrule.[2] In his famous essay, *On Liberty,* John Stuart Mill (1859) held that subjecting arguments to public scrutiny was unconditionally beneficial and provided the most assured way of sorting out good arguments from bad ones.[3] In *Considerations on Representative Government,* Mill (1861) extended the argument to emphasize the virtues of popular participation.[4]

Essentially, meaningful participation in democratic processes requires informed participants. Secrecy reduces the information available to the citizenry, hobbling people's ability to participate meaningfully. Anyone who has sat on a board of directors knows that its power to exercise direction and discipline is limited by the information at its disposal. Management knows this, and often attempts to control the

---

2. "Without publicity, all other checks are fruitless: in comparison of publicity, all other checks are of small account. It is to publicity, more than to everything else put together, that the English system of procedure owes its being the least bad system as yet extant, instead of being the worst" (Bentham 1838-43, vol. iv, p. 317; also quoted in Halévy 1972).

3. Mill argues as follows: "The peculiar evil of silencing the expression of an opinion is, that it is robbing the human race; posterity as well as the existing generation; those who dissent from the opinion, still more than those who hold it. If the opinion is right, they are deprived of the opportunity of exchanging error for truth; if wrong, they lose, what is almost as great a benefit, the clearer perception and livelier impression of truth, produced by its collision with error" (see Mill 1859, p. 205, 1961).

4. "As between one form of popular government and another, the advantage in this respect lies with that which most widely diffuses the exercise of public functions; . . . by opening to all classes of private citizens, so far as is consistent with other equally important objects, the widest participation in the details of judicial and administrative business; as by jury trial, admission to municipal offices, and above all by the utmost possible publicity and liberty of discussion, whereby not merely a few individuals in succession, but the whole public, are made, to a certain extent, participants in the government, and sharers in the instruction and mental exercise derivable from it" (Mill 1861, 1972, p. 325).

flow of information. We often speak of government being accountable to the people, but if effective democratic oversight is to be achieved, then the voters have to be informed: they have to know what alternative actions were available and what the results might have been. Those in government typically have far more information relevant to the decisions being made than those outside government do, just as the management of a firm typically has far more information about the firm's markets, prospects, and technology than do shareholders, let alone other outsiders. Indeed, managers are paid to gather this information.

One might argue that in a society with a free press and free institutions, little is lost by having secrecy in government; after all, other sources of relevant information are available. Indeed, recognizing the importance of information for effective governance, modern democratic societies try to protect the freedom and independence of the press and endeavor to promote independent think tanks and universities, all to provide an effective check on government. The problem is that government officials often represent the only or major source of relevant and timely information. If officials are subjected to a gag order, then the public has no real effective substitute. This is true both with respect to discussions of policy and of data (information), because much of the information that is collected is itself a public good. If the government does not provide the data, no one will, or they will be supplied in insufficient quantity. Governments that are engaged in policies that have the effect of increasing inequality will not want data that show the policies' adverse effects on inequality to become known, at least until the policies are solidly into place. Similarly, policymakers often believe that if they can establish a consensus behind a particular policy in secret, then it will be better able to withstand opposition, but that public disclosure of the direction that the consensus is taking before the consensus has been formed will create sufficient public pressure to prevent that particular consensus, or possibly any consensus, from emerging.

To reiterate, openness is an essential part of public governance. Hirschman (1970) described exit and voice as instruments for discipline in organizations. For members of public organizations, that is, citizens, exit is typically not an option, and therefore greater reliance is placed on voice. In the private marketplace how a firm organizes itself—whether it keeps secrets or not—makes little difference. Customers care about its products and prices, and regardless of how the firm organizes production, if it produces good products at low prices it will succeed. Transparency issues arise of course. Firms often lack the incentive to disclose fully the attributes of their products, and government, accordingly, enforces a variety of disclosure requirements, including truth in advertising, disclosure requirements for loans, disclosure requirements for firms raising new capital publicly, and fraud laws (for a discussion of market incentives for disclosure and the need for government intervention see, for example, Grossman 1981; Stiglitz 1975a,b, 1998).

However, public organizations are not subjected to the same kind of discipline. It is only through voice—through informed discussion of the policies being pursued—that effective governance can be exercised. Because public agencies have an effective monopoly in many of their operating areas, exit is not an option. Consider the difference between doctors in a community that has many physicians and doctors who are the only source of medical care in the community, that is, they have a monopoly. The sole doctor might be tempted to blame the patient when a prescription fails to work by claiming that the patient did not follow the instructions exactly. By contrast, in a community where there is competition among doctors, those whose prescriptions fail to help their patients will eventually end up with a tarnished reputation and their patients will exercise "exit." If there were a single doctor dispensing treatment the doctor might well try to control information. He or she might argue that doing so is necessary to maintain confidence in his or her cures (and because of the placebo effect there may even be a grain of truth in the argument). The doctor knows that competitive pressure will not force him or her to disclose information, because exit is not an effective option.

In all organizations, imperfections of information create agency problems. As a result important disparities may be apparent between, say, the actions of managers and the interests of shareholders. Similarly, in the public sector agency problems may give rise to a disparity between, say, the actions of those governing and those they are supposed to serve. The lack of an exit option may exacerbate the consequences of these agency problems. Obviously, improvements in information can reduce the magnitude and consequences of these agency problems.

The Importance of Openness for Democratic Processes

The previous section presented the traditional arguments for openness, but there are further arguments relate to the more direct impacts of secrecy on democratic processes and participation.

In the private sector management often attempts to control information to limit the ability of shareholders and their elected directors to exercise discipline. By creating information asymmetries managers can create barriers to the entry of outside managers and to takeovers (Edlin and Stiglitz 1995; see also Shleifer and Vishny 1989). By doing so they can increase their managerial rents at the expense of shareholders. The same is true of public managers, namely, elected officials. If outsiders have less information, voters may feel less confident that they will be able to take over management effectively. Indeed, outsiders' lack of information increases the costs of transition and makes it more expensive for society to change management teams. The fact that the alternative management teams have less information means that any proposal they put forward has a higher probability of being ill-suited to the situation. By increasing the mean cost of transition and the subjective variance, secrecy puts incumbents at a distinct advantage over entrants.[5]

By the same token secrecy undermines participation in democratic processes even by voters. Voters are more likely to exercise independent judgments—both to vote and to vote independently of a party—if they feel confident about their views, and this in turn requires that they be informed. Becoming informed implies a cost. Voters have a threshold, that is, a limit to the amount of time and energy they are willing to invest in pursuit of the public interest. Secrecy raises the price of information by inducing more voters who do not have special interests not to participate actively, leaving the field more open to those with special interests. Thus not only do special interests exercise their nefarious activities under the cloak of secrecy, but the secrecy itself discourages others from providing an effective check on the special interests through informed voting.

In addition, secrecy may discourage potential competitors, not only because it reduces their prospects of success in the voting process, but because it increases their own subjective uncertainty about whether they can improve matters. How often have officials been elected on a particular platform only to discover that the budgetary situation is far worse than they had envisioned, forcing them to abandon all their plans and engage in a budget balancing act for which they may have neither a comparative advantage nor a passion?

The adverse effects are, however, even more pervasive. While maintaining secrecy may be in the interests of the government as a whole, it may not be in the interests of particular individuals. Indeed, this is what gives rise to the problem of leaks. As in the case of other forms of collusive behavior, individuals have incentives to deviate. If a secret is shared among a number of individuals any of the individuals can reap the scarcity rents for themselves by disclosing the information to the press. If the decisionmaking process is closed, and especially if it is driven by special interests, those who genuinely disagree with the decision may feel that the only way that a "better" decision will be made is to open up the process. To maintain secrecy the circle of those involved in decisionmaking is often greatly circumscribed, and some of those who are able to provide valuable insights are cut out of the discussion. The quality of decision making is thereby weakened. Again, a vicious circle arises. With more mistakes, public officials become more defensive, and to protect themselves

---

5. In arguing against the Alien and Sedition Acts at the end of the 1700s, James Madison noted how the incumbents "will be covered by the 'sedition-act' from animadversions exposing them to disrepute among the people," while the challengers would have no such protection. So he asked: "Will not those in power derive an undue advantage for continuing themselves in it; which by impairing the right of election, endangers the blessings of the government founded on it?" (see Madison 1799, 1966, p. 225).

they seek even more secrecy, narrowing in the circle still more, and further eroding the quality of decisionmaking.

As the space of informed discourse about a host of important issues becomes circumscribed, attention focuses more and more on value issues. Making judgments about complex economic issues takes an enormous amount of information, while coming to a view on abortion or family values takes far less, or a far different kind of, information. Thus secrecy distorts the arena of politics. Thus the adverse effects of secrecy are multiple: not only are important areas of public policy not dealt with effectively, but also debate focuses disproportionately on issues that are often far more divisive.

Incentives for Secrecy

Secrecy was the hallmark of the totalitarian states that marred the 20th century, yet even though the public may have an interest in openness, public officials have incentives to pursue secrecy even in democratic societies. As noted, this secrecy is corrosive: it is antithetical to democratic values and undermines democratic processes; it serves to entrench incumbents and discourage public participation in democratic processes; and it is based on mistrust between those governing and those governed, and at the same time it exacerbates that mistrust. Secrecy provides fertile ground for special interests and undermines the ability of the press to provide an effective check against the abuses of government. At the same time, by undermining confidence that supposedly democratic processes are working in the general interests, it feeds those who argue against democratic processes.[6]

Compelling as the public interest arguments for openness may be, they run up against powerful private incentives of government bureaucrats, elected officials, and the special interest groups that try to influence them. Public choice theory has emphasized the importance of these incentives (Mueller 1997).

Some of the incentives for secrecy are easily understood: making decisions in secret, without the push and pull of the myriad of forces, is much easier than making them in full public view. Managing democratic processes is not easy, and secrecy provides at least temporary insulation.

Much of the incentive for secrecy is more invidious, however. Secrecy provides some insulation against being accused of making a mistake. If a policy fails to produce the desired results, government officials can always claim that matters would

---

6. A large literature is available on the meaning of democracy that I do not wish to address in this chapter. Certainly, what is meant by democratic processes goes beyond electoral democracy. Electoral democracies in which special interests buy votes lack democratic legitimacy. For the issues at hand, any ambiguity that results from the lack of a precise definition should do little to undermine the analysis of this chapter.

have been even worse but for the government policy. However, the public judges mistakes harshly. A vicious circle results: given the disclosure of too little information, the public must rely on government officials' results in judging their performance. The officials receive credit for good results, whether they deserve the credit or not, and they are condemned for bad results, whether they are the result of government action or inaction. With more information the public might be able to discern the value added of public action more accurately.

Another incentive that public officials have for pursuing secrecy is that secrecy provides the opportunity for special interests to have greater sway. In some societies this takes the naked form of corruption and bribery, but even in societies that view bribery as unacceptable, politicians need campaign funds to get elected and re-elected. The special interest groups that provide the funds do not do so for the greater public good, but because they believe that by doing so they can influence policy in ways that enhance their profits and profitability. If these actions in support of special interest groups are subject to public scrutiny, the scope for favoritism is greatly circumscribed. Secrecy is the bedrock of persistent corruption, which undermines confidence in democratic governments in so much of the world. As the expression goes, sunshine is the strongest antiseptic.

Finally, lack of information, like any form of artificially created scarcity, gives rise to rents. The adverse consequences of rent-seeking have long been of concern. An unhealthy dynamic is at work: public officials have an incentive to create secrets, which earn them rents. In some countries public officials reap these rents through outright bribes or by selling valuable information; in others the process is carried out only slightly more subtly through campaign contributions; and in still others it has a critical—and adverse—effect on the press.

Adverse Economic Effects

While most of this chapter is concerned with the adverse effects of secrecy on the political process, it also has adverse economic effects. The most obvious concern is the economic consequences of political decisions. Many of the decisions taken in the political arena have economic consequences, not only for aggregate output, but also for its distribution.

It is now generally recognized that better and timelier information results in better, more efficient resource allocations. The increasing proportion of the work force involved in gathering, processing, and disseminating information bears testimony to its importance. Ironically, many of these people are engaged in ferreting out information from the public sector, information that one might argue should be publicly available. If better information leads to better resource allocations, does it make sense for the government to deliberately not disclose information instead of letting the market itself decide what is or is not relevant?

Exceptions to the Disclosure of Information

Several exceptions exist to the disclosure of information (for more details see Stiglitz 1999). First, the most important and convincing exception involves privacy matters concerning individuals and organizations. In exercising its duties the government gathers enormous amounts of information on individuals, such as income and health statistics, but few, if any, of the issues discussed here fall within the privacy exception.

Second, a closely related exception concerns certain information that an informed party would never disclose to the government if he or she knew that it would subsequently be made public. The importance of the confidentiality of doctor-patient and lawyer-client relationships has long been recognized, and a limited number of interactions within the public sector should fall within the confidentiality exception.

Third, the importance of secrecy in times of war is indisputable. When a nation's survival is at stake, it must do everything in its power to increase its chance of winning. The success of a military attack may well depend on surprise. The problem is that national security exceptions have been extended to issues where national security is clearly not an issue.

Crying Fire in a Crowded Theater

The disclosure of information can occasionally have life-threatening effects. Typically the issue is not whether to disclose the information, but how. Justice Holmes' famous exception to the right of free speech was based on causing a panic by crying "fire" in a crowded theater.

In economics circumstances arise in which these kinds of concerns are real, for example, disclosing that a bank is likely to have to be closed could—and in the absence of deposit insurance probably would—lead to a run on the bank. The International Monetary Fund's (IMF's) disclosure in Indonesia that it was likely to close down some 16 more banks in addition to those already closed, that depositors would only have limited insurance, but that it had not yet determined which banks were to be closed down, caused enormous damage as depositors withdrew their funds from all private banks.

Often, however, the argument is used to defend secrecy when it should not be used. Under the Clinton administration the secretary of the treasury argued that open discussion of such issues as monetary policy might roil the market, leading to instability. Curiously, those who take this position tend to be those who are strong advocates of markets. While they have great confidence in the market, they evidently believe that market allocations are affected by irrelevant "noise." Should we not have enough confidence in democratic processes and in the market to believe that the market can see through the cacophony of voices, assess the fundamental arguments, and weigh the evidence?

Of course, if the information being discussed or disclosed is of relevance, that is, it affects economic fundamentals, then disclosing the information as soon as possible allows the most efficient allocation of resources. If some political decision might have economic effects, then it makes sense for market participants to appraise the likelihood of alternative actions for themselves. Secrecy deprives them of the information they need to make those assessments.

A particular variant of this analysis focuses on monetary policy. The extent to which central banks should act in secret has been extensively discussed. Should they disclose their proceedings, and if so, with what time lag and in what detail? Again, a certain irony accompanies these discussions. While market advocates praise the price "discovery" function of markets, much of the price discovery function in the bond market is directed at figuring out what the central bankers believe and are likely to do. Rather than having this indirect dance, would it not make far more sense to have the central bank directly disclose that information? If the market believes that it is of value—as evidenced by the huge number of individuals who watch the actions of central banks throughout the world—then should the government not make that information available and in a timely way?

Neither theory nor evidence provides much support for the hypothesis that fuller and timelier disclosure and discussion would have adverse effects. Indeed, as information eventually comes out current procedures that attempt to bottle up information result in periodic disclosures of large amounts of information. Just as the economy is likely to be more stable with frequent small adjustments in exchange rates than with a few large ones, so too is the economy more likely to be stable with a steady flow of information. With a flow of information less attention would be paid to any single piece of information, and revisions in posterior distributions would be smaller. At best, however, the argument that fuller disclosure and discussion might roil markets is only an argument concerning the timing and manner of disclosure, and not an argument for indefinitely postponing public discussion.

Central banks are emblematic of a broader set of problems facing democratic societies today. Democratic societies must find and have found ways of engaging expertise in complicated and technical decisionmaking in a manner that reflects both shared values and expertise. Because of the complexities of the technical issues involved, many countries have devolved responsibility for making critical decisions, for example, issuing regulations, to specialized agencies. Yet the decisions cannot reflect only the interests of the affected industry groups, which are likely to have a disproportionate share of the expertise, but should be forged in ways that leave both the decisions and the framework within which they are made open to democratic processes. In many areas regulatory processes reflect these concerns, for instance, publishing proposed regulations and allowing for a comment period.

To the extent that responsibilities have been delegated more widely, for instance, to independent agencies to engage greater expertise and to isolate the decisionmaking from the vicissitudes of the political process, there is an even greater need for openness and transparency.

Undermining Authority, or Don't Air Your Dirty Linen in Public

The argument that public discussions—including discussions of uncertainties and mistakes—will undermine the authority of public institutions is one of the most corrosive of democratic processes. It is akin to the kinds of arguments that authoritarian regimes conventionally use. On the contrary, I would argue that were governments to deal honestly with their citizenry confidence in government and public institutions would increase, not decrease. Human fallibility is at the cornerstone of the design of our political institutions and is why we have systems of checks and balances. We all know that information is imperfect and that these imperfections of information play out in some of the most important decisions we have to make.

Thus to pretend that any institution is infallible or that it has perfect confidence in the actions being undertaken is to fly in the face of reality. Only those who want to be fooled will be. Admission of fallibility and demonstration that one can learn from one's mistakes should enhance public confidence in an institution, at least by demonstrating that the institution has enough confidence in itself and in democratic processes to engage in open discussions.

The IMF has argued that if open discussions of alternative policies were permitted, this would expose policy disagreements, and the lack of confidence that the policy it recommends or imposes as a condition for a loan may feed the opposition. However, such a stance violates both principles of democracy and principles of science. Science recognizes uncertainty, that the consequences of alternative actions are not fully known, and attempts to quantify the degree of uncertainty associated with different positions. Economic science recognizes the existence of choices, tradeoffs, and risks. Different policies affect different groups within society differently and impose different risks on different groups. There is no single Pareto dominant policy, that is, a single policy that is best for everyone. and democratic processes recognize that in democracies, it should be up to the country to choose from among the alternatives and that such choices cannot and should not be made by technocrats, whether from within the country or outside it.

In the end, the repeated failures of the IMF—of the programs and policies such as the big bailouts and capital market liberalizations that it sold with such confidence, a confidence well beyond what the evidence warranted—has undermined confidence in the institution itself, to the point where even people on Wall Street speak of the "emperor who has no clothes" (Soros 2002). Had it been more open, both about the uncertainties and the choices, confidence in the institution would arguably be greater today. As is so often the case, secrecy also feeds concerns that a special agenda is being pursued that reflects special interests rather than more general interests.[7]

The public might be more effectively convinced that special interests did not dominate the discussion, if that was in fact the case, if more openness was apparent, both in the decisionmaking process and concerning the nature of disagreements. Openness in process assures the public that the decision does not reflect the exercise of special interests,[8] and a summary of the discussion convinces the public that all important arguments were considered, all sides were looked at, and a judgment was made that the weight of evidence came down in favor of the course of action being undertaken. After all, governments are elected in part to make these difficult judgment calls. What the public wants to know is that real deliberation has taken place.

The Role of the Media in Implementing Openness

So far in this chapter I have argued that while the public derives great benefits from greater openness and transparency and secrecy does great harm to democratic processes, government officials have strong incentives for secrecy. Recognizing this, some societies have attempted to circumscribe government behavior by limiting the extent of secrecy and the government's ability to curb those who might bring about greater openness. This is why laws protecting free speech and a free press are so important. This section elaborates both the role of the media in enhancing transparency and openness and how the institutional framework required to protect openness and transparency must go beyond just guaranteeing a free press.

Underlying the creation of a more transparent and open democracy is the creation of a new mind-set, one that sees government as an agent of the citizens for whom it works. Given that the public has paid for the gathering of government information, it is the public that owns the information. It is not the private province of the government official, but belongs to the public at large. Thus the information public officials gather at public expense is owned by the public, just as the chairs, buildings, and other physical assets used by the government belong to the public. We have

---

7. For instance, sentiment is widespread that the IMF's harsh policy toward Argentina after its recent default was intended as much to teach others a lesson—think twice before you default, especially against foreign creditors—as it was to "help" Argentina. Argentineans ridiculed the IMF's position as one of not taking yes for an answer.

8. In the recent U.S. dispute over the energy task force, the public rightly wanted to know who the people were who put together the recommendations, that is, what interests they represented. The Bush administration's determination to keep the members of the task force secret reinforced those worries. When the list eventually became public, their worries proved to be justified: the task force consisted of large campaign contributors with strong energy interests.

come to emphasize the importance of intellectual property. The information that public officials gather and process is intellectual property in the same way that a innovation that could be patented would be. Using that intellectual property for private purposes is just as serious an offense against the public as any other appropriation of public property for private purposes. Naturally fully sharing that information may not be appropriate under some circumstances, that is, the important exceptions to the presumption for openness noted earlier.

In the United States the legal framework underlying the presumption that the public has a right to know is provided by the Freedom of Information Act that Congress passed in 1966. In principle, this law enables any citizen to gain access to any information in the public domain, with narrow exceptions for privacy, but such legislation can only be partially successful unless there is a genuine commitment to openness. Government officials may be careful in what they write down and what remains a "mouth-to-ear" secret, precisely because they do not want to disclose important information to the public. While the law by itself is not enough, it is an important step in the right direction, and in some developing countries it seems that just establishing a law allowing access where none existed before has got people asking for information.

A legal framework is part of the institutional infrastructure required for a transparent and open democracy. So too are a variety of public information institutions designed to ferret out information for the benefit of the public, including a free, and if necessary, adversarial press (as opposed to a captive press); a legitimate opposition; and a myriad of public interest organizations to blow the whistle on the cloaked activities of special interest groups or simply to ensure that all sides of a debate have been heard. Clearly such institutions must have access to information to function effectively.

The press is among the most important of these information institutions. Like any institution the press faces incentives, not all of which work to enhance the overall quality of information and the transparency of decisionmaking. Even if we cannot easily remedy these limitations, we should be aware of the dangers. For instance, it has long been recognized that the existence of secrets gives rise to a press determined to ferret out the secrets; however, earlier I explained how secrecy gives rise to an artificial scarcity of knowledge and how such an artificial scarcity gives rise to rents.

One of the ways in which public officials reap the rents is to disclose secrets to those members of the press that treat them well. As a result, not only is the public deprived of timely information, but government officials use their control of information to distort information in their favor, a distortion that goes well beyond the puff pieces that exaggerate the role and acumen of the officials who are being puffed up. This symbiotic relationship between the press and officialdom undermines confidence in both and interferes with the ability of a free press to carry out its essential functions. Can reporters be effective critics if their access to the information they require can be curtailed following the publication of a critical article? Some government agencies are particularly effective in manipulating the press this way. On one occasion, a reporter from an elite U.S. newspaper repeatedly got front page space for his coverage of a government agency, then remarkably quickly he was reassigned to cover automobiles in Detroit. He had evidently lost access after a critical report, and without access he simply could not get the stories. The lesson was not lost on other reporters.

The complex relationship between the press and transparency is illustrated by leaks, which have come to play an important role in information dissemination. The press must be relied upon not to disclose the source of their information. If reporters do reveal their sources, these sources will dry up. Indeed, if the source of a leak becomes public knowledge others within the government are likely to "sanction" the individual, denying that person access to the information or ostracizing him or her in some other way.

The nature of the bilateral relationship is such as to give an advantage to some public officials over others. It pays reporters to develop a good relationship with someone who leaks more regularly and more exclusively (excessive leaking diminishes the value of the information being leaked), and who is likely to be a source for a long time. (If a reporter has a limited supply of puff pieces to give out, it is better to use them on those for whom the present discounted value of the information they are likely to disclose in the future is high.) Leaks thus become a two-edged sword: they are an important way for getting information that would otherwise be secret into the public domain and an important way for government officials to shape coverage in ways that advance their own interests and causes. Leaks may lead to more information, but also to more distorted information.

The most important check against abuses is a competitive press that reflects a variety of interests. A concentration of media power is thus of concern not just because of the resulting market power, which might lead to advertising rates being higher than they otherwise would be. Media that are excessively tied, for example, to financial interests, will not provide an adequate check against abuse by special interests. The imbalance of resources will put some competitors at a disadvantage, both in ferreting out sources of information and in checking the accuracy of information.

In periods of perceived conflict—such as the U.S. War on Terrorism—a combination of self-censorship and reader censorship may also undermine the ability of a supposedly free press to ensure democratic transparency and openness. Readers may feel that criticism of the government is unpatriotic and boycott critical media, while the media may censor themselves, either because they worry about losing their customer base, or because they too share the sense of patriotism. The Internet, which permits easy access to news coverage from abroad, may in the longer run provide some check, although patriotism itself leads to the discounting of these "foreign" sources.

The press thus plays an essential role in the battle for openness, but is at the same time a central part of the "conspiracy of secrecy." The press must commit itself to working for openness. Expecting reporters to disclose their secret sources inside the government or not to seek out exclusive sources of information is unrealistic, but more reporting on the reporting process itself is needed to expose the dangers of this nefarious system, if not the key players.

Concluding Remarks

Greater openness, as I have argued, can be justified on instrumental grounds, as a means to ends such as reducing the likelihood of the abuse of power. Greater openness is an essential part of good governance, but I also believe that greater openness has an intrinsic value. Citizens have a basic right to know. I have tried to express this basic right in a number of different ways: the public has paid for the information; for government officials to appropriate the information that they have access to for private gain, if only for the nonmonetary return of good newspaper coverage, is as much theft as stealing any other public property. While we all recognize the necessity of collective action and the consequences of collective actions for individual freedoms, we have a basic right to know how the powers that have been surrendered to the collective are being used. This seems to me to be a basic part of the implicit contract between the governed and those they have selected to temporarily govern them.

The less directly accountable a government agency is to the public, the more important it is that its actions be open and transparent. By the same token, the more independent and less directly politically accountable a government agency is, the greater the presumption for openness. Openness is one of the most important checks on the abuse of public fiduciary responsibilities. While such openness may not guarantee that wise decisions will always be made, it would be a major step forward in the ongoing evolution of democratic processes, a true empowerment of individuals to participate meaningfully in the decisions concerning the collective actions that have such profound effects on their lives and livelihoods.

The challenge is to create a truly transparent and open government. The incentives for secrecy are great, and so too are the opportunities for evading the intent of any disclosure regulations. If formal meetings have to be open, then all decisions can be made in informal meetings. If written material is subject to disclosure, then officials will have an incentive to ensure that little is written down, and what is written down will be for the public record. Given these limitations of legalistic approaches, the emphasis must be on creating a culture of openness, where the presumption is that the public should know about and participate in all collective decisions. We must create a mind-set of openness, a belief that the public owns the information that public officials possess, and that using it for private purposes—even if only as an exchange of favors with a reporter—is theft of public property.

A legal framework committed to openness and transparency—including right-to-know laws and ensuring diversified, competitive media—is essential, but insufficient. Also essential are the information institutions, especially free, competitive, and critical media committed to ensuring that government is open and transparent, and as committed to disclosing their own limitations—the symbiotic relationships between the members of their fraternity and the government that so often leads to distorted news coverage—as they are to disclosing the limitations of government.

References

Bentham, J. 1838-43. *The Works of Jeremy Bentham*, 11 vols. Published under the supervision of his executor, John Bowring. Edinburgh: W. Tait.

Bok, S. 1982. *Secrets*. New York: Pantheon.

Carpenter, T. G. 1995. *The Captive Press: Foreign Policy Crises and the First Amendment*. Washington, D.C.: Cato Institute.

Edlin, A., and J. E. Stiglitz. 1995. "Discouraging Rivals: Managerial Rent-Seeking and Economic Inefficiencies." *American Economic Review* 85(5): 1301–12. Also published in 1997 as Working Paper no. 4145, National Bureau of Economic Research, Cambridge, Massachusetts.

Emerson, T. 1967. *Toward a General Theory of the First Amendment*. New York: Vintage Books.

———. 1970. *The System of Freedom of Expression*. New York: Vintage Books.

Grossman, S. 1981. "The Informational Role of Warranties and Private Disclosure about Product Quality." *Journal of Law and Economics* 24(3): 461–84.

Halévy, E. 1972. *The Growth of Philosophic Radicalism*. London: Faber.

Hirschman, A. O. 1970. *Exit, Voice, and Loyalty: Responses to Decline in Firms, Organizations, and States*. Cambridge, Massachusetts: Harvard University Press.

Madison, James. 1799. "The Virginia Report of 1799–1800, Touching the Alien and Sedition Laws." Reprinted in L. Levy, ed., 1966. *Freedom of the Press from Zenger to Jefferson*. Indianapolis: Bobbs-Merrill.

Mill, J. S. 1859. *On Liberty*. Reprinted in M. Cohen, ed., 1961. *The Philosophy of John Stuart Mill*. New York: Modern Library.

———. 1861. *Considerations of Representative Government*. Reprinted in H. B. Acton, ed., 1972. *J. S. Mill: Utilitarianism, On Liberty and Considerations on Representative Government*. London: J. M. Dent.

Mueller, D., ed. 1997. *Perspectives on Public Choice: A Handbook*. Cambridge, U.K.: Cambridge University Press.

Padover, S., ed. 1953. *The Complete Madison*. New York: Harper.

Sen, A. 1980. "Famines." *World Development* 8(9): 613–21.

Shleifer, A., and R. W. Vishny. 1989. "Management Entrenchment: The Case of Manager-Specific Investments." *Journal of Financial Economics* 25(1): 123–39.

Soros, G. 2002. *George Soros on Globalization*. Public Affairs, LLC.

Stiglitz, J. E. 1975a. "Incentives, Risk, and Information: Notes towards a Theory of Hierarchy." *Bell Journal of Economics* 6(2): 552–79.

———. 1975b. "Information and Economic Analysis." In M. Parkin and A. R. Nobay, eds., *Current Economic Problems*. Cambridge, U.K.: Cambridge University Press.

_____. 1998. "The Private Uses of Public Interests: Incentives and Institutions." *Journal of Economic Perspectives* 12(2): 3–22.

———. 1999. "On Liberty, the Right to Know, and Public Discourse: The Role of Transparency in Public Life." Paper presented as the 1999 Oxford Amnesty Lecture, Oxford, U.K.

World Bank. 1998. *Pollution Prevention and Abatement Handbook*. Washington, D.C.

3

Mass Media and Political Accountability

Timothy Besley, Robin Burgess, and Andrea Prat

This chapter examines the media's incentives to produce and disseminate information. Mass media can play a key role in enabling citizens to monitor the actions of incumbents and to use this information in their voting decisions. This can lead to government that is more accountable and responsive to its citizens' needs. Despite the intuitive plausibility of this proposition, comparatively little work in the political economy literature scrutinizes the role and effectiveness of the media in fulfilling this function. A literature is emerging, however, that focuses attention on the importance of the so-called fourth estate of government in the policy process.

This chapter discusses work on political agency problems with a focus on recent work by the authors. Besley and Burgess (2001, forthcoming) looked at the effects of the media on responsiveness to shocks in India, while Besley and Prat (2001) focused on the determinants and consequences of captured media using empirical evidence from cross-country data. At the heart of these papers is the idea that citizens have imperfect information about government actions, and that mass media can therefore enhance citizens' abilities to scrutinize government actions.

Many reasons account for why governments are better informed than voters, and hence act on the basis of privileged information. Politicians know more about their competence than those who vote for them and have access to more policy advice and scenarios from a variety of sources. For example, if a bridge or a dam is being built, citizens can only ascertain whether the authorities have paid the proper attention to the relevant costs and benefits through media scrutiny. Similarly, when natural disasters strike, active mass media increase citizens' ability to monitor their representatives' efforts to protect the vulnerable. This is particularly important in low-income countries, where citizens rely so strongly on the state for social protection. Suppose, for example, that in a region of a country containing 50 villages only 1 village is hit by a flood. Without the media only those directly affected can observe the government's actions; however, mass media enable citizens in all 50 villages to observe whether the government is responsive. This raises politicians' incentives to respond, because citizens in the other 49 villages may use this information in their voting decisions.

For information generated by the media to be valuable, it needs to elicit an appropriate collective response. This may be possible even in autocratic settings; however, it is clearly more likely to happen in a country with democratic institutions, such as free elections. In a democracy, citizens require information that they can use to select politicians who serve their needs and to punish those who do not, otherwise formal democracy has no bite.

While most countries have media of some description, their mere existence is no guarantee that they are an effective vehicle for critical scrutiny of state actions. This requires that media outlets have real information about such actions that they are willing to print or broadcast. This will depend on the extent to which the media are regulated, captured, or repressed, an outcome of a variety of government actions ranging from policy decisions that affect the regulation of entry and ownership of the media to explicit bribery or threats. Many countries, while formally democratic, have limited amounts of press freedom. In a sample of 151 countries for which both a press freedom ranking from Freedom House is available and that have held elections in the past five years, 36 receive one of the bottom two (on a scale of six) press freedom scores and only 59 are in the highest two categories. The "democracies" with low press freedom scores also tend to be low-income countries.

How the government treats the media industry affects the development of news media and the quantity and quality of news generated. The raw data suggest the existence of huge variations in access to the media across the world. Data from the World Bank (1997) show a variation in circulation between 0.008 daily newspaper circulation per 1,000 population in St. Vincent and the Grenadines to 792 per 1,000 in Hong Kong, China. Similarly broad variations are apparent in television ownership, which according to the same data source ranges from 0.1 per 1,000 population in Rwanda to 850 per 1,000 in the United States. Not surprisingly, strong links exist between media development and other development indicators such as income per capita and literacy. After controlling for income per capita and regional dummy variables, the evidence also indicates that newspaper circulation and television ownership are lower in countries that have a larger fraction of state-owned media (Djankov and others forthcoming).

A strongly positive correlation is apparent between media penetration and Freedom House measures of press freedom. Media penetration seems also to go hand in glove with indexes of formal and real democracy. Using data from the Polity IV database (see http://weber.ucsd.edu/~kgledits/Polity.html), countries that are rated as more democratic have higher levels of news media penetration as measured by newspaper circulation and television ownership. Of course, the direction of causation is unclear. A similar positive correlation is found between media penetration and the weaker formal notion of democracy measured by whether a country has held an election in the past five years.

What these raw correlations indicate is that significant costs may be associated with underdeveloped media. Moreover, underdevelopment of the media is often the result of governments' decisions to insulate themselves from scrutiny and criticism. Frequently this takes the form of government ownership, barriers to entry by private media companies, and antidefamation laws. While this may be in the interests of government officials, how it serves the public good is less clear. Deregulation of the media therefore stands out as a powerful policy lever that could be used to promote accountability in the developing world. The challenge is how to implement such deregulation in the face of government opposition.

Intellectual Framework

This section lays out the political agency framework that we view as a useful organizing device for discussing the role of the media in democratic settings.

Political Agency Problems

A good framework for thinking about the role of the media is one in which citizens are imperfectly informed about the government's actions and the track records of their leaders. To the extent that we believe that politicians may behave opportunistically and serve their own private agendas ahead of those of the public at large, then politics is a kind of principal-agent problem. The principals are the citizens of the polity who finance government activities through taxes and are subject to various regulations, and the agents are the elected officials and bureaucrats who determine policy outcomes.[1]

A couple of features of political agency distinguish it from other agency relationships. First, the incentive schemes on offer are typically crude. For example, with politicians, except for cases of gross malfeasance, the only sanction typically available is not to re-elect them. Monetary or other more nuanced incentive contracts are almost never observed. This has the consequence that incentives are mostly implicit, with politicians having to guess what the voters would like them to do rather than the latter posting performance criteria in advance. Even in the case of lobbying, a complete contract that specifies the details of what the principals (the lobbyists) desire is hard to imagine.

---

1. This approach has a long tradition in both political science and economics, beginning with Barro (1973) and Ferejon (1986). For recent reviews see, for example, Przeworski, Stokes, and Manin (1999) and Persson and Tabellini (2000, chapter 4).

The second distinctive feature is the multiplicity of principals. There are many citizens and other actors, such as corporations, that differ in countless ways. Therefore even if the incentives could be made explicit, for the principals to agree on the incentives that they will subject their agents to might be extremely difficult. Thus we could easily find principals with diametrically opposed interests wishing to pull the actions of the agents in different directions.

Information availability is at the heart of this theoretical view of government and politics. When the principals try to influence policy either via the ballot box or by lobbying, then they do so with limited information about the agents whom they are lobbying. Two types of problems arise: problems of hidden action (moral hazard), which occur when an agent has the discretion to make or take a bribe unbeknown to the citizens, and problems of hidden type (adverse selection), which occur when the agent's motivations and/or competence are unknown. Ideally, effective incentives would punish incumbent politicians for bribe taking and/or incompetence, but if such behavior cannot be widely observed, then implementing such incentives is difficult.[2]

Private information gathering exercises by the principals are unlikely to provide sufficient information. This insight is at least as old as Downs (1957), who argued that voters would be "rationally ignorant" about politics, because as only one person out of a mass of voters, they have significant costs of being informed and negligible benefits. This rational ignorance comes on top of the usual free-riding problem in actual voting, when a single voter may not find that the benefits of voting exceed the costs.

This might suggest great pessimism about the ability to find solutions to political agency problems; however, there are at least a few reasons to be more optimistic. First, becoming informed about policy can result in significant private gains. Consider the case of old-age pensions. Any rational individuals planning for their retirement would realize significant private benefits from understanding the evolving public policy debate in this area. Second, the power of forces such as civic duty may make private benefits a poor guide to what happens in practice. Third, the mass media can be a powerful source of information provided to citizens at low cost. By being bundled with other information such as sports or entertainment news, many people may regard the acquisition of information not as a chore, but as a pleasure, thus raising the general level of awareness about policy and public affairs. This, at least, is the rosy-eyed view. Here we will use the framework of political agency to give a tighter specification of the issues. We suggest that discussions of the effectiveness of the media

---

2. Besley and Case (1995) suggested that evidence supports the empirical significance of political agency models applied to U.S. governors, some of whom periodically face a term limit that bars them from running for office again. Incentives for governors to acquire reputations vary at such points: those with re-election incentives have stronger incentives than those without. Besley and Case found distinct policy differences between governors in their initial terms and governors who had reached their term limits.

can be decomposed into two parts: (a) the forces that enable free and independent media to induce governments to better serve the public interest, and (b) the forces that lead the government to intervene successfully to silence the media.

The Media and Agency

Noncaptured media can affect political outcomes through three routes: sorting, discipline, and policy salience.

Sorting refers to the process by which politicians are selected to hold office. Politicians' motivation is a potentially important issue for citizens. Some politicians, albeit rarely, enjoy an almost saintly status, such as Gandhi and Nelson Mandela, while others are reviled. Typically their reputations are somewhere in between these extremes; however, the kind of information the media provide can be important to voters who are deciding who to put in charge. This includes information about candidates' previous track records. Their actions while in office may also be an important source of information about their underlying motivation or competence. By printing news stories that responsibly cast light on this, the media can be a powerful force. To the extent that sorting is effective, ex post incentives are less necessary.

The role of the media in achieving discipline is most relevant in situations of hidden action. Suppose that a politician is thinking of taking or giving a bribe and that the probability that this will become public depends on the media's efficacy in both discovering it and broadcasting it widely. The greater the media's efficacy, the higher the marginal cost of the action, possibly deterring the individual from taking or giving the bribe. Thus we would expect media development to be negatively correlated with such actions, leading to better incumbent discipline.

The media can also affect which issues are salient to voters. Besley and Burgess (forthcoming) consider the case of a vulnerable population in a developing country subject to shocks such as droughts and floods. Such populations depend on state action to mitigate the impact of these shocks, but need political clout to get their interests on the political agenda. One way to achieve this is for politicians to find it worthwhile to develop reputations for being responsive to shocks. This requires that these groups are informed about politicians' actions and if they are informed, that the issue is salient among the many other characteristics of politicians that they care about. Assuming that the government's responsiveness to droughts or floods is a significant enough issue to these citizens, then more information enhances the salience of this issue at the ballot box, and thereby creates incentives for politicians to build reputations for being responsive. Mass media can thus play a central role in enhancing responsiveness by providing information that citizens can use when deciding whom to vote for.

More generally, by publicizing politicians' stances on particular issues the media can change the structure of salient issues in elections. This may mean that the media wield considerable influence. In some countries this can be less than benign, depending on the motives of newspaper owners, for example, news stories can publicize events that enhance the salience of ethnic tensions leading to the victimization of particular ethnic groups.

All three of these effects rely on the media providing reliable information. The quality of the news offered to citizens depends on a number of factors. First, the transparency of the political system is important. In countries without traditions of free information flows, information will tend to be hard to obtain. The extent to which the media will print more speculative news will also depend on the legal environment in which the news media operate. For example, the United States gives public figures less access to libel law and therefore makes it easier for the news media to print stories without fear of libel suits. This contrasts with the United Kingdom, where libel laws make publishing speculative news stories more difficult. Second, the methods and traditions of investigative journalism also affect news quality. This may depend on journalists' training and the extent to which news editors reward investigative activity. It may also rest on some perception of citizens' keenness to be informed, and hence the commercial value of breaking important news stories.

Media Capture

As we have just argued, to keep government accountable to the electorate a country needs effective media. This section looks at one of the main obstacles to media effectiveness: the possibility of political capture.

What motivates the media? First, they want to reach a large audience. This is true both for newspapers, because sale and advertising revenues are linked to circulation, and for television stations because of advertising and, where applicable, cable fees. Competition for audience interest pushes the media to look for interesting news and to establish a reputation for reliability.

While the desire to increase market share is common to most industries, a second motivation derives from the media's special role as political monitors. Any time the media monitor someone, he or she may be tempted to ingratiate or threaten the monitor to get more favorable coverage. In the case of the government and the media this takes a variety of forms. Some are simple, like cash bribes offered to individual journalists, violent threats, or censorship. Some are more subtle and typically not illegal. The government can pass a regulation that benefits the ultimate owner of a particular media outlet. For instance, if a newspaper is owned by an industrial conglomerate that also owns an automobile manufacturing company, beneficial regulation might take the form of a tariff on imported automobiles.

To ascertain which of the two motivations are likely to prevail, Besley and Prat (2001) built a simple model of media capture that includes three classes of players: voters, politicians, and the media. Voters are rational and, for simplicity, have homogeneous preferences. Their problem is that they cannot monitor their politicians directly. All the information they receive comes from the media.

The political side of the model is represented by a standard two-period account-ability problem. In the first period a politician (the incumbent) is exogenously put in power. The type of incumbent (good or bad) is not directly observable. At the end of the first period an election is held in which voters can re-elect the incumbent or replace him or her with a challenger of random type. In the second period the candi-date who wins the election is in power.

The media industry is made up of n identical outlets. With some probability they receive verifiable news on the type of politician, which they can report to the public. (For simplicity the model assumes that all members of the public are either informed or uninformed.) A media outlet cannot fabricate news and an outlet that reports informative news has a larger audience than one that reports no news. Moreover, the audience share of an outlet that reports news decreases the greater the number of other outlets that report news. The best case for an outlet is to be the only one to break news.

The model also assumes that news can only be bad, that is, one may have verifi-able information that a politician is bad, but not that he or she is good. This assump-tion is not restrictive for our purposes, because the government would never want to suppress positive news. The important assumption is that news cannot be fabricated. Allowing for fabrication while keeping the assumption that voters are rational would make the analysis extremely difficult. The credibility of media would depend on a complex signaling game.

The revenues of a media outlet have two components that correspond to the two motivations discussed earlier. The first is an increasing function of audience. The second is a transfer from the government, which should be interpreted loosely as favorable regulation. The cost to the politician of making a transfer of a given value to the outlet depends on transaction costs. This is because some forms of transfer may be illegal or politically costly, while others can be disguised as normal policymaking.

The timing of the game is as follows: (a) the media outlets receive or do not re-ceive verifiable information about the incumbent; (b) the incumbent knows what information the media received and makes them transfer offers; (c) each outlet chooses whether to accept or reject the offer; (d) the outlets that accept the offer suppress their information, while the ones that reject it report their information to voters; and (e) voters re-elect the incumbent or replace the incumbent with a challenger.

In searching for the equilibrium of this game, the main question is whether the incumbent finds that buying off the media industry is profitable or not. If an outlet thinks that all the other outlets are going to be quiet, then its incentive to reject the incumbent's offer rises, because it would be the only one to break the news to voters and would gain a large audience. This means that in an equilibrium in which all media sell out, the incumbent must pay each outlet as if it were the only one who could break news. Even if we keep the potential revenues of the total industry constant, increasing the number of media outlets makes buying their silence more expensive for the incumbent. This is the sense in which media pluralism is good for media independence.

In addition to the number of outlets, the other factors that determine whether or not media are captured are transaction costs and the amount of audience-related revenues. Both decrease the likelihood that the incumbent manages to silence the media. Instead, the probability that the media are informed does not affect media capture, but does increase the probability that voters are informed.

This model can be extended in a number of directions. Besides having a type, the politician may choose the amount of rent extraction activity he or she is engaged in. The larger the rent, the higher the probability that the media are able to spot the politician. In such cases media monitoring not only weeds out bad politicians, but has also a disciplining effect, because it means that dishonest politicians are more likely to be caught. This creates a U-shaped relationship between media effectiveness and political turnover. The probability that the incumbent is replaced is low both when effectiveness is low (because no politician is ever caught) and when effectiveness is high (because no politician dares to extract rent). Other possible extensions include ideological media, vertical differentiation, and endogenous entry (see Besley and Prat 2001 for details).

To summarize, the media capture model yields several testable implications. The probability of media capture, and hence of bad political outcomes such as corruption, depends positively on the following variables: media industry concentration, transaction costs, and audience-related revenues.

Transaction costs are particularly interesting. One would expect them to depend on media ownership. If the outlet is state owned, the government can appoint the management and control the resources. If the outlet is owned by a family or has a controlling shareholder, the government can pass regulations favoring the owners' interests. If the outlet is a widely held corporation, then the government cannot benefit the owners directly, but has to provide some direct transfer to the outlet. Finally, if the owner is a foreign entity transfers may become extremely difficult.

Empirical Evidence

Our analytical framework has served to identify a number of channels through which mass media can influence policymaking. Information provided via the media can be used in voting decisions. This can both increase the salience of particular issues and the probability of selecting politicians who act in the public interest. A free press can also serve as a direct check on politicians' excesses. Therefore we might expect some effects of the media on corruption. In general, finding reliable evidence to match the richness of the theoretical possibilities is not easy. This section reviews the limited available evidence. What we know comes mainly from fairly reduced-form cross-country evidence. This is a notoriously difficult context to study, with directions of causality being virtually impossible to discern and highly imperfect measures of most variables. A more promising approach is to exploit data from countries that for one reason or another exhibit variation in media activity. A case in point is India, where state-level media institutions vary significantly. Given its greater reliability we discuss the within-country evidence first, and follow this with an assessment of cross-country studies.

Evidence from India

The tradition of a free and independent press has permeated somewhat into the developing world. A prominent example is India, which has a newspaper industry that is distinguished from that in the bulk of other low-income countries by being both free and independent (Ram 1991). Sen (1984) attributed a major role to this freedom and independence in explaining why India has not experienced any major famines since achieving independence. He observed that:

> India has not had a famine since independence, and given the nature of Indian politics and society, it is not likely that India can have a famine even in years of great food problems. The government cannot afford to fail to take prompt action when large-scale starvation threatens. Newspapers play an important part in this, in making the facts known and forcing the challenge to be faced (Sen 1984, p. 84).

In contrast, investigators have pointed to China's lack of democracy and of freedom of information as reasons why it experienced a major famine between 1958 and 1961, with excess mortality figures ranging between 16.5 and 29.5 million. They have also identified representative democracy and the media as factors in African countries that have succeeded in preventing famines (see Dreze and Sen 1989). As the quote from Sen makes clear, the media increase the salience of government performance in famine situations by providing information on politicians' actions that citizens can use in their voting decisions.

Though suggestive, Sen's analysis does not establish a robust link between the development of mass media and government responsiveness. Besley and Burgess (forthcoming) extend the analysis of the role of media in influencing government policy. Using panel data for Indian states for 1958–92 they look at two policy response systems: first, public distribution of food as a response to falls in food production associated with droughts, and second, spending on calamity relief as a response to crop damage caused by floods. They then examine how newspapers and politics affect the responsiveness of Indian state governments to these shocks. They find that higher newspaper circulation is associated with increased government responsiveness in both cases. A 10 percent drop in food production is associated with a 1 percent increase in public food distribution in states at the median in terms of newspaper circulation per capita, whereas for states that are in the 75th percentile, a 10 percent drop in food production is associated with a 2.28 percent increase in public food distribution. An interesting finding is that newspapers published in regional languages are driving the results.[3] This makes sense, because regional language newspapers report on localized shocks and local vulnerable groups and politicians are more likely to read them than national newspapers. These results hold up in the face of an array of robustness checks. Thus we have strong evidence that even within India, variation in newspaper circulation can explain how responsive the government is to the needs of its citizenry.

In line with political agency theory, the interplay between mass media and political institutions is what determines government responsiveness. Besley and Burgess (forthcoming) examine how various political factors influence government responsiveness. They find that political turnout increases state governments' responsiveness to drought and flood shocks. Greater political competition is also associated with greater responsiveness. This makes sense, as higher turnout and more intense political competition will increase politicians' incentives to build reputations for being responsive to citizens' needs.

Table 3.1 ranks 16 Indian states on their responsiveness to the need for public food distribution and their per capita incomes and newspaper circulation. The responsiveness measure indicates how much food, on average, the state government distributes as a response to food production changes in that state. According to this measure, Kerala is the most responsive state and Bihar is the least responsive. The striking feature of this responsiveness ranking is how weakly it correlates with the income per capita ranking; however, the newspaper circulation ranking follows the responsiveness ranking quite closely.

These results, along with those in Besley and Burgess (forthcoming), strongly support the notion that the mass media help solve political agency problems and make governments more accountable. By making politicians' actions more transparent, the media are informing citizens about the likelihood that they will be protected in the future. In turn, citizens are using this information in making their voting decisions. Politicians realize this, which creates an incentive for them to be responsive to shocks. Note that this incentive is present even when politicians have no inherent

---

3. Data on newspaper circulation were broken down into 19 different languages. Hindi and English tend to be national in scope, while other languages tend to be state specific. Poor, vulnerable populations will tend to be conversant in the state-specific language. In our regressions we therefore broke out newspaper circulation into Hindi, English, and "other."

Table 3.1. Ranking of 16 Indian States, Selected Variables, 1958–92
(ranking of 1 is the highest)

State	Responsiveness	Per capita income	Per capita newspaper circulation
Kerala	1	13	1
Maharashtra	2	3	2
West Bengal	3	5	4
Tamil Nadu	4	8	3
Gujarat	5	4	6
Assam	6	10	15
Uttar Pradesh	7	11	8
Andhra Pradesh	8	9	10
Karnataka	9	6	7
Rajasthan	10	15	9
Punjab	11	1	5
Orissa	12	12	16
Haryana	13	2	13
Jammu and Kashmir	14	7	11
Madhya Pradesh	15	14	12
Bihar	16	16	14

Source: Besley and Burgess (2001).

interest in protecting citizens, and are only doing so in the interests of garnering the votes of vulnerable citizens. The mass media thus affect responsiveness both by increasing the salience of the social protection issue and by affecting the selection of politicians via voting.

The Indian evidence is consistent with other recent country studies suggesting that the media can affect policymaking. For example, Yates and Stroup (2000) looked at pesticide decisions by the U.S. Environmental Protection Agency and found that it sets more draconian standards when newspapers have published more articles about safety. This fits with the idea that the media can change issue salience. Using data from the United Kingdom, Larcinese (2001) found that the mass media both determine the political knowledge of citizens and drive voter turnout. Strömberg (2001) related New Deal spending in county-level data for the United States to radio ownership, finding a positive association between the two, which suggests that areas with a higher penetration of radios were more successful at attracting New Deal spending.

Evidence from Cross-Country Data

A number of corruption measures have recently become available for different countries. In accordance with the foregoing theoretical discussion, we would expect that greater press scrutiny would be associated with lower corruption. Ahrend (2001) and Brunetti and Weder (1999) carried out exercises along these lines and demonstrated the existence of a negative correlation between press freedom measures and corruption in cross-country data; however, drawing causal influences from such findings is difficult, because if corrupt governments can capture the media and then get away with even greater corruption, then the two would be co-determined without one causing the other. To make further progress, we need to measure features of the media market that may make media capture more or less likely, that is, we need to measure proxies for the transactions costs discussed in Besley and Prat (2001).

One promising route takes advantage of the data on media ownership collected by Djankov and others (forthcoming). A plausible notion is that state ownership of the media will lower the cost of capturing the media. Suggestive of this idea, Djankov and others (forthcoming) found that corruption is lower in countries with fewer state-owned newspapers. They found no effect for television.

Using the same data Besley and Prat (2001) also looked at corruption as an outcome. Using three different sources of data on corruption, they found that corruption is negatively correlated with foreign ownership of the media, a finding that is robust to including a wide variety of different control variables. Besley and Prat interpreted this finding as evidence that foreign ownership may be correlated with factors that make the media more effective at generating information.

Djankov and others' (forthcoming) and Besley and Prat's (2001) results together point to the need for a better understanding of what determines media capture. A rough way of measuring media capture empirically is to look at whether a country's press freedom is given a score of less than or equal to 2 on Freedom House's 6-point scale. We can then ask which characteristics of a country's media market are significantly correlated with media capture so measured. To do this, we exploit the data of Djankov and others (forthcoming). Specifically, we include three variables: the extent of foreign ownership, the extent of state ownership, and a measure of ownership concentration. In line with Besley and Prat's (2001) theoretical predictions, capture is more likely if state ownership of newspapers is more prevalent and newspaper ownership is more concentrated. The latter suggests that media capture is affected by media plurality. Unlike the case of corruption as an outcome, foreign ownership has no significant effect on the probability of capture.

Besley and Prat (2001) also asked whether the observed correlation between media ownership and political outcomes occurs because private or foreign ownership makes media more efficient or because it makes them less susceptible to political capture. Using perceived media independence as an instrumental variable, one can run a test to check whether, conditional on being noncaptured, media ownership influences political outcomes. In the case of private ownership, no efficiency gain is apparent. The beneficial effect of having private media arises only because they are less likely to be captured. In the case of foreign media, the overidentification test fails, and one cannot exclude the possibility that both the efficiency and the noncapture channels are active.

Figures 3.1 and 3.2 present these relationships graphically. Figure 3.1 plots press freedom against the degree of state ownership of newspapers using the data from Djankov and others (forthcoming) and Besley and Prat (2001). A high press freedom score denotes more freedom. If we define press capture as having a press freedom score of less than or equal to 3, we can predict the probability of press capture. We do so on the basis of three variables: state ownership of newspapers, foreign ownership of newspapers, and concentration of newspaper ownership. We then graph the International Country Risk Guide measure of corruption against our predicted probability of capture (figure 3.2). The upward sloping pattern in the data should now be clear: countries with a higher probability of being captured are more corrupt. While the results are crude, they illustrate how the cross-country data can be used to inform the theoretical discussion.

Djankov and others (forthcoming) also cast light on the political salience argument, because they found that a broad array of welfare and policy indicators responds positively to a lower fraction of state ownership of newspapers. If one

Figure 3.1. Press Freedom and State Ownership of Newspapers

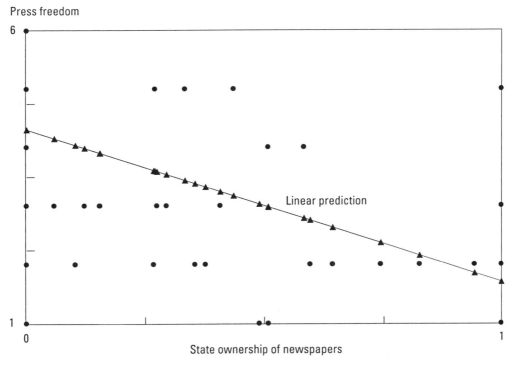

Source: Authors.

Figure 3.2. Corruption and Predicted Probability of Press Capture

International Country Risk Guide measure of corruption

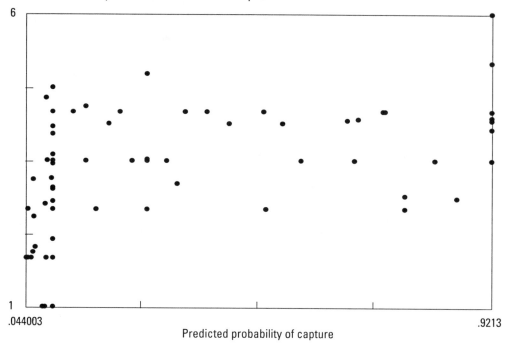

Predicted probability of capture

Source: Authors.

considers ownership to be correlated with the quality of the information generation process, as would be true, for example, if media motivated by profit invest more in researching important news stories, then the changing policy priorities found in the data are consistent with the idea that issue salience changes with the development of the media.

Concluding Remarks

A drive to make governments more accountable to citizens' needs is apparent worldwide. Actors ranging from domestic and international nongovernmental organizations to international financial organizations have pushed the governance agenda. While consensus on the need to improve accountability is widespread, what mechanisms might be used to achieve this is much less clear. This chapter marshals evidence that suggests that a free and independent press working in conjunction with democratic institutions can make governments more responsive to citizens' needs. Political agency models have proved useful in examining the role of the media, because they focus on the importance of information in the political process. We have discussed the various chains of influence by which the media can influence the policy process according to such models. We then argue that the models provide some evidence that ties the electoral process, the media, and government actions together. While the empirical literature is in its infancy, the data certainly suggest that the media have a role to play in political agency. Improved understanding of what makes governments better servants of the people and how strengthening institutions supports this role defines a rich agenda for future work in political economy.

Our central conclusion is that free and independent media should not be viewed as a luxury that only rich countries can afford. Instead our analysis suggests that they should be viewed as a requisite and integral part of representative democracy. Thus a key question is, what kinds of reforms can strengthen the role of the media in promoting accountability? The question of media regulation is central in this context. In the past, most countries had extensive industry-specific rules for the press and for broadcasting. By the 1990s many industrial countries, including the United States and the countries of the European Union, saw a dramatic shift in the philosophy underlying media regulation. The new model is that the media should be governed by the same basic competition policy principles that are applied to other industries, which are mostly based on laissez faire except when consumer welfare is demonstrably hurt. This has led to the elimination of media-specific rules, such as restrictions on ownership, concentration, and pricing. However, because of their role as political watchdogs, the media differ from other industries. Consumer welfare, defined in terms of the interests of customers (viewers and advertisers), is a limiting notion in that it does not take into account the industry's effect on voters' welfare. Future research in the area should re-evaluate existing regulatory regimes in this new light.

References

The word "processed" describes informally reproduced works that may not be commonly available through libraries.

Ahrend, Rudiger. 2001. "Press Freedom, Human Capital, and Corruption." London School of Economics, London. Processed.

Barro, Robert. 1973. "The Control of Politicians: An Economic Model." *Public Choice* 14(Spring): 19–42.

Besley, Timothy, and Robin Burgess. 2001. "Political Agency, Government Responsiveness, and the Role of the Media." *European Economic Review* 45(4–6): 629–40.

———. Forthcoming. "The Political Economy of Government Responsiveness: Theory and Evidence from India." *Quarterly Journal of Economics.*

Besley, Timothy J., and Anne C. Case. 1995. "Does Political Accountability Affect Economic Policy Choices? Evidence from Gubernatorial Term Limits." *Quarterly Journal of Economics* 110(3): 769–98.

Besley, Timothy, and Andrea Prat. 2001. "`Handcuffs for the Grabbing Hand? Media Capture and Political Accountability.'" London School of Economics, London. Processed.

Brunetti, Aymo, and Beatrice Weder. 1999. "A Free Press Is Bad News for Corruption." University of Basel, Basel, Switzerland. Processed.

Djankov, Simeon, Caralee McLeish, Tatiana Nenova, and Andrei Shleifer. Forthcoming. "Who Owns the Media?" *Journal of Law and Economics.*

Downs, Anthony. 1957. *An Economic Theory of Democracy.* New York: HarperCollins.

Dreze, Jean, and Amartya Sen. 1989. *Hunger and Public Action.* Oxford, U.K.: Clarendon Press.

Ferejohn, John. 1986. "Incumbent Performance and Electoral Control." *Public Choice* 50(1–3): 5–25.

Larcinese, Valentino. 2001. "Information Acquisition, Ideology, and Turnout: Theory and Evidence from Britain." London School of Economics, London. Processed.

Persson, Torsten, and Guido Tabellini. 2000. *Political Economics: Explaining Economic Policy.* Cambridge, Massachusetts: MIT Press.

Przeworski, Adam, Susan C. Stokes, and Bernard Manin, eds. 1999. *Democracy, Accountability, and Representation.* Cambridge, U.K.: Cambridge University Press.

Ram, N. 1991. "An Independent Press and Anti-Hunger Strategies: The Indian Experience." In J. Dreze and A. Sen, eds., *The Political Economy of Hunger,* vol. 1. Oxford, U.K.: Oxford University Press.

Sen, Amartya. 1984. "Food Battles: Conflicts in the Access to Food." *Food and Nutrition* 10(1): 81–89.

Strömberg, David. 2001. "Radio's Impact on the New Deal." Department of Economics, Institute of International Economic Studies, Stockholm. Processed.

World Bank. 1997. *World Development Indicators.* Washington, D.C.

Yates, Andrew J., and Richard L. Stroup. 2000. "Media Coverage and EPA Pesticide Decisions." *Public Choice* 102: 297–312.

4

The Media and Markets in the United States

Edward S. Herman

Do the media support markets? There are, of course, a variety of media in virtually every country, as well as major differences in media structures—and media relationships with government and markets—between countries. This suggests that media attitudes toward markets might well vary accordingly, both within and between countries. At the same time recent decades have seen an accelerated trend toward displacing government-sponsored, and sometimes government-owned and government-controlled, noncommercial media with commercial, advertiser-funded media. A steady trend toward concentration and conglomeration has also been apparent, along with more extensive cross-border operations and control of this private sector of the media (see Bagdikian 2000; Herman and McChesney 1997; McChesney 1999).

These trends have made media structures and media outputs across the globe more alike than in the past, partly because of the cross-border flows from common sources like CNN, the BBC, and News Corporation and its affiliates; partly because of increased cross-border ownership and alliances; and partly because commercialization and competition have tended to homogenize media outputs as media managers have sought to reach affluent audiences and please their owners and advertisers. These trends are making the media within the United States more centralized and the media elsewhere more like the media of the United States. The U.S. media system is the most powerful in the world, and much of the spread across borders is associated with the parallel movement abroad of its television channels like CNN, its motion pictures, its syndicated television shows, its advertising agencies, and its overseas alliances and ownership. Even where cross-border growth occurs from outside the United States, as with the Brazilian Globo's and Mexican Televisa's effective production and global sale of Spanish soap operas and other programs, this has closely followed the U.S. model (Herman and McChesney 1997, chapter 7; Straubhar 1996, p. 225).

Because of the centrality of the U.S. media in the global system, their trend-setting character, and their representation of the most mature dominantly commercial system in a world in which commercialization is becoming ever more important, this chapter focuses on the relationship between media and markets in the United States.

A Pro-Market Propaganda Model

Where the mainstream media are privately owned and are funded almost entirely by commercial advertisers, as in the United States, the media themselves are members of and participants in the market. Their attitudes toward the market are obviously heavily shaped by that fact. At issue in this context is the precise meaning of "the market." It could mean a free and fully competitive market; it could merely mean private ownership, whether competitive or monopolistic; or it could describe the preferences of the dominant participants in market activity. This last meaning is not uncommon in everyday parlance, where the market often refers to consensus market opinion that, for example, favors some stock or is hostile to a particular government action. People often say that the market now controls national policy, because of the threat of financial capital flight or possible adverse investment decisions when policies threaten the bottom line.[1] The market in this sense refers to the collective or net actions and preferences of financial and other important market participants.

In this meaning of the market, the market itself will favor private ownership, but whether it will favor free and fully competitive markets is less certain. That may well depend on circumstances. For example, intellectual property rights in the form of patents and copyrights, while defensible on the grounds of encouraging technological advances, clearly interfere with the freedom of trade and are subject to potential abuse through the granting of excessive monopoly time, the possible patenting of assets already in the public domain, and so on. In the United States, however, these monopoly rights accrue to and are sought by powerful corporate interests in the pharmaceutical and other industries, and given this market support the mainstream media do not object to, or encourage significant public debate about the merits of, this exception to free trade.

As another example, in 2001–02 the U.S. steel industry, under stress and threatened by cheap foreign competition, favored protection—at least of steel—and succeeded in getting the government to impose tariff increases to fend off imports (Marsh and Alden 2001; Matthews 2001). Similarly, in the 1980s the U.S. auto industry was seriously threatened by competition from Japan and used its political muscle to get an informal quota system put in place that limited Japanese imports and protected

---

1. As Walter Wriston, former chief executive officer of Citicorp put it: "It's more than 200,000 computer screens in hundreds of trading rooms . . . [that] vote, if you will, on their view of [some policy] action by buying or selling. This market is a harsh disciplinarian" (Wriston 1993).

the domestic industry. In these cases the financial community and mainstream media were also very quiet, reporting the minimal facts, but not stressing or protesting very strenuously the violation of the basic principles of free trade. In addition, at times when foreign competition has widespread scale and learning curve advantages and infant industries are weak, there may be a virtual consensus of the market that protection is in the national interest. However, when national industry and finance have competitive advantages across a wide range of activities and freer trade and improved opportunities for foreign investment would serve their interests, we would expect the market to support "free trade" and oppose protectionism, with opportunistic exceptions as noted (DuBoff 1989, pp. 55–56, 152, 165–66; Schumpeter 1954, pp. 397–406).

At times when the market supports free trade and opposes protectionism, workers and the general public may have a different view. This was the case during the U.S. debates about the North American Free Trade Agreement (NAFTA) in 1993 and 1994 and later controversies about the operations and plans of the World Trade Organization (WTO). Public opinion polls during 1993 and 1994, for example, showed public majorities regularly opposed to NAFTA (for details about media treatment versus polls of citizen opinion see Herman 1999, chapter 14), while elite opinion, and surely the market, was for it. The mainstream media of the United States were also for it, so that in this important, and far from unique, case the media could be said to support the market in the dual senses of supporting an agreement that enlarged the reach of markets and constrained the role of government in economic activity, and also supporting what market opinion favored.

As the general public was hostile to NAFTA, media support for it raises questions about whose interests the media serve. Another question is whether the media covered the issue with the fairness and objectivity consistent with their theoretical role as managers of a public sphere in which sufficient information is provided to make democratic choices and public participation in the democratic process real.

The media's alignment with the market on the NAFTA issue was predictable. As already noted, the mainstream media in the United States are members of the market, so, for example, if they are businesses that hire labor and have to deal with labor unions (and frequently try to fend them off), they are, from the start, in an adversary relationship with labor.[2] This is a structural fact that will almost certainly affect the attitudes of the owners and top managers of media enterprises, and these are the individuals who control the organization, hire the top personnel, and set the tone of its work as a media enterprise. Note that during the NAFTA controversies of 1993 both the *New York Times* (November 16) and the *Washington Post* (September 23) ran editorials criticizing organized labor's attempts to influence the outcome of the

---

2. The *Washington Post*, *New York Times*, Knight-Ridder, Gannett, and others have had serious labor conflicts over the years (see Puette 1992).

struggle, suggesting that this was improper and that labor should know its place. They did not publish comparable criticisms of the efforts of business to influence the legislative outcome, or even of the Mexican government's intervention in the debate represented by an estimated expenditure of US$30 million on public relations within the United States.[3]

The forces that affect media treatment of these kinds of issues can be summarized in a model or framework that focuses on media structures and relationships and reflects the media's integration into the market system and political economy. Herman and Chomsky's (2002, chapter 1) propaganda model attempts to do this, featuring five factors that profoundly influence the media's editorial positions and news choices, namely, (a) ownership and control and bottom-line orientation, (b) funding by advertisers, (c) sourcing, (d) flak, and (e) ideology.

Ownership and Control and Bottom-Line Orientation

The mainstream media in the United States are privately owned and are controlled by wealthy individuals or by other corporations. With stock outstanding, they have fiduciary obligations to their owners to focus on the bottom line, which may well conflict with any theoretical public service obligations. Thus broadcasters did not keep their promises, made in earlier years, to provide public service programming, because the growth of advertising and advertisers' preference for entertainment led them to steadily displace documentaries and other politically enlightening fare with entertainment (see Herman and McChesney 1997, chapter 5, and sources cited therein).

Private owners, especially those of major media, are likely to favor markets, of which they are a part and of which they are major beneficiaries. There is some dispute about the extent to which owners influence media behavior and performance. At a minimum, even where the stock of a media organization is widely distributed, the controlling management will face strong pressure to focus on the bottom line. This in itself has policy implications, as such a focus implies catering to advertisers, cultivating relationships with dominant information sources, and avoiding conflict with other powerful constituencies. The media organization will often have policies in place that affect the treatment of economic and other issues for this and other reasons.

Important media proprietors have had definite, strong political views that they have imposed on their media outlets,[4] and from time to time the evidence indicates

---

3. For an extensive treatment of the U.S. business campaign to push through NAFTA and the Clinton administration's participation in that campaign see McArthur (1999).

4. Famous cases include Henry Luce and his *Time-Life-Fortune* empire, the Hearst press, Colonel Robert McCormick and the *Chicago Tribune*, the Wallace family's *Reader's Digest*, William Knowland's *Oakland Tribune*, Rupert Murdoch's papers and television stations, the Moon-sponsored *Washington Times*, Walter Annenberg's *Philadelphia Inquirer*, and the Copley papers.

that a great many less strongly ideological proprietors have had a distinct and ongoing influence on media policy choices.[5] Close connections and reciprocal service between top media owners and executives, on the one hand, and U.S. presidents and State Department, Central Intelligence Agency (CIA), and Pentagon officials, on the other hand, are also easily documented.[6]

Despite the extensive evidence of proprietary influence, it is often difficult to prove on an ongoing basis. Compelling documentation is frequently accessible only for the past. Policy is likely to be transmitted to the lower echelons in subtle ways: by hiring senior editors known to fit the owner's general outlook and to be sensitive to proprietary demands; by politically biased selection, promotion, and dismissal of reporters;[7] and by editorial instruction on story selection, emphases, and tone that guides underlings as to what is expected of them (see Breed 1955; Soloski 1989).

Equally important, distinguishing between proprietor-editor policy and mere profit seeking is difficult. As noted, however, a decision to focus strictly on profitability is a major and conservative policy decision in its own right. We may distinguish between an explicit and intended policy line and a policy by default, whereby a proprietor who is trying to maximize profits follows the line dictated by dominant sources, which will be cheap ("efficient") and will not offend the powerful.

---

5. Turner Catledge, the top *New York Times* editor for 17 years, noted that the paper's chief owner, Arthur Hays Sulzberger, was in the habit of "making his likes and dislikes known," and that "he sought executives who shared his general outlook, and he tried, by word and deed, to set a tone for the paper" (Catledge 1971, p. 189). Later, when A. M. Rosenthal was managing editor of the *Times* and imposed a distinct structure of policies on the paper, this was clearly in accord with the political preferences of the publisher, Arthur Ochs Sulzberger (see Herman 1999, chapters 6–8). Similar conclusions can be drawn from histories of the *Washington Post* (Davis 1984; Halberstam 1981), CBS (Halberstam 1981; Paper 1987), and the *Los Angeles Times* (Halberstam 1981).

6. On the links between the *New York Times* and the *Wall Street Journal* see Herman (1999, chapters 6–9). David Sarnoff, head of RCA and NBC, received the title of brigadier general during World War II for his armed services propaganda effort. In the late 1940s he chaired an organization called the Armed Forces Communication Association where he promoted numerous Cold War propaganda themes (see Lyons 1966, pp. 270–71). On the extensive connections of Paley and CBS to the government and CIA, see Halberstam (1981) and Paper (1987, pp. 303–4) and Schorr 1978, pp. 204, 275 and following). The revolving door between senior government and media officials has been extremely active. James Hagerty went from being President Eisenhower's press secretary to serving as chief of ABC News. David Gergen went from Reagan's White House media staff to a senior editorial position at *U.S. News and World Report*. Edward W. Barrett resigned as undersecretary of state for public affairs to work for NBC. Before he went to the State Department he was editorial director of *Newsweek*. On the *Washington Post's* official links to government and the CIA see Davis (1984).

7. According to Davis (1984, p. 302), at Ben Bradlee's interview for a top job at the *Washington Post*, Katherine Graham, the publisher, asked him how he planned to cover the Vietnam War, which she consistently supported. "Bradlee said he didn't know, but that he'd hire no 'son-of-a-bitch' reporter who was not a patriot."

Advertising

The mainstream media depend heavily on advertising to fund their operations, ranging from perhaps 70 percent of revenue for newspapers to more than 95 percent for television. Advertisers influence the media not by crude interventions, which are relatively rare, but by their interest in obtaining a programming environment that supports their commercial messages, as well as by their hostility to antibusiness messages.[8] Competition for advertising business is a powerful force that causes the media to program and otherwise structure their activities so as to meet the demands of these primary sources of revenue (see Barnouw 1978). Avoiding flak from advertisers is a major concern of media managers (see the section on "Flak").

Sourcing

The major media want steady and reliable sources of news, which they can obtain mainly from other large governmental and business organizations. Fishman (1980, p.143) calls this "the principle of bureaucratic affinity: only other bureaucracies can satisfy the input needs of a news bureaucracy." The symbiotic relationship that develops from this mutual dependency and service gives the large nonmedia organizations an edge in framing the news, and both governmental and large business organizations tend to favor markets, although conflicts about particular policy issues may exist between government and business, or even among business organizations, for example, as in the case of the recent protectionist actions favoring steel producers, where corporate users of steel were strongly against protection and in favor of free trade.

Flak

Flak refers to negative feedback to news and other media offerings, which may take the form of individual calls and letters of protest, organized actions such as picketing and boycotts, law suits, and even congressional hearings and regulatory actions. Flak is most threatening to the media, and most effective in influencing their behavior, when it comes from people and organizations that can seriously harm them, like advertisers and organizations and government bodies that can withdraw their patronage, humiliate them, and rule or legislate against them. Thus when CBS produced a documentary critical of the Pentagon and its contractors ("The Selling of the

---

8. Procter and Gamble had a written policy as follows: "There will be no material on any of our programs which could in any way further the concept of business as cold, ruthless, and lacking all sentiment or spiritual motivation." It is not alone in such a policy. For more information see Bagdikian (2000, pp. 155–73).

Pentagon," shown on February 23, 1971), CBS was forced to defend itself before a congressional committee, a somewhat chilling experience for CBS and a lesson to other media. When public television station WNET showed the program "Hungry for Profit," which criticized transnational corporate behavior in the developing world, Gulf & Western withdrew its funding support from the station, and the *Economist* ("Castor Oil or Camelot?" December 5, 1987) noted that "Most people believe that WNET would not make the same mistake again."

Flak that seriously worries the media derives mainly from the same large bodies, such as the Pentagon and its contractors, companies like Gulf & Western, and advertisers, that are important information sources and also tend to be friendly to markets. There are even institutions created to produce flak, such as Accuracy in Media, The Center for Media and Public Affairs, Freedom House, and The Media Institute, funded mainly by the corporate community, that attack the media for any incipient populist tendencies and press them to support deregulation, privatization, and an aggressive foreign policy.

Ideology

U.S. ideology flows from the strength of the property-owning and business class, and has long been characterized by anticommunism, possessive individualism, belief in the merits of private enterprise and markets, and hostility toward the government except in its role of maintaining law and order and serving business interests abroad (Herman and Chomsky 2002; Katznelson and Kesselman 1979, chapter 2).

These elements of ideology have a firmer grip on the business community and on the elite than on blue-collar workers and others who are not as clear beneficiaries of the status quo. The leaders of the media are members of that elite, and so are many of the journalists of the leading media organizations (Croteau 1998; Gans 1985). Sociologist and media analyst Gans (1979, pp. 42–55) lists a number of assumptions, such as "ethnocentrism," "altruistic democracy," and "responsible capitalism" that he also calls "enduring values," and which he contends U.S. journalists take for granted. He gives this set of premises and values the name "para-ideology." There is evidence that for many journalists the belief that free enterprise and free trade are good and government enterprise and regulation and constraints on free trade are bad are important elements of their para-ideology. The forces of ideology and para-ideology add to the other factors that tend to make journalists favorable to the market.

Contesting Viewpoints

Conservatives commonly express the view that the media are liberal, and sometimes even claim that they are adversarial to the government and to the powerful. These claims often come from media pundits, and even from owners whose own power position in the media is enviable, and the allegations frequently constitute a form of flak and are part of an attempt to discipline the media and push them from the center to the right.[9] These claims are commonly supported by reference to polls showing that media personnel vote disproportionately for Democrats and have opinions on social issues to the left of blue-collar citizens (see Croteau 1998; *EXTRA!* 1998, p. 10; Gans 1985). Such polls, however, ignore the fact that owners and top managers control the media enterprises, shape their aims and direction, and fix overall and sometimes specific policy and assume that lower echelon media employees operate with no constraints from above. In addition, in focusing on social issues these analyses also ignore the fact that on such matters the highly educated and the business elite have opinions to the left of blue-collar workers. The analyses also tend to ignore economic issues, an area in which journalists are more conservative than blue-collar workers and share the perspectives of the business community (see Croteau 1998; Gans 1985).

A more serious claim against the model and its implications is that media personnel are professionals, who work on the basis of professional values, which could, if valid and sufficiently powerful, override any demands and pressures from above or from the outside. Professional values encompass two things: first, objectivity, meaning presenting a variety of sides to a story, searching out facts without political constraint, and presenting those facts fairly and impartially; and second, deciding what is newsworthy on the basis of consistently applied news values, unaffected by a political agenda or biased by ideological premises or compromised by strategic or profitability considerations.

The claim that professional values affect news work is no doubt true to some extent. Many journalists say that these are operative values, and because journalists have a certain (and variable) degree of autonomy, they do sometimes deviate from established policies, principles, or beliefs. But how strong is the force of professional values relative to the factors incorporated into the propaganda model? Can they seriously disturb the perspectives of news and commentary that follow from the widespread internalization and use of the dominant language, frameworks, ideological assumptions, and policy positions on important issues tacitly or explicitly in place at many media institutions?

One reason why professional values are not likely to offset structural and power factors is that the hiring, job security, and advancement of journalists depends on their conforming to established principles and policies. Insofar as journalists are initially out of step, they learn on the job and adapt (see Breed 1955; Bonner 1984, pp.

---

9. In 1996 John Malone and Rupert Murdoch, two extremely powerful owners of mainstream media institutions, announced that they were going to produce a new news service to combat the left bias of the mainstream media (see Herman 1999, pp. 1–5).

340–41; Herman and Chomsky 2002).[10] Another reason is that the rules of objectivity themselves, especially as they work out in practice, encourage source dependence on powerful actors, which gives government officials and corporate executives a privileged position in defining and framing the news. Journalists often find that the uncritical transmission of official information is easy and acceptable practice, whereas looking beyond this is arduous and risks alienating major newsmakers. This produces a nominal rather than substantive objectivity, but describes common news practice (Herman 1999, chapter 5; Tuchman 1972).

Finally, as noted earlier, journalists tend to accept the dominant ideologies of their society, which enter into news work as implicit value judgments or premises about facts that are debatable and rest on value judgments. Belief in the merits of markets and free trade falls into this category. Gans (1979) contends that the presence of these ideological elements as an underpinning of news work does not constitute a violation of objectivity. He maintains that because they are already built into news judgments "they do not conflict with objectivity—in fact, they make it possible. Being part of news judgment, the enduring values are those of journalism rather than of journalists; consequently, journalists can feel detached and need not bring in their personal values" (Gans 1979, pp. 196–97). However, if premises that reflect the dominant ideology are already incorporated into news judgments, objectivity is compromised in advance and Gans's journalists do not have to introduce personal values because this is already done for them. He salvages journalistic objectivity by the semantic shift of the ideological bias and nonobjectivity toward journalism and away from journalists,[11] but the penetration of ideology, including para-ideology, into the newsmaking process at any stage is incompatible with meaningful conceptions of objectivity and professional values.

Case Studies

The filtering effect of the elements of the propaganda model on media performance should be similar to the effects of money on elections. In an important analysis of electoral processes, political scientist Thomas Ferguson (1995, pp. 28–29) argues that where those who fund elections agree on an issue, the parties will not compete on

---

10. Bonner (1984) is a brief account of how he was attacked by the *Wall Street Journal* for reporting on the El Mozote massacre in El Salvador. Shortly after this attack the management of the *New York Times* removed him from his job.

11. Gans also contends that para-ideology is less biasing than other ideologies: "In the final analysis it encourages them [reporters] to be somewhat more open-minded than would an integrated ideology" (1979, pp. 277–78). This claim is unconvincing. Journalists who do not even recognize their bias are hardly likely to be more objective than those who do. The former need not makes any concessions for balance, as the truth is entirely clear.

that issue even if most of the general public might be interested in another option. By analogy, where those who own the media and their advertisers agree on an issue, the propaganda model would lead us to expect that the media will support the position of the owners and advertisers and not allow extensive debate and critical news on such a topic. As the owners and advertisers are important members of the market and will reflect any market consensus, this is tantamount to saying that the media position on such an issue will reflect the preferences of the market.

National Defense and the Defense Budget

The U.S. corporate community has supported a large military budget for years, because it provides a great deal of valuable business directly, has been a source of major funding and subsidizing of new technologies, and provides the military forces that have opened up market opportunities for U.S. transnational firms. The benefits to ordinary citizens are less clear, and for years polls have shown that except in times of war or widespread fear or panic, the general public would like less defense and more education and other civil expenditures (for a major study see Kull 1996; for public opposition to excessive defense spending even during the Reagan era see Ferguson and Rogers 1986, pp. 19–24). However, given the corporate—that is, market—consensus, the major parties do not compete on this issue and the major media do not insist on candidates addressing this issue nor do they themselves address it.

This was reflected in the 2000 presidential election campaign, during which neither George W. Bush nor Al Gore considered any tradeoffs between civilian and defense expenditures; indeed, they both proclaimed the need for enlarged defense funding and competed only on their declarations of devotion to defense and on the size and composition of proposed increases. Third party candidate Ralph Nader did call for cuts in the defense budget, but he was not allowed to participate in the national debate with Bush and Gore. In justifying his exclusion from the debates, the *New York Times* (editorial, June 30, 2000) explained that the two major parties reflected all the options the public needed. It noted that Nader did not need to run because the two parties offered a "clear-cut choice" so there was "no driving logic for a third-party candidacy this year." The *New York Times* and the mainstream media in general followed the Bush-Gore lead in this matter, simply not allowing any serious discussion of the defense-civil society budget tradeoff. In doing this, the media may be said to have followed the market's preference.

Globalization and Free Trade

The dominant members of the market have also been in the forefront of the globalization process and in support of policies advancing that process, such as trade agreements and grants and backing for the WTO, the International Monetary Fund (IMF), and the World Bank. As in the case of defense versus civilian budgets, the corporate community and the general public have disagreed on these issues. As noted earlier, polls taken before the enactment of NAFTA showed substantial majorities opposed to its passage—and later to the bailout of investors in Mexican securities—but the elite favored enactment.

On these issues the mainstream media have aligned themselves almost uniformly on the side of the corporate community, supporting the trade agreements, the WTO, the IMF, the World Bank, and fast-track authority both in editorials and in news coverage. The media's position has been that free trade is good and brings benefits to people at home and abroad, and across class lines; that the trade agreements, the WTO, the IMF, and the World Bank serve free trade and the opening of markets and therefore deserve support; and that the opposition to these servants of free trade is based on the self-serving motivation of special interests and has no justification in economic analysis or the distribution of benefits and losses. The points seem so obvious to the leading mainstream editorialists and journalists that they are impatient with counterclaims and repeat that "free trade is good" as a self-evident mantra.[12]

The use of the term special interests is itself revealing, pointing to the media's own integration into the corporate community and the market. The media do not consider the corporate community, or its constituent parts that support free trade, to be special interests, but rather to represent the national interest. The special interests were admittedly people who might be losers in the free trade game, "predominantly women, blacks and hispanics" and "semiskilled production workers" (Lueck 1993), whose large numbers underlie the poll findings of majority opposition to NAFTA and other trade agreements. In one notable case Meg Greenfield, the op-ed column editor of the *Washington Post*, answering criticism of imbalance in the paper's opinion columns on NAFTA, stated that "On that rare occasion when columnists of the left, right and middle are all in agreement. . . . I don't believe it is right to create an artificial balance when none exists" (quoted in Kurtz 1993). However, with polls showing a majority of the public opposing NAFTA, the pro-NAFTA unity of the *Post's* pundits simply highlights the huge class bias of mainstream punditry.

Another manifestation of the integration of media and corporate opinion on trade issues is displayed in the media's willingness to join with advertisers in pushing for free trade. The most notable case was a three-part "advertorial" in the *New York Times*, beginning in April 1993, based on a solicitation by the paper to advertisers to "present the positive economic and social benefits of NAFTA." A leak of this solicitation led to some protests at the paper taking a definite stance on the issue in this

---

12. A front-page backgrounder in the *New York Times* (Passell 1993), cheerleads in a literal sense: "Free trade means growth. Free trade means growth. Free trade means growth. Just say it 50 more times and all doubts will melt away." Needless to say this primer contains no voices that challenge the cheerleading.

manner, and subsequently at its refusal to allow dissenters from this support to place advertisements in these advertorials.[13]

The media have also done poorly in allowing any debate on free trade issues. While occasionally admitting that there were losers as well as winners, they have been extremely reluctant to go into details on effects on labor bargaining power and inequality, and often explicitly or implicitly denied that there were any losers. They regularly used the friendly phrase free trade to describe arrangements that were first and foremost about investor rights, not trade, and failed even to mention those investor rights. They have also persistently ignored the fact that intellectual property rights, like patents, are monopoly rights that interfere with the freedom of trade, and in urging the benefits of free trade to developing countries, the media have failed to acknowledge that all the great industrialized countries—including Germany, Japan, the United Kingdom, and United States—and the Asian Tigers used protectionism for extended periods to help them compete globally before taking off into sustained growth (Amsden 1989; Wade 1990). The U.S. media have not only failed to allow this argument to be made, they have even denied it and made the historical error of claiming that free trade was the route to such development (for an example of this error see Nasar 1991).

Free Trade and Democracy

The undemocratic and antidemocratic thrust of the media's treatment of free trade issues goes well beyond their denial of labor's right to try to influence legislation. For example, critics of the ongoing globalization process have contended that the process has suffered from secrecy, decisionmaking behind closed doors, and lack of debate, as well as from the establishment of agreements and mechanisms that deprive democratic governments of the rights to serve their noncorporate citizens. In the context of widespread public opposition to many of these actions, the pushing through of these agreements has arguably been an attack on democracy in favor of what Ralph Nader and other critics of corporate globalization have called a "corporate bill of rights." However, the market has favored these actions, and the media have followed in the market's wake. They have never criticized editorially or given any but marginal attention to the secrecy, top-down character of the new laws and rules or their limiting effects on democratic rule.

Indeed, the mainstream media have positively lauded some of the antidemocratic effects of the new institutions and agreements. For example, one of the main arguments for NAFTA was that its would "lock in" Mexico to the "reforms," making it

---

13. The *Times* letter of solicitation, dated April 6, 1993, and a letter of protest to the editor sent by 10 prominent media critics, was published in *Lies of Our Times* (1993, pp. 20–21).

impossible for its government to change course. Six of ten *New York Times* editorials on the NAFTA debate in 1993 mentioned this merit of the agreement. The fact that the Mexican leader who negotiated the agreement had won an election widely believed to have been fraudulent did not affect the *Times'* (or other media's) view of the appropriateness of Mexico being locked in by the agreement.

After the onset of crisis in Mexico in December 1994, U.S. officials and economists pointed out that Mexico was now blocked from using import quotas and restricting access to foreign currency to protect itself, and would have to deflate painfully to reach a new equilibrium. The undemocratic character of this system of constraints never struck the U.S. mainstream media, as their news and opinions on this set of issues paralleled those of the general business community.

Although street protests are a long-recognized feature of the democratic process, the mainstream media's treatment of the protests in Seattle, Washington, D.C., Quebec, and Genoa have been almost uniformly derisive and hostile, with a clear pro-police and antiprotester bias and, most important, a regular failure to address substantive issues. In a throwback to their biased treatment of the protests of the Vietnam War era (Gitlin 1980; Morgan 2000), they have exaggerated protester violence, played down police provocations and violence, and shown great complaisance at illegal police tactics designed to limit all protester actions, peaceable or otherwise (Ackerman 2000; Coen 2000; DeMause 2000). Even though the Seattle police resorted to force and used chemical agents against many nonviolent protesters well before a handful of individuals began breaking windows, both then and later the media reversed this chronology, stating that the police violence was a response to protester violence.[14]

The media's hostility to the protests, closely aligned with that of the rest of the corporate establishment, caused them to display their devotion to the First Amendment in a way they never have when their own rights and privileges have been at stake.

The Chemical Industry

Another striking case of media support of markets is reflected in their treatment of the chemical industry and its regulation. Because of the industry's power, as well as the media's receptivity to the demands of the business community, the media have normalized a system described by Carson (1962, p. 183) as "deliberately poisoning us, then policing the results." Industry is permitted to produce and sell chemicals

---

14. Zachary Wolfe, legal observer and coordinator for the National Lawyers Guild, concluded that "Police sought to create an atmosphere of palpable fear," and that anyone even trying to hear dissident views ran a risk of police violence "just for being in the area where speech was taking place" (quoted in Coen 2000).

(and during the 1990s bioengineered foods) without independent and prior proof of safety, and "policing" by the Environmental Protection Agency (EPA) has been badly compromised by underfunding and political limits on both law enforcement and testing (see Fagin and Lavelle 1996, chapters 4–5). A major study by the National Research Council in 1984 (Thornton 2000, pp. 99–100) found that health hazard data were unavailable for 78 percent of the chemicals used in commerce, and a dozen years later an Environmental Defense Fund update found that little had changed. The government's National Toxicology Program tests about 10 to 20 chemicals a year for carcinogenicity (but not for the numerous other possible adverse effects); meanwhile 500 to 1,000 new chemicals enter commerce annually, and thus our knowledge base declines steadily.

This system works well for industry, because it wants to sell without interference, and leaves virtually all the research and testing for safety in its hands, allowing it to decide when the results are worth transmitting to the EPA. This is a classic fox guarding the henhouse arrangement. The system has worked poorly for the public, and the industry's power to influence, sometimes even capture, the EPA has reinforced its inadequacy (Fagin and Lavelle 1996, chapters 4–5; Herman 1999, chapter 17). Nevertheless, the industry often contends that the safety of chemicals is assured by EPA (or Food and Drug Administration) regulation,[15] which the industry does its best to keep weak, and which, as noted, has failed to deal with the great majority of chemicals in the market.

With the media's help the chemical industry has also gained wide acceptance of its view that chemicals should be evaluated individually on the basis of an analysis of their risks to individuals and individual tolerances. However, measuring such risks and tolerances for humans is extremely difficult, because controlled experiments are not possible, damage may not show up for many years, the forms of damage may not be known in advance, chemicals may interact with others in the environment and may be bioaccumulative, and the breakdown products of chemicals may have their own dangers. Furthermore, if thousands of chemicals enter the environment, many long-lasting, bioaccumulative, and interacting with other chemicals, a public policy that ignores their additive and interactive effects on people and the environment is deeply flawed and irresponsible.

Policy based on the precautionary principle, bitterly opposed by the chemical industry with the support of the U.S. government,[16] would not allow chemicals to

---

15. Monsanto's publicity director, Phil Angell, stated that "Our interest is in selling as much of it [a bioengineered product] as possible. Assuring its safety is the F.D.A.'s job" (quoted in Pollan 1998).

16. At a January 2000 meeting on the biosafety protocol, the U.S. government's insistence on WTO "good science" while the European Union was urging application of the precautionary principle almost broke up the meeting (Pollack 2000a,b).

enter the environment without full testing, would prohibit the use of chemicals that accumulate in human tissues and whose breakdown products are threatening or unknown, and would compel the use of nonthreatening alternatives for untested chemicals and those known to be risky where such alternatives could be found or developed at reasonable cost (for a good discussion of the case for applying the precautionary principle see Thornton 2000, chapters 9–11).

In successfully avoiding application of the precautionary principle, industry spokespersons have argued that the existing system is based on sound science, but science does not tell us that industry has any right to put chemicals into the environment that carry any risk at all, let alone telling us what risks are acceptable—these are political decisions. Furthermore, if the chemicals in the environment have not been tested for all relevant variables, such as their long-term effects on the immune system and reproduction, their potential carcinogenicity, and the effects of their breakdown products on the environment, and none of them have been so tested, the political, not scientific, basis of sound science is evident.

The chemical industry has produced, and long denied, any harm from, innumerable products—from tetraethyl lead in gasoline and PCBs in batteries to asbestos, the pesticide DDT, and the defoliant Agent Orange—that are now well established as seriously harmful, only withdrawing them (often only from domestic use) under overwhelming legal and regulatory pressure. For the products they have wanted to sell they have always found scientists who would testify to their harmlessness or who would note that claims of harm were not scientifically proven. A consistent sharp difference has been apparent between the results of industry-sponsored science and those of independent researchers working the same terrain. In addition, numerous cases of fraud in industry testing, industry use of testing laboratories that manipulated the data so as to find industry products acceptable, and political manipulation to weaken regulatory standards have come to light (Fagin and Lavelle 1996, chapters 3–5; Herman 1999, chapter 17).

Despite these industry abuses of science, the media have largely accepted the industry's claim that it supports sound science, in contrast with its critics' use of junk science. For example, from 1996 through September 1998, 258 articles in mainstream newspapers used the phrase junk science, but only 21 (8 percent) used it to refer to corporate abuses of science, whereas 160 (62 percent) applied it to science used by environmentalists, other corporate critics, or tort lawyers suing corporations. Seventy-seven (30 percent) did not fit into either of these categories (Herman 1999, p. 235). In short, the media have internalized industry's self-legitimizing usage, just as they have normalized a status quo of *caveat emptor* (buyer beware) rather than of safety first.

In accord with industry domination of the media's environmental perspective, the media portray the EPA as a powerhouse organization that is perhaps too aggressive and adversarial in its pursuit of the public interest. The reality—a seriously underfunded organization, unable to do its job properly, sometimes captured and often driven to industry-friendly compromises—can only be grasped, if at all, by a close, often between-the-lines study of media reporting (see Fagin and Lavelle 1996; Steingraber 1997; issues of *Rachel's Environment & Health Weekly*). The media have normalized the fact that, contrary to the stated aim of the 1976 Toxic Substances Control Act, the EPA has been unable to cope with the toxic chemical flood, and an estimated 75 percent of the chemicals in wide use have still not been tested for toxicity.

The media also do not pay serious attention to the evidence that the system of leaving safety testing to industry has failed. For example, in the course of a struggle with Monsanto between 1986 and 1990 about the company's right to introduce Santogard, the EPA discovered that some years previously Monsanto had found negative effects of Santogard in a study that the company had failed to submit to the EPA, contrary to law. Monsanto was fined US$196,000, although by law the fine should have been US$19.7 million (Reisner 1992). The company was then allowed to search for other delinquent toxicity studies, and turned up 164, for which it was fined another nominal $648,000. Realizing that other chemical companies were also probably failing to submit studies the EPA arranged an amnesty with the industry, promising only nominal fines for the next three years in exchange for the industry turning over previously hidden studies. Under this amnesty the industry produced some 11,000 documents (Reisner 1992; see also *Rachel's Environment & Health Weekly* 1997). Despite the implications, the media did not find this story of even passing interest.

For decades the chemical industry has fought against disclosure of the effects of its products on the grounds of proprietary information and the free speech right to be silent. Although full disclosure would seem especially urgent when products can harm and potential victims need to know as much as possible to deal with any damage, the industry has been remarkably successful in preserving its right to silence and the public's right not to know. Worker knowledge of the effects of workplace chemicals came only after decades of struggle, and it was not until 1986, after Bhopal (and a leak of the same chemical in West Virginia), that Congress finally passed the Emergency Planning and Community Right-to-Know Act. The act was passed over furious industry opposition, with many key provisions passing by one vote.

Under the act the larger chemical producing firms were obliged to make public information about their releases into the environment of some 654 named chemicals. The mainstream media did not find the industry's resistance to informing the public, or the passage of the act and the act itself or its effects, of great interest. Steingraber (1997, p. 102) cites industry admissions that this enforced disclosure compelled industry members to pay attention to the chemicals they were pouring into the environment, a point that would seem of enormous significance to public health. While the Toxic Release Inventory showed startling figures—several billion pounds of toxic chemicals released each year—even with the limited coverage of companies and chemicals, self-reporting, and many refusals to comply, you will look in vain in the mainstream media for detailed reports of these releases, calls for better data, discussions of the health consequences of these releases, or indignation at a system that permits such large-scale emissions of poisons.

Since 1993 business has got 24 states to pass audit privilege laws, which give companies the right to carry out their own environmental audits, to report this information to state authorities along with promises to correct noted deficiencies, and then to be free of any requirement to disclose environmental information to the public or in court proceedings. EPA official Steven Herman (1998) states that such laws are "anti-law enforcement, impede public right-to-know, and can penalize employees who report illegal activities to law enforcement authorities. They interfere with government's ability to protect public health and safety. They prevent the public from obtaining potentially critical information about environmental hazards." Once again, however, the mainstream media have been exceedingly quiet about this regressive process, giving the topic a few back-page articles, but without featuring this development or giving it critical editorial attention.

An important right-to-know issue has also arisen in connection with the new biotechnology products. Many consumers and environmentalists have insisted that the milk produced by cows given Monsanto's growth hormones, soybeans, and other farm products that are bioengineered should be labeled as such. Vermont and other states have tried to legislate labeling, and a number of European countries have been concerned about allowing such products entry as well as sale without labeling. Deeper problems are at stake here than disclosure to consumers, including animal and human health and ecological effects, but notably the U.S. mainstream media do not consider any of these issues of great importance. They have been given back-page treatment at best, and no editorial criticism in the national media. The *New York Times* editorially condemned the "food disparagement" laws in the case of Oprah Winfrey versus the Texas cattle ranchers (editorial, "Free Speech about Food," January 19, 1998), but neither it nor the other national papers have spoken out in favor of labeling bioengineered products. In these cases producer sovereignty apparently overwhelms any concern for either biological threats or the consumer's right to choose.

The media have also regularly dismissed concerns about chemical threats as unwarranted scares, such as the alleged scares about dioxin and the danger of Alar on apples, but these and other scares often turn out to be based on genuine health hazards (Herman 1999, chapter 17). Meanwhile, the media rarely report on or examine in any depth the frequent evidence of the inadequacy of regulation and testing and of the real costs of the "chemicalization" of the environment (Herman 1999, chapter 17). For example, the International Joint Commission, a joint Canadian-U.S. venture dating back to 1978, was given the formidable task of trying to halt the flow of toxic chemicals into the Great Lakes. It reports each year that it is failing, and since 1992 has called for the ending of the manufacture of chlorine as essential to fulfilling its task. The national media virtually ignore this appeal, and the commission's U.S. co-chairman, Gordon Durnil, has remarked that "we have a societal problem about how to deal with this, but 90 percent of the population doesn't even know there is anything to worry about" (quoted in Herman 1999, p. 240; see also Thornton 2000, chapter 9). Here once again the media serve the market, not the general public.

Conclusion

The U.S. mainstream media are an integral part of the corporate system, privately owned, dependent on advertising for their revenues and on the government and the business community for much of their information and protection (in the case of the government). As part of the market the media are unlikely to be hostile to the market and oppose policies that dominant members of the market support. Theoretically, their editorial positions might be biased in favor of markets while their news is unbiased. However, the structural factors incorporated into the propaganda model point to bias across the board, and empirical evidence supports this conclusion.

The mainstream media strongly support markets, in the sense of privatization and reliance on markets, on the one hand, and in the sense of what the dominant elements in the market want, on the other hand. However, in reflecting market preferences, an element of opportunism is apparent in media stances toward markets, so that if the market wants government intervention and protection in specific cases (wars opening up markets abroad, import quotas and subsidies when particular industries are in crisis), the media may well support these exceptions to their faith in the market.

This support of markets also does not preclude occasional sharp criticism of market participants and practices that violate accepted business norms, injure innocents, and jeopardize the market system as a whole. These criticisms often come belatedly, as in the case of the Long Term Capital Management and Enron collapses, and before that the savings and loan industry debacle, but not always. Harsh criticism of market abuses within the mainstream media comes more often from powerful institutions that serve an elite audience, like the *Wall Street Journal*, rather than media that serve a broader audience, such as the television networks or newspapers like *USA Today*, or even the *New York Times*. The *Journal's* audience does not need as much ideological pampering.

Whether the existing strong pro-market bias of the mainstream media is desirable is debatable. On the one side one could argue that as markets are good, strengthening them is desirable, and that this is therefore a beneficent media order. On the other side one may argue that the media are not serving their democratic and public sphere responsibilities if they are failing to allow market initiatives to be fully and honestly debated, especially when the majority seems to have doubts about the steady displacement of government services and deregulation. The pro-market bias may even serve the market badly by failing to provide the informational and political basis for constraining its excesses and failures, thereby contributing to Enron-like disasters and potentially far worse outcomes.

Reform of the media in the direction of making it more responsive to the interests of the general public, insofar as that is deemed desirable, faces an arduous task. Insofar as the media's stance on markets follows from their integration into the market, it would take a quasi revolution, with the emergence of a strong noncommercial media, for a change in perspective to occur. The ongoing drift toward deregulation, a weakening of constraints on concentration, and the declining support here and abroad for noncommercial media put such basic media reform further out of reach. Media support of markets, in the senses noted here, is likely to strengthen in the future.

References

Ackerman, Seth. 2000. "Prattle in Seattle: WTO Coverage Misrepresented." *EXTRA!* (January-February): pp. 13–17.

Amsden, Alice. 1989. *Asia's Next Giant: South Korea and Late Industrialization.* New York: Oxford University Press.

Bagdikian, Ben. 2000. *The Media Monopoly,* 6th ed. Boston: Beacon Press.

Barnouw, Erik. 1978. *The Sponsor.* New York: Oxford University Press.

Bonner, Raymond. 1984. *Weakness and Deceit.* New York: Times Books.

Breed, Warren. 1955. "Social Control in the Newsroom: A Functional Analysis." *Social Control* (May).

Carson, Rachel. 1962. *Silent Spring.* Greenwich, Connecticut: Fawcett.

Catledge, Turner. 1971. *My Life and Times.* New York: Harper and Row.

Coen, Rachael. 2000. "Whitewash in Washington: Media Provide Cover as Police Militarizes D.C." *EXTRA!* (July–August): 12–14.

Croteau, David. 1998. "Challenging the "Liberal Media' Claim." *EXTRA!* July-August, pp. 4–9

Davis, Deborah. 1984. *Katherine the Great.* Bethesda, Maryland: National Press.

DeMause, Neil. 2000. "Pepper Spray Gets in Their Eyes: Media Missed Militarization of Police Work in Seattle." *EXTRA!* (March–April): 8–9.

DuBoff, Richard. 1989. *Accumulation and Power: An Economic History of the United States.* Armonk, New York: E. Sharpe.

Economist. 1987. "Castor Oil or Camelot." December 5.

EXTRA! 1998. "The 89 Percent Liberal Media." July–August.

Fagin, Dan, and Marianne Lavelle. 1996. *Toxic Deception: How the Chemical Industry Manipulates Science, Bends the Law, and Endangers Your Health.* Secaucus, New Jersey: Birch Lane Press.

Ferguson, Thomas. 1995. *Golden Rule.* Chicago: University of Chicago Press.

Ferguson, Thomas, and Joel Rogers. 1986. *Right Turn.* New York: Hill & Wang.

Fishman, Mark. 1980. *Manufacturing the News.* Austin: University of Texas Press.

Gans, Herbert. 1979. *Deciding What's News.* New York: Vintage.

————. 1985. "Are U.S. Journalists Dangerously Liberal?" *Columbia Journalism Review* (December).

Gitlin, Todd. 1980. *The Whole World Is Watching.* Berkeley: University of California Press.

Halberstam, David. 1981. *The Powers That Be.* New York: Alfred Knopf.

Herman, Edward S. 1999. *The Myth of the Liberal Media.* New York: Peter Lang.

Herman, Edward S., and Noam Chomsky. 2002. *Manufacturing Consent: The Political Economy of the Mass Media,* 2nd ed . New York: Pantheon.

Herman, Edward S., and Robert McChesney. 1997. *The Global Media.* London: Cassel.

Herman, Steven. 1998. "EPA's 1998 Enforcement and Compliance Assurance Priorities." *National Environmental Enforcement Journal* (February).

Katznelson, Ira, and Mark Kesselman. 1979. *The Politics of Power,* 2nd ed. New York: Harcourt Brace Jovanovich.

Kull, Steven. 1996. "Americans on Defense Spending: A Study of U.S. Public Attitudes." Center for Study of Public Attitudes, College Park, Maryland.

Kurtz, Howard. 1993. "The NAFTA Pundit Pack: Sure, They Backed It. How Could They Lose." *Washington Post,* November 19.

Lies of Our Times. 1993. "NAFTA: The Times for Sale?" (October).

Lueck, Thomas. 1993. "The Free Trade Accord: The New York Region." *New York Times,* November 18.

Lyons, Eugene. 1966. *David Sarnoff.* New York: Harper and Row.

Marsh, Peter, and Edward Alden. 2001. "A Lot to Hammer Out: Efforts to Cut Global Steel Capacity Must Face up to U.S. Protectionism." *Financial Times,* December 17.

Matthews, Robert Guy. 2001. "A Big Stick: The U.S. Won't Take 'No' for an Answer at Paris Steel Summit." *Wall Street Journal ,* December 14.

McArthur, John. 1999. *The Selling of "Free Trade."* New York: Hill & Wang.

McChesney, Robert. 1999. *Rich Media, Poor Democracy.* Urbana: University of Illinois Press.

Morgan, Edward P. 2000. "From Virtual Community to Virtual History: Mass Media and the American Antiwar Movement in the 1960s." *Radical History Review* 78(fall): 85–122.

Nasar, Sylvia. 1991. "Industrial Policy the Korean Way." *New York Times,* July 12.

New York Times. 1998. "Free Speech about Food." January 19.

Paper, Lewis J. 1987. *Empire: William S. Paley and the Making of CBS.* New York: St. Martin's Press.

Passell, Peter. 1993. "How Free Trade Prompts Growth: A Primer." *New York Times,* December 15.

Pollack, Andrew. 2000a. "Talks on Biotech Food Turn on a Safety Principle." *New York Times,* January 28.

————. 2000b. "130 Nations Agree on Safety Rules for Biotech Food." *New York Times,* January 30.

Pollan, Michael. 1998. "Playing God in the Garden." *New York Times Magazine,* October 25.

Puette, William J. 1992. *Through Jaundiced Eyes.* Ithcaca, New York: Cornell University Press.

Rachel's Environment & Health Weekly. 1997. "On Regulation." March 20 (no. 538).

Reisner, Jeff. 1992. "EPA Program Trades Leniency for Toxicity Data." *Journal of Commerce,* January 14.

Schorr, Daniel. 1978. *Clearing the Air.* New York: Berkeley Medallion Books.

Schumpeter, Joseph. 1954. *History of Economic Analysis.* New York: Oxford University Press.

Soloski, John. 1989. "News Reporting and Professionalism: Some Constraints on the Reporting of News." *Media Culture & Society* (April): 207–28.

Steingraber, Susan. 1997. *Living Downstream*. Reading, Massachusetts: Addison-Wesley.

Straubhar, Joseph. 1996. "The Electronic Media in Brazil." In Richard Cole, ed., *Communication in Latin America*. Wilmington, Delaware: Scholarly Resources, Inc.

Thornton, Joe. 2000. *Pandora's Poison: Chlorine, Health, and a New Environmental Strategy*. Cambridge, Massachusetts: MIT Press.

Tuchman, Gaye. 1972. "Objectivity as Strategic Ritual." *American Journal of Sociology* 77(4): 66–79.

Wade, Robert. 1990. *Governing the Market*. Princeton, New Jersey: Princeton University Press.

Wriston, Walter. 1993. "Clintonomics: The New Information Revolution and the New Global Market Economy." Speech delivered at the Independent Policy Forum, January 25, Washington, D.C.

5

Irrational Exuberance in the Media

Robert J. Shiller

The history of speculative bubbles begins roughly with the advent of newspapers.[1]

This chapter is an extract from chapter 4 of the author's book *Irrational Exuberance* (Princeton University Press, 2000). It was also published in the *Harvard International Review* (spring) 2001. It is reprinted with permission from the *Harvard International Review* and the Princeton University Press.

1. No doubt there were speculative price movements before there were newspapers, but I have found no pre-newspaper accounts of widespread public attention to speculative price movements that are described by contemporaries as wild and inexplicable or as due only to investors' exuberance. The first regularly published newspapers appeared in the early 1600s. Once publishers discovered how to generate public interest, increase circulation, and make a profit, papers sprung up rapidly in many European cities. We might date the beginning of the mass media somewhat earlier, to the invention of printing itself, when publication became no longer dependent on patrons. Innumerable pamphlets, broadsides, and religious and political tracts were printed during the 1500s. Historian of printing Zaret (1999, p. 136) notes that "printing put commerce squarely at the center of textual production. Unlike that of scribal production, the economics of text production increasingly involved calculation, risk taking, and other market behaviors in which printers oriented production to vague estimations of popular demand for printed texts." The advent of printing brought with it an increased incentive for literacy; by the 1600s many if not most urban people in Europe could read. Histories of speculative manias, such as that by Kindlberger (1989), give no examples of speculative bubbles before the 1600s, and my polling of local historians provided none either. However, I cannot claim to have researched their history exhaustively. Indeed, there are probably some stories that *could* be regarded as an exception to my generalization about the coincidence of the first manias and the first newspapers, although other interpretations are also possible. Yale historian Paul Freedman offered me the example of pepper as a possible exception: its price in the spice trade seems at times to have been surprisingly high, and in the 1500s it was very volatile. There are ancient and medieval examples of grain prices soaring at times of famine. Land price movements were also remarked in history. For example, in a letter to Nepos around A.D. 95, Pliny the Younger (1969, pp. 437–38) writes, "Have you heard that the price of land has gone up, particularly in the neighborhood of Rome? The reason for the sudden increase in price has given rise to a good deal of discussion." By saying there was much discussion, he is suggesting word-of-mouth effects, but he really does not tell a mania story.

One can assume that, although the record of these early newspapers is mostly lost, they regularly reported on the first bubble of any consequence, the Dutch tulip mania of the 1630s.[2]

Although the news media—newspapers, magazines, broadcast media, and now the Internet—present themselves as detached observers of market events, they are themselves an integral part of these events. Significant market events generally occur only if there is similar thinking among large groups of people, and the news media are essential vehicles for the spread of ideas.

In this chapter I consider the complexity of the media's impact on market events. As we shall see, news stories rarely have a simple, predictable effect on the market. Indeed, in some respects, they have less impact than is commonly believed. However, a careful analysis reveals that the news media do play an important role both in setting the stage for market moves and in instigating the moves themselves.

To understand the effects of the transmission of ideas via the *news media*, we must also understand how they interact with *word-of-mouth* transmission of ideas. I discuss evidence in this chapter about how the effects of the news media are achieved through word-of-mouth, and this discussion will set the stage for further analysis of word-of-mouth effects later in this book.

The Role of the Media in Setting the Stage for Market Moves

The news media are in constant competition to capture the public attention they need to survive. Survival for them requires finding and defining interesting news, focusing attention on news that has word-of-mouth potential (so as to broaden their audience), and, whenever possible, defining an ongoing story that encourages their audience to be steady customers.

The competition is by no means haphazard. Those charged with disseminating the news cultivate a creative process, learning from each others' successes and failures, that aims to provide emotional color to news, to invest news stories with human interest appeal, and to create familiar figures in the news. Over the years, experience in a competitive environment has made the media professions quite skilled at claiming public attention.

---

2. There were Dutch newspapers by 1618, and Holland, in contrast to other countries at the time, allowed the printing of domestic news, not just foreign news. On these pioneering Dutch newspapers, see Desmond (1978). The primary surviving source of information about the tulip mania is a pamphlet published in Holland during the peak of the mania. The anonymous 1637 document, in the form of a dialogue between two men, gives detailed news of the speculation as it was then happening. Numerous other pamphlets about the mania, published just after its end, also survive (see Garber 2000). These surviving pamphlets confirm the existence of well-developed print media capable of disseminating information about the tulip mania as it happened.

The news media are naturally attracted to financial markets because, at the very least, the markets provide constant news in the form of daily price changes. Certainly other markets, such as real estate, are sources of news. But real estate does not typically generate daily price movements. Nothing beats the stock market for sheer frequency of potentially interesting news items.

The stock market also has star quality. The public considers it the Big Casino, the market for major players, and believes that on any given day it serves as a barometer of the status of the nation—all impressions that the media can foster and benefit from. Financial news may have great human interest potential to the extent that it deals with the making or breaking of fortunes. And the financial media can present their perennial lead, the market's performance, as an ongoing story—one that brings in the most loyal repeat customers. The only other regular generator of news on a comparable scale is sporting events. It is no accident that financial news and sports news together account for roughly half of the editorial content of many newspapers today.

Media Cultivation of Debate

In an attempt to attract audiences, the news media try to present debate about issues on the public mind. This may mean creating a debate on topics that experts would not otherwise consider deserving of such discussion. The resulting media event may convey the impression that there are experts on all sides of the issue, thereby suggesting a lack of expert agreement on the very issues that people are most confused about.

I have over the years been called by news people asking me if I would be willing to make a statement in support of some extreme view. When I declined, the next request would inevitably be to recommend another expert who *would* go on record in support of the position.

Five days before the 1987 stock market crash, the MacNeil/Lehrer News Hour featured Ravi Batra, author of *The Great Depression of 1990: Why It's Got to Happen, How to Protect Yourself*. This book took as its basic premise a theory that history tends to repeat itself in exact detail, so that the 1929 crash and subsequent depression had to repeat themselves. Despite Batra's significant scholarly reputation, this particular book of his is not one that would be viewed with any seriousness by serious scholars of the market. But it had been on the *New York Times* best-seller list for 15 weeks by the time of the crash. On the News Hour, Batra confidently predicted a stock market crash in 1989 that would "spread to the whole world"; after it, he declared, "There will be a depression."[3] Batra's statements, made as they were on a nationally respected show, may—even though they predicted a crash two years hence—have contributed in some small measure to an atmosphere of vulnerability that brought us the

---

3. Transcript 3143, "McNeil/Lehrer NewsHour," WNET/13, New York, October 14, 1987, p. 10.

crash of 1987. Although Batra's appearance on the News Hour just before the crash might be considered just a coincidence, one must keep in mind that predictions of stock market crashes are actually quite rare on national news shows, and so the proximity in time of his appearance to the actual crash is suggestive at least that it is representative of the process that brought us the crash.

Should the media be faulted for presenting debates on topics of little merit? One can argue that they ought to focus on a variety of topics of interest to general audiences so that the public can refine their views. Yet in doing so the media seem often to disseminate and reinforce ideas that are not supported by real evidence. If news directors followed only their highest intellectual interests in judging which views to present, the public might indeed find its consciousness constructively broadened. But all too often they are swayed by competitive pressures to skew their presentations toward ideas best left alone.

Reporting on the Market Outlook

There is no shortage of media accounts that try to answer our questions about the market today, but there is a shortage within these accounts of relevant facts or considered interpretations of them. Many news stories seem to have been written under a deadline to produce *something, anything,* to go along with the numbers from the market. The typical such news story, after noting the remarkable bull market, focuses on very short-run statistics. It generally states which groups of stocks have risen more than others in recent months. Although these stocks are described as leaders, there is no good reason to think that their performance has caused the bull market. The news story may talk about the "usual" factors behind economic growth, such as the Internet boom, in glowing terms and with at least a hint of patriotic congratulations to our powerful economic engine. The article then finishes with quotes from a few well-chosen "celebrity" sources, offering their outlook for the future. Sometimes the article is so completely devoid of genuine thought about the reasons for the bull market and the context for considering its outlook that it is hard to believe that the writer was other than cynical in his or her approach.

What are the celebrity sources quoted as saying in these articles? They typically give numerical forecasts for the Dow Jones Industrial Average, tell stories or jokes, and dispense their personal opinions. For example, when Abby Joseph Cohen of Goldman, Sachs coins a quotable phrase—as with her warnings against "FUDD" (fear, uncertainty, doubt, and despair) or her phrase "silly putty economy"—it is disseminated widely. Beyond that, the media quote her opinions but pay no critical attention to her analysis. In fact, although she no doubt has access to a formidable research department and performs extensive data analysis before forming her opinions, they are ultimately reported as just that—her opinions. Of course she should not be faulted for this, for it is the nature of the sound-bite-driven media that superficial opinions are preferred to in-depth analyses.

Record Overload

The media often seem to thrive on superlatives, and we, their audience, are confused as to whether the price increases we have recently seen in the stock market are all that unusual. Data that suggest that we are setting some new record (or are at least close to doing so) are regularly stressed in the media, and if reporters look at the data in enough different ways, they will often find *something* that is close to setting a record on any given day. In covering the stock market, many writers like to mention "near-record one-day price changes," measured in points on the Dow rather than percentage terms, so that records are much more likely. There may be some increased enlightenment about reporting points on the Dow in recent years, after so many records have been set, but still the practice persists among media accounts.

This *record overload*—the impression that new and significant records are constantly being set—only adds to the confusion people have about the economy. It makes it hard for people to recognize when something truly and importantly new really *is* happening. It also, with its deluge of different indicators, encourages an avoidance of individual assessment of quantitative data—a preference for seeing the data interpreted for us by expert sources.

Do Big Stock Price Changes Really Follow Big News Days?

Many people seem to think that it is the reporting of specific news events, the serious content of news, that affects financial markets. But research offers far less support for this view than one would imagine.

Victor Niederhoffer, while he was still an assistant professor at Berkeley in 1971 (before he became a legendary hedge fund manager), published an article that sought to establish whether days with big news stories corresponded to days that saw big stock price movements. He tabulated all very large headlines in the *New York Times* (large type size being taken as a crude indicator of relative importance) from 1950 to 1966; there were 432 such headlines. Did these days correspond to big movements in stock prices? As the standard of comparison Niederhoffer noted that the Standard and Poors Composite Index over this period showed substantial one-day increases (of more than 0.78 percent) on only 10 percent of the trading days, and substantial one-day decreases (of more than 0.71 percent) on only another 10 percent of the trading days. Of the 432 "big news days," 78 (or 18 percent) showed big price increases, and 56 (or 13 percent) showed big decreases. Thus big news days were only slightly more likely to show large price movements than other days (Niederhoffer 1971, p. 205; see also Cutler, Poterba, and Summers 1989).

Niederhoffer claimed that, on reading the stories under these headlines, many of the news events reported did not seem likely to have much impact on the fundamental value represented by the stock market. Perhaps what the media *thought* was big national news was not what was really important to the stock market. He speculated that news events that represented national crises were more likely to influence the stock market.

Defining a national crisis as a time when five or more large headlines occurred within a seven-day period, Niederhoffer found 11 crises in the sample interval. These were the beginning of the Korean war in 1950, the capture of Seoul by the communists in 1951, the Democratic National Convention of 1952, Russian troops' threatening Hungary and Poland in 1956, the Suez crisis of 1956, Charles de Gaulle's taking office as French premier in 1958, the entry of U.S. marines into Lebanon in 1958, Russian premier Nikita Khrushchev's appearance at the United Nations in 1959, Cuban tensions in 1962, the Cuban arms blockade in 1962, and President John Kennedy's assassination in 1963. During these crises, so defined, 42 percent of the daily price changes were "big" changes, as compared with 20 percent for other, "normal" time periods. Thus the crisis periods were somewhat, but not dramatically, more likely to be accompanied by big stock price changes.

Note that there were only 11 such weeks of "crisis" in the whole 16 years of Niederhoffer's sample. Very few of the aggregate price movements in the stock market show any meaningful association with headlines.

Tag-Along News

News stories occurring on days of big price swings that are cited as the causes of the changes often cannot, one suspects, plausibly account for the changes—or at least not for their full magnitude. On Friday, October 13, 1989, there was a stock market crash that was clearly identified by the media as a reaction to a news story. A leveraged buyout deal for UAL, the parent company of United Airlines, had fallen through. The crash, which resulted in a 6.91 percent drop in the Dow for the day, had begun just minutes after this announcement, and so it at first seemed highly likely that it was the cause of the crash.

The first problem with this interpretation is that UAL is just one firm, accounting for but a fraction of 1 percent of the stock market's total value. Why should the collapse of the UAL buyout have had such an impact on the entire market? One interpretation at the time was that the deal's failure was viewed by the market as a watershed event, portending that many other similar pending buyouts would also fail. But no concrete arguments were given why this was really a watershed event; rather, calling it so seemed to have been nothing more than an effort to make sense of the market move in response to the news.

To try to discover the reasons for the October 13, 1989, crash, survey researcher William Feltus and I carried out a telephone survey of 101 market professionals on the Monday and Tuesday following the crash. We asked: "Did you hear about the UAL news before you heard about the market drop on Friday afternoon, or did you hear about the UAL news later as an explanation for the drop in the stock market?"

Only 36 percent said they had heard about the news before the crash; 53 percent said they had heard about it afterwards as an explanation for the drop; the rest were unsure when they had heard about it. Thus it appears that the news story may have *tagged along* after the crash, rather than directly caused it, and therefore that it was not as prominent as the media accounts suggested.

We also asked the market professionals to interpret the news story. We queried:

Which of the following two statements better represents the view you held last Friday:

1. The UAL news of Friday afternoon will reduce future takeovers, and so the UAL news is a sensible reason for the sudden drop in stock prices.

2. The UAL news of Friday afternoon should be viewed as a focal point or attention grabber, which prompted investors to express their doubts about the market.

Of the respondents, 30 percent chose 1 and 50 percent chose 2; the rest were unsure. Thus they were mostly reacting to the news as an *interpretation of the behavior of investors* (Shiller and Feltus 1989). It may be correct to say that the news event was *fundamental* to this stock market crash, in that it represented a "story" that enhanced the feedback from stock price drops to further stock price drops, thereby preserving the feedback effect for a longer period than would otherwise have been the case. Yet it was unlikely to have been its cause.

The Absence of News on Days of Big Price Changes

We can also look at days of unusually large price movements and ask if there were exceptionally important items of news on those days. Following up on Niederhoffer's work, David Cutler, James Poterba, and Lawrence Summers compiled in 1989 a list of the 50 largest stock market movements in the United States since World War II, and for each tabulated the explanations offered in the news media. Most of the so-called explanations do not correspond to any unusual news, and some of them could not possibly be considered serious news. For example, the reasons given for large price movements included such relatively innocuous statements as "Eisenhower urges confidence in the economy," "further reaction to Truman victory over Dewey," and "replacement buying after earlier fall" (Cutler, Poterba, and Summers, 1989, p. 10).

Some would argue that perhaps we should not expect to see prominent news on days of big price changes, even if markets are working perfectly. Price changes in a so-called efficient market occur, so the argument goes, as soon as the information becomes public; they do not wait until the information is reported in the media. Thus it is not surprising, according to this line of reasoning, that we often do not find new information in the newspaper on the day of a price change: earlier information, appearing to the casual observer as tangential or irrelevant, has already been interpreted by perceptive investors as significant to the fundamentals that should determine share prices.

Another argument advanced to explain why days of unusually large stock price movements have often not been found to coincide with important news is that a confluence of factors may cause a significant market change, even if the individual factors themselves are not particularly newsworthy. For example, suppose certain investors are informally using a particular statistical model that forecasts fundamental value using a number of economic indicators. If all or most of these particular indicators all point the same way on a given day, even if no single one of them is of any substantive importance by itself, their combined effect will be noteworthy.

But both of these interpretations of the fact that news and market movements are only tenuously related are based on the assumption that the public is paying continuous attention to the news. By these interpretations, the public is supposed to be reacting sensitively to the slightest clues about market fundamentals, or is every single moment carefully adding up all the pieces of evidence. But that is not the way public attention works; attention is much more quixotic and capricious. The news functions more often as an initiator of a chain events that fundamentally change the public's thinking about the market.

News as a Precipitator of Attention Cascades

The role of news events in affecting the market seems often to be delayed, and to have the effect of setting in motion a sequence of public attention. Attention may be to facts that may already have been well known, or to images or stories. The facts may have been ignored or were in the past judged as inconsequential, but attain newfound prominence after some news event. These sequences of attention may be called cascades, as one thing attracting attention leads to another and then to another.

At 5:46 A.M. on Tuesday, January 17, 1995, an earthquake measuring 7.2 on the Richter scale struck Kobe, Japan. It was the worst earthquake to hit urban Japan since 1923. The reaction of the stock markets of the world to this event provides an interesting case study, since in this case we know without doubt that the precipitating event, the earthquake, was truly exogenous and not itself generated by human activity or business conditions, not a response to a subtle hint of economic change, nor the result of a confluence of unusual values of conventional economic indicators. In the Cutler, Poterba, and Summers list of media explanations for the 50 largest postwar movements in the Standard and Poors Index in the United States referred to earlier, not a single one of the explanations referred to any substantial cause that was definitely exogenous to the economy.[4]

---

4. That is, there is none unless one counts as substantial President Dwight Eisenhower's heart attack on September 26, 1955.

The earthquake took 6,425 lives. According to estimates by the Center for Industrial Renovation of Kansai, the total damage caused by the earthquake was about US$100 billion. The reaction in financial markets was strong, but delayed. The Tokyo stock market fell only slightly that day, and prices of construction-related companies generally rose, reflecting the expected increased demand for their products and services. Analysts reported at that time that the probable effects of the earthquake on corporate value were as yet ambiguous, since the wave of rebuilding after the quake might stimulate the Japanese economy.

The biggest reaction to the earthquake did not come until a week later. On January 23, the Japanese Nikkei share index fell 5.6 percent on no apparent news except the gradual unfolding of numerous news accounts of earthquake damage. Over the 10 days following the earthquake, the Nikkei lost over 8 percent of its value. If viewed as the direct result of the earthquake damage alone, the loss of value would be an overreaction.

What was going on in investors' minds over the 10 days following the earthquake? Of course, there is no rigorous way to find out. We know only that over this period the Kobe earthquake dominated the news, created new and different images of Japan, and may have led to very different impressions about the Japanese economy. Moreover, the quake sparked discussions about the risk of an earthquake centered in Tokyo. Despite the fact that geological evidence suggesting that Tokyo is at risk for a major earthquake was already known, greater attention was now focused on this potential problem. The damage that an earthquake of the severity of the 1923 quake could cause to modern-day Tokyo was put at US$1.25 trillion by Tokai Research and Consulting, Inc. ("The Tokyo Earthquake: Not 'If' but 'When,'" *Tokyo Business Today*, April 1995, p. 8).

Even more puzzling than the direct effect of the Kobe earthquake on domestic Japanese markets was its effect on foreign stock markets. On the day that the Nikkei fell 5.6 percent, the Financial Times Stock Exchange 100 Index in London fell 1.4 percent, the Compagnie des Agents de Change 40 Index in Paris fell 2.2 percent, and the Deutscher Aktien Index in Germany fell 1.4 percent. The Brazilian and Argentine stock markets both fell about 3 percent. These diverse countries around the world suffered no earthquake damage on this occasion.

The best interpretation of the effects of the Kobe earthquake on the stock markets of the world is that news coverage of the earthquake, and of the accompanying stock market declines, engaged the attention of investors, prompting a cascade of changes that brought to the fore some more pessimistic factors.

Another market reaction to news illustrates how media attention may, through a sequence of events, foster a belief that some news that would normally be considered nonsense and irrelevant by nearly all investors may eventually be widely taken seriously. A sequence of news stories about Joseph Granville, a flamboyant market forecaster, appear to have caused a couple of major market moves. The only substantive content of these media stories was that Granville was telling his clients to buy or sell, and that Granville himself was influential.

Granville's behavior easily attracted public attention. His investment seminars were bizarre extravaganzas, sometimes featuring a trained chimpanzee who could play Granville's theme song, "The Bagholder's Blues," on a piano. He once showed up at an investment seminar dressed as Moses, wearing a crown and carrying tablets. Granville made extravagant claims for his forecasting ability. He said he could forecast earthquakes and once claimed to have predicted six of the past seven major world quakes. He was quoted by *Time* magazine as saying, "I don't think that I will ever make a serious mistake in the stock market for the rest of my life," and he predicted that he would win the Nobel Prize in economics (Santry 1980a,b).

The first Granville episode took place on Tuesday, April 22, 1980. With the news that he had changed from his recommendation (from short to long), the Dow rose 30.72 points, or 4.05 percent. This was the biggest increase in the Dow since November 1, 1978, a year and a half earlier. The second episode occurred on January 6, 1981, after Granville's investor service changed from a long recommendation to a short recommendation. The Dow took its biggest dive since October 9, 1979, over a year earlier. There was no other news on either of these occasions that might appear responsible for the market change, and on the second occasion both the *Wall Street Journal* and *Barrons* squarely attributed the drop to Granville's recommendation.

Can we be sure that media reporting of Granville and his supposed powers of prognostication caused these changes? Many people wondered if the Granville effect was not just a coincidence that the news media exaggerated. We *can* be sure that a sequence of news stories about Granville's pronouncements had a cumulative effect on national attention, and that public reactions to his pronouncements and to market declines at the time of his announcements were fundamentally altered by this cascade.[5]

References

Cutler, David, James Poterba, and Lawrence Summers, 1989, "What Moves Stock Prices?" *Journal of Portfolio Management* 15(3): 4–12.

---

5. Professors Gur Huberman and Tomer Regev, of Columbia University wrote a case study of the soaring price of an individual company's stock in response to a newspaper story that, while compellingly written, actually revealed no news. The share price of EntreMed rose from 12 to 85 from the close of the market the day before to its opening on the day of a front-page *New York Times* story that described the potential of the company's drugs to cure cancer. They document that every fact in the story had already been published five months earlier (see Huberman and Regev 1999.) It is plausible—although the authors do not document this—that many of the buyers of EntreMed shares on that day knew there was no news in the story, but merely bought thinking that a story that was so well written and featured so prominently would boost the share price.

Desmond, Robert W. 1978. *The Information Process: World News Reporting to the Twentieth Century.* Iowa City: University of Iowa Press.

Garber, Peter. 2000. *Famous First Bubbles: The Fundamentals of Early Manias.* Cambridge, Massachusetts: MIT Press.

Huberman, Gur, and Tomer Regev. 1999. "Speculating on a Cure for Cancer: A Non-Event That Made Stock Prices Soar." Columbia University, Graduate School of Business, New York. Unpublished manuscript.

Kindlberger, Charles P. 1989. *Manias, Panics and Crashes: A History of Financial Crises*, 2nd ed. London: Macmillan.

Niederhoffer, Victor. 1971. "The Analysis of World News Events and Stock Prices." *Journal of Business* 44(2).

Pliny the Younger. 1969. *Letters and Panegyrics,* book 6, no. 19. Translated by Betty Radice Cambridge, Massachusetts: Harvard University Press.

Santry, David. 1980a. "The Long-Shot Choice of a Gambling Guru." *Business Week*, May 12, p. 112.

———. 1980b. "The Prophet of Profits." *Time*, September 15, p. 69.

Shiller, Robert J., and William J. Feltus. 1989. "Fear of a Crash Caused the Crash." *New York Times*, October 29, section 3, p. 3, col. 1.

Tokyo Business Today. 1995. "The Tokyo Earthquake: Not 'If' but 'When.'" April.

Zaret, David. 1999. *Origins of Democratic Culture: Printing, Petitions, and the Public Sphere in Early-Modern England.* Princeton, New Jersey: Princeton University Press.

6

Distributing News and Political Influence

David Strömberg

The mass media affect both who receives political information and what information they receive. This influences public policy, because politicians tend to favor informed voters and well-covered issues. Politicians do so for good reason: not only are well-informed voters more likely to vote than uninformed voters, but they are also more likely to vote for those candidates who further their interests. For example, Delli Carpini and Keeter (1996) found that in the 1988 U.S. presidential election nearly 9 out of 10 of the most knowledgeable 10 percent of survey respondents voted, while only 2 out of 10 of those in the least informed decile did so (see also Larcinese 2001). In addition, Stein and Bickers (1994) found that people who are well informed in general are also more likely to be aware of new projects in their districts. Furthermore, voters who are aware of new projects are more likely to vote for their incumbent representative, controlling for the actual increase in awards to the district. This chapter discusses my recent work on how the mass media may affect policy formation.

Theory

This section describes the salient features of my theoretical model (Strömberg 1999, 2001a, forthcoming) and discusses some key results. Instead of looking for evidence of the impact of mass media, this section explores the question: If the mass media have a systematic influence on the political system, what should we expect this influence to be?

How the mass media affect policy depends on how politicians compete to gain and remain in power and on how media coverage affects their actual and proposed policies. It also depends on how the mass media compete for audience ratings and profits and on how their news coverage depends on politicians' actions. To analyze media influence I (Strömberg 1999, 2001a, forthcoming) combine a model of mass media competition with a model of political competition (for other media models see Anderson and Coate 2000; Masson, Mudambi, and Reynolds 1990; Spence and Owen 1977; Steiner 1952). In this hybrid model the distribution of informed and uninformed voters arises endogenously through the deliberate and purposeful actions of the mass media, voters, and politicians. It indicates that some common features of the mass media have important political consequences.

One such feature is that the mass media operate under increasing returns to scale. For example, once a television program has been produced, the extra cost of an additional viewer is small. For a newspaper the cost of gathering, editing, and writing news to produce the first newspaper is high, but once this fixed cost has been borne, the variable cost of selling additional newspapers is just the cost of printing and delivering them (for the cost structure of newspapers see Litman 1988; Rosse 1970). This cost structure induces media motivated by profits to cover issues that concern large groups while frequently neglecting minority groups and special interests.

The resulting news bias has political consequences. For example, in a world without mass media trade policies are likely to ignore dispersed consumer interests and favor special interests with highly concentrated benefits from trade barriers (see Lohmann 1998; Olson 1965). In a country without mass media, for a politician to advocate reducing trade barriers may be difficult. Few consumers have individual incentives to keep themselves informed about the effects of trade barriers and of politicians' positions on this issue. Special interests will, however, surely keep themselves informed, thereby inducing pressure on the politicians. The mass media may counter this bias, because they provide politicians with a megaphone that reaches the large, dispersed consumer groups. In a similar vein, without the mass media we might expect policies to ignore dispersed taxpayers' interests and favor those that receive concentrated benefits from some small government program. The mass media might counter this bias, because their cost structures make covering politicians' positions on taxes more profitable than covering their positions on small government programs.

If this was the only aspect of news reporting, newspapers would never report on, say, operas, whose audiences consist of a tiny share of the population, yet clearly they do. One reason for this may be that a main source of revenue for many newspapers and television stations is advertising, and for advertisers not only the size, but also the characteristics of the audience are important. In the newspaper industry examples abound of newspapers that have increased their sales only to see profits fall as a consequence of falling advertising revenue. One of the most cited examples involves the English newspaper the *Times*. Michael Mander, deputy chief executive of the *Times* in the late 1960s put it this way (Mander 1978, p. 75):

From 1967 to 1969 the Times . . . sales shot up from 270,000 to 450,000—a remarkable achievement. But its higher sales made it no more attractive as an advertisement medium . . . adding to the readership just watered down the essential target group and increased the cost of reaching it. A reversal of policy changed the situation with a consequent dramatic improvement of profitability. The circulation is back down to 300,000.

In a frequently cited case from American television the show "Gunsmoke" was canceled even though it had high ratings. The show's audience was evidently too old and too rural to be worth much to advertisers (Barnouw 1978, p. 73). Apparently the mass media try to cover issues that groups valuable to advertisers find interesting. This media bias translates into a political bias favoring these groups.

A third feature arises because surprising events are more newsworthy than expected events. In the model, news about government programs is valuable to readers because these programs affect their everyday lives and they need to take actions to adjust to them. For example, news about rural public works may help famine victims find employment. Similarly, early news about changes in agricultural subsidies help farmers produce the right crops to realize the full value of these subsidies. In this setting unexpected developments will therefore be valuable and thoroughly covered by the media. By contrast, news about a program that develops as expected will not be very valuable and will be scantily covered by the media. This behavior of the media induces politicians to boost unexpected increases in programs and moderate unexpected cutbacks. The reason is that unexpected spending hikes attract the attention of the media, making such hikes more politically profitable. Similarly, unexpected program cutbacks receive extra news coverage, making them more politically costly. These information management concerns induce politicians to launch a few large spending initiatives in the hope of garnering media coverage, balanced by small cuts in a large number of programs in the hope of avoiding media coverage. Because of this convex response, over time the media will induce politicians to focus more on programs whose high variability in demand attracts frequent media coverage, such as famines, and less on programs with a constant demand and scarce media coverage, such as endemic hunger. This particular case has been argued by Drèze and Sen (1990), who found that India, which has free media, has avoided famines, but not endemic hunger, more successfully than China, which lacks free media.

A final feature is that the amount of news coverage depends on the cost of delivering news. Although trivial, this has important and testable implications, because the major mass media—radio, newspapers, and television—have very different delivery costs. As distributing radio waves is less expensive than distributing newspapers to remote areas, the model predicts that radio will increase the share of well-informed rural voters, and that this should cause an expansion in programs that benefit these voters. This hypothesis is tested in the following section.

Evidence

If the mass media affect public policy or voting behavior, then revolutions in media technology, such as the invention of the radio, television, and the Internet, should leave some visible impact. This section looks for this impact by studying whether the county allocation of funds in a large, early New Deal program was affected by the increasing use of radio, and is based on Strömberg (1999, 2001b).

The Program under Study

I tested the hypothesis about the effects of radio on policy on the Federal Emergency Relief Administration (FERA) program. The purpose of this program was to provide assistance to people with inadequate incomes. It was implemented from 1933–35 and distributed a total of US$3.6 billion, which can be compared with total annual federal, state, and local government expenditures at the time of about US$12 billion. The program's funds were widely distributed, at their peak reaching around 16 percent of all Americans, or more than 20 million people. The federal government was responsible for the allocation between states, and governors were responsible for county allocations within states.

I chose the FERA program because it was implemented in the middle of the period when radio was becoming widespread. If radio increased the political strength of certain groups or regions, then one should expect a new, major program to target these groups, to some extent. At the beginning of the FERA program radio had become established as an important mass medium used for news broadcasts and political campaigns. Nevertheless, radio ownership was still unevenly distributed across the United States. From county to county the share of households with a radio receiver ranged from 1 to 90 percent. This wide variation in radio use should make it easier to identify the effects of radio use on FERA spending, because the variation in government spending because of the effects of radio should also have been exceptionally large.

In line with the earlier discussion, radio may have affected spending if the information transmitted by radio increased voter turnout or helped voters to vote for the political candidate who best furthered their interests. As concerns the FERA program, radio broadcasts of the time covered ongoing developments in relation to FERA projects. Radio was also used in political campaigns. In a typical campaign speech, broadcast over the radio in 1934, Governor Lehman of New York stated:

> In 1932, I promised that the State under my administration would recognize that it was its obligation to see that no citizen should be lacking in food, shelter, or clothing. I am proud of the fulfillment of that promise during the two years of my administration. Between November 1931 and August, 1934, we expended $482,000 000 from public funds, Federal, State, and local.

The address goes on to take credit for projects such as roads from farms to markets and the provision of relief to specific groups such as homeowners and teachers. Radio was apparently used to remind voters of past favors as well to make new campaign promises.

Both these uses of radio probably changed the political benefits of government programs, because information about past favors and campaign promises helped voters to identify and vote for politicians who had furthered their interests in their last term in office or who promised to do so in the coming term. For example, if a governor in the early 1920s would have promised to start building roads from farms to markets, the return in the form of rural votes might have been meager, because many of those people concerned lived in rural areas, did not have a daily newspaper, and would not have been aware of this promise. Ten years later this governor could go on the radio and make this promise directly to an increasing number of such voters. This, of course, increased the political benefits of such projects. Similarly, before the advent of radio many of the people living in rural areas would not have known whom to credit for the roads they benefited from, while 10 years later a governor could go on the radio and tell an increasing number of these voters directly that the credit was his or hers. This increased the incentive to launch such projects.

The incentives created by radio could also have worked at the local level. According to Dunn (1936), a local relief chairman reportedly laments when the FERA is cutting back its activities: "'This is likely to hinder my chances for re-election,' since there would undoubtedly be a feeling of bitterness created on the part of a number of people whom he might find it necessary to refuse." My model suggests that the chairman would be more reluctant to refuse people who were likely to vote and people who were likely to know that he was responsible for their refusal.

If politicians were affected by the incentives to provide favorable policies to informed voters is an empirical question. If this were true, the patterns we would expect in the data would be high spending in areas with high voter turnout where many voters have radios and few voters are illiterate.

Results

Before a more structured investigation of the data, it may be helpful to look at some univariate correlations. Illiteracy, low voter turnout, and low radio ownership are negatively correlated with government spending, whereas unemployment is positively correlated with spending and low bank deposits are only weakly correlated with spending.

In a multivariate regression analysis of the determinants of spending, a similar pattern emerges. Factors related to low socioeconomic status are positively related to spending if they indicate a need for income assistance (high level of unemployment, low bank deposits, low house values) and negatively related to spending if they indicate low levels of political participation and information (low voter turnout, high levels of illiteracy, low radio use). Thus poor counties are not automatically politically weak. This makes sense, because the votes of the poor may be more easily swayed by economic favors. The weakness comes about because the poor participate less in politics and are not well informed.

The estimated effects of radio use and voter turnout on government spending are sizable. The estimate coefficients from the foregoing regression imply that a 1 percent increase in the share of households with radios in a county is associated with an increase in relief spending of 0.52 percent, and a 1 percent increase in voter turnout is associated with a 0.61 percent increase in relief spending.

Next I used a panel of county data from 1920–30 to investigate whether voter turnout was related to the increasing use of radio. In a fixed effects regression I found an extremely significant positive correlation between increasing radio use and increasing voter turnout. The estimated coefficients from this regression imply that a 1 percent increase in radio use is associated with a 0.12 percent increase in voter turnout.

Figure 6.1 summarizes radio's total estimated effects on relief spending. A 1 percent increase in the share of households with radios in a county is estimated to increase relief spending by 0.52 percent directly as people in the county become better at attracting public funds. As every 1 percent increase in voter turnout increases spending by 0.61 percent, radio's effect on spending via voter turnout is 0.07 percent. Thus the total increase in relief spending from a 1 percent increase in radio ownership is estimated to be 0.59 percent.

A possible concern is that the correlation between the share of households with a radio and relief spending may arise simply because counties where many people have radios have a greater need for relief spending; however, the opposite seems more likely. Counties where many people have radios have characteristics that suggest a lower need for relief spending, that is, lower unemployment, higher wages, higher property values, and so on.[1]

Discussion

The effects of radio ownership on both relief spending and voter turnout are significantly higher in rural than in urban counties. This is expected given the cost structure

---

1. To further investigate whether it really is radio penetration that matters, radio ownership was instrumented using ground conductivity, a geological feature that the Federal Communications Commission uses to predict the propagation of AM signals across the United States, and the sum of the power of all AM antennas in 1934, weighted by the inverse square root of the distance between the county seat and the antenna. The instruments are strongly correlated with the share of households with radios in the expected way. The instrumental variables estimates show significant effects of radio on both spending and turnout. However, while the instrumental variables-estimated effect of radio on turnout remains significant after the inclusion of state effects, this is not true for the spending equation.

Figure 6.1. Estimated Effects of Radio

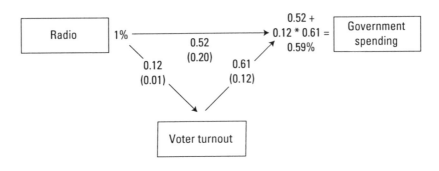

Note: Figures in parentheses are standard errors.
Source: Author.

of radio and newspaper news delivery. It is also in line with contemporary accounts of how radio reduced the informational disadvantage of rural populations. In a symposium on radio and rural life organized in 1935 by E. Brunner, a professor of education at Columbia University, radio's effectiveness in breaking down rural isolation was repeatedly stressed. For example, R. F. Fricke (1935, p. 26) stated:

> I believe the radio to be a very important factor in giving to the farmer a much broader knowledge in public affairs . . . I believe the radio has meant more to the farmer than to the city person, and that he uses it more especially in listening to programs dealing with public affairs and for that reason, I believe the farmer to be better informed than the average city man, thanks to the radio.

My results (Strömberg 1999, 2001a) indicate that radio not only broke rural isolation, but in doing so also increased the political power of rural counties. The effect was considerable. Estimates indicate that radio increased FERA funds allocated to a rural county, relative to an identical urban county, by 20 percent.

Moreover, radio's effect on voter turnout is interesting in its own right. The aggregate effects of increasing radio use on voter turnout are far from negligible. In 1920 fewer than 1 percent of the U.S. population used radios. By 1940 around 80 percent of households had radios. The estimate suggests that this would have led to an increase in votes per capita of around 5.5 percent. Between 1920 and 1940 votes per capita in the United States increased by about 12 percent, from 25 to 37 percent, in both gubernatorial and presidential elections. According to the estimates the increase would only have been about half as large without radio. The estimates are based on time series variation using year dummy variables, so they are not merely picking up the time trend in both series.

I estimated the media's impact on policy in the United States in the early 1930s, that is, for an industrial, democratic country with a free press (Strömberg 1999, 2001a). This impact may, of course, be different in other settings, though Besley and Burgess (forthcoming) found a similar impact in a developing country. They found that Indian states with higher newspaper circulation are more effective in attracting public food distribution and calamity relief expenditure in cases of drought. However, the findings of Djankov and others (forthcoming) that state ownership is negatively correlated with good government and of Besley and Prat (2001) that less press freedom is associated with lower government turnover indicate that in a less democratic country with less free press the effects are likely to be smaller.

Extension: Television 1950–60

I carried out a similar study on the effects of the expanding use of television. Although the effects of television on voter turnout are as precisely estimated as those of radio, the estimated effects on spending are cruder, because I did not look at one large program with well-defined goals, but used a 1962 cross-section of all intergovernmental transfers from U.S. states to counties. This included spending on education, highways, public welfare, and for other purposes, and thus carefully controlling for other determinants of spending was much more difficult. Unfortunately, the 1950 census took place before the large-scale expansion of television, when only 9 percent of U.S. homes had television, and the 1960 census took place after most of the expansion, when 87 percent of homes had a television. So the cross-sectional variation is not as great as in the radio study.

While radio was important for rural areas, television seemed to have been important for African-Americans and people with low education. McCombs (1968) found that during the 1952–60 expansion of television, the share of the population that used neither television nor newspapers extensively fell from 71 to 49 percent among African-Americans with less than a high school education. Among whites at the same educational level the share of low media users actually grew by 5 percent. Among whites with a high school education or more, the share of low media users doubled from 16 to 38 percent. Judging from these studies, television seems to have reduced the informational disadvantage of African-Americans and people with a low level of education. I therefore tested whether television increased the political strength and participation of these groups.

The statistical analysis took the same form as in the study of radio: one regression studied the determinants of intergovernmental transfers and another studied the determinants of changes in voter turnout during 1950–60. The results show that while high voter turnout is correlated with receiving more government transfers, television ownership is only significantly correlated with government transfers in counties with many African-Americans. Furthermore, an increase in television use is clearly associated with increases in voter turnout, especially in counties with many people with low education levels. The effects of television are weaker than those of radio: the positive effect of television on voter turnout is only a third of that of radio. Perhaps this indicates increasing media saturation.

The results indicate that television increased the ability of African-Americans and people with a low level of education to attract government funds. For African-Americans the effect seems primarily to be that television directly increased their ability to attract government funds, perhaps by helping them to vote more accurately for politicians who furthered their interests. In contrast, television seems to have increased the political power of people with low levels of education by increasing their voter turnout more than for the average citizen.

That the increasing use of television significantly increased voter turnout is somewhat surprising. Watching television news is often not a significant predictor of political knowledge in cross-sectional studies of survey data (Delli Carpini and Keeter 1996). However, this may indicate that people who watch much television are less knowledgeable to start with, not that they do not learn from television (Price and Zaller 1993). Critics of television further claim that instead of stimulating viewers' interest and involvement in social action, television news may instead spread a political malaise that discourages political participation (Putnam 2000; Robinson 1976). My analysis (Strömberg 1999, 2001a) strongly rejects the idea that the increasing use of television created a political malaise in the 1950s. Instead my findings suggest that television increased political participation.

Conclusions

The mass media may affect policy because they provide voters with politically relevant information. This information makes voters both more likely to vote, and more likely to vote for politicians who further their interests. In consequence, politicians should target well-informed voters.

Who will be informed by the media depends on the media's cost and revenue structures. The theoretical section of this chapter argues that increasing returns to scale will induce mass media to provide less news to small groups of voters. This news bias will translate into a bias in public policy. Minority groups and special interest groups will receive less favorable policies because of the provision of information by mass media firms. Mass media may, for this reason, help dispersed consumer and taxpayer interests to decrease the prevalence of trade barriers and of small "pork barrel" projects sought by special interest groups.

The media may also affect how politicians respond to changes in demand for different government-provided services. They are likely to induce politicians to propose drastic increases or initiatives in a few programs to attract positive media attention, financed by many small cutbacks to avoid media attention. Thus over time more resources will be devoted to programs with highly variable demand, such as famines, than to programs with a more constant demand, such as endemic hunger.

The empirical evidence suggests that U.S. politicians of the 1930s allocated more relief funds to areas where a larger share of the population had radios and where more people voted. The effects are not only highly statistically significant, but also economically important. The estimates imply that for every percentage point increase in the share of households with radios in a certain county the governor would increase per capita relief spending by 0.6 percent. A one standard deviation increase in the share of households with radios would increase spending by 10 percent.

Politicians allocated fewer relief funds to areas with a large share of illiterate people. Illiteracy impedes the gathering of political information. Like people not using the mass media, illiterates are less politically powerful than those who are literate, because they are both less likely to vote and less likely to vote for candidates who further their interests. The estimated effects of illiteracy are highly significant and considerable: for every percentage point increase in the illiteracy rate politicians cut spending by an average of 2 percent.

One way to put the estimated effects of radio and literacy in perspective is to compare them with the effects of voter turnout. The estimated gain in political power from, say, a 10 percent increase in literacy and mass media access in disadvantaged counties is of the same order of magnitude as a 10 percent increase in voter turnout. An uninformed vote seems to create similar political pressure as no vote at all.

The innovation of radio and television changed the political strength of different groups by affecting who was informed and who was not. In particular, radio improved the relative ability of rural America to attract government transfers. In total, radio increased the funds allocated to a rural county relative to an identical urban county by an estimated 20 percent. Similarly, preliminary results also indicate that African-Americans and people with little education gained from the introduction of television in the 1950s. Today the spreading use of the Internet is likely to have a similar political impact, creating both losers and gainers. An interesting topic for future study would be to identify these groups and to measure the political impact of the Internet.

References

The word "processed" describes informally reproduced works that may not be commonly available through libraries.

Anderson, Simon P., and Stephen Coate. 2000. "Market Provision of Public Goods: The Case of Broadcasting." Cornell University, Ithaca, New York. Processed.

Barnouw, Erik. 1978. *The Sponsor.* New York: Oxford University Press.

Besley, Timothy, and Robin Burgess. Forthcoming. "The Political Economy of Government Responsiveness: Theory and Evidence from India." *Quarterly Journal of Economics.*

Besley, Timothy, and Andrea Prat. 2001. "Handcuffs for the Grabbing Hand? The Role of the Media in Political Accountability." London School of Economics, London. Processed.

Delli Carpini, Michael X., and Scott Keeter. 1996. *What Americans Know about Politics and Why it Matters.* New Haven, Connecticut; London: Yale University Press.

Dunn, Catherine. 1936. *What Price Poor Relief?* Chicago: American Public Welfare Association.

Djankov, Simeon, Caralee McLiesh, Tatiana Nenova, Andrei Shleifer. Forthcoming. "Who Owns the Media?" *Journal of Law and Economics.*

Drèze, Jean, and Amartya Sen. 1990. *The Political Economy of Hunger*, vol. 1. Oxford, U.K.: Clarendon Press.

Fricke, R. F. 1935. In Edmund Brunner, ed., *Radio and the Farmer.* New York: Radio Institute of the Audible Arts.

Larcinese, Valentino. 2001. "Information Acquisition, Ideology, and Turnout: Theory and Evidence from Britain." London School of Economics, London. Processed.

Litman, Barry. 1988. "Microeconomic Foundations." In Robert G. Picard, James P. Winter, Maxwell E. McCombs, and Stephen Lacy, eds., *Press Concentration and Monopoly.* Norwood, New Jersey: Ablex.

Lohmann, Susanne. 1998. "An Information Rationale for the Power of Special Interests." *American Political Science Review* 92(4): 809–27.

Mander, M. 1978. "The Integration of Advertising and Circulation Sales Policies." In H. Henry, ed., *Behind the Headlines: The Business of the British Press: Readings in the Economics of the Press.* London: Associated Business Press.

Masson, Robert T., Ram Mudambi, and Robert J. Reynolds. 1990. "Oligopoly in Advertiser Supported Media." *Quarterly Review of Economics and Business* 30(2): 3–16.

McCombs, Maxwell E. 1968. "Negro Use of Television and Newspapers for Political Information, 1952–1964." *Journal of Broadcasting* XII(3): 261–66.

Olson, Mancur. 1965. *The Logic of Collective Action.* Cambridge, Massachusetts: Harvard University Press.

Price, Vincent, and John Zaller. 1993. "Who Gets the News? Alternative Measures of News Reception and Their Implications for Research." *Public Opinion Quarterly* 57: 133–64.

Putnam, Robert D. 2000. *Bowling Alone: The Collapse and Revival of American Community.* New York: Simon & Schuster.

Robinson, Michael J. 1976. "Public Affairs Television and the Growth of Political Malaise." *American Political Science Review* 70: 409–42.

Rosse, James N. 1970. "Estimating Cost Function Parameters without Using Cost Data: Illustrated Methodology." *Econometrica* 38(2): 256–75.

Spence, Michael, and Bruce Owen. 1977. "Television Programming, Monopolistic Competition, and Welfare." *Quarterly Journal of Economics* 91: 103–26.

Stein, Robert M., and Kenneth N. Bickers. 1994. "Congressional Elections and the Pork Barrel." *Journal of Politics* 56(2): 377–99.

Steiner, Peter O. 1952. "Program Patterns and Preferences, and the Workability of Competition in Radio Broadcasting." *Quarterly Journal of Economics* 66(2): 194–223.

Strömberg, David. 1999. "The Politics of Public Spending." Ph. D. Dissertation, Princeton University, Princeton, New Jersey.

———. 2001a. "Mass Media and Public Policy." *European Economic Review* 45(4–6): 652–63.

———. 2001b. "Radio's Impact on Public Spending." Stockholm University, Stockholm. Processed.

———. Forthcoming. "Mass-Media Competition, Political Competition, and Public Policy." *Review of Economic Studies*.

7

The Corporate Governance Role of the Media

Alexander Dyck and Luigi Zingales

In April 1992 the *Wall Street Journal* published a strange advertisement. It was a full-page picture of a silhouette of the board of directors of Sears Roebuck with the title: "The non-performing assets of Sears." The advertisement, paid for by shareholder activist Robert Monks, exposed all the directors, who were identified by name, as responsible for the poor performance of Sears' stock. The directors, greatly embarrassed by the advertisement, chose to adopt many of the proposals advanced by Robert Monks, even though he had received only 12 percent of the votes in the previous election for board members and had failed to get a seat on the board. The market welcomed this change with a 9.5 percent excess return the day these changes were announced and a 37 percent excess return during the following year (Monks and Minow 1995, pp. 399-411).

On March 8, 1988, all the major U.S. networks broadcast a tape of a Panamanian tuna boat, the *Maria Luisa*, killing hundreds of dolphins while fishing for tuna. Building on public outrage, the Earth Island Institute, Greenpeace, and the Humane Society launched a boycott of tuna. Restaurant chains took tuna off the menu and school boards across the country stopped using tuna until it was "dolphin safe," that is, fished with nets that were not killing tuna. On April 12, 1990, Heinz announced that it would only sell dolphin-safe tuna. Within hours the two other largest tuna producers made a similar commitment (Reinhardt and Vietor 1994a,b).

Other contributions in this volume focus on the media's influence on development through their impact on politicians and the political process, but these episodes

We thank Mehmet Beceren for assistance in preparing the data and Rakhesh Khurana, Jay Lorsch, Forest Reinhardt, Richard Vietor, Andy Zelleke, and seminar participants at the Harvard Business School for helpful comments on an earlier draft. Alexander Dyck gratefully acknowledges financial support from the Division of Research of Harvard Business School and Luigi Zingales from the George Stigler Center at the University of Chicago.

suggest that the media may also play a role in shaping corporate policy. Are these isolated incidents or are they representative of the media's influence? If the media do have such an influence, why do they have it? As the media do not vote and do not set managers' compensation, what mechanisms force directors to pay attention to what the media say? How does the media's power relate to and interact with other corporate governance mechanisms, such as the legal and competitive environment? In what direction does media influence lead corporate policy?

These two examples alone suggest that an answer to these questions is not straightforward. In both examples the media play the role of a lever, but a lever used by two very different groups: disenfranchised shareholders in the first case, environmentalists in the second. The way the media were used is also different. In the first case a dissenting shareholder paid out of his own pocket for an advertisement that communicated his position about the shortcomings of managers and directors. In the second case the television networks included a tape filmed by an environmental group in their regular programming.

Finally, the outcome is also different. In the first example the public pressure resulting from the advertisement ended up forcing the directors of Sears to increase shareholders' value, an objective they should have pursued to begin with. In the second case it forced them to bow to environmentalist groups, a constituency to which they have no fiduciary duty. One could argue that Heinz managers responded to their customers' preferences and that the media were simply instrumental in bringing crucial facts to the attention of customers. In this case, however, we have evidence that contradicts this hypothesis. As some marketing studies show, a big gap exists between consumer complaints communicated through the press and their willingness to pay. "If there is a dolphin-safe can of tuna next to a regular can, people choose the cheaper product even if the difference is just one penny" (Reinhardt and Vietor 1994a, p. 3). It is not even clear that the media forced the directors to behave in society's interest. There is no evidence that the societal loss caused by the killed dolphins is compensated for by the additional cost of fishing dolphin-safe tuna. In fact, some environmentalists have criticized this decision by claiming that it has reduced biodiversity, because it shifted tuna fishing entirely to the western Pacific, where catching tuna does not kill dolphins, but does kill many other species that, unlike dolphins, are on the endangered species list.

All these questions regarding the media's role receive limited attention in the academic literature.[1] This is no accident. The process of diffusion of information plays

---

1. In his survey of the state-of-the-art in corporate finance, Zingales (2000) mentions this as one important force that has been neglected. Skeel (2001) analyzed the role of shaming in corporate law. Baron (1996, 2001) investigated the role of the media in lobbying efforts and in private politics more generally. Djankov and others (2001) studied the effects of the ownership of the press.

a small role in economic models. Agents are assumed to be informed or not. If not, sometimes they are given the option of acquiring information at a prespecified cost. There is no role for information aggregators, which selectively reduce the cost of acquiring information. In the real world the media play this role. People obtain much of their information from the media, which play an important part in selecting which pieces of information to communicate to the public and in adding credibility to information provided through other sources. By selectively reducing agents' cost of collecting and evaluating information, the media play a major role in shaping the creation and accumulation of reputation.

The media can play a role in corporate governance by affecting reputation in at least three ways. First, media attention can drive politicians to introduce corporate law reforms or enforce corporate laws in the belief that inaction would hurt their future political careers or shame them in the eyes of public opinion, both at home and abroad.

Second, media attention could affect reputation through the standard channel that most economic models emphasize. In the traditional understanding of reputation (see, for example, Fama 1980; Fama and Jensen 1983), managers' wages in the future depend on shareholders' and future employers' beliefs about whether the managers will attend to their interests in those situations where they cannot be monitored. This concern about a monetary penalty can lead mangers not to take advantage of opportunities for self-dealing so as to create a belief that they are good managers.

Third, and what we emphasize here, media attention affects not only managers' and board members' reputations in the eyes of shareholders and future employers, but media attention affects their reputation in the eyes of society at large. As Monks describes the Sears advertisement: "We were speaking to their friends, their families, their professional associates. Anyone seeing the ad would read it. Anyone reading it would understand it. Anyone understanding it would feel free to ask questions of any board member they encountered" (Rosenberg 1999, pp. 269–70). Heinz shareholders may have been extremely unhappy about the decision to fish only dolphin-safe tuna, as might any of the managers' potential employers. Heinz's managers and directors acted in part to protect their public image. They did not want to be harassed by their children when they went home or to feel embarrassed when they went to church or to their country club. Nell Minow, Robert Monks' business partner, told us that to this day Sears' directors hate Robert Monks, because at their local country club they are still laughed at as a result of Monks' advertisement. No insurance policy for managers or directors can protect them from such reputational penalties.

Thus the media do play a role in shaping the public image of corporate managers and directors, and in so doing they pressure them to behave according to societal norms. Depending on the situation this pressure can lead to shareholders' value maximization, as in the case of Sears, or to deviations from it, as in the case of Heinz.

Thus far we have only raised the possibility that managers and directors care about their public image, and thus respond to media pressure. Before concluding that the media do indeed play a role in corporate governance we have to establish that this is more than a theoretical possibility supported by two anecdotes. This is what we do in the rest of this chapter. We start by reviewing a series of examples where the media do affect corporate policy. These examples sharpen intuition that we seek to clarify in a theoretical section on issues that determine the impact of the media on corporate behavior. We then move on to more systematic evidence. In Dyck and Zingales (2001) we showed that the diffusion of the press affects the amount of corporate value that insiders appropriate for themselves, the so-called private benefits of control. In this chapter we look at the effects of the press on the private sector's responsiveness to environmental issues. As our main measure of the importance of the press in a country we use the circulation of daily newspapers normalized by population. While the press cannot be important if it is not read, this is clearly a rough indicator of its importance, but one of the few available in a large cross-section of countries. We then test the robustness of our results using other indicators of press freedom and independence. As a measure of the average corporate environmental standards of firms in a country we use an index produced as a component of the 2001 environmental sustainability index. This private sector responsiveness index is a combination of five firm-based indicators ranging from the number of ISO 14001 certified companies per million dollars of gross domestic product (GDP) to the rating of firms' environmental sustainability in the Dow Jones global index.

We found that countries with a larger newspaper circulation have better environmental responsiveness, on average. This is true even after controlling for the extent of environmental regulation, the availability of information on environmental outcomes, and the level of economic development measured as GDP per capita. The effect is also economically significant. One standard deviation increase in the diffusion of the press increases the environmental index by 15 percentage points, equal to 28 percent of its standard deviation.

As the diffusion of the press may itself be endogenous or spuriously correlated with other institutional factors, we try to explain the press diffusion using exogenous variables. Religion is a major factor affecting the literacy of a country and its propensity to read. Another important factor is the degree of ethnolinguistic fractionalization. These two factors alone can explain 41 percent of the cross-sectional variation in press diffusion. When we use these two factors as instruments in our regressions on the effects of the press on environmental standards and on the size of private benefits, we obtain similar results. This supports the idea that our results are not driven by spurious correlations or reverse causality.

From a policy perspective, this evidence on the importance of media in corporate governance has two important consequences. First, previous research has mostly focused on the legal and contractual aspects of corporate governance. The evidence provided in this chapter and in Dyck and Zingales (2001) suggests that this focus should be broadened, and that the policy debate should undergo a similar shift in focus.

Second, the press pressures managers to act not just in shareholders' interest, but in a publicly acceptable way. This finding brings the role of societal norms to the forefront of the corporate governance debate. With a few notable exceptions, for example, Coffee (2001), the role of these norms has been ignored, yet they may present an opportunity for reformers if they can increase communication about behavior that violates norms and those norms support effective corporate governance. However, they might also represent a major obstacle to any attempt to improve a country's corporate governance system. In countries where firing workers to increase profits is viewed negatively, creating the incentives for managers to do so will be extremely difficult, especially in highly visible companies. This should be openly considered in any realistic plan to reform a country's corporate governance system.

Some Examples of the Effects of the Media on Corporate Policy

To illustrate that the two examples provided in the introduction are not isolated anecdotes, but the tip of an iceberg, this section provides additional case studies that link media pressure to changes in corporate behavior. What is remarkable about all the examples is that these changes took place even in the absence of any legal requirement to act or legal liability not to act.

Corporate Strategy toward the Environment

Following the passage of the Pollution Prevention Act in 1990, U.S. firms were required to disclose their annual releases of each listed chemical by facility. Unlike accounting information, which constituency could legally make use of this information is unclear. Nevertheless, this information requirement has become an extremely important tool for changing corporate behavior, because it allowed polluters to be identified by firm and by individual facilities. As the Environmental Protection Agency noted: "The information is a lever for action, as citizens exact pledges from local manufacturing facilities to reduce toxic discharges" (Vietor 1993, p. 3).

Environmental groups like the Natural Resource Defense Council and the National Wildlife Federation have aggregated the information and communicated it to the press by means of publications with such titles as *The Who's Who of Toxic Polluters* and *The Toxic 500*, which have then been selectively picked up by the broadcast and print media. Given the high appeal of any news about the environment, environmental groups are generally spared the expense that Robert Monks had to face in his Sears battle (the *Wall Street Journal* advertisement alone cost more than US$100,000) to communicate their information to the public. This differential appeal of news to the broader public might lead to systematic distortions in the targets of these campaigns, and thus in the media's corporate governance role.

The public opinion pressure created by this information about polluters had an impact. Firms that were high on the list, such as Allied (ranked third in 1990) and DuPont (ranked first in 1990), have made getting off that top 10 list a point of corporate strategy, and doing so as fast as possible, even in the absence of any legal requirement. Allied, for example, more than tripled its expenditures on environmental control facilities and voluntary cleanup following the release of this information (Vietor 1993, exhibit 1). The industry has also responded, with the Chemical Manufacturers Association developing a code for responsible manufacturing and handling principles and making these principles mandatory for members, with this "draconian self-policing" viewed as "necessary to reverse the public's overwhelmingly negative opinion of the chemicals industry" (Vietor 1993, p. 3).

Corporate Governance and the Press

The press also intersects with various corporate governance mechanisms.

SHAREHOLDER ACTIVISTS AND THE PRESS. While activists such as Robert Monks and Nell Minnow have found the press useful in their fights with management in the United States, does the press have a similar effect in emerging markets? Recent events in the Republic of Korea indicate that it does.

Korea has long been known as a place where controlling shareholders in the largest Korean firms (*chaebol*) take advantage of their position at the expense of small investors. National corporate laws convey few rights to outside investors—they score only 2 out of 5 in La Porta and others' (1998) index that measures the strength of protection for minority shareholders—and expectations in relation to law enforcement are low. According to an index designed to assess countries' law and order tradition, Korea has a level half of the average in the industrial countries.

The beginning of efforts to force change in Korea dates to 1996 and the formation of the People's Solidarity for Participatory Democracy (PSPD) driven by Jang Ha-Sung of Korea University. As in the United States, this investor activist has focused his attention on changing corporate policies in the largest Korean firms, and has relied both on legal pressures, including proxy battles, criminal suits, and derivative suits, and on the use of the press to shame corporate leaders into changing their policies. Perhaps to an even greater extent than in the United States, the success stories have resulted more from the creation of public opinion pressure than from legal sanctions.

The most successful challenge to date has been the battle to stop insider dealings in SK Telecom. SK Telecom was an extremely profitable company, but its financial results did not show this because the company used transfer pricing to benefit two companies almost 100 percent owned by the chairman of SK Telecom and his rela-tives.[2] The PSPD drew attention to these policies. After the London-based *Financial Times* picked up the story, a media campaign ensued to attract proxy votes. This campaign involved publishing advertisements in newspapers and using television and radio. In March 1998 SK Telecom's directors capitulated and agreed to the PSPD's requests.

This success stands in sharp contrast with the failure of legal actions. For ex-ample, shareholders' proposals are severely restricted and cannot involve the re-moval of directors or auditors. Perhaps the only successful legal challenge has been the one to ensure investors' rights to speak at meetings, though the right to speak can only be used to affect the reputation of the parties involved, not to trigger any legal remedy. For example, the press gave extensive coverage to the fact that the Samsung shareholders' meeting lasted 13 hours. The effect of shareholder and public opinion pressure was an increase in the transparency of Samsung's financial statements.

INSTITUTIONAL INVESTORS. While institutional investors have many legal mecha-nisms to encourage change in corporate policies, the presence of an active press in-creases their influence. It provides a relatively cheap way to impose penalties on companies and to coordinate the response of other investors in availing themselves of potential legal protection.

The California State Pension Fund for Public Employees (CalPERS), for example, has adopted a policy of identifying underperforming firms and generating wide-spread media attention as an important tool in its efforts to change corporate policies to increase their returns. CalPERS identifies a long list of poorly performing firms according to criteria such as shareholder returns, economic value added, and corpo-rate governance. Armed with this list CalPERS representatives talk to companies to try to get them to change their policies, with the threat that if they do not, CalPERS may launch a proxy contest and will go ahead and reveal the firms in a "focus list." This threat of public exposure is an important part of CalPERS' approach. CalPERS

---

2. According to PSPD (2002, p. 3): "It was confirmed that SK Telecom channeled huge profits to Sunkyung Distribution, in which Sunkyung Group Chairman Choi Jong-Hyun holds 94.6% shares, and Daehan Telecom, owned 100% by Choi's son and his son-in-law. It was revealed that SK Telecom transferred profits to Sunkyung Distribution and Daehan Telecom by paying exorbitant service fees or purchasing equipment at high prices. Due to SK Telecom's internal transactions, SK Group affiliate Daehan Telecom's business profits increased from only 64 mil-lion won to 13.7 billion won, and Sunkyung Distribution's business profits increased from –4.1 billion won to 6.6 billion won. In contrast, SK Telecom, which as the strongest company in 1996 recorded sales of 2.6 trillion won, began showing sharply increased sales costs and sharply decreased profits since becoming part of the SK Group in 1994. The sales profit, which was as high as 31% in 1994, decreased to only 14% in 1996, and the sales cost/income ratio increased greatly from 58% to 76%."

found that when it removed this publicity threat its strategy did not work. In 1991, when several chief executive officers (CEOs) convinced CalPERS that a "kindler, gentler" strategy would be less antagonistic and more effective, only 2 of the 12 targeted companies negotiated acceptable agreements with CalPERS and 3 resisted even meeting with CalPERS officials. As CalPERS CEO Dale Hanson commented: "'Kindler, gentler' is not working. It has shown us that a number of companies won't move unless they have to deal with the problem because it's in the public eye" (Dobrzynski 1992, p. 44). In 1992 CalPERS returned to the policy of publicizing its target lists.

Another example is the case of investors in Russian firms. William Browder, CEO of Hermitage Capital Management, the largest public equity fund in Russia, reported to us that "the single most important corrective mechanism we have against misgovernance is the press" (email, May 21, 2002). For example, Browder brought misdeeds at Gazprom in October 2000 to the media's attention, and was thereby able to generate publicity about management's failures, with stories in the international business press, including *Business Week*, the *New York Times*, the *Financial Times*, the *Wall Street Journal*, and the *Washington Post*. Such media pressure, reportedly, had the beneficial effect of facilitating coordination by institutional investors and shaming them to take action to vote for a special audit of the firm, something that required the approval of 10 percent of the shareholders, and of contributing to other changes in corporate policies. Press reporting on misgovernance can also shame politicians and managers who care about their international reputations to act to improve policies in firms. Interestingly, press attention is viewed as equally important to legal challenges. As William Browder reported to us: "The press is one of the reasons why we pursue lawsuits. We have pursued 24 lawsuits so far and lost 23. That is the way it is in Russia. But the advantage is the publicity."

PRIVATE AND GOVERNMENT REGULATORS. Public opinion pressure generated by an active press is also essential to efforts by private sector organizations to use self-regulation to improve corporate governance. Consider the approach in the United Kingdom to the range of financial scandals of the 1980s, including the collapse of the Bank of Credit and Commerce International and the Maxwell Group. Instead of legislation that proscribed certain activities matched by court sanctions and fines, the United Kingdom pursued self-regulation, enforced through disclosure. The Cadbury Commission, dominated by the private sector, defined corporate governance standards and developed mechanisms to compel the disclosure of performance relative to standards, allowing the force of public pressure generated by disclosure and news stories to change practices. This publicity route had the advantage that the self-regulatory organization had the power to impose it and the penalty could be introduced quickly. Alternative sanctions, such as fines and court-enforced penalties, were either unavailable or could be delayed through court proceedings, thereby limiting their effectiveness.

The Cadbury Commission, which issued its report in December 1992, was the first effort at reform by means of disclosure and public pressure. The key element of the report was a code of best practice with 19 recommendations, including an enhanced role for independent directors, a minimum number of independent directors, and the separation of the roles of the chair and the CEO. Since 1993 the London Stock Exchange has made a requirement of listing that a company include a statement of performance relative to the code and a written explanation for any variation in its annual reports. It has since become common practice for company statements issued to the press and for independent press reports to identify performance relative to code standards, with a lack of compliance described largely as a failure of corporate governance by the company and its directors. A similar approach regarding company practices toward executive compensation was adopted in the Greenbury report, issued in July 1995, and in the Hampel report, released in January 1998. All these best practices have been consolidated into a "supercode" published by the London Stock Exchange in June 1998, again with requirements for disclosure rather than compliance.

This approach—reliance on disclosure supported by widespread communication by the press of performance relative to standards—has led to remarkable changes in firm practices within a short time. A recent study (Dahya, McConnell, and Travlos 2002) showed that while two-thirds of a sample of London Stock Exchange firms were not in compliance with Cadbury standards when they were enacted in 1992, 93 percent had complied by 1996. In addition, firms that adopted the standards have seen increased management accountability, as CEOs' tenure has become more sensitive to their firms' performance. This remarkable response was undoubtedly facilitated by the press's (and the public's) acceptance of the standards, so that reports of noncompliance would lead to widespread condemnation of managers and directors.

The extent and success of a disclosure and publicity approach is widespread. In Hong Kong, China, the stock exchange has historically not had the legal authority to impose penalties on companies that misbehave. Instead, it uses the media as a sanction, taking out advertising space to notify the public about a firm's security violations. The threat is usually enough. Shaming is both a personal penalty for the executives involved and may introduce a financial penalty if others now update their beliefs about the reliability of the executives and company and increase their terms for financing projects suggested by the executives. The effects of this policy were highlighted by Dyck and Zingales (2001), who reported that the average size of private benefits in Hong Kong, China, is only 0.7 percent, versus an international average of 14 percent.

The New York Stock Exchange is currently considering a similar approach of publishing reprimand letters to members that fail to implement revised listing guidelines relating to, for example, auditor independence and committee structures, requiring firms to publish these letters in their annual reports and relying on the press to communicate the content of such letters. In short, relying on what James Landis, architect of the U.S. security laws after the crash of 1929, described as "the penalizing force of pure publicity" (McCraw 1984, p. 172).

THE PRESS VERSUS OTHER MECHANISMS FOR ADDRESSING GOVERNANCE PROBLEMS. In some markets the penalties that can be imposed by the press are at least as important as other mechanisms for fighting misgovernance that the literature more commonly focuses on. Consistent with this contention is a recent survey in Malaysia that asked institutional investors and equity analysts to identify the factors that were most important in assessing corporate governance and deciding to invest in publicly listed corporations (Low, Seetharaman, and Poon 2002). The analysts thought that the frequency and nature of public and press comments about the company were more important than a host of other factors that receive more attention in academic debate, such as the company's relationship with the regulatory authorities, the number of independent nonexecutive directors and their qualifications, the existence of remuneration and audit committees, and the identity of company auditors.

BUSINESS SCHOOL GOVERNANCE AND *BUSINESS WEEK* RANKINGS. In 1988 the magazine *Business Week* started to publish a ranking of the top U.S. business schools. Despite its arguable criteria (most students experience no more than one business school, yet their responses are used to rank them), this ranking gained a lot of attention, and soon assumed the role of a standard in the industry.[3] While we are not aware of any systematic study of the effect of the introduction of these rankings on the governance of business schools, their impact is undoubtedly huge. Suddenly teaching ratings became important and faculties were held accountable, new programs were introduced to cater to students' needs, and some schools were even caught coaching their students how to respond to the *Business Week* questionnaires.

In this case the reason why the media pressure works seems even more complex, because business schools are nonprofit institutions with peculiar governance structures. While a number of factors undoubtedly help to explain this response, including the belief that the ranking will affect the quality of applicants and the expected salaries of graduates, we cannot discount the factor we have emphasized, namely, managers' concerns about their own reputations. The moment the business school rankings were introduced and were considered an important measure for judging business schools, deans started to care because the rankings would affect their own reputations.

---

3. In the last year or so new competitors have entered the market: the *Financial Times* and the *Wall Street Journal* have elaborated their own rankings. To date, however, the *Business Week* ranking is by far the most important.

Business Week's ranking of business schools was not the first. *U.S. News and World Report* ranked all university departments, including business schools, before *Business Week* entered the game, but *U.S. News and World Report* does not have the circulation and credibility of *Business Week*, especially in the business community. However, this proves our point that the way the media affect corporate behavior is by reducing the cost of collecting and certifying relevant information. The more authoritative and diffused a magazine is, the more influential it will be, because it will be better able to affect the reputations of the parties involved.

A CONTROLLED EXPERIMENT. All these examples show an apparent correlation between media exposure of certain practices and some companies' actions to modify these practices. Yet concluding that this link is necessarily a causal one is hard. One could easily argue that the media reported this information because a demand for it existed, and that demand for it existed because pressure to change the course of action was already present. Thus the correlation between media reporting and a change in the course of action is spurious. The next section deals with this problem systematically by using instrumental variables. Before doing that, however, we report on a small, controlled experiment that lends support to the view that this correlation is causal.

One of us used to write a Sunday column in the leading Italian newspaper, *Il Corriere della Sera*. Fascinated with the Sears' story, in January 1999 he wrote a column pointing to the importance of the role of newspapers in shaping the reputation of directors and thereby enforcing better corporate practices. To set an example he singled out the worst-performing company among large publicly traded companies in Italy in the previous three years and published the names of all the directors. To his surprise he received no public response. Two months later, however, the CEO of the company resigned, providing no explanations for his departure. Another magazine linked the two events and called the writer "the torpedo professor."

Theoretical Framework

While the anecdotal evidence is useful in documenting the existence of this phenomenon and illustrating how this influence takes place, more systematic evidence is needed to prove its importance. For this reason we turn to a cross-country analysis of the effects of the media on corporate policy. Before doing so, however, we need to be more specific about the channels through which this influence occurs.

A first channel of influence is that media attention can drive corporate law reforms or the enforcement of corporate laws. The likely motivation for such changes is politicians' belief that inaction would hurt their future political careers or shame them in the eyes of public opinion, both at home and abroad. This is an important dimension of the media's impact that Besley and Prat (2001) and others have explored. It is developed in other chapters in this volume.

We focus on the links between the media and managers' and directors' reputations. Consider a model of reputation building like that presented in Diamond (1989). Agents can be of two types, good or bad, which differ in their cost of taking a certain action. In our case an environmentally-friendly manager will find polluting more painful than somebody who does not care about the environment. Let us assume, as it is likely, that the environmentally sensitive decision carries a higher cost for the manager, say, it requires more effort. Thus the good (environmentally-friendly) manager will not pollute while the bad manager will pollute.

Let us now assume, consistent with our previous discussion, that being identified as an enemy of the environment carries a cost. If we really want to incorporate this cost in the typical career concern models (see, for example, Harris and Holmstrom 1982), we can say that this cost arises from the possibility that the manager might move into politics, where a bad environmental record represents a genuine liability. More broadly, we can think of this cost as the personal disutility of a dent on the manager's public image. The social norm is that managers should be environmentally friendly, therefore being identified as a bad environmental manager produces social shaming. People simply dislike being singled out as "bad" people.

If the payoff of being recognized as environmentally conscious is large enough (or the disutility of being identified as a polluter is significant enough), even bad managers can be induced to take the "right" action by their desire to mimic the good type, and in so doing being recognized as environmentally friendly (see Diamond 1989). As only the bad manager will want to pollute, polluting immediately identifies a manager as bad. Hence if the payoff of being identified as a polluter is sufficiently negative, the bad manager will choose to disguise himself or herself as environmentally conscious by not polluting.

This type of reputation model is based on the assumption that the information about the manager's action is revealed to the public with probability 1. In practice, this is not the case. Information does not descend on individuals: they acquire it at a cost that is affected by the media. Governments, firms, and interest groups generate and aggregate information that the media then process and selectively communicate.

The broader the media coverage, the more likely that the public at large will acquire this information. Similarly, the more attention the media command, the more widely this information will travel. In our empirical analysis we will use the second dimension, and as a measure of the attention the media command we use newspaper readership normalized by population.

Clearly in this type of reputation model, if we introduce the idea that outsiders learn of managers' actions only with a certain probability, then the higher this probability is, the higher the likelihood that managers will behave in an environmentally-conscious way. In particular, if a higher diffusion of the press leads to a higher probability of detection, then the higher the diffusion of the press, the more likely that managers will behave in an environmentally-conscious way.[4] This is the proposition we will test.

Similarly, we will test the proposition that the higher the diffusion of the press, the more likely managers are to protect minority shareholders' interests. The foregoing discussion can be recast in these terms simply by substituting "shareholder friendly" for "environmentally conscious." The only difference is that in this latter case we do not have to appeal to managers caring about their public image to obtain the results, but could simply have talked about managers' reputation in the labor market. Nevertheless, in most countries managers are appointed by majority shareholders, thus whether their career opportunities are enhanced by acting in the interests of minority shareholders is not clear.

Where Do the Media Get Their Information?

The previous discussion highlighted the role of the media in aggregating, certifying, and diffusing crucial information, but where do the media get their information? For the media to collect their own information about managers' actions is costly, thus they often rely on information provided to them. An important source is the government, which either directly, or indirectly through mandated disclosure, for instance, requires financial or environmental disclosures. Government-mandated information is the most reliable, because it is not affected by selectivity and is not provided in exchange for something. With greater government-mandated disclosure, such as the toxic release inventory, it is easier for interest groups to aggregate the information and for journalists to use this aggregated information when they communicate to the public.

Journalists also obtain information directly from the source, that is, managers, employees, and so on. Not only is this information selective, it is often provided to the journalist on a quid pro quo basis, such as favorable treatment in the news story. In the long run, the use of this channel will undermine the credibility of the media.

A similar problem arises with the third potential source of information, namely, interest groups such as the shareholder activists, institutional investors, and environmental activists described earlier. Interest groups both generate information, for

---

4. More generally, any organization or institution can enhance reputation penalties if it can increase the likelihood of identifying, certifying, and disseminating information about a manager's or owner's type to a community that can impose sanctions. The key issue with effective informal contract enforcement is to increase expected penalties associated with breach of trust, which normally involves moving from bilateral sanctions ("I will refuse to trade with you again") to multilateral sanctions ("We will all refuse to trade with you again and will penalize you in additional ways as well such as shaming"). The importance of such private order institutions that rely on norms supported by repeated interactions is developed in Ellickson (1991), historical work on trading associations and ethnic groups is described by Greif (1997) and McMillan and Woodruff (2000).

instance, the tape of dolphins being killed, and aggregate and synthesize information from other outlets, such as the list of toxic polluters. Other aggregators of information in corporate governance include equity and bond analysts. While the media are important to all these groups, the media are particularly important to activists who seek to mobilize and coordinate the actions of a dispersed set of citizens, such as for a boycott or a proxy fight.

Selective Coverage and Media Credibility

So far we have treated the media as a single entity that aggregates and then communicates information. A critical issue we have ignored is the credibility of the information the media communicate to the public, which is, of course, extremely important. The fact that the *Financial Times* reported on the SK Telecom and Gazprom insider deals brought credibility to the stories, because even in Korea and Russia the *Financial Times* is more credible than local newspapers. Similarly the *Business Week* ranking of business schools had a much greater impact than the *U.S. News and World Report* ranking because the former is not only more diffused, but also more authoritative than the latter.

The issue of credibility is particularly delicate because it opens up the question of newspapers' incentives to conduct further investigations to establish the validity of the information reported to them and their incentives to report the information they receive accurately. It is precisely when newspapers do have an impact that they have an incentive to enter into side deals with the parties involved and be paid not to reveal damaging information. Threats to increase (or withhold) future advertising revenues in exchange for stories that reflect well (badly) on company management and directors are one example of side deals. Of course, such side deals might hurt the reputation of a newspaper in the long run, and hence its credibility.

If—as is likely—it is more difficult for an individual newspaper to build a reputation of integrity in a market where all the other newspapers are colluding, the possibility for multiple equilibria arises. One equilibrium is where newspapers have credibility and thus avoid side deals for fear of losing it. Another is where newspapers do not have credibility and happily accept bribes not to publish damaging information or to publish false damaging information.

Important factors that determine which equilibrium prevails are the competitive environment in which newspapers operate, the ownership structure of the media, and libel laws. In a competitive market a newspaper agreeing not to publish bad news is likely to be scooped by another newspaper and to lose credibility. Thus the more competitive the environment is, the less likely is the collusive equilibrium. Similarly, an independent newspaper whose survival rests solely on its own success is less likely to collude with established business interests. By contrast, a newspaper owned by a business group is naturally less likely to publish bad news about the group itself. This in turn affects its credibility in correctly reporting other news, thereby reducing its incentives to build a reputation (and increasing its incentives to collude).[5] More stringent libel laws reduce the likelihood of a newspaper publishing information that suggests that managers are "bad," again reducing the information content of the media.

Empirically, we lack most of this information. No internationally comparable indicators of the stringency and enforcement of libel laws are available. Djankov and others (2001) reported the fraction of media owned by the government, and Freedom House (1999, 2000) reported the degree to which each country permits the free flow of information. In our case, however, these indicators are not the most important pieces of information. We would like to know which media are owned by business groups with other important business interests and which ones have fewer ties to nonmedia firms and are independently owned, like the *New York Times* or the *Washington Post*. Political freedom of the press is not the same as freedom from economic influences.

The extent of newspaper readership that we will be using, however, indirectly gets at the credibility question. In a market where newspapers are more likely to collude, and are thus less credible, they also become a less valuable source of information, and therefore, other things being equal, they are less likely to be read. Hence our measure of newspaper readership captures both the diffusion of the newspapers and their overall credibility.

Consumer Demand and Selective Coverage

The media's impact also depends on the entertainment value of news. "It was all too complicated and boring to interest many mainstream journalists," said Ellen Hume of the *New York Times* to explain the delay in media attention to the U.S. savings and loan crisis (cited in Baron 1996, p. 62). Similarly, when asked why television had paid relatively little attention to the crisis even after it had made headlines in 1988, the president of NBC news, Michael Gartner, observed that the story did not lend itself to images, and without such images "television can't do facts" (cited in Baron 1996, p. 62).

Environmental issues naturally generate images (the dying dolphins) that can capture the public's attention, while corporate scandals do not. For this reason we expect the print media to be more central to corporate governance issues than broadcast media.

---

5. Chapter 3 in this volume by Besley, Burgess, and Prat and related work by Besley and Prat (2001) sketch out a model that picks up many of the issues described in this section, although they focus on possible collusion between the government and the media rather than private sector firms and media outlets.

Demand considerations also lead to a selective focus on stories with wide interest, like executive compensation levels, rather than on other elements of good corporate governance, like the composition of boards and the role of auditors, even after scandals such as Enron and Worldcom. Readers may not be able to appreciate the nuances of corporate situations, leading to news stories that simplify firm performance relative to environmental or corporate governance standards in too stark a way. In the United Kingdom, for example, while the recommendations developed in the Cadbury, Greenbury, and Hampel reports are often qualified, they are rarely reported that way. The "public" version is a gross oversimplification around bright line rules, producing "box checking" and intense pressure to conform to standards different from those intended.

Finally, demand for corporate governance news might depend on the structure of corporate ownership. Thus the extent of coverage and the consequent sanctioning role of the press are likely to be more important when a broad group of citizens have a personal interest in the outcomes, because of their direct or indirect (through pension funds) shareholdings. The important corporate governance role played by the media in Korea and Malaysia described earlier is probably attributable to the widespread dispersion of ownership in publicly traded firms in these two countries.

Reputational Penalties and Social Norms

As noted previously, media activity can hurt managers' reputations in the eyes of shareholders and future employers as well as of family, friends, professional associates, and the public at large. Reputational penalties can be long-lasting. As Jean Lamierre, the president of the European Bank for Reconstruction and Development said: "People may not necessarily change," in defense of a policy of keeping a secret blacklist of companies and individuals with which the bank will not do business (Wagstyl 2002).

The strength and nature of shared social norms influence the impact of the media. Where maximizing shareholders' value is the norm, any media account of underperformance has a significant impact. In the United States, for instance, a well-developed set of publications, including the *Wall Street Journal*, the *New York Times*, the *Financial Times*, *Business Week*, *Fortune*, *Forbes*, and *Harvard Business Review*, emphasizes both business heroes and villains. Executives seek to be identified in these publications for the status it brings them. Where such status is valued, the media are particularly powerful because they can both build and destroy reputations.

This power of U.S. and British media to pressure managers transcends domestic borders. After becoming rich, executives in emerging markets seek broader acceptance in the international community by joining the World Economic Forum at Davos, seeking positions on the boards of trustees of prominent international institutions, and so on. While the Russian oligarch Vladimir Potanin was successful in his efforts to join the trustees of the Guggenheim Museum in April 2002, oligarchs such as Oleg

Deripaska were "disinvited" from participating in the Davos meeting, and Deripaska was stripped of his designation as "one of the global leaders of tomorrow" following negative press coverage of civil lawsuits alleging bribery, money laundering, and worse (*Financial Times* 2001; Wagstyl 2002). Interestingly, these leaders are not as sensitive to their public image in their own country, perhaps because of the lack of credibility of the local media, the lack of shared norms, or both. In any case, these episodes suggest that the U.S. and British media play a nontrivial role in exporting the Anglo-American model to other countries.

We should reiterate, however, that the norms communicated by the media are not necessarily in shareholders' interests. In countries like Japan, where lifetime employment is a shared value, the media are likely to describe workers' dismissals in a negative light. This sanction might deter firings even when they enhance value from a shareholder's perspective.

Data on Corporate Policy and the Importance of the Press

In Dyck and Zingales (2001) we analyzed, among other things, the impact of the diffusion of the media on corporate governance. As a measure of corporate governance we used an estimate of the value of control obtained from control block transactions. On average, parties are willing to pay more for control only if they expect to enjoy some private benefits. Private benefits of control represent the wedge between the physical return to investments and the amount external financiers can appropriate. They are therefore a good indicator of how much dispersed shareholders' rights are respected.

We found that private benefits of control are lower, and thus governance is better, in countries where the press is more diffused. This is true even after controlling for the degree of legal protection offered to minority shareholders, for the quality of accounting standards, and for the level of economic development as measured as GDP per capita. The effect is also economically significant. One standard deviation increase in the diffusion of the press reduces the average value of private benefits by 5 percentage points, 18 percent of their standard deviations.

In this chapter we perform a similar analysis with respect to environmental practices.

Dependent Variable: Private Sector Responsiveness to Environmental Issues

As an indicator of the importance that private sector firms place on environmental issues we use an index of private sector responsiveness to environmental concerns developed through the collaboration of the World Economic Forum and researchers from Columbia and Yale universities. This index is based on five variables: the number of ISO 14001 certified companies per million dollars of GDP, the number of World Business Council for Sustainable Development Members per million dollars of GDP, Innovest's EcoValue rating of firms' environmental performance, the Sustainable Asset

Management rating of the environmental sustainability of firms in the Dow Jones global index, and the levels of environmental competitiveness based on firm surveys. Each variable is based on firm-level data and assigned equal weight in the index. Table 7.1 describes and defines all the variables used in this chapter and shows their sources.

Private sector responsiveness is clearly related to per capita income. The five highest ranked countries are Switzerland, Japan, Germany, the United Kingdom, and New Zealand, while the five lowest ranked countries are Venezuela, Indonesia, Greece, Colombia, and the Philippines. However, responsiveness is not driven solely by per capita income. Italy and the United Kingdom, for example, have similar per capita incomes, but very different measures of private sector responsiveness: Italy's index is –0.35, ranking it 35th in our sample, while the United Kingdom's index is 1.02, ranking it 4th.

Measures of the Importance of the Press

We focus on two principal measures of the press that recent studies have highlighted. The first measure, and the focus of the analysis, is a measure of the diffusion of the press based on the circulation of daily newspapers in the country normalized by the country population. This measure captures, to some extent, the possibility for the press to affect public opinion, because it provides one measure of the reach of the press. It also captures, to some extent, the presence of an active and competing press, because wider circulation is presumably accompanied by more intense competition among competing firms.

Cross-country variation in the diffusion of the press is significant. The five economies in our sample with the highest readership are Hong Kong (China), Norway, Japan, Finland, and Sweden. The five lowest countries in our sample are Kenya, Zimbabwe, Pakistan, South Africa, and Egypt. Again, income explains much of the variation, but even for countries with similar incomes great disparities are apparent, for instance, in the United Kingdom the average circulation is 331 per 1,000 inhabitants, while in Italy it is 104.

The press measures used more often in the literature are derived from Freedom House (see examples cited in chapter 3 by Besley, Burgess, and Pratt in this volume). We focus on three measures: the freedom of the press, the frequency of violations against broadcast media, and the frequency of violations against print media. The freedom of the press is an index that measures the "degree to which each country permits the free flow of information" (Freedom House 1999).[6] The frequency of

---

6. Freedom House reports a measure of press freedom that is scaled from 0 to 100, where 90 out of the 100 points are based on Freedom House's subjective evaluation of the laws and regulations and of political pressures and economic influences over media content, and 10 of the 100 points are based on actual violations against the media, including murder, physical attacks, harassment, censorship, and self-censorship. Half of the index total comes from an evaluation of broadcast media and half from an evaluation of print media.

Table 7.1. Variables and Sources

Variable	*Description*
Environmental governance indicator: private sector responsiveness to environmental concerns	The index of private sector responsiveness is based on five variables: the number of ISO 14001 certified companies per million dollars of GDP, the number of World Business Council for Sustainable Development members per million dollars of GDP, Innovest's EcoValue rating of firms' environmental performance (firms' weight determined by market capitalization), Sustainable Asset Management rating of the environmental sustainability of firms in the Dow Jones global index (proportion of firms in global index classified in top 10 percent of sustainability), and the levels of environmental competitiveness based on firm surveys. Each variable is based on firm-level data, assigned equal weight in the index, and using data for 122 countries has been normalized to have mean 0 and variance 1. 2001 Environmental Sustainability Index, annexes 4, 6.
Press indicator 1: newspaper diffusion	Circulation of daily newspapers/population. UNESCO (1998), reporting values for 1996. For Taiwan (China) based on Editors and Publishers' Association Year Book and AC Nielsen, Hong Kong (China), as reported in "Asian Top Media—Taiwan" (http://www.business.vu.edu).
Press indicator 2: press freedom rating	This index indicates the degree to which each country permits the free flow of information. Freedom House (1999) reports a measure of press freedom that is scaled from 0 to 100, where 90 out of the 100 points are based on Freedom House's subjective evaluation of laws and regulations and political pressures and economic influences over media content, and 10 of the 100 points are based on actual violations against the media, including murder, physical attacks, harassment, censorship, and self-censorship. Half of the index total comes from an evaluation of broadcast media and half from print media. We have rescaled the data so that higher free rating values correspond with greater press freedom. *Source:* Freedom House (1999).
Press indicator 3a: violations against broadcast media	An index based on actual violations against the media, including murder, physical attacks, harassment, and censorship. The scores for 1999 and 2000, both of which vary from 0 to 5, are combined and rescaled to produce an index that ranges from 0 to 10 with higher values corresponding to greater freedom. *Source:* Freedom House (1999, 2000).
Press indicator 3b: violations against print media	An index based on actual violations against the media, including murder, physical attacks, harassment, and censorship. The scores for 1999 and 2000, both which vary from 0 to 5, are combined and rescaled to produce an index that ranges from 0 to 10 with higher values corresponding to greater freedom. *Source:* Freedom House (1999, 2000).

(Table continues on the following page.)

Table 7.1. (continued)

Variable	Description
Environmental regulation and management	Index of stringency of legal and regulatory restrictions on firms. The index is based on four variables: stringency and consistency of environmental regulations, degree to which environmental regulations promote innovation, percentage of land area under protected status, and number of sectoral guidelines on environmental impact assessment. Each variable has equal weight and has been normalized. 2001 Environmental Sustainability Index, annexes 4, 6.
Environmental information	This index is based on three variables: the availability of sustainable development information at the national level, environmental strategies and actions plans, and the number of environmental sustainability index variables missing from selected datasets. Each variable has equal weight and has been normalized. 2001 Environmental Sustainability Index, annexes 4, 6.
Ethnolinguistic fractionalization	Average value of five different indices of ethnolinguistic fractionalization. Its values range from 0 to 1. The five component indices are: (1) index of ethnolinguistic fractionalization in 1960, which measures the probability that two randomly selected people from a given country will not belong to the same ethnolinguistic group (the index is based on the number and size of population groups as distinguished by their ethnic and linguistic status); (2) probability of two randomly selected individuals speaking different languages; (3) probability that two randomly selected individuals do not speak the same language; (4) percent of the population not speaking the official language; and (5) percent of the population not speaking the most widely used language. *Source:* Easterly and Levine (1997).
Primary religion	Identifies countries' primary religion as Protestant, Catholic, Muslim, or other. *Source:* Stulz and Williamson (2001).
Log of school attainment	The log of school attainment for those over the age of 25 taken over five-year periods (1960–1965, 1970–1975, 1980–1985). Each value is the logarithm of (1+ average years of school attainment during the respective periods). *Source:* Barro and Lee (1993) for raw data; LaPorta and others (1998) for constructed variables.
The market share of state-owned print media	The market share of state-owned print media as a percentage of the total market share of the top five print media outlets. *Source:* Djankov and others (2001).

Source: Authors.

violations against the media, be they broadcast media or print media, is an index based on "actual violations against the media, including murder, physical attack, harassment and censorship" (Freedom House 1999).[7]

A clear relationship between diffusion and the rating of press freedom is apparent, with a correlation of 0.55. However, the variables do capture different components of the press, and for countries with similar levels of freedom quite significant differences in readership can be noted, for instance, Spain and the United Kingdom have similar levels of press freedom, but Spain has less than one-third the readership.

We do not look at other possible press measures, such as the measure of ownership of the media used by Djankov and others (2001). They focused on what fraction of the media is owned by the government, but our sample has too few countries where ownership of the press is in other than private hands.

Other Institutional Factors

As we already pointed out, countries where the press is very diffused are also countries with a higher GDP per capita and better law enforcement (tables 7.2, 7.3, and 7.4). To reduce the likelihood that we are attributing to the influence of the press the role of some other institutional factors, correlated with press diffusion, our regressions control for the most important ones.

LEGAL ENVIRONMENT. Our claim is that the media have an impact on corporate behavior beyond any legal requirement. Therefore when studying the private sector's responsiveness to environmental issues we should control for the extent of environmental laws and regulations. As an indicator of the stringency of legal and regulatory restrictions on firms we use the 2001 environmental sustainability index (Yale

Table 7.2. Dependent Variable of Private Sector Responsiveness

Item	Public sector environmental responsiveness
Number of observations	122
Mean	−0.13
Standard deviation	0.55
Minimum	−0.89
Maximum	2.12
25th percentile	−0.48
75th percentile	0.05

Source: Authors' calculations.

---

7. The scores for 1999 and 2000, both of which vary from 0 to 5, are combined and rescaled to produce an index that ranges from 0 to 10, with higher values corresponding to greater freedom.

Table 7.3. Independent Variables

Item	Log per capita income	Rule of law	Press diffusion	Press freedom	Absence of violations against print media	Absence of violations against broadcast media	Environmental regulation and management	Environmental information
Number of observations	120	49	112	119	119	119	122	122
Mean	7.32	6.85	116.50	56.49	6.05	8.06	−0.09	0.00
Standard deviation	1.38	2.63	134.73	22.81	3.91	2.80	0.64	0.73
Minimum	4.72	1.90	0.20	6.00	0.00	0.00	−1.32	−1.44
Maximum	10.15	10.00	593.00	95.00	10.00	10.00	1.54	2.25
25th percentile	6.23	4.82	22.00	39.00	2.00	7.00	−0.57	−0.65
75th percentile	8.19	9.23	168.00	73.00	10.00	10.00	0.35	0.58

Source: Authors' calculations.

Center for Environmental Law and Policy 2001), which is based on four variables: the stringency and consistency of environmental regulations, the degree to which environmental regulations promote innovation, the percentage of land area under protected status, and the number of sectoral guidelines on environmental impact assessments. Each variable has equal weight and has been normalized.

Table 7.4. Correlation Matrix

Item	Log per capita income	Rule of law	Press diffusion	Press freedom	Absence of violations against print media	Absence of violations against broadcast media	Environmental regulation and management	Environmental information
Log per capita income								
Rule of law	0.88	1.00						
Newspaper circulation	0.71	0.60	1.00					
Press freedom	0.73	0.77	0.55	1.00				
Absence of violations against print media	0.63	0.74	0.57	0.76	1.00			
Absence of violations against broadcast media	0.39	0.44	0.47	0.49	0.61	1.00		
Environmental regulation	0.72	0.81	0.44	0.63	0.56	0.42	1.00	
Environmental information	0.46	0.54	0.44	0.38	0.31	0.38	0.54	1.00

Source: Authors' calculations.

INFORMATION ENVIRONMENT. More disclosure can have an effect independent of the role of the press. For this reason, we want to control separately for the degree of disclosure. When we examine the private sector's responsiveness to environmental issues we control for environmental disclosure. As we lack firm-based measures of environmental disclosure, we instead use the extent of environmental disclosure as captured by the index of environmental information compiled for the 2001 environmental sustainability index.

Empirical Results

We start by analyzing the link between the diffusion of the press and the indicator of private sector responsiveness to environmental issues. We first use univariate analysis and then turn to multivariate analysis to try to control for the other important institutional factors. Panel A of table 7.5 shows a strong positive correlation between the diffusion of the press and private sector responsiveness to environmental issues. As column (1) shows, the diffusion of the press alone explains 42 percent of the cross-country variation, slightly more than the explanatory power of per capita income (38 percent). Not surprisingly, the private sector's responsiveness to environmental issues is also positively correlated with the level of environmental regulation (column 2), environmental information (column 3), and per capita income (column 4).

In column (5) we combine readership with the legal and disclosure variables, and readership continues to have a statistically significant impact: including readership increases the explanatory power from 45 to 58 percent. Of course, there is the possibility that readership is just picking up the impact of some third omitted variable. To attempt to capture this possibility we also include the level of per capita income (column 6), but readership continues to have a significant effect. Finally, in columns (7) and (8) we include other institutional variables, such as the rule of law and ownership concentration, but the diffusion of the press continues to be significant. An interesting finding is that ownership concentration has a negative and statistically significant effect on the private sector's responsiveness to environmental issues. Where large shareholders run firms they feel freer to ignore the public opinion pressure in favor of the environment, another piece of evidence that this is not a course of action that maximizes value.

In panel B we substitute the diffusion of the press with the freedom of the press, the frequency of violations against broadcast media, and the frequency of violations against print media. In a univariate setting all three of these variables help explain a significant amount of the cross-country variation. In a multivariate analysis, however, the statistical significance is reduced, and in the case of violations against broadcast media it drops below conventional standards. The traditional indicators of press freedom thus have an effect similar to the diffusion of the press, but statistically weaker. This is not surprising, because these other indicators are meant to capture freedom from political influences rather than the credibility of reporting about corporations.

Table 7.5. Institutional Determinants of Private Sector Responsiveness to Environmental Issues
(dependent variable: private sector environmental responsiveness)

Panel A

Independent variables	Ordinary least squares regressions								Instrumental variable regressions
	(1)	*(2)*	*(3)*	*(4)*	*(5)*	*(6)*	*(7)*	*(8)*	*(9)*
Newspaper circulation	0.268***				0.200***	0.125*	0.198***	0.136*	.255***
	(0.048)				(0.054)	(0.069)	(0.072)	(0.073)	(0.070)
Environmental regulation		0.487***			0.300***	0.288***	0.351**	0.450**	.293***
		(0.074)			(0.090)	(0.085)	(0.137)	(0.158)	(0.104)
Environmental information			0.374***		-0.008	-0.021	-0.148	-0.122	-0.073
			(0.061)		(0.075)	(0.074)	(0.135)	(0.152)	(0.086)
Log per capita income				0.246***		0.104***			
				–0.033		(0.038)			
Rule of law							0.044		
							(0.029)		
Ownership concentration								-1.135*	
								(0.566)	
Constant	-0.426***	-0.089**	-0.134***	-1.934***	-0.320***	-0.988***	-0.537***	.390	-0.389***
	(0.045)	(0.044)	(0.043)	(0.221)	(0.060)	(0.229)	(0.128)	(.398)	(0.078)
R-squared	0.42	0.32	0.25	0.38	0.51	0.54	0.59	0.58	0.54
Number of observations	113	122	122	120	113	112	49	38	96

Panel B									Instrumental variable regressions
			Ordinary least squares regressions						
Independent variables	(1)	(2)	(3)	(4)	(5)	(6)	(7)	(8)	(9)
Press freedom	0.011***			0.004*			0.000		
	(0.002)			(0.002)			(0.002)		
Absence of violations against broadcast media		0.038**			0.016				
		(0.15)			(0.014)				
Absence of violations against print media			0.041***			0.022**		0.001	
			(0.012)			(0.009)		(0.009)	
Environmental regulation				0.322***	0.352***	0.338***	0.286***	0.285***	
				(0.089)	(0.091)	(0.090)	(0.077)	(0.078)	
Environmental information				0.159**	0.200***	0.194***	0.076	0.076	
				(0.073)	(0.069)	(0.070)	(0.075)	(0.071)	
Log per capita income							0.167***	0.166***	
							(0.031)	(0.033)	
Constant	−0.746***	−0.431***	−0.375***	−0.320***	−0.234*	−0.235***	−1.329***	−1.327***	
	(0.105)	(0.114)	(0.060)	(0.110)	(0.124)	(0.066)	(0.227)	(0.217)	
R-squared	0.21	0.04	0.09	0.38	0.37	0.39	0.50	0.50	
Number of observations	119	119	119	119	119	119	118	118	

*Significant at the 10 percent level.
**Significant at the 5 percent level.
***Significant at the 1 percent level.

Note: The dependent variable is an index of private sector responsiveness to environmental issues. The explanatory variable to identify the role of the press in panel A is newspaper circulation/population. The press variables in panel B include the aggregate index of press freedom, actual violations against the broadcast media, and actual violations against print media. Additional explanatory variables include an index of the stringency of legal and regulatory restrictions on firms, an index of the availability of environmental information, rule of law index, and ownership concentration. More complete descriptions of variables are provided in table 7.1. The instruments used in specification (9) are primary religion (Protestant, Catholic, Muslim, other) and average ethnolinguistic fractionalization. Huber-White standard errors, which are presented in parentheses, are consistent in the presence of heteroscedasticity.

Source: Authors' calculations.

What Determines the Diffusion of the Press?

Our cross-country regressions suffer from two problems that are common to this genre of regressions. First, there are so many institutions that differ across countries and so few degrees of freedom that one always wonders whether the results are due to an omitted variable that drives both press diffusion and environmental responsiveness. We have tried to address this problem by controlling for the most obvious determinants of environmental responsiveness, but we can never be sure that we have controlled for all the important factors. The second problem, which is less of an issue here, is one of reverse causality. Is the press more diffused because companies are more sensitive to environmental policies?

To address both these problems we resort to instrumental variables. A good instrument is one that is correlated with our variable of interest (the diffusion of the press), but is not correlated with the error in our regressions of the diffusion of the press on corporate behavior.

One precondition for the diffusion of the press is the diffusion of education, and we could use the average level of school attainment as a determinant. However, the same factors that determine schooling policy could also be correlated with environmental responsiveness. For this reason we prefer to use historically predetermined factors that have caused these differences in the level of education. We introduce two, the degree of linguistic fractionalization and the dominant religion in a country.

The more languages are spoken in a country, the more fragmented the newspaper market. In a more fragmented market fewer newspapers can survive, and it is more difficult for them to acquire reputation and credibility. Ethnolinguistic fractionalization should therefore have a negative impact on the diffusion of the press.

Religions differ in their approach to education and to the extent they encourage the development of critical judgment by their followers. Catholicism, for instance, traditionally did not encourage education among its followers except for the clergy. Catholics were not encouraged to read the Bible, nor were they supposed to develop an individual capacity to interpret it. The Catholic Church saw itself not only as the intermediary between God and individual believers, but also as the only official interpreter of the word of God. By contrast, the Reformation, with its emphasis on individual reading and interpretation of the Bible, favored individual education. Martin Luther translated the Bible into German and promoted the literacy of his followers. Hence we would expect Protestant countries to have a better level of schooling and exhibit a higher diffusion of the press. Our third and fourth categories are Islam and other religions, which includes Judaism and Buddhism.

We test these conjectures in table 7.6, column (1). As a dependent variable we have the diffusion of the press. As independent variables we have three indicator variables for the dominant religions (Catholic, Protestant, Muslim) and an indicator of ethnolinguistic fractionalizaiton used in the literature (see Easterly and Levine 1997). The latter is based on the probability that two randomly selected people from

Table 7.6. Determinants of Diffusion of Press
(dependent variable: circulation of daily newspapers)

Independent variables	(1)	(2)	(3)	(4)	(5)	(6)	(7)
Catholic	114.3***	−76.93**	−87.14***	−82.13***	−66.29***	−79.26***	−92.23***
	(13.38)	(35.99)	(26.61)	(29.63)	(22.76)	(28.63)	(25.44)
Muslim	49.93***	−0.469					
	(15.91)	(42.37)					
Protestant	235.6***						
	(41.75)						
Other	119.7***	28.38					
	(35.22)	(59.97)					
Log of school attainment		207.62***	204.7***	202.9***	158.9***	153.63***	38.98
		(29.41)	(23.75)	(24.34)	(23.68)	(29.16)	(26.69)
State-owned newspapers' market share				−63.28*		−53.28	−79.42**
				(32.17)		(31.92)	(32.76)
Short-term democracy					7.553**	9.774*	0.690
					(3.633)	(4.951)	(3.615)
Log per capita income							72.43***
							(10.45)
Constant		−144.3	−129.3	−133.1	−116.1***	−109.2	−432.0***
		(58.94)	(22.48)	(29.37)	(20.08)	(26.11)	(51.62)
R-squared	0.50	0.52	0.52	0.59	0.58	0.61	0.74
Number of observations	115	85	85	60	84	60	60

*Significant at the 10 percent level.
**Significant at the 5 percent level.
***Significant at the 1 percent level.
Source: Authors' calculations.

a given country will not belong to the same ethnolinguistic group. As column (1) shows, all our explanatory variables have the expected impact on the diffusion of the press. In all the cases except for the Catholic dummy, these coefficients are statistically significant. Most important, from the point of view of their quality as instruments, they together explain 41 percent of the variation in press diffusion. Hence they appear to be good instruments.

We use these instruments to re-estimate by instrumental variables our basic specifications for the determinants of environmental policy.[8] The environmental policy

---

8. We have performed a similar test with a country-level version of the corporate governance relation estimated in Dyck and Zingales (2001). The instrumental variable point estimate is slightly lower than the ordinary least squares one, and significant only at the 10 percent level. Thus spurious correlation might explain a tiny bit of the impact of the diffusion of the press, but not the bulk of it.

regressions, reported in column (9) of table 7.5, produce similar results to the ordinary least squares estimates. The instrumental variable point estimate of the impact of the diffusion of the press is actually larger than the ordinary least squares counterpart, rejecting the hypothesis that the result is due to omitted variables.

Thus far we have limited our search of the determinants of press diffusion to factors that (a) are likely to be uncorrelated with the determinants of environmental pressure and protection of minority shareholders; and (b) are predetermined, and as such are legitimately exogenous. However, the question of what drives the diffusion of the press is of independent interest. If the diffusion of the press plays a role in corporate governance, then from a policy point of view we are interested in finding out what factors under the control of the government play a role in spreading newspapers' readership.

For this reason, in table 7.6, columns (2) through (4), we consider the empirical significance of other potential determinants of the diffusion of the press. First we consider the average degree of schooling (column 2) measured as the log of school attainment for those over the age of 25 taken over five year periods (1960–1965, 1970-1975, 1980–1985) (Barro and Lee 1993). As expected, countries with a higher level of schooling have a more diffused press. All the other variables except the Muslim dummy maintain their predicted effect, although the statistical significance of the religion dummies decreases, as is to be expected if they affected the diffusion of the press mainly through their effect on education.

In column (3) we also insert the market share controlled by state-owned newspapers. The more newspapers the government controls, the less credible they are, the less they will be read, and perhaps the harder it will be for competitors to enter the market. We take the market share of state-owned newspapers as a percentage of the total market share of the top five newspaper outlets from Djankov and others (2001). As expected, the impact of government ownership of the media is negative and statistically significant. All the other variables maintain their predicted effect.

Finally, we want to make sure that the effects we have described are not just due our failure to control for any indicator of the level of economic development of a country. While the cause-effect relationship is more ambiguous here, seeing that the estimated effects are similar once we insert the log of per capita income, is reassuring (column 4).

Conclusion

Others chapters in this book focus on the important role of the media in affecting the functioning of government institutions, but the media play an equally important role in shaping corporate policy. Our contribution is a first attempt to outline the theoretical channels through which this influence takes place and to show their practical relevance.

We argued that the media selectively reduce the cost of acquiring and verifying information. This information is crucial in shaping the reputation of the key players who determine corporate policy. The reputation that decisionmakers seem to care about is not just the reputation in the eyes of current and future employers, but more broadly, their reputation in the eyes of the public at large, that is, their public image. Only concerns about their public image would explain the responsiveness of corporate directors to environmental issues, which have a zero or negative impact on the wealth of their ultimate employers, that is, the shareholders.

These effects of the media are not only anecdotal. The more diffuse the press in a country is, the more companies are responsive both to environmental issues and to minority shareholders' concerns, even after controlling for the presence of specific laws and regulations and the level of law enforcement. These results suggest that the corporate governance role of the media is more complex than the one we identified in Dyck and Zingales (2001). The media can help shareholders or can hurt them. We conjecture that while the strength of the impact of the media depends on their credibility, the direction of their net effect depends on societal norms and values, but much more research is needed before coming to any definite conclusion on this matter. The only definite conclusion we can draw at this point is that the media are important in shaping corporate policy and should not be ignored in any analysis of a country's corporate governance system.

From a policy point of view our contribution provides both good and bad news. The good news is that even countries with inadequate laws and malfunctioning judicial systems can experience some of the benefits of better governance if the pressure of the press is sufficiently strong and the norms support good governance. The bad news is that the direction in which the press exercises its influence depends on societal values, which cannot be easily changed by the legislators or by international policymakers. Moreover, the extent of press influence may be largely outside policymakers' control. Our analysis of the ultimate determinants of the diffusion of the press indicates that these lie in a country's cultural and ethnic tradition.

References

The word "processed" describes informally reproduced works that may not be commonly available through libraries.

Baron, David. 1996. *Business and its Environment*. Upper Saddle River, New Jersey: Prentice Hall.

———. 2001. "Private Politics." Working Paper. Stanford University, Palo Alto, California.

Barro, Robert J., and Jong-Wha Lee. 1993. "International Comparisons of Educational Attainment." *Journal of Monetary Economics* 32(3): 363–94.

Besley, Timothy, and Andrea Prat, 2001, "Handcuffs for the Grabbing Hand? Media Capture and Government Accountability," London School of Economics and Political Science, London. Processed.

Coffee, John. 2001. "Do Norms Matter? A Cross-Country Examination of Private Benefits of Control." Columbia University Law School, New York. Processed.

Dahya, Jay, John McConnell, and Nickolaos Travlos. 2002. "The Cadbury Committee, Corporate Performance, and Top Management Turnover." *Journal of Finance* LVII(1): 461–83.

Diamond, Douglas. 1989. "Reputation Acquisition in Debt Markets." *Journal of Political Economy* 97(4): 828–62.

Djankov, Simeon, Carilee McLeish, Tatiana Nenova, and Andrei Shleifer. 2001. "Who Owns the Media." Working Paper no. 8288. National Bureau of Economic Research, Cambridge, Massachusetts.

Dobrzynski, Judith. 1992. "CalPERS Is Ready to Roar, but Will CEO's Listen?" *Business Week*, March 30.

Dyck, Alexander, and Luigi Zingales. 2001. "Private Benefits of Control: An International Comparison." Working Paper no. 8711. National Bureau of Economic Research, Cambridge, Massachusetts.

Easterly, William, and Ross Levine. 1997. "Africa's Growth Tragedy: Policies and Ethnic Divisions." *Quarterly Journal of Economics* 112: 1203–50.

Ellickson, Robert. 1991. *Order without Law: How Neighbors Settle Disputes.* Cambridge, Massachusetts: Harvard University Press.

Fama, Eugene F. 1980. "Agency Problems and the Theory of the Firm." *Journal of Political Economy* 88(2): 288–307.

Fama, Eugene, and Michael Jensen. 1983. " Separation of Ownership and Control." *Journal of Law & Economics* 26(2): 301–25.

Financial Times. 2001. "Oleg's Out." Observer column, January 25.

Freedom House. 1999. *Press Freedom Survey 1999.* Available on: http:// www.freedomhouse.org.

———. 2000. *Press Freedom Survey 2000.* Available on: http:// www.freedomhouse.org.

Greif, Avner. 1997. "Contracting, Enforcement, and Efficiency." In Boris Pleskovic and Joseph Stiglitz, eds., *Annual World Bank Conference on Development Economics.* Washington, D.C.

Harris, Milton, and Bengt Holmstrom. 1982."A Theory of Wage Dynamics." *Review of Economic Studies* 49: 315–33.

La Porta, Rafael, Florencio Lopez-de-Silanes, Andrei Shleifer, and Robert W. Vishny. 1998. "Law and Finance." *Journal of Political Economy* 106(6): 1113–55.

Low, Kevin, Arumugan Seetharaman, and Wai Ching Poon. 2002. "The Sustainability of Business Corporate Governance: Evidence from Publicly Listed Companies in Malaysia." Multimedia University, Faculty of Management, Cyberjaya, Malaysia.

McCraw, Thomas. 1984. *Prophets of Regulation.* Cambridge, Massachusetts; Belknap Press.

McMillan, John, and Christopher Woodruff. 2000."Private Order under Dysfunctional Public Order." *Michigan Law Review* 38: 2421–59.

Monks, Robert, and Nell Minow. 1995. *Corporate Governance.* Cambridge, Massachusetts: Blackwell.

PSPD (People's Solidarity for Participatory Democracy). 2002. *Shareholder History, the Year 1998.* Available on: http://www.psped.org/pspd/archive/history_2.html.

Reinhardt, Forest, and Richard Vietor. 1994a. *Starkist (A).* Harvard Business School Case no. 794-128. Cambridge, Massachusetts: Harvard Business School Press.

———. 1994b. *Starkist (B)*. Harvard Business School Case no. 794-139. Cambridge, Massachusetts: Harvard Business School Press.

Rosenberg, Hilary. 1999. *A Traitor to His Class: Robert A. G. Monks and the Battle to Change Corporate America*. New York: John Wiley.

Skeel, David. 2001. "Shaming in Corporate Law." *University of Pennsylvania Law Review* 149: 1811–68.

Stulz, Renee, and Rohan Williamson. 2001. "Culture, Openness, and Finance." Working Paper no. 8222. National Bureau of Economic Research, Cambridge, Massachusetts.

UNESCO (United Nations Educational, Cultural, and Scientific Organization). 1998. *Statistical Yearbook*. Paris.

Vietor, Richard. 1993. *Allied Signal: Managing the Hazardous Waste Liability Risk*. Harvard Business School Case no. 793-044. Cambridge, Massachusetts: Harvard Business School Press.

Wagstyl, Stefan. 2002. "The Road to Recognition." *Financial Times*, April 6/7, p. I.

Yale Center for Environmental Law and Policy. 2001. *2001 Environmental Sustainability Index*. Available on: http://www.ciesin.columbia.edu/indicators/ESI.

Zingales, Luigi. 2000. "In Search of New Foundations." *Journal of Finance* 55: 1623–53.

Part II

WHAT ENABLES THE MEDIA

8

Media Ownership and Prosperity

Simeon Djankov, Caralee McLiesh,
Tatiana Nenova, and Andrei Shleifer

In modern economies and societies the availability of information is central to better decisionmaking by citizens and consumers. In political markets citizens require information about candidates to make intelligent voting choices. In economic markets, including financial markets, consumers and investors require information to select products and securities. The availability of information is a crucial determinant of the efficiency of political and economic markets (Simons 1948; Stigler 1961; Stiglitz 2000).

In most countries citizens and consumers receive the information they need through the media, including newspapers and television. The media serve as the intermediaries that collect information and make it available to citizens and consumers. Thus a crucial question is how the media should be optimally organized. Should newspapers and television channels be state owned or privately owned? Should the media industry be organized as a monopoly or competitively? While some theoretical discussion of these issues has taken place, our empirical knowledge of the possible forms of organization of the media industry and their consequences for economic and political markets remains extremely limited.

Consider some theoretical issues first. An economist who believes that governments maximize the welfare of consumers would conclude that information should be provided by a government-owned monopoly for two main reasons. First, information is a public good. Once it has been supplied to some consumers, keeping it away from others who have not paid for it is costly. Second, the provision and dissemination of information is subject to strong increasing returns. Organizing information gathering and distribution facilities entails significant fixed costs, but once

This chapter is a follow-up to our previous work summarized in Djankov and others (2001).

these costs have been incurred, the marginal costs of making the information available are relatively low. For both these reasons, one can make a strong case for organizing the media as a government-owned monopoly.

In contrast, those who believe in less than fully benevolent government are led to a different conclusion. In their view a government monopoly in the media would distort and manipulate information to entrench the incumbent government, preclude voters and consumers from making informed decisions, and ultimately undermine both democracy and markets. Because private and independent media supply alternative views to the public, they enable voters and consumers to choose among political candidates, commodities, and securities with less fear of abuse by unscrupulous politicians, producers, and promoters than in a monopoly situation (Besley and Burgess forthcoming; Sen 1984, 1999). Moreover, competition among media firms assures that, on average, voters and consumers obtain unbiased and accurate information.

These debates notwithstanding, little evidence is available on the organization of media industries in different countries and its consequences. Our research fills this gap. In a previous paper (Djankov and others forthcoming) we collected data on ownership patterns of media firms (newspapers and television) in 97 countries. Our research provides a first systematic look at the extent of state and private ownership of media firms around the world, of the different kinds of private ownership, and of the prevalence of monopoly across countries and segments of the media industry. Our basic finding is that the two dominant forms of ownership of media firms around the world are state ownership and ownership by concentrated private owners, that is, by controlling families.

Demsetz (1989) and Demsetz and Lehn (1985) hypothesized that the "amenity potential," also known as "the private benefits of control" (Grossman and Hart 1988), arising from owning media outlets is extremely high. In other words, the nonfinancial benefits, such as fame and influence, obtained by controlling a newspaper or a television station are considerably higher than those obtained from controlling a firm of comparable size in, say, the bottling industry. Our findings are broadly consistent with these predictions.

Having established the importance of state ownership of the media, we first asked: In which countries is government ownership of the media higher? We found that government ownership of the media is higher in countries that are poorer, that have more autocratic regimes, and where overall state ownership in the economy is higher. These results cast doubt on the proposition that state ownership of the media serves benevolent ends.

We then considered the consequences of state ownership of the media as measured by freedom of the press, development of economic and political markets, and social outcomes. To this end we ran regressions of a variety of outcomes across countries on state ownership of the media, holding constant the level of development, the degree of autocracy, and overall state ownership of the economy. We found pervasive evidence of "bad" outcomes associated with state ownership of the media, especially the press, holding country characteristics constant. The evidence is inconsistent with the benevolent view of state ownership of the media. Nevertheless, as we only have a cross-section of countries, we cannot decisively interpret this evidence as causal, that is, as showing that state ownership of the media rather than some omitted country characteristic is responsible for the bad outcomes. We note, however, that the omitted characteristic must be quite closely related to the government's inclination to control information flows, because we are controlling for a number of dimensions of "badness" in the regressions.

Ownership Data

This section focuses on patterns of ownership in the media industry. Because ownership bestows control (Grossman and Hart 1988), it shapes the information provided to voters and consumers. Of course ownership is not the only determinant of media content. In many countries, even those with private ownership, the government regulates the media industry, provides direct subsidies and advertising revenues to media outlets, restricts access to newsprint and information collection, and harasses journalists. We discuss these modes of control as well.

Construction of the Database

In Djankov and others (forthcoming) we gathered new data on media ownership in 97 countries. We focused on newspapers and television, because these are the primary sources of news on political, economic, and social issues. Our selection of sample countries was driven by data availability. First, we identified the countries for which we had information on the control variables. As we were interested in the consequences of state ownership of the media we needed to make sure that our results were not driven by differences in the levels of economic development, the level of political competition, or of broad state intervention in the economy. To this end we controlled for general levels of state ownership in the economy, a measure of autocracy, and gross national product (GNP) per capita. We used the Fraser Institute (2000) index of the involvement of state-owned enterprises (SOEs) in the economy, which is based on the number of SOEs, their prevalence in particular sectors of the economy, and their share of gross domestic output.

Within countries we selected media outlets based on their market share of the audience and their provision of local news content in 1999. This approach focuses on who controls the majority of information flows on domestic issues to citizens. We excluded entertainment and sport media, as well as foreign media outlets, if they did not provide local news content. Our sample included the five largest daily newspapers as measured by their share in the total circulation of all dailies, and the five largest television stations as measured by the share of viewing.[1] We consulted three primary data sources to selecting these outlets. First, we used Zenith Media's *Market and Media Fact Book 2000* publications, which are organized by region, including the Americas, Asia and the Pacific, Central and Eastern Europe, the Middle East and Africa, and Western Europe (Zenith Media 2000a,b,c,d,e). We checked Zenith Media's rankings of newspapers with the World Association of Newspapers *World Press Trends 2000* report. We also used the association's data as the source for total newspaper circulation, which Zenith Media does not report. Finally, we used the European Institute for the Media "Media in the CIS" report as a primary source for countries in the former Soviet Union (European Institute for the Media 2000). We sought alternative sources in two cases: when an inconsistency was apparent in data reported by primary sources or when none of the sources covered the country in question. When this occurred we used local media survey firms, World Bank external affairs offices, U.S. Department of State information offices, and direct contact with the media outlets.

Where possible, we relied on companies' annual reports and the WorldScope database for information on the ownership of media firms. Many of our sample companies are not covered by WorldScope and operate in countries with limited disclosure requirements. Accordingly, we also used business news reports in Lexis Nexis and the *Financial Times* databases, country-specific company handbooks, media surveys, and Internet information services (see table 8.1 for a description of the variables and the main data sources). In all cases we verified the ownership and other information by contacting World Bank external affairs offices; embassies in Washington, D.C.; and regional or in-country media organizations.

Ownership data are for December 1999 or the closest date for which reliable data were available. For most firms in the sample ownership structures have been stable over time. Timing is a significant issue only in the transition economies, where many media enterprises have been privatized or have increasing rates of foreign ownership. For these countries we strictly enforced the December 1999 date of ownership information, even when we had more recent data.

---

1. Following the World Association of Newspapers definition, newspapers are considered dailies if they are published at least four times per week. In the initial phase of the data gathering (first 12 countries) we focused on the top 10 media enterprises in the daily newspaper and television markets. We subsequently reduced the sample to 5 firms per medium for two reasons. First, the difference in market coverage obtained by increasing the sample of companies from 5 to 10 was marginal. In the first 12 countries the top 5 newspapers accounted for an average of 62.4 percent of total circulation and the top 10 for 74.1 percent. The correlation between the two is 94.2 percent. For the sample as a whole, the top 5 newspapers accounted for an average of 66.7 percent of total circulation. Television markets were even more concentrated: on average the top 5 firms covered 89.5 percent of total viewing. Second, 20 countries in our sample did not have more than 5 daily newspapers and 42 countries did not have more than 5 television stations.

Table 8.1. Variables and Data Sources

Variable	*Description and source*
Media ownership[a]	
State ownership of press, by count	The percentage of state-owned newspapers out of the five largest daily newspapers (by circulation), 1999.
State ownership of press, by share	The market share of state-owned newspapers out of the aggregate market share of the five largest daily newspapers (by circulation), 1999.
State ownership of television, by count	The percentage of state-owned television stations out of the five largest television stations (by viewership), 1999.
State ownership of television, by share	The market share of state-owned television stations out of the aggregate market share of the five largest television stations (by viewership), 1999.
Controls	
GNP per capita	GNP per capita, 1999, in thousands of U.S. dollars. *Source:* World Bank (2000b).
SOE Index	An index from 0 to 10 based on the number, composition, and share of output supplied by SOEs and government investment as a share of total investment. Countries with more SOEs and larger government investment received lower ratings. When there were few SOEs and those are mainly in utility sectors, and government investment was less than 15 percent of total investment, countries were given a rating of 10. When there were few SOEs other than those involved in industries where economies of scale reduce the effectiveness of competition, for example, power generation, and government investment was between 15 and 20 percent of the total, countries received a rating of 8. When there were, again, few SOEs other than those involved in utility industries and government investment was between 20 and 25 percent of the total, countries were rated at 7. When SOEs were dominant in utility sectors and government investment was 25 to 30 percent of the total, countries were assigned a rating of 6. When a substantial number of SOEs operated in many sectors, including manufacturing, and government investment was between 30 and 40 percent of the total, countries received a rating of 4. When a substantial number of SOEs operated in many sectors and government investment was between 40 and 50 percent of the total, countries were rated at 2. A zero rating was assigned to countries where more than 50 percent of the economy's output was produced by SOEs and government investment exceeded 50 percent of the total. *Source:* Fraser Institute (2000) for all countries except Armenia, Azerbaijan, Belarus, Ethiopia, Moldova, and Turkmenistan. Data for these six countries were constructed by the authors based on the World Bank (2000a).

(Table continues on the following page.)

Table 8.1. (continued)

Variable	*Description and source*
Autocracy	Index of authoritarian regimes, 1999. Based on an 11-point autocracy scale that is constructed additively from the codings of 5 component variables: competitiveness of executive recruitment, openness of executive recruitment, constraints on chief executive, regulation of participation, and competitiveness of political participation. Values were rescaled from 0 to 1 with 0 being high in autocracy and 1 being low in autocracy. *Source:* Polity IV Project (2000).
Media freedom	
Journalists jailed	The number of journalists held in police custody for any length of time in 1999, rescaled from 0 to 1, with higher values indicating less opression. *Source:* Reporters Sans Frontiéres (2000).
Media outlets closed	The number of media outlets closed in 1999, rescaled from 0 to 1, with higher values indicating less opression. *Source:* Reporters Sans Frontiéres (2000).
Journalists jailed	The number of journalists held in police custody for any length of time per year, average over 1997–99, rescaled from 0 to 1, with higher values indicating less opression. *Source:* Committee to Protect Journalists (2000).
Political markets	
Political rights	Index of political rights rescaled from 0 to 1, with higher values indicating better political rights. Higher ratings indicate countries that come closer to the "ideals suggested by the checklist questions of: (1) free and fair elections; (2) those elected rule; (3) there are competitive parties or other competitive political groupings; (4) the opposition has an important role and power; (5) the entities have self-determination or an extremely high degree of autonomy." *Source:* Freedom House (2000b).
Civil liberties	Index of civil rights rescaled from 0 to 1, with higher values indicating better civil liberties. Higher ratings indicate countries that enjoy "the freedoms to develop views, institutions, and personal autonomy apart from the state." The basic components of the index are: (1) freedom of expression and belief, (2) association and organizational rights, (3) rule of law and human rights, and (4) personal autonomy and economic rights. *Source:* Freedom House (2000b).
Corruption	Assessment of the corruption in government, 1997, on a scale of 1 to 6. Lower scores indicate that "high government officials are likely to demand special payments" and "illegal payments are generally expected throughout lower levels of government" in the form of "bribes connected with import and export licenses, exchange controls, tax assessment, policy protection, or loans." *Source:* Political Risk Services (2000).

Variable	Description and source
Economic markets	
Security of property	A rating of property rights in each country in 1997, rescaled from 0 to 1, with higher values indicating more secure property rights. The rating assesses the issue of "Are property rights secure? Do citizens have the right to establish private businesses? Is private business activity unduly influenced by government officials, the security forces, or organized crime?" *Source:* Freedom House (2000a).
Risk of confiscation	Assessment of the legal security of private ownership rights, 1997. Ranges from 0 to 10, with higher values indicating lower risk. *Source:* Fraser Institute (2000).
Quality of regulation	An aggregated measure focused on national regulatory policies. "It includes measures of the incidence of market-unfriendly policies such as price controls or inadequate bank supervision, as well as perceptions of the burdens imposed by excessive regulation in areas such as foreign trade and business development." *Source:* Kaufmann, Kraay, and Zoido-Lobaton (1999).
Social outcomes	
School attainment	A measure of the highest grade of primary education in which individuals are enrolled. The data reflect the attainment rates for the population that is over age 25 as of 1990. *Source:* Barro and Lee (1996).
Enrollment	Total enrollment at the primary educational level, regardless of age, divided by the population of the age group that typically corresponds to that level of education, as of 1995. The specification of age groups varies by country, based on different national systems of education and the duration of schooling at the primary level. *Source:* UNESCO (1999).
Pupil/teacher ratio	The number of pupils enrolled in primary school divided by the number of primary school teachers (regardless of their teaching assignment), an average over 1990–99. *Source:* World Bank (2000b).
Life expectancy	Life expectancy at birth (years), average over 1995–2000. *Source:* UNDP (2000).
Infant mortality	Infant mortality rate (per 1,000 live births) in 1998. Rescaled from 0 to 1, with higher values indicating lower mortality. *Source:* UNDP (2000).
Nutrition	Daily per capita supply of calories, 1997. *Source:* UNDP (2000).

a. Authors' calculations.
Source: Authors.

We followed La Porta, Lopez-de-Silanes, and Shleifer (1999) in identifying the ultimate controlling shareholder of each media outlet. We focused explicitly on voting rights as opposed to cash flow rights in relation to the ownership of firms. For each firm we identified the legal entities and families that own significant voting stakes.[2] This provided us with the first level of ownership. For each legal entity we then identified its ownership structure by determining all significant vote holders, giving us the second level of ownership. We continued to identify vote holders at each level of ownership until we reached an entity for which we could not break down the ownership structure any further.

We defined the entity that ultimately controls the highest number of voting rights, but no less than 20 percent at every link of the chain, as the ultimate owner. Such control can be gained through direct ownership of more than 20 percent of the voting rights of a media enterprise, or indirectly through a chain of intermediate owners. For example, an individual X may control newspapers Z when he or she holds more than 20 percent of the voting rights in Company Y, which in turn owns more than 20 percent of the voting rights in Z. With indirect holdings we defined the percentage of ultimate ownership as the minimum holding along the chain of control.

After identifying the ultimate owner, we classified each media outlet into one of the four main categories of owners: the state, families (we used families as a unit of analysis and did not look within families), widely held corporations, and "other." Examples of other controlling entities are employee organizations, trade unions, political parties, religious entities, not-for-profit foundations, and business associations. We defined a corporation as widely held if there is no owner with 20 percent or more of the voting rights. We also kept track of whether the ultimate owner is a foreign family, an entity, or a government.[3]

Examples of Media Ownership

The construction of the ownership variables is best illustrated through examples of the ownership structures of individual firms. We start with a simple case of family ownership. In Argentina the third largest newspaper, with a daily circulation of 177,000, is *La Nacion*. The owner of each share in *La Nacion* is entitled to one vote. The paper has two large shareholders (figure 8.1): the Saguier family with 72 percent of the capital and votes and Grupo Mitre with 28 percent of the capital and votes. In

---

2. The cut-off level of voting stakes depends on the mandatory disclosure levels in the country. In no case, however, is that threshold higher than 5 percent.

3. In a few instances the owner of voting rights in a media firm does not hold the broadcast license. In these cases firm ownership and not license ownership determines control. We took this view because control of all broadcast licenses ultimately belongs to the government, and licenses can be revoked depending on the strength of property rights in a country.

Figure 8.1. Ownership of *La Nacion,* Argentina

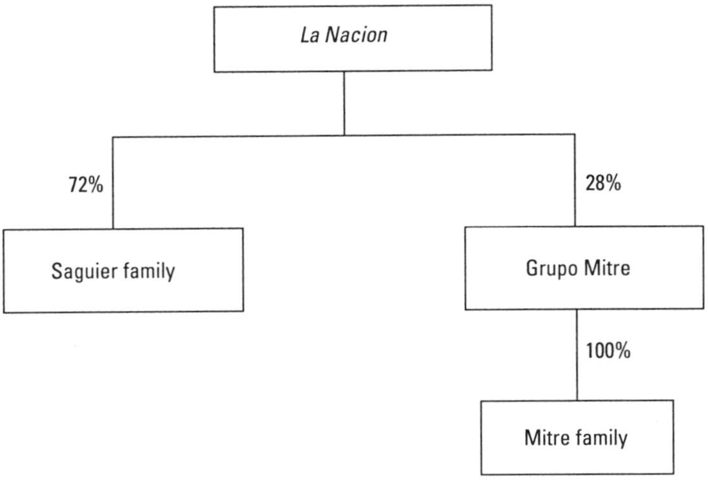

Source: Authors.

turn, the Mitre family owns 100 percent of Grupo Mitre. Although the Mitre family holds indirect control of 28 percent in *La Nacion*, we followed the chain of control of the largest shareholder at each level of ownership. We therefore recorded the Saguier family as the ultimate owner and classified *La Nacion* as family owned.

A more complex example of family ownership is the Norwegian television station TV Norge (TVN). TVN is the second largest television station with local content in Norway, as measured by the share of viewing. It is 50.7 percent controlled by Scandinavian Broadcasting Systems (SBS) and 49.3 percent by the largest Norwegian television station, TV2 (figure 8.2). We followed the chain of control along SBS rather than TV2, because SBS holds the majority of votes in TVN. Although Harry Sloan, the chairman and chief executive officer of SBS, holds a 9.8 percent share of voting rights in SBS, the only voting interest above 20 percent is held by Netherlands United Pan-Europe Communications SV Netherlands (UPC), with 23.3 percent of the vote. The majority shareholder of United Pan-Europe Communications is United Global Com with 51 percent. United Global Com is in turn controlled by the Schneider family through a combination of three direct interests totaling 21.9 percent, as well as 50 percent control of a voting agreement with 69.2 percent control of votes. We thus classified TVN as family owned and the Schneider family as the ultimate owner.

State ownership takes different forms. The British Broadcasting Corporation (BBC) is classified as state owned. It is funded by government license fees and advertising. The board of governors is appointed by royal prerogative, in practice the prime minister, and is accountable to the government, but the BBC Charter specifies a number

Figure 8.2. Ownership of TVN, Norway

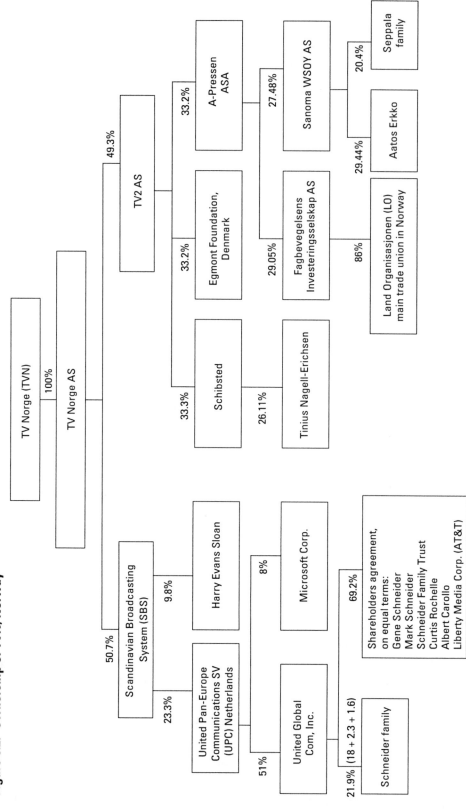

Source: Authors.

of safeguards to ensure its independence from government interference. By comparison, the Ministry of Information and Culture directly controls the largest television station in Myanmar and the Myanmar military controls the second largest station. In both cases the state retains full powers to manage content and appoint and remove staff. Similarly, in Turkmenistan the state maintains direct control over the press: President Niyazov is officially the founder and owner of all newspapers in the country.

In a number of cases we needed to distinguish between state and political party ownership. In Kenya the ruling party, the Kenyan African National Union, is the ultimate owner of the daily newspaper the *Kenya Times*, the country's fourth largest daily; however, we do not classify the *Kenya Times* as state owned, because if the government changed the ownership would still remain with the Kenyan African National Union. In contrast, control of the Kenyan Broadcasting Corporation would remain with the state regardless of the political party in power, so we classified the Kenyan Broadcasting Corporation as state owned. Ruling party ownership also occurs in Malaysia and Côte d'Ivoire. We placed these firms in the other category along with more clear-cut cases of media owned by opposition political parties. In several cases family ownership is closely associated with the state. In Kazakhstan President Nazarbayev's daughter and son-in-law together control 7 of the 12 media outlets in our country sample. In Saudi Arabia members of the royal family are the ultimate owners of two of the five most popular dailies. In cases where a direct family relationship exists between the ultimate owner and the head of state and the governing system is a single-party state, we classified the media enterprise as state owned.

Other associations between families and the state are prevalent throughout our sample. In Ukraine the deputy prime minister holds more than 30 percent of the top television station, while in Malawi the owner of the *Nation* newspaper is the minister of agriculture and vice-president of the ruling United Democratic Front party. Neither of these positions are equivalent to head of state in single-party governments, and we therefore classified both media outlets as family owned. Other unofficial links to the state were documented in country files, but did not influence our classification of ultimate ownership. In Russia the close associations between the owner of one of the main television stations, Boris Berezovsky, and then President Boris Yeltsin are well documented.[4] In Indonesia the daughter of former President Suharto still controls one of the main television stations. In an effort to be conservative in our measures of state control, in all these cases we classified the media outlets as family owned, because a change in government would sever the link between the politician and the media owner.

---

4. Berezovsky (2000, p. A27) wrote as follows: "We helped Yeltsin defeat the Communists at the polls, using privately owned TV stations."

Variable Construction

We constructed two ownership variables from these data. First, we computed the percentage of firms in each category, state or private. For example, we classified two out of the top five newspaper enterprises and three out of the top five television stations in the Philippines as state owned. We recorded Philippine newspaper market ownership as 40 percent state owned when measured by count, and television market ownership as 60 percent state owned when measured by count. Second, we weighted the ownership variable by market share. In the Philippines the two state-owned newspapers account for 22.2 percent and 21.3 percent of circulation for the top five newspapers, respectively, so the newspapers are 43.5 percent state owned when measured by market share. As for television, the three state-owned Philippine stations account for only 17.5 percent of the share of viewing for the top five television stations, so the television market is 17.5 percent state owned as measured by market share.

The market share variables, while more precise as a measure of state control, have the disadvantage that in countries with regional newspapers, such as the United States, the market share of any single firm is small. As a consequence, the variables we define are not properly compared with those in countries with national newspapers. This criticism, of course, is less compelling for television firms, which are typically national. The regressions presented later use market share variables, but our results are virtually identical using the counts.

Patterns in Media Ownership

Next we turn to a description of the data.

Descriptive Statistics

Our first significant finding is that families and the state own the media throughout the world (figure 8.3). In the sample of 97 countries, only 4 percent of media enterprises are widely held. Fewer than 2 percent have other ownership structures, and a mere 2 percent are employee owned. In relation to ownership by count, on average, family-controlled newspapers account for 57 percent of the total and family-controlled television stations for 34 percent of the total. State ownership is also vast. On average, the state controls approximately 29 percent of newspapers and 60 percent of television stations. The state also owns a huge share—72 percent—of the top radio stations. Based on these findings, for the remaining analysis we classified ownership into three categories: state, private (the sum of the family, widely held, and employee categories), and other.

Figure 8.3. Newspaper and Television Ownership Worldwide

Press Ownership by Count

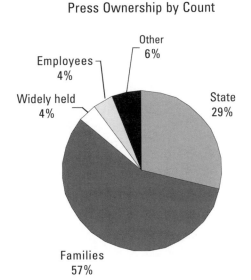

Television Ownership by Count

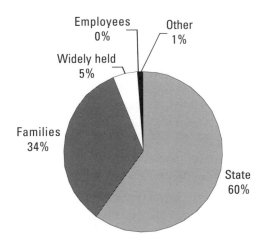

Press Ownership by Share

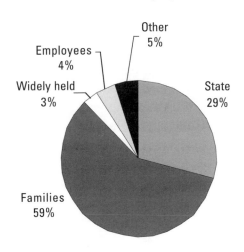

Television Ownership by Share

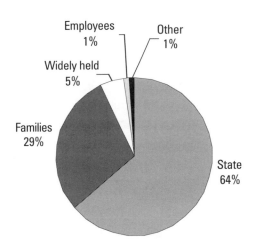

Source: Authors.

The nearly total absence of firms with dispersed ownership in the media industry is extreme, even by comparison with the La Porta and others (1999) finding of high levels of ownership concentration in large firms around the world. This result is consistent with the Demsetz (1989) and Demsetz and Lehn (1985) insight that the large amenity potential of ownership media outlets creates competitive pressures toward ownership concentration. In a sense, both the governments and the controlling private shareholders obtain the same benefit from controlling media outlets: the ability to influence public opinion and the political process.

We consider that the state has a monopoly in a media market if the share of state-controlled firms exceeds 75 percent. A total of 21 countries have government monopolies of daily newspapers, and 43 countries have state monopolies of television stations with local news. Families and the state control the media regardless of whether ownership is measured by count or weighted by market share.

Television has significantly higher levels of state ownership than newspapers.[5] To explain this finding a supporter of state ownership would focus on public goods and note that television broadcasts are, at least in part, nonexcludable and nonrivalrous. Television also has higher fixed costs than publishing and more significant economies of scale. Thus the private sector might underprovide broadcasting services, particularly in smaller markets serving remote areas, ethnic minorities, or students. These theories are central to many of the laws governing public broadcasters in Europe. Alternatively, from the political perspective privately-owned newspapers are easier to censor than privately-owned television. Because television can be broadcast live, control of content is more likely to require ownership. In this case, governments that want to censor news would own television stations.[6]

The simple statistics presented so far raise many questions. The evidence suggests that media ownership confers large private benefits. Throughout the world media are controlled by parties likely to value these private benefits, that is, families and the state. In particular, the extent of state ownership of the media, particularly television and radio, is striking, suggesting that governments extract value by controlling information flows in the media. We cannot as yet tell from this evidence whether high government ownership derives from a benign attempt to cure market failures and protect consumers or from a less benign attempt to control the flows of information. In the subsequent analysis we attempt to distinguish between these two hypotheses.

---

5. Only five countries (Ghana, the Philippines, Uganda, Ukraine, and Uzbekistan) have more state control of the top five newspapers than the top five television stations.

6. A further argument is that the extent of required regulation of television is higher because of difficulties in defining property rights for broadcasting frequencies. From an efficiency standpoint it may be optimal for the state to control television stations directly, as opposed to regulating the sector and spending resources on monitoring compliance. These arguments have been disputed by Coase (1959) and others, who do not see any need for government ownership and regulation arising from the peculiar technological features of broadcasting frequencies.

Determinants of Media Ownership

In this section we examine how ownership patterns are associated with different characteristics of countries. We examine the basic determinants of media ownership, such as the country's geography, the level of development, the government's proclivity to intervene in the economy, and the political regime. For all these characteristics arguing that causality runs from media ownership to these basic country characteristics rather than the other way around is hard.

State ownership of newspapers and television is significantly higher in African countries and in the Middle East and North Africa than elsewhere. On average, African governments control 61 percent of the top five daily newspapers and reach 85 percent of the audience for the top five television stations. Two-thirds of African countries have state monopolies in television broadcasting. With the exception of Israel, all countries in the Middle East and North Africa have a state monopoly over television broadcasting, and state ownership of newspapers, which averages a 50 percent share of circulation, is also high in these countries.

By contrast, newspapers in Western Europe and the Americas are predominately privately held. In Western Europe none of the top five daily newspapers is owned by the state. In the Americas single families have owned and managed most newspapers for many decades. State ownership of television is also overwhelmingly lower in the Americas than in other regions. None of the top five stations in Brazil, Mexico, Peru, and the United States is state owned; this occurs in only one other country (Turkey) in our sample. In Western Europe, in contrast, a substantial number of public broadcasters pushes the regional state ownership average to 48 percent by count and 55 percent by share.

Countries in the Asia-Pacific region, Central and Eastern Europe, and the former Soviet Union have ownership patterns closer to the sample mean, although ownership within each of these regions varies dramatically, for example, Indonesia and Thailand have low state ownership of the media compared with the full state monopolies in the People's Democratic Republic of Korea and Myanmar. Similarly, the predominantly privately-owned media in Estonia and Moldova contrast with the full state control apparent in Belarus and Turkmenistan.

Poorer countries have higher state ownership of newspapers and television (table 8.2). State ownership is reported after dividing the sample into quartiles of GNP per capita in 1999. The average state ownership of newspapers (by share) falls sharply from 49.7 percent for the lowest income quartile to zero for the highest income quartile. For television, the lowest income quartile averages 78 percent state ownership (by share), compared with 52.7 percent for the highest income quartile.

Countries with higher state ownership in the economy as a whole also have higher ownership of the media (table 8.3). Countries in the lowest quartile of the SOE index,

8.2. State Ownership of the Media and GNP per Capita
(means by quartile)

GNP per capita quartile	Press, by count	Press, by share	Television, by count	Television, by share
1 (low)	0.486	0.497	0.667	0.780
2 (mid-low)	0.550	0.565	0.792	0.781
3 (mid-high)	0.129	0.106	0.463	0.473
4 (high)	0.000	0.000	0.474	0.527

Note: Means by GNP per capita quartile. Media owned by the state by count and share.
Source: Authors' calculations.

which reflects high economywide state ownership, average 48.5 percent state newspaper ownership (by share) and 78.6 percent television ownership (by share). In contrast, countries in the highest quartile of the SOE index, that is, with low economywide state ownership, average only 20.3 percent state ownership of newspapers (by share) and 60.4 percent state ownership of television (by share).

Table 8.4 shows that autocratic governments are more likely to own media outlets. The relationship is monotonic over the autocracy quartiles.

Table 8.5 looks at whether per capita income, the SOE index, and autocracy have independent influences on state ownership of the media. Generally, all three variables have a significant effect in a regression. In the analysis of the consequences of state ownership of the media, we accordingly control for per capital income, the SOE index, and the autocracy measure.

The preliminary evidence presents considerable challenges to the benign view of government ownership of the media. The less developed, more interventionist, and more autocratic countries are the ones with higher state ownership of the media. The market failure argument for state ownership suggests the opposite: the richer, more democratic countries should cure market failures through state ownership. In the

Table 8.3. State Ownership of Media and SOE Index
(means by quartile)

SOE quartile	Press, by count	Press, by share	Television, by count	Television, by share
1 (high)	0.488	0.485	0.768	0.786
2 (mid-high)	0.444	0.459	0.702	0.786
3 (mid-low)	0.339	0.338	0.622	0.672
4 (low)	0.202	0.203	0.535	0.604

Note: Means by SOE quartile. Media owned by the state by count and share.
Source: Authors' calculations.

Table 8.4. State Ownership of Media and Autocracy
(means by quartile)

Autocracy quartile	Press, by count	Press, by share	Television, by count	Television, by share
1 (high)	0.717	0.737	0.917	0.920
2 (mid-high)	0.529	0.576	0.900	0.907
3 (mid-low)	0.460	0.454	0.524	0.655
4 (low)	0.100	0.094	0.470	0.608

Note: Means by autocracy quartile. Media owned by the state by count and share.
Source: Authors' calculations.

following analysis we pursue the same issue by examining the consequences of state ownership of the media.

Consequences of State Ownership of the Media

In this section we consider some of the consequences of state ownership of the media for a number of social indicators, such as freedom of the press, functioning of political and economic markets, and social outcomes such as infant mortality and educational attainment. In this analysis it is important to us to be able, to the extent possible, to link the various outcomes to state ownership of the media rather than other characteristics of society. We have shown that poor countries with interventionist and nondemocratic governments exhibit higher state ownership of the media. Accordingly, we control for GNP per capita, an index of the involvement of SOEs in the economy, and the autocracy score in all regressions. Such controls do not assure us an unambiguous causal interpretation of the relationship between state ownership of the media and the various outcomes. While state ownership of the media may still

Table 8.5. Determinants of State Ownership of the Media

Variable	GNP per capita	SOE index	Autocracy	Constant	R^2	N
State ownership press (by share)	−0.0084* (0.0027)	−0.0185*** (0.0112)	−0.8345* (0.1462)	1.0948* (0.1075)	0.5574	97
State ownership television (by share)	0.0043 (0.0035)	−0.0356* (0.0133)	−0.5652* (0.0908)	1.1879* (0.0572)	0.3779	97

*Significant at the 1 percent level.
**Significant at the 5 percent level.
***Significant at the 10 percent level.
Source: Authors' calculations.

proxy for some unobserved aspect of "badness," if state ownership helps predict bad outcomes holding constant our extensive controls, it must be closely related to the omitted badness. For example, the omitted characteristic of a country must reflect the state's interest in controlling the information flows or something close to that.

For ease of interpretation we coded all the outcome variables, as well as the controls, so that high is good. Thus a high value of the corruption or infant mortality variable corresponds to low corruption and low infant mortality, respectively.

Freedom of the Press

Perhaps the clearest way to compare alternative theories of state ownership of the media is by focusing on freedom of the press. After all, the main implication of the good government theories is that greater government ownership should, if anything, lead to greater press freedom, because the media avoid being captured by individuals with extreme wealth or extreme views.

Table 8.6 presents the results from the regressions of "objective" measures of media freedom on state ownership of the media. We measured media freedom by actual cases of harassment of journalists and media outlets compiled from Reporters Sans Frontiéres (2000) reports on journalists jailed and media outlets closed by governments. We constructed another measure from reports by the Committee to Protect Journalist (2000) on the actual numbers of journalists jailed. We also looked at a measure of Internet censorship.

Table 8.6 shows a negative impact of government ownership of the media on media freedom, holding per capita income, interventionism, and autocracy constant, with just under half of the coefficients being statistically significant. Media tend to be more independent and journalists tend to be arrested and jailed less frequently when the media are privately owned. A closer look at the data reveals a complex picture. Journalist harassment is high in Kenya, Nigeria, and Turkey, where the media are predominately privately owned, perhaps because harassment substitutes for state control through ownership. However, harassment is also high in some countries with high state ownership of the media, such as Angola, Belarus, Iran, and China. Furthermore, some countries with state media monopolies, such as the Democratic People's Republic of Korea and the Lao People's Democratic Republic, exhibit a "Castro effect": state control is so powerful that further restricting freedom through journalist harassment becomes unnecessary.

Political Markets

We examine the consequences of media ownership for two aspects of political development. First, we consider the effect of media ownership on the civil and political rights of a country's citizens. If information flows are essential for the exercise of

Table 8.6. Media Freedom

Variable	State owner-ship, press (by share)	State owner-ship, television (by share)	GNP per capita	SOE index	Autocracy	Constant	R^2	N
Journalists jailed (RSF)	−0.0815*** (0.0487)		0.0013 (0.0011)	0.0014 (0.0044)	0.0412 (0.0536)	0.9223* (0.0542)	0.1650	97
		−0.0247 (0.0423)	0.0022* (0.0009)	0.0024 (0.0045)	(0.0691) (0.0661)	0.8531* (0.0825)	0.1355	97
Media outlets closed	−0.0514 (0.0547)		0.0018 (0.0018)	−0.0045 (0.0060)	0.0599 (0.0559)	0.9170* (0.0567)	0.0771	97
		0.0622 (0.0730)	0.0020 (0.0013)	−0.0013 (0.0048)	0.1309** (0.0606)	0.7930* (0.0926) 0.8726*	0.0802	97
Journalists jailed (CPJ)	−0.4136* (0.1571)		0.0065*** (0.0037)	−0.0012 (0.0182)	−0.0841 (0.2128)	0.8966* (0.2030)	0.1929	97
		−0.3753** (0.1617)	0.0119* (0.0040)	−0.0042 (0.0184)	−0.0277 (0.2213)	0.9395* (0.2432)	0.1699	97

*Significant at the 1 percent level.
**Significant at the 5 percent level.
***Significant at the 10 percent level.
CPJ Committee to Protect Journalists.
RSF Reporters Sans Frontiéres.
Note: All dependent variables are rescaled so that larger values correspond to better outcomes. Media freedom refers to the press freedom index for newspapers and the broadcast freedom index for television and radio. Standard errors in parentheses.
Source: Authors' calculations; CPJ (2000) data; RSF (2000) data.

citizens' rights, and if government ownership of the media influences information flows, we should see an association between government ownership and rights. Second, information flows may facilitate public oversight of government and increase the accountability of politicians for bad conduct. In this case government ownership of the media would increase corruption (Besley and Burgess forthcoming; Sen 1984, 1999). In this analysis we again control for per capita income, government ownership of SOEs, and autocracy.

The results are reported in table 8.7. Government ownership of the press typically has a negative effect on citizens' rights and corruption. In many instances the effect of government ownership of the press is statistically significant, while government ownership of television generally is not. These results are most naturally consistent with the view that government ownership of the press restricts information flows to the public, thereby diminishing the value of citizens rights and the effectiveness of government.

Table 8.7. Political Markets

Variable	State owner-ship, press (by share)	State owner-ship, television (by share)	GNP per capita	SOE index	Autocracy	Constant	R^2	N
Political rights	−0.1872* (0.0613)		0.0107* (0.0019)	−0.0011 (0.0071)	0.7772* (0.0780)	−0.0511 (0.0779)	0.8112	97
		−0.1278*** (0.0682)	0.0130* (0.0019)	−0.0011 (0.0079)	0.8275* (0.0692)	−0.0816 (0.0852)	0.8132	97
Civil liberties	−0.1531* (0.0532)		0.0105* (0.0017)	−0.0002 (0.0063)	0.5334* (0.0748)	0.1145*** (0.0703)	0.7507	97
		−0.0804 (0.0659)	0.0122* (0.0017)	0.0006 (0.0071)	0.5886* (0.0685)	0.0608 (0.0875)	0.7529	97
Corruption	−0.6819*** (0.4174)		0.0661* (0.0114)	−0.0289 (0.0450)	0.8072*** (0.4833)	2.5209* (0.4524)	0.4863	79
		0.0193 (0.4455)	0.0728* (0.0123)	−0.0174 (0.0457)	1.2313** (0.5496)	1.8852* (0.6688)	0.4863	79

*Significant at the 1 percent level.
**Significant at the 5 percent level.
***Significant at the 10 percent level.
Note: All dependent variables are rescaled so that larger values correspond to better outcomes. Standard errors in parentheses.
Source: Authors' calculations.

Our results are generally much stronger for the press than for television. For the latter, the effects of government ownership are generally insignificant. One reason might be that the presence of a private press, which is more common, provides a check on state television, ensuring freer flows of information than would occur if both were in state hands. The data confirm that the outcomes are worse when the state owns both newspapers and television than when it owns only one of them.

Economic System

The supply of information by the media can also improve the performance of the economic system. When citizens are better informed they may, through political action, become more effective in limiting the government's ability to hurt them economically by, for example, confiscating property or over-regulating businesses. Economic governance indicators, such as the security of property rights from confiscation and intervention and the quality of regulation, should therefore be higher in countries where the media function more effectively.

Table 8.8. Economic Markets

Variable	State owner- ship, press (by share)	State owner- ship, television (by share)	GNP per capita	SOE index	Autocracy	Constant	R^2	N
Security of property	−0.2415* (0.0676)		0.0114* (0.0019)	0.0295* (0.0080)	−0.1035 (0.1106)	0.5720* (0.1070)	0.5892	91
		−0.0088 (0.0611)	0.0135* (0.0018)	0.0342* (0.0081)	0.0429 (0.1230)	0.3611* (0.1236)	0.5893	91
Risk of confiscation	−2.8428* (0.6998)		0.0650* (0.0222)	0.1105 (0.1010)	−1.5156 (1.1106)	9.2214* (0.9643)	0.3112	81
		−2.1013** (1.0370)	0.1007* (0.0272)	0.0975 (0.1144)	−1.2372 (1.4425)	9.3301* (1.6183)	0.3084	81
Quality of regulation	−0.5496* (0.1748)		0.0204* (0.0046)	0.0627* (0.0178)	0.5395** (0.2427)	−0.5032** (0.2412)	0.6046	97
		−0.1458 (0.1593)	0.0261* (0.0048)	0.0701* (0.0197)	0.8219* (0.2643)	−0.8656* (0.2834)	0.6062	97

*Significant at the 1 percent level.
**Significant at the 5 percent level.
***Significant at the 10 percent level.
Note: All dependent variables are rescaled so that larger values correspond to better outcomes. Standard errors in parentheses.
Source: Authors' calculations.

Table 8.8 indicates that higher state ownership of the media is associated with weaker security of property, as measured by the Freedom House security of property rights index and Political Risk Services' measure of confiscation risk. Countries with higher state ownership of the media also exhibit lower quality of regulation, as measured by the World Bank. The results are statistically stronger for the press than for television and radio.

The results for the security of property again suggest that government ownership of the media hurts. Taken together with our earlier evidence on freedom of the press and political competition, this evidence is broadly supportive of the view that governments own the media—especially the press—not to improve the performance of economic and political systems, but to improve their own chances of staying in power.

Social Outcomes

Our analysis has focused on political and economic freedom, but one could presumably argue that the true benefits of state ownership of the press accrue to the disadvantaged members of society. Freed from the influence of capitalist owners, state-controlled media can serve the social needs of the poor and disadvantaged and thereby improve social outcomes. A skeptic would argue, in contrast, that the government would use its ownership of the media to muzzle the press and to prevent disadvantaged groups from having a mechanism for voicing their grievances. Government ownership should then be associated with inferior social outcomes.

The contrasting predictions of the two views can be evaluated empirically. Table 8.9 reports the relationships between state ownership of the media and education

Table 8.9. Social Outcomes

Variable	State ownership, press (by share)	State ownership, television (by share)	GNP per capita	SOE index	Autocracy	Constant	R^2	N
School attainment	−12.4252*** (6.8314)		−0.2927 (0.1882)	0.6594 (0.6836)	11.2771 (10.9235)	31.1315* (10.8036)	0.1791	67
		−18.6429* (7.1035)	−0.0990 (0.2068)	0.2327 (0.6922)	5.8109 (9.4805)	44.3819* (10.8167)	0.2221	67
Enrollment	−17.6477** (9.0161)		0.1021 (0.1762)	0.5956 (0.7532)	−10.0709 (10.9333)	106.0125* (10.9157)	0.1137	92
		−15.5171*** (9.4133)	0.3166 (0.1983)	0.5261 (0.7678)	−7.6437 (10.8303)	107.4779* (12.8582)	0.1155	92
Pupil/teacher ratio	−0.1909* (0.0627)		0.0076* (0.0017)	0.0004 (0.0079)	−0.1646* (0.0641)	0.8529* (0.0562)	0.3976	89
		−0.2537* (0.0651)	0.0107* (0.0019)	−0.0042 (0.0077)	−0.1904* (0.0758)	0.9724* (0.0834)	0.3879	89
Life expectancy	−11.1692* (3.1662)		0.4709* (0.0694)	0.3563 (0.3664)	−5.7165*** (3.5440)	69.7560* (3.6037)	0.4680	95
		−10.8742* (3.3970)	0.6196* (0.0726)	0.2580 (0.3609)	−4.9429 (3.8853)	72.0350* (4.7135)	0.4741	95
Infant mortality	−0.2692* (0.0833)		0.0086* (0.0015)	0.0007 (0.0082)	−0.1184 (0.0891)	0.9052* (0.0944)	0.4142	95
		−0.2548* (0.0835)	0.0122* (0.0020)	−0.0015 (0.0086)	−0.0953 (0.0936)	0.9514* (0.1133)	0.4170	95
Nutrition	−332.0943** (159.8358)		26.9430* (4.8200)	4.7406 (16.2370)	−155.0844 (205.9862)	2841.2880* (214.3279)	0.4102	93
		−327.5296** (167.5104)	30.8943* (4.5334)	0.0288 (17.5395)	−96.7649 (197.5197)	2889.1050* (254.9896)	0.4265	93

*Significant at the 1 percent level.
**Significant at the 5 percent level.
***Significant at the 10 percent level.

Note: All dependent variables are rescaled so that larger values correspond to better outcomes. Standard errors in parentheses.

Source: Authors' calculations.

and health indicators, holding per capita income, government ownership of firms, and autocracy constant. In countries with higher state ownership of the media we observe inferior school attainment, enrollment, and pupil to teacher ratios. Health outcomes, such as life expectancy, infant mortality, and malnutrition, are also worse in countries where the government owns more media outlets. Media ownership structures that are associated with better economic and political variables are also beneficial for social outcomes. The results for social outcomes are generally stronger than for economic and political variables, and hold for television as well as for the press.

Ownership or Monopoly?

The results of the previous sections raise an important question: Are the adverse effects of state ownership of the media driven solely by the instances of monopoly or near monopoly? Alternatively, is more state ownership always worse, even at lower market shares? At the time the BBC was created in the United Kingdom, the advocates of state ownership insisted on monopoly. In recent years a softer argument has prevailed, particularly in Western Europe, whereby some state ownership, particularly of television, is considered sufficient to provide the public with exposure to particular content that might be unavailable through private media. As none of the countries in our sample have private monopolies of either newspapers or television, the monopoly question pertains solely to state ownership.

To address this argument we divided our sample of countries into groups (of unequal sizes) by the degree of state control of newspaper circulation and of the television audience. Thus we created dummies for state control of newspaper circulation being between 0 and below 25 percent, between 25 and below 50 percent, between 50 and 75 percent, and above 75 percent. We created corresponding dummies for state control of television audiences. We refer to countries with state control exceeding 75 percent as having state monopolies in the relevant market. We reran the regressions shown in tables 8.6–8.9 with the dummies (for newspapers and television separately) rather than with the linear specification of the effects of state ownership of the media. The omitted dummy is always that corresponding to the second quartile, that is, state control between 25 and 50 percent. We looked at how the various outcomes compared across quartiles.

The results for media freedom and political and economic markets do not indicate that the adverse consequences of state ownership on the various outcomes are driven solely by state monopolies. In general, no clear pattern emerges from the data, as both third and fourth quartile state ownership often has large negative effects. However, most coefficients on quartile ownership dummies are statistically insignificant. For brevity, we do not present these results.

The results are clearer for social outcomes. Typically, though not always, for both newspapers and television, the coefficients on the first quartile dummy are positive while those on the third and fourth quartile dummies are negative. This evidence suggests that social outcomes deteriorate over the whole range of increases in government ownership of the media. The more competition in the media, the better are the outcomes. If the adverse outcomes were driven solely by monopoly, we would have seen, in contrast, zero coefficients on the first and third quartile dummies. This said, we also note that—especially in the case of television—the largest and most statistically significant adverse effects on social outcomes appear in the cases of state monopolies.

Conclusion

This chapter presents a range of evidence on the adverse consequences of state ownership of the media, holding key country characteristics constant. Government ownership of the media is detrimental to economic, political, and—most strikingly—social outcomes. The latter finding is particularly important in light of the commonly made argument justifying state ownership in a variety of sectors, including the media, by citing the social needs of the disadvantaged. If correct, our findings thoroughly debunk this argument. The evidence shows, to the contrary, that increasing private ownership of the media through privatization or the encouragement of entry can advance a variety of political and economic goals, and especially the social needs of the poor.

References

Barro, Robert and Jong-Wha Lee. 1996, "International Measures of Schooling Years and Schooling Quality." *American Economic Review* 86(2): 218–23.

Berezovsky, Boris. 2000. "Our Reverse Revolution: Under Yeltsin, We Oligarchs Helped Stop Russia from Reverting to its Old, Repressive Ways." *Washington Post*, October 26.

Besley, Timothy, and Robin Burgess. Forthcoming. "The Political Economy of Government Responsiveness: Theory and Evidence from India." *Quarterly Journal of Economics*.

Committee to Protect Journalists. 2000. *Attacks on the Press in 1999: A Worldwide Survey by the Committee to Protect Journalists.* Available online: http://www.cpg.org.

Coase, Ronald H. 1959. "The Federal Communications Commission." *Journal of Law and Economics* 2(5): 1–40.

Demsetz, Harold. 1989. "The Amenity Potential of Newspapers and the Reporting of Presidential Campaigns." In H. Demsetz, ed., *Efficiency, Competition, and Policy.* London: Basil Blackwell.

Demsetz, Harold, and Kenneth Lehn. 1985. "The Structure of Corporate Ownership: Causes and Consequences." *Journal of Political Economy* 93(6): 1155–77.

Djankov, Simeon, Caralee McLiesh, Tatiana Nenova, and Andrei Shleifer. "Who Owns the Media." Working paper. National Bureau of Economic Research, Cambridge, Massachusetts.

———. Forthcoming. "Who Owns the Media?" *Journal of Law and Economics.*

European Institute of the Media. 2000. "Media in the CIS." Duesseldorf, Germany.

Fraser Institute. 2000. *Economic Freedom of the World.* Vancouver, Canada.

Freedom House.2000a. *The Annual Survey of Press Freedom 2000.* New York. Available on: http://www.freedomhouse.org/research/presssurvey.htm.

———. 2000b. *Freedom in the World: Annual Survey of Freedom Country Ratings 1999/2000,* Available online: http://www.freedomhouse.org/research/freeworld/2000/index.htm.

Grossman, Sanford J., and Oliver Hart. 1988. "One Share-One Vote and the Market for Corporate Control." *Journal of Financial Economics* 20(1-2): 175–202.

Kaufmann, Daniel, Aart Kraay, and Pablo Zoido-Lobaton. 1999. "Governance Matters." Policy Research Working Paper no. 2196. World Bank, Washington, D.C.

La Porta Rafael, Florencio Lopez-de-Silanes, and Andrei Shleifer. 1999. "Corporate Ownership around the World." *Journal of Finance* 54(2): 471–517.

La Porta, Rafael, Florencio Lopez-de-Silanes, Andrei Shleifer, and Robert Vishny. 1999. "The Quality of Government." *Journal of Law, Economics, and Organization* 15(3): 222–79.

Polity IV Project. 2000. *Polity IV Dataset: Political Regime Characteristics and Transitions, 1800–1999.* College Park, Maryland: University of Maryland, Center for International Development and Conflict Management. Available online: http://www.cidcm.umd.edu/inscr/polity.

Political Risk Services. 2000. *International Country Risk Guide.* East Syracuse, New York: Institutional Reform and Informational Sector.

Reporters Sans Frontiéres. 2000. *Annual Report 2000.* Available online: http://www.rsf.fr.

Sen, Amartya. 1984. *Poverty and Famines.* Oxford, U.K.: Oxford University Press.

———. 1999. *Development as Freedom.* New York: Alfred A. Knopf.

Simons, Henry. 1948. *Economic Policy of a Free Society.* Chicago: University of Chicago Press.

Stigler, George. 1961. "The Economics of Information." *Journal of Political Economy* 69(3): 213–25.

Stiglitz, Joseph E. 2000. "The Contributions of the Economics of Information to Twentieth Century Economics." *Quarterly Journal of Economics* 115(4): 1441–78.

UNDP (United Nations Development Programme). 2000. *Human Development Report 2000.* New York.

UNESCO (United Nations Educational, Scientific, and Cultural Organization). 1999. *Annual Statistical Yearbook.* Paris, France: Institute for Statistics.

World Association of Newspapers. 2000. *World Press Trends 2000.* Paris: Zenith Media.

World Bank. 2000a. *Database of Enterprise Indicators on Transition Economies, Europe, and Central Asia Region.* Washington, D.C.

———. 2000b. *World Development Indicators 2000.* Washington, D.C.

Zenith Media. 2000a. *Americas Market and Mediafact.* London, the United Kingdom.

———. 2000b. *Asia Pacific Market and Mediafact.* London.

———. 2000c. *Central and Eastern European Market and Mediafact.* London.

———. 2000d. *Middle East and Africa Market and Mediafact.* London.

———. 2000e. *Western European Market and Mediafact.* London.

9

Media as Industry:
Economic Foundations of Mass Communications

Bruce M. Owen

Often we look at mass media in developing countries through a political lens, asking such questions as whether they are subject to state control or censorship and the extent to which democratic objectives such as transparency in government and freedom of expression are advanced through the work of journalists. Examination of the role of the media in development also often focuses on the media's effects on audiences and on cultural values (see World Bank 2001, chapter 10). This chapter looks at the media simply as businesses.

The direct contribution of mass media to economic output is modest; the sector is a relatively small one in almost every economy, rich or poor. For example, in 1999 radio and television contributed 0.7 percent of U.S. gross domestic product; all printing services, including newspapers and periodicals, contributed 1.06 percent, and motion pictures contributed 0.3 percent. Nevertheless, the political and other non-economic effects of mass media are clearly of great importance, and the media's indirect economic effects on economic development are hardly less important. Advertising-supported media are a major source of consumer and commercial information and a vehicle for disseminating knowledge, and both these activities contribute to economic growth. The availability of commercial information contained in advertising greatly reduces consumers' transaction and search costs and creates the possibility of mass marketing with its economies of scale and scope. Similarly, the dissemination of commercial information, such as commodity prices and wage rates, facilitates productivity in small-scale enterprises. Mass communication also serves important, perhaps even transcendent, political, cultural, and educational ends.

Yet none of the political, cultural, or indirect economic benefits of mass media can exist, at least in market economies, if the media are not successful businesses. Therefore understanding the economic factors that explain the commercial basis and structure of media enterprise is important. For the owners of media enterprises commercial success must either be an end in itself or a condition necessary to achieve and maintain prestige, power, and influence. This is because they cannot gain power and influence alone without commercial success except in the absence of competition. The content that best serves those media owners whose goal is power and influence is not, in general, the same content required for commercial success—and therefore perhaps survival—in a competitive market environment (see Owen 1975 for an extensive discussion of the relationship between media structure and economic competition affecting content).

Economic Characteristics of Media Products

Media produce two products: content and advertising. While interdependent, the two products have different characteristics.

Content

Mass media sell content such as information and entertainment to consumers. In doing so, media attract audiences that often can be sold to advertisers. Thus in general, media have two outputs or sources of revenue: content and audiences. Examples of media at all extremes are available. For instance, media such as traditional commercial television broadcasters rely wholly on the sale of audiences to advertisers; other media, such as motion picture studios and book publishers, rely wholly on the sale of content to consumers and sell no audiences to advertisers; and certain other media, such a billboards, flyers, and certain periodicals, consist wholly of advertising.

The earliest mass media beyond the pulpit were newspapers and periodicals. By the mid-19th century, newspaper publishers in many countries were beginning to enjoy the benefits of advertising revenues from new mass marketers of consumer goods. Many factors came together to support the resulting surge in newspaper circulations: new transportation technology facilitated the development of mass markets as well as wider newspaper circulation, increasing literacy contributed to circulation demand, and new printing technology and increased supplies of cheap newsprint supported larger circulations and lower subscription prices.

As a consumer product, media content has two fundamental economic characteristics. First, content is a public good. This simply means that producing a given body of content, say a newspaper story, for the first reader costs no more than it does for the 10,000th reader. If a story costs US$500 to produce, the cost per reader is US$500 if there is one reader and US$0.05 if there are 10,000 readers. In short, the production of mass media content is characterized by enormous economies of scale. This applies to all mass media, from newspapers to satellite television broadcasters.

The second basic characteristic of media content is that it is heterogeneous or differentiated. No two items of media content are identical, in part because media have intellectual property rights in the content they produce, and in part because for commercial reasons media need to differentiate their content to compete successfully with media having larger audiences, and therefore lower unit costs. Product differentiation is a costly activity that generally faces decreasing returns to scale.

The structure of the newspaper industry illustrates these factors. Economies of scale in spreading the first copy costs of content creation over an increasing number of readers would suggest that a newspaper might be a natural monopoly. As newspapers with larger circulations have lower unit costs, they should be able to drive smaller newspapers out of the market. Yet in most countries more than one newspaper serves both national and local markets. The presence of multiple newspapers does not necessarily mean that the market is in disequilibrium, on the path to monopoly. It may simply mean that the competing newspapers have found ways to appeal to different audiences or different advertisers, each with tastes that cannot be satisfied simultaneously by a single content provider. Differentiation may take many forms. Some media, such as local newspapers, specialize by locality. The *Bombay Times* cannot compete in Calcutta because it cannot efficiently cover local Calcutta news in depth while remaining attractive to readers and advertisers in Bombay. Similarly, Ulaanbaatar, Mongolia, is highly unlikely to have been able to support 18 "principal" newspapers in 1994 if these newspapers had not been sharply differentiated along political and other lines (Williams 1995).

In many countries newspapers are also specialized by political affiliation. Noncommercial, party-sponsored newspapers are common. Some readers may not trust content from newspapers aligned with an opposition party, or may simply enjoy having their own opinions reinforced by like-minded content. Publishers seeking to compete in an industry with economies of scale naturally gravitate to clusters of consumers with such tastes. Similar specialization takes place with respect to language, ethnicity, and cultural factors. Both newspapers and broadcast media have some ability to serve different tastes within the same medium. Newspapers have sections, news and sports, for example, that cater to different audience segments. Radio and television broadcasters often serve different audience segments, such as children versus adults, by offering different content at different times of day. Mongolia is again an interesting case. While the country only had four broadcast channels in 1995, viewers reported in interviews that it had as many as seven. Each channel offered programming in different languages at different times of day, and viewers perceived these languages as being offered on different channels (Williams 1995).

In the case of newspapers, technology and geography also play a role in setting limits on newspaper scale. Urban newspapers face increasing transport costs (and costs associated with delivery delays) as they attempt to serve areas outside the city, costs that increase more than proportionately with distance because of declining population density. Smaller countries are more likely than larger ones to have national newspapers for this reason. In recent times national and regional newspapers have addressed this problem by using advanced communications technologies that permit a given newspaper to be printed simultaneously in multiple locations. Geography is somewhat less important to radio and television than to newspapers. Broadcast media are instantaneous and can be simultaneously transmitted cheaply from antennas all over a country. Hence the United States had national radio and television networks long before it had any national newspapers.

A number of economic models of competing advertiser-supported media reach the conclusion that such media will tend to cater to mass interests, or least common denominator mass interests, wastefully duplicating similar programming and neglecting minority tastes (Steiner 1952; see Owen and Wildman 1992, chapter 3, for a literature review.). One might conclude from this that multiple media channels owned by a monopolist would produce greater content diversity than the same number of channels each independently owned and operated; however, more general models cast doubt on such a conclusion. Today economists recognize that the extent of content diversity produced by a competitive, profit-maximizing media industry depends on consumer and advertiser preferences, program costs, and other factors, and there is no basis for assuming that a monopolist would produce more diverse programming (Owen and Wildman 1992, chapter 4).

The term diversity is often used in discussions of mass media. Content diversity refers to the range of content made available; source diversity refers to the range of content selectors or gatekeepers. Presumably what matters for favorable political outcomes is source diversity, or perhaps the absence of barriers to entry at the gatekeeping level. From an economic point of view, however, recognizing that content diversity rather than source diversity affects consumer welfare is important. There is no necessary relationship between source diversity and content diversity.

The quality of mass media content is multidimensional and difficult to measure or to compare; however, the factors of production of commercially successful content are scarce and typically earn economic rents. This is why, for example, popular movie stars earn large incomes. If one is willing to associate commercial success with quality, then it follows that the rents that accrue to scarce inputs create a correlation between production cost and quality. Therefore, with appropriate qualifications, the quality of media content can be measured by its production cost. At least within the same genre, more costly content attracts larger audiences. The U.S. motion picture industry, for example, owes its worldwide success in part to the huge production budgets of its films.

Advertising

Advertising (or the sale of audiences) is no less important than content in understanding media economics. The demand for mass media advertising is based on its ability to generate additional sales of consumer goods and services. Much advertising, such as newspaper classified advertisements, contains detailed and specific information that facilities buyers' and sellers' searches for favorable transaction opportunities. Other advertising appeals mainly to more subjective needs. The psychological and economic mechanism by which advertising is effective is complex, and beyond the scope of this chapter. In brief, media advertising conveys information that, when processed, alters consumers' valuations of advertised and unadvertised goods. Some advertising, of course, is aimed at changing opinions or institutional images rather than at selling commercial goods.

Advertisers seek to reach a target audience consisting of those consumers most likely to be influenced favorably by their messages. Mass media such as broadcast television are extremely effective in reaching large, relatively undifferentiated audiences. Such media are useful vehicles for advertisers selling products such as soap, beverages, foodstuffs, or retail services that nearly every household might use. Broadcast television is inefficient, however, for advertisers seeking small or specialized target audiences, such as potential buyers of expensive antiques. An antique dealer seeks to reach potential customers who are both geographically concentrated near the dealer's location and suitable in terms of income and taste. Such an advertiser would use certain periodicals; local newspapers; flyers; and, where available, direct mail solicitation.

In addition to seeking to reach an audience with certain target characteristics, advertisers seek to avoid wasteful duplication of coverage. Therefore advertisers prefer media able to deliver larger audiences of a given composition to media that deliver smaller audiences of that composition. Put differently, advertisers will prefer a medium with a given reach (circulation) among the target audience to media with a lesser reach, because using several smaller media typically results in duplication of advertising to overlapping members of the audience.

The efficiency of mass media for advertisers is summarized in an index number: the cost per thousand (CPM). Advertising media promote themselves by offering large audiences with attractive (low) CPMs. Media CPMs are defined both for the overall audience and for specialized demographic segments defined by location, age, sex, education, and income. Segments are defined in a way that approximates the target audiences of particular advertisers or types of advertisers. Some media such as periodicals specialize in content that is attractive to a particular demographic segment to produce audiences that have low CPMs for advertisers seeking to reach that segment.

A medium dependent both on subscription payments from the audience and on advertising revenues must recognize the interdependence of advertising revenues and subscription pricing. Higher subscription prices reduce circulation and therefore lower advertising revenue. Because many members of the audience may value advertisements, especially those with pricing and other specific information, as well as noncommercial content, a reduction in advertising resulting from higher prices for advertisements reduces circulation.

Government legislation influences the economics of advertising, especially in broadcasting. For example, the U.S. government regulates advertising on children's programs, limits the advertising of proprietary drugs, and forbids the advertising of tobacco products; however, the courts struck down voluntary industry agreements limiting the number of commercial minutes as violating antitrust laws. In contrast, Germany limits private television broadcasting companies to a maximum of 20 percent of daily broadcasting time devoted to advertising.

The dissemination of information by the government can be an important source of advertising revenue for some media, as well as a subtle vehicle for the exercise of political control. Many local governments in the United States, for example, are required by law to publish various legal notices in "a local newspaper of general circulation." For smaller newspapers these notices can be a significant revenue source, and hence one not lightly jeopardized by aggressive political content.

Media Structure and Pricing

Both the public good characteristics of content and the greater advertising efficiency of large circulations within a given audience segment tend to favor the economic success and survival of larger media, but some audiences' demand for specialized or differentiated content, together with some advertisers' demand for specialized target segments, pulls in the opposite direction. In highly developed economies this produces a thickly populated spectrum of media, with clusters of competitors around each concentration of advertiser or consumer demand. Clearly the extent to which the spectrum of potential media locations in content space is populated depends in part on the extent of demand by advertisers and members of the audience. Developing economies have fewer occupied niches along this spectrum, and thus fewer competitors around each cluster of audience and advertiser demand characteristics.

Large, dense clusters of consumer demand for content of a given kind (by definition, popular content) combined with concentrated demand by advertisers for the audiences produced by such content will tend to produce multiple media channels with like content. Only when so many competing media have divided the mass audience will more specialized media content appear, because only at that point will a large share of a smaller audience exceed a small share of the larger mass audience in profitability. In a developing economy this is probably fortunate, because it supports the growth of mass consumer markets from both the demand and supply sides. Nevertheless, commercial mass media offering popular content with little differentiation inevitably attract criticism from articulate groups concerned about the absence of programming that appeals to minority cultural or elitist tastes.

Theoretically, the provision of public goods such as media content is impossible in a competitive market system. Competition drives prices toward marginal cost, and the marginal cost of an additional audience member is zero. At a zero price, there is no revenue. This leads either to no production of the public good at all or to production by a monopolist or a cartel charging inefficiently high prices. In reality, several market solutions to this problem are available. Competing broadcast media such as traditional radio and television stations exist even though they charge an economically efficient (zero) price for content, thanks to their ability to sell advertising, a private good with nonzero marginal costs. Media that cannot rely chiefly on advertising revenue, such as motion pictures, specialized periodicals, and book publishers, can survive if intellectual property rights exist and are enforced, so that competitors must produce differentiated rather than identical products. This permits content prices to be greater than zero despite competition. The relative welfare loss from pricing above marginal cost diminishes as the growing market and increased crowding of content space reduces the number of consumers inefficiently excluded.

Economists often cite the fact that mass media, especially broadcasters, deal in public goods as a reason for public subsidies or outright government ownership of the media. Both ownership and subsidies raise difficulties if the media's role is to promote political freedom. Moreover, from an economic point of view, neither state ownership nor subsidies are necessarily helpful, because the information that even an entirely benign intervention would require in order to improve consumer welfare is not observable. Efficient centralized resource allocation in the provision of public goods would require detailed knowledge of each consumer's preferences.

Stages of Media Production and Vertical Integration

Mass media have certain common stages of production: creation of content, selection of content and financing of production, and distribution of the resulting package.

Content creation includes producing video entertainment programs, gathering news, putting on sporting events, producing motion pictures, writing, composing and recording music, and like activities. Perhaps because of its creative nature, content production often takes place on an extremely small scale. Entry is generally easy, with low or zero capital requirements or other barriers; however, the usual outcome of entry is commercial failure. Creative enterprises at this earliest stage of media production are extremely risky. For example, for every published article, musical recording, newspaper feature, or video program hundreds or thousands of proposals are often rejected. Entry at this stage of production persists partly because the creative process is rewarding in itself and on account of optimism, but also because the rewards of success can be great. Skillful entrepreneurship and efficient management are major ingredients of success. Hollifield (2001) surveyed research results on transnational media management. Kaiser (2001) told the story of Vyacheslav Dagayev, a young Russian entrepreneur, and his successful struggle to establish a commercial weekly newspaper in Ulan-Ude, Russia, in 1992.

From an economic perspective, distinguishing news or explicit political content from entertainment content is not useful. The mass media as businesses exist to make money by offering attractive products that will produces revenues from audiences and advertisers. They will only offer news, political content, or other "serious" content to the extent that it is profitable. As noted earlier, media owners protected from competition may choose to spend their economic rents on less profitable projects, such as political propaganda. In other cases, government regulation may forbid some profitable programming, for instance, pornography, or advertising, such as for liquor or tobacco products. Dagayev, for example, began his newspaper without any political or news content because he found that other content was more profitable. Moreover, material that is classified as entertainment may often have important political content, for instance, political cartoons. Audiences value some "serious" material in part because it is entertaining. In any event, the stages of production are much the same, regardless of the nature of media content.

The remaining stages of production typically require more substantial scale and capital investment. Much entertainment content fails to become popular, and so media must acquire a portfolio of properties to diversify their risk. In broadcasting, a network, studio, or station will select among proposed projects and finance their production. In newspaper publishing editors seeking to satisfy diverse reader demands select material for publication. Financing of the creative effort is important for certain kinds of content, such as motion pictures and video entertainment, where first copy costs loom large. In other fields, such as magazine publishing, financing may be limited to paying small advances to writers. While the efficient scale of production at the creative stage may be small, as in weekly newspaper publishing, the optimal scale of physical distribution is usually much larger. Thus entry into publishing may require the existence of commercial printing and distribution industries that rely largely on non-newspaper revenue sources.

Selection or editing of content and its subsequent bundling is a crucial function in any mass medium. Of the tens of thousands of messages vying for the public's attention and money, only a few will be financially successful. It is the role of the editor (whatever his or her title) to select those messages that best satisfy the demands of the reader or viewer. Competition among editors, program directors, or other content selectors ensures that market forces will prevent any arbitrary exercise of the power of selection (see Crawford 2001 for a review of some of the extensive economic literature on product bundling and market power in the specific context of cable television service).

Not all media rely heavily on a reputation for specific content or predictable quality. Motion picture studios, for example, are more likely to value their reputation with investors than with movie goers; movie goers' enjoyment of a particular movie provides little indication that they will like any other movie distributed by the same studio. Consumers rely instead on the reputations of actors and directors and on the effects of extensive promotions in choosing among motion pictures. The editorial or selection process is most often integrated with finance, because its outcome is a portfolio of risky assets. Selection of content for a given media channel thus serves not only to create packages of content attractive to readers or viewers, but also to manage risk.

Physical distribution of mass media generally requires substantial investment. In the case of print media, a network of agents and delivery vehicles is required. Terrestrial broadcasters require transmitters and spectrum and rely on audiences to purchase receiving equipment. Cable television providers must invest in a network of cables, amplifiers, and other equipment. Satellite broadcasters require spectrum, orbital slots, satellites, and terrestrial facilities for uplinks, as well as receiving equipment at consumer locations. The distribution stage of the mass media is usually the stage at which promotion takes place. Most media spend heavily on promotional programs aimed at potential readers or viewers, motivated partly by a desire to spread the first copy costs of content creation and selection over as large an audience as possible, and partly by a desire to have additional audience members to sell to advertisers. The proportion of funds spent on distribution, as opposed to content, varies with the size of the audience. If the audience is small, the costs are chiefly for content, and if the audience is large, the costs are chiefly for distribution.

Almost everywhere controversies are created by disparities in the scale at which media content is created and the scale at which the remaining stages are most efficient. Creative individuals (actors, writers, directors, reporters, columnists, photographers) often perceive a disparity in economic power between themselves and the large enterprises that purchase (or reject) their services or works. Similar disparities in size appear at other stages in the mass media. For example, as noted earlier, the editorial process that produces a magazine or other periodical can be managed at extremely small scales compared with the efficient scale at which printing and physical distribution take place. Thus magazines and weekly newspapers seldom own their own printing presses, and most rely on independent distributors who handle many periodicals. At the local level, periodical distribution is often a monopoly.

In contrast to magazines, daily newspapers are vertically integrated. While daily newspapers buy content such as features and wire service news from third parties, they also employ reporters and other content creators. Daily newspapers generally own their own presses and use most of the presses' capacity. Similarly, daily newspapers frequently use employees rather than independent distributors to deliver copies to readers or newsstands. One reason for the vertical integration found in daily newspapers is the need to coordinate the production process so that the newspaper can be produced and delivered on a tight and regular schedule. This is often easier to do within a firm than through contractual arrangements among firms.

Electronic media tend to purchase content from third parties. This is especially true of entertainment content for two reasons. First, virtually all media, even national media, are "local" with respect to entertainment content with broader appeal, that is, much entertainment programming must appear on multiple media to obtain access to its widest audience. For third parties to produce, or at least to distribute, content that can appear on multiple media makes sense, because that lowers the unit cost of the content, making it competitively more attractive. Of course, a given mass medium may produce some content of its own and sell it to other media, but this is simply partial vertical integration. Second, electronic entertainment content is often exploited in "windows" (Owen and Wildman 1992, chapter 2). Each window is a period of time during which the content is offered exclusively to a particular audience or through a particular medium. Windows provide an opportunity for suppliers to engage in price discrimination. Audiences willing to pay high prices are offered the material first, then the same content is successively offered to audiences willing to wait in exchange for lower prices. The simplest example of this is the release of paperback or mass market books after a period during which only hardbound books are offered at a relatively high price. Another advantage of windows is that they permit particular media to reap the rewards of advertising and other promotional expenditures that would otherwise spill over to the advantage of competing media. This happens because the distributors in each window enjoys exclusive rights in their respective territories.

Vertical integration is sometimes blamed for media concentration (OECD 1993). Ownership of key resources may present one competitor with opportunities to raise rivals' costs or to exclude them entirely. Vertical foreclosure in developing nations is likely to be a problem chiefly in vernacular programming given the substantial supply of popular foreign programming that would be difficult to foreclose from competitors. In Mexico, for example, for many years Televisa controlled television and radio broadcasting, and Televisa's dominance was commonly attributed to its extensive vertical integration into the production of Spanish-language television programming (Barrera n.d.). An independent program production industry might have facilitated entry by broadcasters seeking to compete with Televisa.

Nevertheless, despite the vertical integration, competition did develop in Mexican broadcasting when the government privatized additional broadcast frequencies in the 1990s. These channels and other media assets were awarded to Azteca, a new entrant that appears to have been successful. Thus Televisa's long dominance may have been attributable not to its vertical integration, but to horizontal concentration, that is, to its ownership of all available private broadcast channels, a circumstance attributable to government policy. Moreover, in the case of Televisa, vertical integration may have been responsible for Mexican television's relative lack of dependence on foreign sources of programming, and has certainly helped to promote Mexico's success in exporting Spanish-language television programming to the United States and to the rest of Latin America.

The Mexican example underscores the importance of avoiding inefficient vertical disintegration of media stages in response to perceived media concentration problems.

Vertical integration may produce efficiencies by permitting media to control or optimize risk. A policy tradeoff seems to exist between economies of vertical integration and the competitive benefits of easier entry in the absence of such integration. The point of the Mexican example is that even though vertical integration was blamed for the media ownership concentration and lack of competition, in reality the government's spectrum policies sustained the monopolist. In the United States, in the past regulators have sometimes restricted vertical integration by television and cable networks into programming to increase competition or source diversity, but these restrictions are now generally regarded as contrary to consumer interests and are being repealed.

Media Production Technologies

On the technical side, media have much in common. A mass medium by definition involves the transmission (broadcast) of the same content from one or a small number of centers to many audience members, organized like the spokes of a wheel. In contrast, a narrowcast transmission involves point to point communication of unique, often two-way, messages, as in a telephone network. The sharing of content among many members of the audience of a mass medium is what leads to economies of scale.

The production capacity of a mass medium can be measured in many ways. Most media have one or more channels, which may be marketed individually or in bundles by a single economic entity. Each channel has a distinct identity that consumers may associate with a specific kind and quality of content, as with a trade name or mark. Channels offer content either continuously or periodically, and seek to induce repeated patronage by consumers. A newspaper, magazine, television station, or radio broadcaster can each be thought of as a channel of mass communication. As discussed previously, the total number of competing channels and the number of channels under the common control of each economic entity determines the extent of content diversity. As technology has advanced, the number of channels under common control has tended to grow, as in the contrast between a local broadcaster and a local cable television system. Increasingly, the structure of media involves competition among multichannel providers, as when direct-to-home satellite broadcasters compete with cable television systems. A newspaper, with its different sections organized by topical content, can also be regarded as a multichannel medium.

The physical capacity of a given channel can be measured in terms of its ability to transfer information per unit of time. For electronic media this is done in terms of bandwidth (for analog channels) or bits per second (for digital channels). Print media have analogous physical measures, but most of today's print media use electronic transmission at some point in their production. However, the aesthetic appeal and substantive content of a mass media message may have little to do with physical measures of capacity. For example, both consumer willingness to pay and critical reception for a message transmitted or printed in grayscale may readily exceed that accorded a color message that requires many more bits of information.

Networks

The structure or topology of a communication network helps define the nature of the messages it can effectively carry. Several important distinctions are useful here. A mass media broadcast, defined earlier, is a one-to-many, one-way communication path that can transmit messages over the air or in print. Print media convey a public good (the message) by means of a private good (the book, magazine, or newspaper). In over-the-air broadcasting both the message and the medium are public goods, which typically conveys a substantial cost advantage. Two-way or interactive networks are organized in a fundamentally different way than broadcast networks. Interactive networks conserve capacity by relying on time-sharing of common facilities. Connecting all pairs of users directly all the time, with nearly all the links unused at any given time, would be much too costly. Instead, providers use switching (time-sharing) to provide access to trunk facilities or employ other methods of dividing common capacity. These methods all rely on the assumption that users are not all simultaneously and continuously engaging in communication. For this reason an ordinary telephone network could not be used to broadcast even one radio station to all households simultaneously, and the Internet as structured today has similar limitations that prevent its use as a mass medium. Therefore, at least using current terrestrial technologies, two-way telecommunications networks and one-way mass media networks are distinct entities that are not functionally interchangeable as providers of mass communications.

Printing

Printing is the oldest mass media technology. Commercial newspapers first appeared in Europe early in the 17th century, and mass circulation newspapers could be found throughout the world by the mid-19th century except where governments suppressed them. Many innovations in printing technology have taken place over the centuries, generally with the effect of making newspapers and periodicals cheaper to print at higher quality and in greater quantity. The availability, beginning in the mid-19th century, of cheap newsprint manufactured from softwood pulp was key. Improvements in printing technology are typically embodied in capital equipment whose manufacture is currently concentrated in a few countries, notably Germany and Japan. The most recent innovations in printing technology rely on computers and telecommunications that facilitate the organization, selection, and creation of content. Many newspapers and magazines now distribute their content electronically as well as in printed form, but the future of this method of distribution remains uncertain. Few publishers have been successful in imposing user fees, and advertising demand for electronic distribution remains constrained by issues of measurement and effectiveness.

Terrestrial Broadcasting

Although use of the electromagnetic spectrum for radio and video broadcasting is only a century old, there have been several generations of improved transmission methods. Any message traveling from one person to another at a distance must be impressed upon a medium (such as paper, magnetic tape, or carrier wave) by encoding (for example, typesetting, digitizing, or modulating) to suit the features of the medium, and then decoded or transformed back into terms accessible to human senses. For many years electronic communication used analog modulation for this purpose, because it was one of the most cost-effective ways to get the job done. In recent years, however, the cost of digital processors has fallen greatly. If the information to be transmitted is in digital form, such computers can be used to lower the cost of communicating any given amount of information by conserving relatively expensive bandwidth. This is done by compressing the information in each signal into a smaller package, using digital processing to remove bits that can be computed or interpolated at the receiving end. Digital coding is still more expensive than analog coding, but the bandwidth savings compensates for this disadvantage. For example, new digital television broadcasting standards permit the use of a single current analog television channel to broadcast six or more digital television signals in the same area. Owen (1999) surveyed the economic implications of recent advances in electronic mass communication technology, including the possible convergence of mass media technology with the computer and information network technologies.

The implications of digital transmission and processing go beyond terrestrial broadcasting. The technology is generally applicable to any electronic transmission path and greatly reduces the cost of distributing mass media messages. Lower distribution costs can have significant implications for developing economies, which will no longer have to build more than one television tower and transmitter to broadcast up to six television signals, each of which can be programmed independently.

Multichannel Video Distribution

Multichannel video distribution systems encompass a variety of technologies, both wired and wireless. Examples include cable television; multipoint, multichannel distribution systems; local multichannel distribution systems; and direct-to-home satellite broadcasting. These technologies have in common the packaging of many simultaneous video channels into a single service, in contrast to conventional broadcasters, who commonly operate a single channel. As noted earlier, in this respect multichannel video distributors resemble certain print media, especially daily newspapers, in their need to select and package content not only over time, but also across channels. This permits the medium to appeal to more consumers than a single-channel medium could hope to do; however, bundling (that is, selling multiple channels as a package) may require some consumers to acquire access to unwanted content as part of their subscription packages. This bundling effect often gives rise to competition policy disputes because competitors may be discouraged from entering if they cannot offer the same range of content as an incumbent medium. Bundling may either increase or decrease consumer welfare.

In several industrial countries multichannel distribution has already become the dominant mode of video distribution. In the United States more than 80 percent of television viewers use cable or satellite rather than off-air antennas. As fewer consumers depend on over-the-air broadcasts and as demand for spectrum by mobile communications providers grows, one can expect countries gradually to abandon terrestrial broadcasting.

Satellite Broadcasting

Satellites that orbit the earth directly over the equator at an altitude of about 35,785 kilometers have an orbital speed that exactly matches the speed of the Earth's rotation. Hence they appear to remain stationary over a single point on the equator and can be used as if they were extremely tall fixed antennas. Satellite broadcasting is a special case of multichannel distribution. Increasingly powerful direct-to-home satellites operate on ever higher frequencies, permitting smaller and smaller receiving antennas. Satellites will be launched in the next year that operate in the Ka frequency band, which lies beyond 20 gigaHertz (20 billion cycles per second). As antennas shrink they become easier to conceal, addressing both aesthetic and, in some countries, political concerns. Satellite broadcasts, both audio and video, easily bypass the authority of local and national governments. They also bypass relatively expensive terrestrial distribution systems. Content can be uplinked to a broadcast satellite from outside the area to which the satellite is broadcasting. Ka band satellites may provide not just multichannel video distribution, but also inexpensive two-way service to homes, and perhaps individual users, including telephone and Internet access. The political implications of direct broadcast satellites are obvious, but in peace time national governments maintain, by treaty, the right to regulate or limit broadcasts to their populations. These matters, as well as the allocation of relevant portions of the spectrum and orbital slots among countries, are worked out within the framework of the United Nations' International Telecommunications Union (for information about the union go to http://www.itu.int).

One interesting implication of satellite technology, especially the next generation, is that repressive governments may be less able to control access by their populations to outside political and cultural influences. Another implication is that the low per unit distribution costs associated with satellites (compared with terrestrial distribution) may greatly expand the quantity of media content offered in response to a given level of consumer and advertiser demand. Finally, low distribution costs will probably increase the tendency for content to be distributed more widely, enhancing the trend toward globalization of the media and facilitating the further globalization of popular culture.

The Internet

The Internet is often touted as the newest mass medium. As a technology, however, the Internet is more closely analogous to point-to-point telephone or postal networks than to point-to-points broadcast networks. Nevertheless, the speed and low cost of access to the Internet in most countries makes it a preferred mechanism for distributing media content akin to that found in small periodicals and newsletters. The Internet also supports rapid dissemination of low bandwidth, non-real-time content, such as email, that may be a close substitute for politically significant mass media content and is much less easily regulated by governments. (However, Internet access is more readily blocked by repressive governments than access to transnational radio broadcasts or black market sources of printed and recorded content.)

The current design of the Internet makes it inherently inefficient as a broadcast medium. While a television broadcaster sends out one signal that millions of people can receive, an Internet broadcaster seeking to reach millions must send a separate signal to each recipient, thereby tying up bandwidth proportional to the size of the audience. Future Internet designs may change this. The Internet as it currently exists has not demonstrated an ability to compete successfully with conventional media for advertising revenue. Indeed, failure to produce sufficiently large, verifiable audiences attractive to advertisers contributed to the 1999–2000 demise of hundreds of "dotcom" ventures throughout the world. (Most Internet advertising has been based on barter transactions in which two dotcoms agree to show each others' advertisements.) Thus, whatever the strength of its role in the marketplace of ideas, the Internet is not yet and may never be an important mass medium (Owen 1999).

Economic Regulation

Governments commonly seek to regulate the mass media. Censorship of the printed media, an old story, is outside the scope of this chapter. Economic regulation also affects the media, print as well as electronic. For example, newspaper publishers may face scrutiny from competition policy agencies when seller concentration is high or when mergers are proposed. Some countries prohibit or limit cross-ownership of competing media in an effort to ensure greater diversity of sources of news and opinion (see OECD 1999 for a comprehensive overview of ownership and cross-ownership policies in member countries).

There has traditionally been a sharp distinction in the degree of regulation (and state ownership) of mass media depending on the technology employed.[1] Freedom of the printed media from government regulation or ownership has long been an important measure of the degree of political freedom in a society. One reason for this attitude may be that the print media have long been structurally competitive, or at least monopolistic only locally, so that societies did not have to choose between private monopoly and government regulation. By contrast, the assumption from the outset seems to have been that electronic mass media were far more powerful, and therefore posed a greater threat to social and political stability, and that this together with government ownership of the electromagnetic spectrum justified regulation or state ownership.

Early use of the electromagnetic spectrum for safety, rescue, and maritime and military services led to nationalization of the spectrum in most countries early in the last century. Because radio waves are not hampered by national frontiers, treaties and international agencies (the International Telecommunications Union) define acceptable uses and users of different portions of the spectrum to encourage equipment compatibility and to reduce interference problems. In most countries government ownership of the airwaves led to government nationalization of first radio and then television broadcasting. Even those nations that permitted private broadcasting strictly limited the number of broadcast frequencies, creating an artificial scarcity of channels. Thus in some countries a broadcast permit is virtually a license to print money often used to reward the government's political supporters.

One marketplace reaction to government-owned or controlled broadcast outlets, especially to a restriction of the number of video entertainment channels, was the growth of cable television systems, and more recently, of direct satellite broadcast television. Compared with over-the-air broadcasting, cable television is an expensive means of distributing video programming. If the number of broadcast channels had not been restricted as a matter of policy in many countries, substantial investment expense in cable television systems might have been avoided. More recently, however, the use of broadcast frequencies for use in mobile telephone applications has increased the opportunity cost of broadcast spectrum. Given the availability of alternative multichannel transmission methods, over-the-air broadcasting may now be an inefficient method of distributing video mass media.

Beginning in the 1980s, many industrial and developing countries started to privatize and deregulate broadcasting. More significantly, in many parts of the world the electromagnetic spectrum is being privatized through the use of spectrum auctions

---

1. For example, in 1968 the United States Supreme Court upheld federal government licensing and regulation of radio broadcast content on the grounds that radio frequencies were inherently "scarce," even though most communities had many competing stations (*Red Lion Broadcasting v FCC* 395 U.S. 367). In 1974 the same court held that a newspaper, even though it was a local monopolist, could not constitutionally be required by statute to print the reply of a political candidate whom it had attacked (*Miami Herald v Tornillo* 418 U.S. 241).

and other techniques. For example, spectrum auctions have been held in Australia, Chile, New Zealand, the United States, Venezuela, and many other countries and in the European Union. This has greatly facilitated the rapid growth of wireless telephony, and to a much lesser extent, of broadcast competition. Despite this liberalization, however, restrictions on how the privatized spectrum can be used and on resale continue to limit the economic efficiency of this important resource.

Although it is still early, the general effect of privatization and deregulation of electronic mass media (whether as a result of policy changes or of technological improvements that permit bypassing the traditional media) seems to have been to increase competition and to reduce concentration. This has reduced the power and influence of individual media outlets, in turn further reducing the rationale for government regulation. From a consumer point of view, these changes have resulted in a great increase in the variety of programming available, presumably enhancing welfare, but the very process of increasing diversity also eliminates a previously available choice, namely, the opportunity to consume content that is also consumed by most other viewers. In the United States, for example, the percentage of the audience viewing what used to be the only three television networks has declined in 20 years from more than 90 percent to less than 50 percent.

Policy Issues

Both economies of scale and limited markets tend to promote seller concentration. Government intervention through state ownership, licensing, and import controls also promotes concentration.[2] Seller concentration is a particular problem in relation to mass media because of the media's central role in democracy. Concentration is also, of course, an economic policy problem. A major cross-sectional study of media ownership in 97 countries found that concentration was often high, media were frequently family or government owned, and that these factors were associated with poor outcomes, such as low rates of economic growth, poverty, and oppressive regimes (Djankov and others forthcoming). This study did not take an economic perspective, so we do not know whether the extent of media concentration (or of family or government ownership) is greater or smaller than in other domestic industries of similar capital intensity in the same countries. Similarly, whether a causal relationship exists between media concentration and poor socio-political outcomes, and if so, in which direction it runs, is not clear.

The public good character of content can lead to other policy problems, as when government see imports of foreign or transnational media content as a threat to local culture or social norms. American motion pictures and, to a lesser extent, video programs, are often mentioned in this connection. The source of the difficulty is that

---

2. In Mongolia, for example, government controls on newsprint imports are a problem despite a great expansion in the number of newspaper voices since 1990 (Williams 1995).

competition to serve large and generally rich English-speaking audiences supports expensive and attractive content—content so attractive that it can surmount the obstacles of language and culture. Content produced initially for smaller national or local audiences must necessarily be less expensive and is less attractive to broader audiences. Developing countries without a common language or culture face special problems in this regard. In a competitive world the economics of mass media do not favor the survival of languages or cultures that are not supported by large populations or substantial specialized economic demand. This is a consequence not of advertent cultural imperialism by the more successful media, but simply of the superior ability of such media to deliver consumer satisfaction at an attractive price. Some nations choose to subsidize demand for local media content to offset such effects.

Threats to the preservation of local culture and language from foreign or the increasingly important transnational media (Pathania-Jain 2001; Shrikhande 2001) are not unique to developing economies. The same underlying economic forces also threaten local cultures and dialects, if not languages, in highly developed economies. In 1909 New York City had about 85 daily newspapers, many in foreign vernaculars native to recent immigrants (Owen 1975, p. 70). Within a few decades New York had only a handful of surviving newspapers as advertisers found they could reach the same readership more efficiently through the general circulation press and readers were unwilling to pay for the increasingly expensive specialized press.

Media ownership often raises important policy issues. Government ownership of the press or of broadcast facilities may imply the absence of certain political freedoms. A concentration of media ownership among private citizens can sometimes reflect political power in the hands of an elite group. From an economic perspective, concentration raises concerns if it results in a monopoly or facilitates collusion leading to increased prices and reduced output. Generally speaking, relevant economic markets for purposes of assessing threats to competition are much narrower than what is often called the marketplace of ideas. Concentration among, say, radio broadcasters located in a given city might, in principle, raise economic competition issues with respect to certain advertisers even if numerous other vehicles are available for the expression of ideas, including political dissent, such as television, the press, magazines, and online services. Where concentration is insufficient to raise concerns about competition policy, it is unlikely to raise significant issues in relation to freedom of expression. Thus even though many countries attempt to limit media concentration (OECD 1999; World Bank 2001, section 10.47), such efforts may be based on a too narrow definition of the marketplace of ideas.

Conclusion

Private mass media (the press) perform a key role in any system of government that features political liberty and accountability. Mass media are also critical to the flow of economic information in an economy, including information that permits more informed consumption and production decisions. However, private mass media exist chiefly to make profits from the sale of subscriptions and advertising. Except where government policy restricts entry, mass media are generally competitive rather than monopolistic in structure. Modern technology has tended to reduce distribution costs, increasing the potential number of economically viable media and increasing the geographical scope in which they can be distributed profitably. This increases consumer choice and reduces the leverage of governments seeking to control content for political or cultural reasons.

References

Barrera, Eduardo. n.d. *Mexico*. Available on: http://www.mbcnet.org/archives/etv/M/htmlM/mexico/mexico.htm.

Crawford, Gregory. 2001. "The Discriminatory Incentives to Bundle: The Case of Cable Television." Working paper. Duke University, Durham, North Carolina.

Djankov, Simeon, Caralee McLiesh, Tatiana Nenova, and Andrei Shleifer. Forthcoming. "Who Owns the Media?" *Journal of Law and Economics.*

Hollifield, C. Ann. 2001. "Crossing Borders: Media Management Research in a Transnational Market Environment." *Journal of Media Economics* 14(3): 133–46.

Kaiser, Robert G. 2001. "The Rise of a Press Baron: An Unlikely Entrepreneur Builds Buryatia's Biggest Weekly." *The Washington Post*, August 13.

OECD (Organisation for Economic Co-operation and Development). 1993. *Competition Policy and a Changing Broadcast Industry*. Paris.

———. 1999. *Communications Outlook*. Paris.

Owen, Bruce M. 1975. *Economics and Freedom of Expression: Media Structure and the First Amendment*. Lexington, Massachusetts: Ballinger.

———. 1999. *The Internet Challenge to Television*. Cambridge, Massachusetts: Harvard University Press.

Owen, Bruce M., and S. Wildman. 1992. *Video Economics*. Cambridge, Massachusetts: Harvard University Press.

Pathania-Jain, Geetika. 2001. "Global Parents, Local Partners: A Value-Chain Analysis of Collaborative Strategies of Media Firms in India." *Journal of Media Economics* 14(3): 169–88.

Shrikhande, Seema. 2001. "Competitive Strategies in the Internationalization of Television: CNNI and BBC World in Asia." *Journal of Media Economics* 14(3): 147–68.

Steiner, Peter O. 1952. "Program Patterns and Preferences and the Workability of Competition in Radio Broadcasting." *Quarterly Journal of Economics* 66(May): 194–223.

Williams, John W. 1995. "Mass Media in Post-Revolutionary Mongolia." Principia College, Elsah, Illinois. Processed.

World Bank. 2001. *World Development Report 2000/2001: Attacking Poverty*. New York: Oxford University Press.

10

The Legal Environment for News Media

Peter Krug and Monroe E. Price

There are many steps to shaping an effective democratic society, and the formation of media law and media institutions is one of the most important. Too often, governments undertake efforts to build effective media systems that advance democracy without sufficient understanding of the many aspects of the legal environment that influence this process. We seek to identify certain components of the complex legal process that contribute to an environment that enables media to advance democratic goals. A number of factors indicate whether a free and independent media sector can flourish, for instance, the general level of literacy; the signals to a society that a critical, informed perspective for shaping political leadership is welcomed; the nature of the electoral system; and the stability and nature of the institutions that make the production and distribution of information possible.

Among the key elements, complementing others, is a set of legal institutions, that is, the law-related aspect of an enabling environment. The nature of the legal environment—the cluster of laws, legal institutions, and legal actors—in which news media operate obviously has a profound impact on the degree to which journalists and news organizations are free to engage effectively in gathering news and disseminating information and ideas.[1] Consideration of a satisfactory legal enabling environment for effective news media activity must encompass issues such as media ownership and the role of civil society in addition to the specific elements of the legal system itself.

This chapter focuses primarily on aspects of legislation in a legal enabling environment for news media activity. In this regard, four aspects of the legal setting in which news media operate warrant our attention: news gathering; content-based

---

1. In this discussion the term journalist is used to encompass print media publishers and electronic media owners and executives, as well as editors, commentators, and reporters.

regulation; content-neutral regulation that has the potential to influence content indirectly; and protection of journalists in their professional activity, including protection against physical attacks.

Our review is based largely on a set of rules and principles that have evolved in and characterize media law practices in Western democracies, but also take into account practices that have been adopted in a wide variety of global settings, including certain of the more successful post-Soviet transition countries. The adoption of formal laws is never a guarantee that they will be fully and generously implemented in practice, even in the most advanced democratic societies. Many are the states in which well-drafted laws languish because the environment for implementation falters. Indeed, the whole concept of an enabling environment implies that specific laws exist in a context in which the spirit of the laws is engaged and the processes for realizing their impact are implemented.

News Gathering

One can conceive of a system in which journalists are independent, in that they can print what they wish, but are severely hampered because they have constricted access to information. Of course, in some ways all journalists are hampered. They have deadlines that prevent as much investigation as they desire, they have budgetary constraints, and they have editors who limit their travel or the direction of their journalistic inquiry. Nevertheless, one can examine the nature of a state's enabling environment specifically in terms of journalists' capacity to gather information. Information gathering by journalists is a vital component of freedom of information. Without access to information, journalists are engaged primarily in presenting opinions. While openness in the statement of opinions is an important element of a democratic society, it is insufficient for its development and maintenance. An informed citizenry depends on journalists' ability to have access to sources. Without this kind of journalistic effectiveness, a society can have free and independent media, but their utility in advancing democratic institution building is severely limited.

Access to Information

An essential condition of effective and professional journalism is journalists' ability to gather information held in tangible files, often dusty and hard to find, that are held by or controlled by public authorities. An enabling legal environment will include legal guarantees for the conduct of this gathering activity. Such guarantees are often found in generally applicable legislation that recognizes the rights of public access to documents. Although these laws often do not expressly cite the rights of journalists, naturally news media representatives share the rights of access with the general public.

The fundamental characteristic of effective freedom of information legislation is an expressly articulated presumption of openness. The presumption of openness is grounded in the principle that information in the control of the public authorities is public unless it is covered by an exception expressly set forth in a legislative act. The principle therefore places the burden of justification for refusal to disclose on the public custodian.

Many legal systems impose some kind of standard on people who request access to documents, such as a requirement that they demonstrate that the requested information affects their rights and legal interests or that it is of a particular level of importance. The effectiveness of freedom of information legislation is significantly reduced if, instead of a presumption of openness, burdens are imposed on requesters. The problem with such requirements is that they create an opportunity for arbitrary refusals to disclose based on the custodian's assessment of the status of the requester or the importance of the document. Regarding the latter, custodians naturally tend to be more reluctant to disclose documents that might be deemed "important," and therefore perhaps damaging to governmental or corporate interests, a situation that would be counterproductive to the goals of freedom of information.

APPLICATION OF FREEDOM OF INFORMATION TO PUBLIC INSTITUTIONS. Effective freedom of information legislation must apply broadly to public institutions. The broader the scope of public access rights, the more democratic a freedom of information law will be. For example, are legislative bodies covered? If so, a comprehensive right of access to legislative documents would include a right of access to draft legislation and to hearings at the legislative committee level, not just at plenary sessions of the legislature. This would give journalists the opportunity to inform the public of crucial determinations made at the committee level, rather than only at the plenary level, when the important policy debate might already have been concluded. A broadly based freedom of information law would also include a general right of access to documents in judicial proceedings.

A number of specific issues might arise in regard to documents produced by or under the control of particular branches of government. For example, a right of access to legislative documents should be general and should not include specific categorical exclusions based on the status of the document, but only on its subject matter. For example, not only should the minutes of legislative sessions be available, but so should written reports considered in the legislative proceedings unless they are insulated under an exception covering specific subject matter. In addition, minutes of legislative committee meetings, as well as those of the plenary legislative body, should not be shielded from disclosure.

EXCEPTIONS TO THE RIGHT OF ACCESS. Exceptions to the right of access must be limited to those that are expressly and narrowly defined in legislation, and are necessary in a democratic society to protect legitimate interests that are consistent with international norms. It is universally recognized that freedom of information access rights are not absolute, that their existence does not automatically mean unlimited and unconditional access to public sector information. Instead, it is accepted that the protection of certain countervailing secrecy interests will constitute exceptions to those rights of access. At the same time, however, any exception to the presumption of openness should satisfy certain requirements. First, it must be prescribed in legislation. This means that the legislature has the exclusive power both to identify the secrecy interests to be protected and to define the particular parameters of the exception. Second, it means that the exceptions must be set forth in detail, and cannot be presumed simply on the basis of perceived legislative intent or ambiguous language in the law. Thus the legislative norms must be carefully defined, not open-ended. As concerns national security, for example, a common legislative practice is to prohibit the disclosure of "state secrets"; however, a regime inclined toward democratic principles will permit the use of this exception only when a particular category into which the document in question falls has been identified in advance.

Certain core secrecy interests are generally deemed necessary in a democratic society, and exception categories fall into two general groups. The first group seeks to advance general or public secrecy interests, and includes national security, state economic or financial interests, law enforcement, internal administration of government departments, and policymaking deliberations. The second group protects the interests of individual legal or natural persons, for example, personal privacy and commercial confidentiality.

CRIMINAL, CIVIL, AND ADMINISTRATIVE LIABILITY. Journalists should be insulated from criminal, civil, or administrative responsibility for publishing secret documents or information from those documents unless they knowingly participated in a scheme to obtain the documents in an illegal fashion and knew that the documents were lawfully protected against disclosure. Moreover, an effective freedom of information regime will shield a journalist from liability even in circumstances of knowing participation if the public interest in disclosure outweighs the harm threatened or caused by such disclosure. Sometimes a journalist will obtain documents that are legally protected from disclosure. In such circumstances, a blanket imposition of liability for publication of such documents or information from them would have a chilling effect on the exercise of press freedoms that would be detrimental to the goal of democratic governance.

EFFECTIVE ENFORCEMENT. Articulation of rights of access must be accompanied by effective means of enforcing those rights. This requirement has several elements: effective remedies; effective, independent review of custodial denials of disclosure; threat of sanctions for willful violation by public officials; and designation of an independent freedom of information "umpire." Such enforcement remedies should include the possibility of appealing to the courts or some other review body outside the administrative structure. In this regard, a public access law should require that a denial of access be accompanied by a written statement informing the requester of the opportunity to file an appeal with the independent reviewing body. The nature of the reviewing body's enforcement authority is also important. A scheme that simply imposes monetary penalties on the custodial body will not be effective. Instead, a court or other reviewing body should have the power to order the custodian to do what the requester wanted in the first place, that is, to make the information in question available.

At the same time, legislation should also provide for sanctions against illegal refusals to disclose documents. It advances the purposes of freedom of information if either the right of access legislation or the criminal codes contain provisions that buttress the rights of access found elsewhere by establishing liability for public officials who unlawfully deny requests. In this regard, however, the use of sanctions should be approached with caution lest it have a counterproductive effect. An important component in making freedom of information effective is the designation of an independent official who is empowered to mediate disputes and provide effective interpretations, so that public employees do not find themselves subject to personal liability for decisions they have made in good faith.

Protection of Confidential Sources

An enabling environment recognizes the societal value of journalists' ability to protect confidential sources and information obtained from those sources. In many legal systems laws and professional codes of conduct reflect the conclusion that the protection of journalists' sources is a fundamental condition for effective news gathering in a democratic society.[2] Without the confidence that journalists will not be compelled to disclose their identity, sources of information may be deterred from providing information on matters of public interest, thereby diminishing the effectiveness of the news media's watchdog role. This situation can take on a constitutional dimension: that of the public's right to receive information from the news media.

Exceptions to journalists' protection of confidential sources, if permitted at all, should be prescribed in law, narrowly defined, and available only to advance interests necessary in a democratic society. Under optimal conditions for an enabling

---

2. Two Internet sources containing numerous examples of professional codes, as well as other relevant material, are the EthicNet web site of the University of Tampere, Finland (http://www.uta.fi/ethicnet), and the Media Ethics web site of Claude-Jean Bertrand (http://www.u-paris2.fr/ifp/Deontologie/ethic).

environment, a journalist's protection of confidential sources is absolute, with disclosure not justified under any circumstances; however, many legal systems do establish an exception to a legal or ethical duty not to disclose when certain public authorities have ordered disclosure. In such circumstances an enabling environment will require that only a court, in a decision grounded in legislative norms, issue such an order, but the goals of democratic governance will not be advanced if courts enjoy open-ended discretion to compel disclosure.

A controversial question is whether any public interest would ever be of sufficient weight to require a journalist to disclose a confidential source in a noncriminal proceeding. The European Court of Human Rights confronted this issue in its March 27, 1996, decision in the case of *Goodwin v the United Kingdom*. In that case, a confidential source provided a journalist with detailed information from the confidential records of a business enterprise that reflected the company's precarious financial position. Because of the perceived threat of harm to the company resulting from public disclosure of the information, the English courts ordered the journalist and his publication not to make the information public. They also required the journalist to identify the confidential source, who was believed to have obtained the information illegally. Reviewing the English courts' orders, the European Court found that they constituted an interference with the journalist's exercise of rights under the free press guarantees of Article 10 of the European Convention on Human Rights, and that the interests advanced by compelled disclosure of the information were not of sufficient weight to be necessary in a democratic society. The court stated that limitations on the confidentiality of journalistic sources call for the most careful judicial scrutiny.

Licensing of Journalists

The licensing of journalists, that is, the outlawing of the unlicensed practice of journalism, poses risks to democratic governance. A number of countries, many of them in response to proposals from the United Nations Educational, Scientific, and Cultural Organization in the 1970s, have recognized the practice of journalism as a licensed profession. According to its proponents, licensing promotes journalistic ethics and responsibility, and takes the form of establishing qualifications in the form of educational standards, such as graduation from a recognized journalism training program. By contrast, detractors of licensing maintain that it can operate as a form of censorship by allowing the authorities to license only those journalists who do not incur the government's displeasure.

In 1985, in an advisory opinion, the Inter-American Court of Human Rights ruled that in general, laws licensing journalists are incompatible with the individual and collective rights guaranteed under Article 13 ("Freedom of Thought and Expression") of the American Convention on Human Rights. In that case the government of Costa

Rica advanced three arguments in support of its statutory licensing scheme: (a) that licensing is the normal method of regulating the practice of a profession, (b) that licensing of journalists is necessary to promote the public interest in journalistic ethics and responsibility, and (c) that licensing serves as a way to guarantee journalists' independence from their employers. While recognizing that these goals fell into the general category of ensuring public order—one of the legitimate interests supporting restrictions on the exercise of rights under the convention—the court concluded that none was sufficient for legitimate interference with journalistic freedoms. In response to Costa Rica's first argument, the court concluded that journalism differs from the practice of other professions because it entails activity expressly protected under the convention.

The court also rejected the claim that a restriction on freedom of expression could serve as a means of guaranteeing it, concluding instead that the greatest possible amount of information is essential to public welfare. Finally, while articulating its agreement with the goal of protecting the independence of journalists, the court found that this goal could be achieved without placing limits on who may enter the practice of journalism.

Direct Regulation of Media Content

Universally, it is understood that freedoms of speech and of the press are not absolute. All legal systems tolerate content regulation to some extent to advance certain state, collective, and individual interests. A good deal of such regulation takes place through the mechanism of direct regulation of content, effected through legislative, executive, and judicial acts. We will take a broad view of content regulation, which we perceive as any form of external intrusion into the professional activities of gathering, editing, and reporting public sector information and disseminating opinion on public matters. Again, an enabling environment is one in which this takes place according to the rule of law.

Although rights of free expression are not absolute, an enabling environment is one in which the political culture recognizes the value of the free flow of information and ideas for democratic society. This recognition of the centrality of freedom of expression to fundamental values and democratic society has been expressed on numerous occasions by the European Court of Human Rights:

> [F]reedom of expression constitutes one of the essential foundations of a democratic society and one of the basic conditions for its progress and for each individual's self-fulfillment. . . . It is applicable not only to 'information' or 'ideas' that are favorably received or regarded as inoffensive or as a matter of indifference, but also to those that offend, shock or disturb. Such are the demands of that pluralism, tolerance and broadmindedness without which there

is no 'democratic society' (*Nilsen and Johnsen v. Norway*, paragraph 43, judgment of November 25, 1999).

Of particular significance is the court's recognition of the essential function that the news media—both print and electronic—play in advancing the goals of democratic society:

> One factor of particular importance . . . is the essential function the press fulfils in a democratic society. Although the press must not overstep certain bounds, in particular in respect of the reputation and rights of others and the need to prevent the disclosure of confidential information, its duty is nevertheless to impart—in a manner consistent with its obligations and responsibilities—information and ideas on all matters of public interest. In addition, the Court is mindful of the fact that journalistic freedom also covers possible recourse to a degree of exaggeration, or even provocation (*Bladet Tromso and Stensaas v Norway*, paragraph 59, judgment of May 20, 1999).

According to the court, this essential role informs not only the rights of news media organizations and their representatives, but also the public's right to receive the information and ideas that the news media have imparted. In this regard the court has cited the news media's "vital role" of "public watchdog" in imparting information of serious public concern. The court has also emphasized that freedom of the news media affords the public one of the best means of discovering and forming an opinion about the ideas and attitudes of political leaders (*Lingens v. Austria* paragraphs 42 and 44, Judgment of June 24, 1986a).

Manifestation of this recognition of value should be found throughout the normative structure, including international, constitutional, and legislative norms, and in their application in executive and judicial acts. Indeed, an enabling environment should include textual recognition of news media freedoms in international instruments to which the state is a party and in the state's constitution. Moreover, these norms must be directly applicable by the courts and superior to any legislative or administrative acts.

In a properly functioning enabling environment the legal system will provide adequate safeguards against abuse, including prompt, full, and effective judicial scrutiny of the validity of the restriction by an independent court or tribunal. As stated earlier, the application of legal norms that interfere with news media freedoms must be subject to independent judicial control.

An enabling environment will take a broad view as to what acts—governmental or private—constitute an interference with the exercise of news media freedoms. An interference with news media activity is not in itself a violation of fundamental standards of media freedoms, but without the recognition that certain acts can potentially violate news media rights, a political and legal order can easily limit the exercise of protected news media freedoms.

All acts by public authorities—the legislative, executive, and judicial branches of government—that have a practical impact on news media activity must be taken into account as a matter of law. This does not mean that freedom of expression will always prevail in a clash with other fundamental rights or public interests. Such an approach would make free press rights absolute, which they are not. Rather, it means that free press rights must be taken into account in determining the legitimacy of state action.

A functioning enabling environment is one that recognizes that self-censorship poses a threat to democratic governance. The threat of legal liability imposes a chilling effect on those engaged in news media activity. A key element in advancing news media freedoms in regard to content regulation has been the courts' recognition that the role of the news media is of such fundamental importance to democratic governance that media representatives must be insulated from self-censorship to a reasonable extent.

An enabling environment will recognize that private acts can also implicate the exercise of news media rights. The legal system must recognize the "third-party effect," namely, that fundamental guarantees of news media freedoms are broader in scope than simply offering protection against acts by those in public authority. The principle of the third-party effect provides, for example, that a news media organ should not automatically lose its constitutional protection in a lawsuit against it simply because that lawsuit has been initiated by a private person and not a public entity.

Forms of Content Regulation

Three forms of content regulation can be distinguished: registration of media outlets, prepublication review, and postpublication punishment.

REGISTRATION SYSTEMS. A number of legal systems require some form of registration of media outlets; however, in most systems this registration is not subject to discretion by the authorities on the basis of the applicant's anticipated content. Systems in which registration is subject to discretion based on an official's judgment concerning the content of the media organ are suspect in an enabling environment, and will be incompatible with it unless accompanied by effective rule of law protections, including a right of appeal to an independent judiciary.

PREPUBLICATION REVIEW. Systems of formal pre-publication review are incompatible with the basic principles of free press and democratic governance. In the second half of the 20th century international human rights law recognized that formal administrative censorship is inconsistent with fundamental tenets of human rights and democracy. This principle is explicitly expressed, for example, in Article 13(1) and (2) of the American Convention on Human Rights:

> Everyone has the right to freedom of thought and expression. This right includes freedom to seek, receive, and impart information and ideas of all kinds, regardless of frontiers, either orally, in writing, in print, in the form of art, or through any other medium of one's choice.
>
> The exercise of the right provided for in the foregoing paragraph shall not be subject to prior censorship but shall be subject to subsequent imposition of liability, which shall be expressly established by law to the extent necessary to ensure:
>
> - Respect for the rights or reputations of others; or
> - Protection of national security, public order, or public health or morals.

In accordance with this recognition of the incompatibility of censorship with democratic governance, most countries no longer employ such structures. Instead, as the American Convention on Human Rights permits, they employ regimes of subsequent punishment of perceived abuses of news media freedoms.

SUBSEQUENT PUBLISHMENT. Systems of subsequent punishment must be consistent with generally applicable international standards governing criminal and civil procedure. Systems of subsequent punishment for alleged abuses of news media freedoms often take the form of criminal sanctions, thereby triggering the need for recognition of international standards in criminal law and procedure, including the presumption of innocence. In addition, they often take the form of civil procedure in relation to the protection of individual interests. It is subsequent punishment that poses the threat of self-censorship, therefore the fundamental propositions of fairness, impartiality, and objectivity set forth earlier are applicable.

Protection of State Interests

Throughout history governments have sought to impose controls on the flow of information and opinions to further a range of state interests. This is to be expected, because much of constitutional law represents the effort to find a balance between the exercise of constitutional rights and the state's perceived duty to serve the public interest by such measures as protecting national security and preserving public order. Thus these public interests include restraints in the name of national security; sanctions against violence and public disorder; and protection of the honor of state institutions, officials, and symbols.

Governments have often imposed these controls by means of formal systems of prepublication censorship, but even where formal censorship is absent, they are advanced by criminal laws that provide for subsequent punishment. In addition, controls are also applied in a number of media registration laws that prohibit the granting of approval to operate a news outlet if the authorities conclude that the content of the applicant will constitute an abuse of free press rights.

NATIONAL SECURITY. Legal systems everywhere, as well as international principles, recognize that national security can be a basis for regulating free expression. At the same time, governments can enlist this broad, ambiguous concept to stifle or suppress free expression and criticism. The Johannesburg Principles on National Security, Freedom of Expression, and Access to Information, a compilation of fundamental propositions adopted in 1995 by a group of experts in international law, national security, and human rights, closely address the sensitive matter of national security. For example, Principle 1.2 states:

> Any restriction on expression or information that a government seeks to justify on grounds of national security must have the genuine purpose and demonstrable effect of protecting a legitimate national security interest.

Principle 1.3 states:

> To establish that a restriction on freedom of expression or information is necessary to protect a legitimate national security interest, a government must demonstrate that (a) the expression or information at issue poses a serious threat to a legitimate national security interest; (b) the restriction imposed is the least restrictive means possible for protecting that interest; and (c) the restriction is compatible with democratic principles.

Finally, Principle 2 addresses the question of a legitimate national security interest:

> A restriction sought to be justified on the ground of national security is not legitimate unless its genuine purpose and demonstrable effect is to protect a country's existence or its territorial integrity against the use or threat of force, or its capacity to respond to the use or threat of force, whether from an external source, such as a military threat, or an internal source, such as incitement to violent overthrow of the government. In particular, a restriction sought to be justified on the ground of national security is not legitimate if its genuine purpose or demonstrable effect is to protect interests unrelated to national security, including, for example, to protect a government from embarrassment or exposure of wrongdoing, or to conceal information about the functioning of its public institutions, or to entrench a particular ideology, or to suppress industrial unrest.

PREVENTION OF DISORDER, INCLUDING CRIMINAL PROSECUTION OF VIRULENT EX-
PRESSION. International standards recognize that inflammatory speech can be
responsible for inciting violence and disorder, therefore those standards permit restrictions on such speech. Enforcement of a broadly stated and construed criminal
law against incitement to violence, disorder, or hatred can be an effective means of
imposing self-censorship on news media representatives. It will not be conducive to
an enabling environment if the authorities impose or threaten to impose criminal
sanctions based solely on the degree of virulence in the expressive activity in question. Instead, the dispositive question in a democratic society is not the degree of
virulence, but instead the question of whether the speaker is advocating violence
and whether his or her statements are likely to produce a violent result.

LAWS PROTECTING THE HONOR OF GOVERNMENT INSTITUTIONS, OFFICIALS, AND
SYMBOLS. Many countries have criminal laws that seek to protect the honor of state
institutions, officials, and symbols against insult. In this field of law, often called
seditious libel, the perceived harm is not in presenting false factual assertions, but in
disparaging or degrading symbols of state power or national unity.

In an enabling environment such laws and their application must be presumed to
be incompatible with fundamental human rights and employed, if ever, only in extreme circumstances. Perhaps more than any other area, seditious libel laws
criminalizing "insult" of state institutions and officials have been subject to abuse by
public officials seeking to insulate themselves from the scrutiny and criticism of the
news media and the public.

An important aspect of these laws tends to be that the truth of the statement is not
a defense, and the indeterminacy of the concept of insult lends itself to arbitrary
enforcement. The existence and enforcement of laws that are not limited to protecting individual dignity or reputation, but instead are available to shield the authorities from criticism, will retard progress toward an enabling environment.

The key perspective from which seditious libel should be approached is whether
the application of such laws is necessary in a democratic society. In this regard an
enabling environment will recognize that the limits of permissible criticism should
be even wider with respect to the government than to individual public officials.

ELECTION LAWS. One element of the enabling environment directly affects the political process, namely, election-related media law. Such laws may pertain to access to
the media by candidates, editorializing and expressions of bias by the broadcaster,
manipulation of the broadcasting system by the government, and rules concerning
political advertisements. Some countries regulate broadcasts of public opinion poll
results, for example, they may prohibit the dissemination of poll results shortly before an election.

The Council of Europe has called on the governments of its member states to

[E]xamine ways of ensuring respect for the principles of fairness, balance, and impartiality in the coverage of election campaigns by the media, and consider the adoption of measures to implement these principles in their domestic law or practice where appropriate and in accordance with constitutional law" (Recommendation Number R [99] 15, Committee of Ministers, Council of Europe, "On Measures Concerning Media Coverage of Elections," adopted by the Committee of Ministers on September 9, 1999).

The council encouraged self-regulatory measures by media professionals in the form of codes of conduct that would set out good practice guidelines for responsible, accurate, and fair coverage of electoral campaigns.

No absolutely correct model is available for the set of laws that deals with these questions. After 1989, during the first bloom of transition in Eastern Europe, social reformers recommended that each candidate receive equal time on a national or regional broadcasting entity. However, those who considered that democratic institutions are furthered by a stable contest between a limited number of political parties found this system chaotic and counterproductive. European licensing regimes, meanwhile, have preferred an approach in which the broadcasting station is viewed as objective and impartial, a position inconsistent with editorializing. European rules also tend to limit or prohibit political advertising on the grounds that excessive access to the media through paid advertising gives too much of an advantage to the wealthy candidate.

Many of the transition countries of Eastern Europe have few means of shielding broadcasters—private, public service, or government—from coercion by the ruling party during the election process. Or to put it differently, many broadcasters, indebted to the government for the availability of their license and their continued vitality, have used their valuable asset to serve their patrons. Few elements of interaction between governments and broadcasters are more adverse to rule of law notions than the pressured exploitation of the power of radio and television to affect the outcome of elections.

Thus an enabling environment for stable democratic institutions must seek to design institutions that minimize the abuse of government authority during elections. For example, in 1993 Russia set up a special arbitration tribunal to receive complaints during the election process, whether complaints by candidates about the media or from the media about the government. This tribunal and its successor entity, abolished on June 3, 2000, by President Putin, had little power except—as is often the case with such panels—to render a decision and publish it. In addition, several countries establish special election commissions that are empowered to impose fines for abuses of privileges by media entities or to sanction candidates who seek to circumvent or violate election laws concerning the media.

PROTECTION OF JUDICIAL ADMINISTRATION. An enabling environment will strive to achieve a balance between protecting the integrity of judicial proceedings, exercising news media freedoms, and retaining the need for public supervision of the work of the courts. Promoting the impartial, effective administration of justice is a goal of all democratic legal systems adhering to rule of law precepts. In a number of legal systems news media can be penalized for disseminating information and commentary concerning ongoing judicial proceedings. In some cases the intent is to protect the fair trial rights of criminal suspects and defendants, while in others they are viewed as necessary to maintain the orderly administration of justice and public respect for the judicial system.

This is an area that exemplifies the need for recognition and application of the fundamental propositions of fairness, impartiality, and objectivity. For example, a thin line exists between what might be a legitimate interest in protecting respect for the administration of justice and an illegitimate desire to protect the judiciary from public criticism. In the same way, while protecting the rights of criminal suspects and defendants is widely recognized as a fundamental human right, this principle could be subject to abuse if the authorities seek to shield the criminal process from public scrutiny. In sum, an approach that does not sufficiently take news media freedoms into account in such circumstances will not be compatible with an enabling environment.

Protection of Collective Interests

Laws protecting collective interests, broadly speaking, seek to accomplish a number of objectives, including the protection of public peace, of the dignity of identifiable groups by regulating hate speech, and of public morals and religious beliefs. These are extremely sensitive areas of public policy, to be determined through the democratic process according to a society's values. While one cannot point to any particular approach to these matters as more or less indicative of an enabling environment, one must remember that the fundamental propositions of fairness, impartiality, and objectivity should apply.

Of value in this complex area are the following principles articulated by the Committee of Ministers of the Council of Europe in their recommendation of October 30, 1997, on "Hate Speech." According to Principle 6:

> National law and practice in the area of hate speech should take due account of the role of the media in communicating information and ideas which expose, analyze and explain specific instances of hate speech and the underlying phenomenon in general as well as the right of the public to receive such information and ideas.
>
> To this end, national law and practice should distinguish clearly between the responsibility of the author of hate speech on the one hand and any

responsibility of the media and media professionals contributing to their dissemination as part of their mission to communicate information and ideas on matters of public interest on the other hand.

Principle 7 adds the following:

In furtherance of principle 6, national law and practice should take account of the fact that:

- Reporting on racism, xenophobia, anti-Semitism or other forms of intolerance is fully protected by Article 10, paragraph 1, of the European Convention on Human Rights and may only be interfered with under the conditions set out in paragraph 2 of that provision;
- The standards applied by national authorities for assessing the necessity of restricting freedom of expression must be in conformity with the principles embodied in Article 10 as established in the case law of the Convention's organs, having regard, *inter alia*, to the manner, contents, context, and purpose of the reporting;
- Respect for journalistic freedoms also implies that it is not for the courts or the public authorities to impose their views on the media as to the types of reporting techniques to be adopted by journalists.

Protection of Individual Interests

Legal systems throughout the world seek to protect individuals' reputation, privacy, and dignity. Generally these protections take the form of criminal and civil proceedings in defamation, privacy protection, and insult. An important feature of this complex area of law is that in many legal systems these interests rise to the level of fundamental rights guaranteed in constitutional and international norms. Once again, this interaction between competing rights and interests must be subject to the fundamental propositions of fairness, impartiality, and objectivity.

An enabling environment will recognize the sensitivity of the issues and values at stake in the intersection of free news media and competing individual interests. In the area of individual rights protection, a dominant theme throughout the world is the high level of use and visibility of defamation law actions brought under both criminal and civil law. The prevalence of such actions, including the threat of penal and/or monetary sanctions, poses the threat of self-censorship. For this reason a number of legal systems have recognized that lawsuits to protect individual rights and interests also impose burdens on the exercise of protected forms of expression. The European Court of Human Rights, for example, has developed an extensive body of case law that includes significant protection for statements made regarding matters of public interest. These include the maxim that public officials must tolerate considerably more criticism than private individuals, and that the burden of evidentiary proof cannot be imposed on a defendant to prove the truth of a value judgment or statement of opinion.

ISSUES IN DEFAMATION LAW. In an enabling environment the legal system will recognize that its application of defamation laws interferes with the exercise of news media freedoms, and that in some circumstances the interference is not justified. A defamatory statement is one that is deemed to lower a person's reputation in the community. Defamation laws are found in all legal systems, and protection of an individual's reputation is a right recognized in international instruments. Legal norms intended to protect these interests are often found in criminal codes and in civil code or tort law provisions recognizing the interests as civil rights that can be enforced by claiming monetary damages.

However, unless certain protections are available, defamation laws can be used to repress the news media in their reporting on matters of public interest. News media activity, by its very nature, will often present information and ideas that criticize individuals, that may be construed as depicting individuals in a negative way, or that may be viewed as invading an individual's personal privacy. Unless defamation law takes news media freedoms into account, the threat of criminal sanctions or civil money damages awards will effectively cause self-censorship, to the detriment of democratic governance.

In this regard, if a legal system takes an approach that categorically places false statements of fact or expressions of opinion deemed to be excessively critical completely outside the protection of fundamental guarantees of news media freedoms, this is detrimental to news media freedoms. The status of the plaintiff is one of the many crucial variables that should be considered in developing a defamation law approach that is compatible with an enabling environment.

PROTECTION OF INDIVIDUAL DIGNITY. An enabling environment will seek to balance the protection of individual dignity against the threat to news media freedoms by limiting the application of insult laws and treating them with caution. Insult laws carry an inherent threat to the exercise of news media freedoms, especially because of their ambiguous nature and the absence of truth as a defense. It is widely accepted that protection of an individual's sense of self-worth can be implicated, and perhaps violated, by disseminating personal attacks. Thus many legal systems have established criminal and/or civil sanctions against insulting statements in which the crucial question is not the truthfulness of the statement in question (truth is not a defense), but the speaker's or writer's intent. Insult laws can be dangerous for the exercise of news media freedoms if not construed and applied narrowly, limited strictly to circumstances in which the statement carried no information of public importance, and clearly expressed with intent solely to injure the victim.

PROTECTION OF INDIVIDUAL PRIVACY. In adjudicating disputes concerning claims of violations of personal privacy, legal systems must strive to develop standards for distinguishing between public and private information. Many legal systems place a high priority on protecting individuals against the dissemination of statements that violate their personal or family privacy. The important point here is that reasonable construction of the notion of privacy is necessary. It should not be a shield behind which to hide acts of public importance from public scrutiny.

RIGHT OF REPLY OR CORRECTION. Legal obligations to provide an opportunity to reply or to demand a correction concerning media content can serve to address perceived abuses of journalistic freedoms in a form that is less threatening to media independence than regulation by such means as defamation lawsuits. However, the advancement of an enabling environment will be impeded if such obligations sweep too broadly or intrude too deeply into the exercise of editorial discretion.

In many legal systems legislative acts such as civil codes or mass media laws provide judicial remedies of reply or correction to persons whose legal rights or interests have been violated by the dissemination of media content. Under a right of reply a news media outlet is obliged to disseminate a statement that the injured party prepares. The right of correction (or retraction), by contrast, requires the media outlet to disseminate its own statement correcting its earlier offending statement. The availability of such remedies is often viewed as a more efficient and effective means of satisfying the concerns of people who believe they have been injured by offensive media content. At the same time, such remedies can in themselves threaten journalistic freedoms if not kept within limits that reflect respect for the rights of journalists and of the public to receive information.

Content-Neutral Regulation and the Risk of Manipulation

An enabling environment will be one in which legal institutions can provide the media with sufficient substantive and procedural protections against indirect manipulation. In all legal systems an almost limitless range of opportunities exists for public officials or private actors to attempt to manipulate the media if they are inclined to do so. These opportunities are found in the manipulation of laws that are not explicitly targeted against news media content, but instead are seemingly content-neutral, while still capable of influencing the editorial decisionmaking of the media. Ways to influence media content will always exist and public authorities have many opportunities for indirectly seeking to influence media content. Subsidies, customs regulations, copyright, newsprint availability, costs of doing business with state entities (publishing houses), taxation, general anticompetition laws, public access requirements, and election campaign requirements are just a few examples.

These methods of indirect influence can occur by way of both substantive rules and their application. For example, regarding the former, the authorities could establish discriminatory tax classifications that impose higher taxes on some media outlets than on others. In relation to the latter, tax classifications as a matter of normative law may be equal, but different media outlets may be subject to selective enforcement.

Therefore the tax laws, and in particular the manner in which they are administered and enforced, can pose obstacles to the development and maintenance of an enabling environment. The authorities have often used nonpayment of taxes as a pretext to raid, harass, or close newspapers. One element of the rule of law, significant in relation to the press, is a ban on selective enforcement. Of course, no statute is fully enforced against all those who engage in violations, but selective enforcement is often the culprit in actions against print media or broadcasting stations.

Simply stating that such substantive rules should be outlawed in an enabling environment is not possible. These measures are enacted as part of the lawmaking and enforcement authority found in all legal systems. Therefore the best attributes of an enabling environment in this regard will be the existence of adequate rule of law protections and consideration of the fundamental propositions of fairness, impartiality, and objectivity.

Protection of News Media Against Private Acts

Much of our discussion has centered on relations between news media and public authorities; however, in some circumstances affirmative government measures might be necessary to protect the exercise of news media activity from acts by private persons.

Internal Press Freedom

At times, disagreements over content will arise between media owners and their editorial staffs. An important task for an enabling environment will be determining whether laws are needed in such situations, and if so, what kind, to maintain a balance between these respective parties that will advance societal needs in the dissemination of information and ideas. For example, some legal systems attempt to accommodate these competing interests by providing incentives for developing editorial guidelines and setting up systems for the resolution of disputes.

Physical Protection

An enabling environment is one in which the authorities are willing and able to prosecute those who physically intimidate or attack media representatives, so that those who seek to act violently against news media representatives will not be able to do so with impunity. The news media cannot function effectively if the authorities do not enforce generally applicable criminal laws or do so in an arbitrary, selective fashion.

In a 1996 recommendation, the Committee of Ministers of the Council of Europe addressed this issue, calling on member states to "investigate instances of attacks on the physical safety of journalists occurring within their jurisdiction" and to "use all appropriate means to bring to justice those responsible for such attacks" (Recommendation Number R 96[4], Committee of Ministers, Council of Europe, "On the Protection of Journalists in Situations of Conflict and Tension, adopted by the Committee of Ministers on May 3, 1996). In this regard journalists' and professional organizations for those working in the media can play a positive role exerting collective pressure, when necessary, on the public authorities.

Conclusion

Isolating any particular aspect of social formation and describing it as essential or critical to the enabling environment for free and independent media is difficult. We have attempted to identify components of complex legal processes that contribute to an environment that enables the media to advance democratic goals. We recognize that while these are insufficient for guaranteeing free and independent media activity in themselves, they are necessary to foster and sustain it.

Naturally, other factors are critical in determining the success of news media activity in a given society. The structure of the media depends on how a readership or audience supports media activity. Advertising revenue depends on the structure of consumption. The role and nature of subsidies (from within or without) depends on guarantees of autonomy and the subsidizing agency's thirst for control. The general level of education in a society also can shape the nature of the media and the way they are used in the political process.

Delicately interwoven with all these issues is the role of law. We have sought to examine the role of specific practices, identified as significant legislative steps that affect the prospects for achieving strong media institutions contributing to democratic practices.

11

Insult Laws

Ruth Walden

In more than 100 nations, individuals—including journalists—can be imprisoned or fined for insulting or offending government officials and institutions. Insult laws are still on the books in many of Western Europe's oldest democracies as well as in the world's most authoritarian regimes. Many countries with constitutional provisions guaranteeing freedom of expression and opinion nonetheless continue to enforce laws that punish criticism of the government.

The titles and wording of insult laws differ (see the appendix to this chapter for examples). In many former British colonies seditious libel laws criminalize words that allegedly cause hatred, contempt, or disaffection toward the government. In Latin American nations *desacato* (disrespect or contempt) laws provide criminal penalties for showing disrespect to public officials. In many monarchies traditional *lèse majesté* laws prohibit affronts to the royal family, and in Islamic nations blasphemy laws mandate penalties as severe as death for insults to religious leaders. Many such laws make offending the honor and dignity of specific, high-ranking officials and bodies, representatives of foreign countries, and national symbols and emblems a crime. Others prohibit insults to all public officials because of their positions or while they are performing their duties. Some countries have only general insult laws penalizing offensive words aimed at any individual. Although such laws theoretically cover insults to private as well public persons, high-ranking government officials, politicians, and civil servants invoke them most often.

Regardless of what the laws are called or how they are worded, the result is the same: they are used to stifle and punish political discussion and dissent, editorial comment and criticism, satire, and investigative journalism. They constitute one of the most pervasive, repressive, and dangerous forms of media regulation.

Criminal Defamation and Insult Laws

At first glance, an insult law may appear to be just another form of criminal defamation law, but significant theoretical and practical differences exist. Criminal defamation laws are designed to enable individuals to protect their reputations. They establish criminal penalties for slander (oral defamation) and libel (written defamation).

Theoretically, the harm caused by defamation lies in the impact the defamatory words have on others' opinions of the defamed individual: other people think less of the defamed individual as a result of the publication. Defamation laws often define the crime in terms of this third-person impact, for example, words that tend to expose a person to public hatred, ridicule, or contempt. Insult laws, by contrast, are more concerned with protecting the feelings of the insulted individual, that is, his or her personal sense of honor and dignity.

Practically, defamation laws are supposed to be aimed at false assertions of fact. They are designed to ensure that an individual's reputation is not unjustly harmed by the publication or dissemination of falsehoods. As many national and international courts have recognized, truthful statements—as well as unverifiable statements of opinion—are not legally actionable as defamation. In contrast, because insult laws are designed to protect honor and dignity rather than reputation, they are used to punish truth as well as falsehood, opinions as well as factual assertions, satire, invective, and even bad manners.

Two recent European cases are illustrative. In one, Greek journalist Vassilis Rafailidis was charged with both defamation and insult for calling the mayor of Prototsani "a miserable little mayor" in an editorial. The Greek court dismissed the defamation claim, apparently because the statement was obviously an opinion, but sentenced Rafailidis to four months in prison for insult. In the other case, Austrian journalist Gerhard Oberschlick was charged with violating both Article 111 of the Austrian Criminal Code, which prohibits defamation, and Article 115, which prohibits insult to any person, for calling Austrian Freedom Party leader Georg Haider an "idiot." The former provision, however, applies only to false statements, and since the term "idiot" was clearly a statement of opinion, not provably true or false, the Austrian courts found Oberschlick guilty of violating only the insult law. That decision was ultimately overturned by the European Court of Human Rights.

The wording of laws in many countries also recognizes the distinction between libel and insult. For example, the law in Croatia states that "if the defendant proves the truth of the allegations or that he had justified reason to believe they were true, he shall not be punished for defamation but may be punished for insult." Likewise, Moroccan law recognizes that an assertion of fact is necessary for defamation, but goes on to say: "Any gravely offensive expression, contemptuous term or invective that does not contain an imputation of any fact is an insult."

While in theory insult and defamation laws differ, in practice the distinction is often blurred. Vaguely worded criminal libel statutes are hard to distinguish from insult laws and are often used to punish what would more accurately be characterized as insult or disrespect rather than defamation. For example, in a 1996 Cambodian case Chan Rotana, editor of the *Voice of Khmer Youth*, was sentenced to a year in prison and a fine of approximately US$2,000 for defaming Cambodia's first and second prime ministers in a satirical article headlined "Prince Ranariddh is more stupid than Hen Sen three times a day." Cambodia's Penal Code does not contain an explicit insult provision, but, as in several other countries, the general criminal defamation statute is used to punish critical opinions about government leaders.

Criminal libel laws that place the burden of proving truth on the defendant, as many do, rather than requiring the prosecutor or complainant to prove falsity, are used to punish antigovernment opinions. A criminal libel law that recognizes truth as a defense invites prosecutions for statements of opinion, which by definition cannot be proven true, and thus often functions as an insult law. Furthermore, in some nations truth is not a complete defense to a criminal defamation charge. For example, in the Republic of Korea the law provides that truth is a defense to defamation only if published "solely for the public interest." In India truth is a defense "if it be for the public good that the imputation should be made or published." Such a public interest or good motives restriction on the use of a truth defense is fairly common in criminal defamation laws and also serves to convert libel laws into insult laws. My research (Walden 2000) showed that criminal defamation actions are often the result of critical reports about government officials and institutions, which further supports the conclusion that criminal defamation laws can and do serve as substitutes for insult laws.

Origins of Insult Laws

The roots of current insult laws can be traced to the fifth century B.C. Roman Law of the 12 Tablets, which contained provisions concerning *iniuria*, generally translated as insult or injury. In its earliest use, *iniuria* probably referred only to assaults or bodily harm; however, a series of edicts expanded the concept of *iniuria* to include verbal attacks, insult, or outrage. Because the action for *iniuria* was designed to protect honor and dignity, husbands could recover for insults to their wives and fathers for insults to their children. As with modern insult laws, *iniuria* was based on an individual's feelings of insult and outrage, not on economic loss. Therefore the penalty was based on the position of the parties and the severity of the outrage rather than on any proof of loss. Initially a type of civil action for damages, over time criminal remedies developed as well.

When Emperor Justinian ordered a compilation of Roman law in the sixth century A.D., the Digest contained a section devoted to "insulting behavior and scandalous libels." It provided that "the term 'injury' is used to indicate an outrageous insult. The term 'insult' is derived from the verb 'to despise.' . . . Every insult is either inflicted upon the person or relates to someone's dignity or dishonor" (see Kolbert 1979). While the ancient Roman law of *iniuria* was designed to protect all citizens' dignity—with those of higher status entitled to greater compensation—most of today's insult laws are much narrower, offering protection only to the government, public officials and bodies, royal families, national symbols, and/or foreign dignitaries. Modern insult laws seem to have replaced the ancient Roman law's concern for individual honor and dignity with government officials' concerns for self-preservation and freedom from criticism. In that respect, modern insult laws are more closely related to the old British common law of seditious libel.

Seditious libel, quite simply, consists of criticism of government, true or false, justified or unjustified. It was no accident that the law of seditious libel originated in England shortly after the introduction of the printing press in that country by William Caxton in the 15th century. The English monarch's first defense against this new and potentially dangerous communication tool was to establish stringent licensing and prepublication censorship schemes. When allegedly seditious publications began to slip through the cracks in the licensing and censorship system, an ancient medieval law prohibiting the spreading of false and scandalous tales was modified by the common law courts to criminalize any and all criticism of government.

The United States repudiated the concept of seditious libel some two centuries ago, but it lives on today throughout much of the world in the form of *desacato* and insult laws, sedition laws, and often criminal defamation and blasphemy laws, all of which can be and often are used to punish criticism of government and government officials.

Colonialism was responsible for the spread of insult laws throughout much of the world. Most former British colonies still retain the seditious libel laws that were imposed under British rule. Most Latin American *desacato* laws are based on Spain's old law, which was partially eliminated in 1995 when Spain revised its entire Criminal Code. In the former Dutch colony of Indonesia, the so-called Hate-Sowing Articles prohibit public expressions of "feelings of hostility, hatred, or contempt toward the government." While similar provisions were never part of the Criminal Code of the Netherlands, the Dutch used the Hate-Sowing Articles to suppress the pre-World War II nationalist movement in Indonesia. Perhaps the best known of all insult laws, the French law of 1881, was the model for insult laws throughout francophone Africa. The governments of developing nations continue to use the French law as justification for enacting, retaining, and enforcing their insults laws.

Insult Laws in Action

The exact number of insult laws currently on the books is unknown, but they exist in more than 100 nations. My study (Walden 2000) identified the texts of approximately 90 such laws in countries in every region of the world. Even in countries that do not have formal insult provisions, criminal defamation laws often serve as convenient substitutes.

Some of the most egregious recent examples of reliance on insult and criminal defamation laws to stifle reporting on and criticism of government have occurred in the former Soviet states. In these countries journalists face not only ingrained traditions of censorship and official hostility toward the press, but also an entrenched legacy of protecting honor and dignity. Despite constitutional provisions guaranteeing freedom of speech and of the press, government officials in several postcommunist nations continue to invoke insult laws against the media and opposition political leaders, often in an attempt to prevent revelations of corruption and other abuses of power. A case in Kazakhstan illustrates the disastrous effects of insult laws on freedom of the press and on democratic processes in general.

In April 2001 the editor of the Kazakh opposition weekly *SolDat*, was convicted of "publicly insulting the dignity and honor" of the president. The editor, who was sentenced to a year's imprisonment and ordered to pay approximately US$280 in court costs, was immediately pardoned under a presidential amnesty, but remains a convicted criminal banned from leaving the country. In July 2001 he was prevented from boarding a plane to the United States to testify before a congressional hearing on human rights in Central Asia.

The editor's conviction resulted from *SolDat*'s reprinting of an Internet article about the so-called Kazakhgate scandal that included allegations that the president and other top officials had funneled millions of U.S. dollars into Swiss bank accounts. The author of the Internet article, the editor's co-defendant in the trial, was acquitted, apparently because he wrote the article for the Internet, not for publication in a Kazakh paper. Ironically, the issue of *SolDat* containing the article had never even circulated in Kazakhstan, because customs officials impounded it at the border. The paper had been printed in Russia because all the Kazakh publishing companies had refused to print it, reportedly because of government pressure.

This case was just one battle in a long-running conflict between the opposition press and Kazakh officials. Other papers that have published reports on government corruption, often reprints of stories from foreign news outlets and Internet sites, have also faced criminal charges, loss of printing facilities, and other forms of intimidation. For example, the Committee to Protect Journalists reported that the state-owned printing company Dauir refused to continue publishing the Russian-English biweekly *Vremua Po* after it reprinted articles from *Newsweek* and the *Wall Street Journal* on the corruption scandal, and Bigeldy Gabdullin, the editor of the weekly *XXI Vek*, was charged with criminal libel as a result of two articles published in October 2000 charging President Nazarbayev with corruption. The Almaty prosecutor dropped those charges in April 2001.

Officials in other former Soviet states also turn to insult laws to punish their critics. In 1999 a journalist with the newspaper *Baku Boulevard* in Azerbaijan was found guilty of "insulting the honor" of the president's brother, a member of parliament, for describing him as "king of the oil industry." The journalist received a one-year suspended prison sentence and was barred from leaving the country. The same year Irina Khalip, editor-in-chief of the Belarussian independent weekly *Imia*, was charged with offending the honor of the chief of the presidential staff and of the prosecutor general by accusing them of corruption in a July 15, 1999, article. In Ukraine, the Kiev Municipal Court ordered the arrest of Oleg Liachko, editor-in-chief of *Politika*, an opposition paper, in December 1998. Liachko was accused of defamation and insult under Articles 125 and 126 of the Criminal Code after he published stories suggesting wrongdoing by three high-ranking police officials. Earlier the Public Prosecutor's Office had frozen the paper's bank account after it ran a series of articles about individuals close to the president.

Turkish officials also continue to enforce their country's sweeping insult laws, especially Article 159 of the Criminal Code, which provides for up to six years imprisonment for anyone who "publicly insults or vilifies the Turkish nation, the Republic, the Grand National Assembly, or the moral personality of the Government or the military or security forces of the State, or the moral personality of judicial authorities." In September 2000 journalist and author Nadire Mater was finally found not guilty of violating Article 159 after spending more than a year defending herself. In August 1999 she had been charged with insulting the army in her book, *Mehmed's Book: Soldiers Who Have Fought in the Southeast Speak Out*, which a court banned in June 1999. The book consists of interviews with 42 Turkish soldiers discussing the war against Kurdish rebels.

Another case arising under Turkey's Article 159 demonstrates that insult laws can be used against new media as well as the traditional press. Eighteen-year-old Emre Ersöz was given a 10-month suspended prison sentence in June 1998 for "publicly insulting the state security forces" after he posted criticism of the police for allegedly mistreating a group of blind people protesting against potholes in Ankara's pavements on the Internet.

Perhaps nowhere are the disastrous effects of Western Europe's insult and sedition laws more evident than in the nations of Sub-Saharan Africa. South Africa does not have such a law and Kenya repealed its sedition provisions in 1997; however, virtually every French-speaking African nation has its own version of France's infamous 1881 law, and most of the former British colonies retain sedition laws and provisions prohibiting insults to "foreign princes." In 1996 Anthony Akoto Ampaw, Ghanaian barrister and general secretary of the New Democratic Movement, told a conference of the Council of Europe in Strasbourg that African governments were using Western-style laws to throttle the press. "In Africa, you can be sure that there will be the worst interpretations of law, even if the worst interpretations are unlikely in Europe," Ampaw stated. A few examples of recent African cases demonstrate Ampaw's point.

In one of the most publicized cases in the region, in June 1996 an appeals court in Côte d'Ivoire affirmed the two-year prison sentences of three journalists with the opposition daily *La Voie* for insulting President Hénri Konan Bédié. The publisher, an editor, and a writer were all imprisoned, and *La Voie* was fined CFAF 3 million and suspended from publishing for three months. The convictions stemmed from two December 1995 satirical articles suggesting that the presence of President Bédié at the African Championship Cup Final had brought bad luck to the Ivorian soccer team, the Asec Mimosas, which lost to the visiting South Africans. One article was headlined "He should have stayed home," and the other, headlined "He cursed ASEC," referred to Bédié as Lucifer and said the championship "that was in the bag for the Ivorians went elsewhere, as if in a nightmare." The three journalists were released from prison on January 1, 1997, after serving about a year of their sentences.

In March 2000 two Angolan journalists with the Luanda-based weekly *Agora* were sentenced to prison for an article saying that the country's president should be held accountable for the near collapse of Angola amid government corruption fostered by civil war. According to the Associated Press, after a trial from which defense witnesses and evidence were barred, writer Rafael Marques was sentenced to six months in prison and editor Aguiar dos Santos to two months.

In Swaziland the only independent paper, the *Times of Swaziland*, got into trouble in September 1999 for reporting that the young woman King Mswati III had chosen to be his eighth wife had been expelled from high school for playing hooky. Charges were reportedly dropped after the paper agreed to fire the editor responsible for publishing the article. In June 2001 the Committee to Protect Journalists reported that King Mswati had enhanced the government's weapons again royal insults by signing a decree that authorized the banning of any publication for any reason and providing penalties of up to 10 years' imprisonment and fines of US$6,200 for anyone who "insults, ridicules, or puts into contempt the King or the Queen."

Three African heads of state sought to use France's insult law to punish one of their critics. The presidents of Chad, the Republic of Congo, and Gabon filed a complaint against Francois-Xavier Verschave, author of the book *Noir Silence*, which traces the relationship between France and its former African colonies. The complaint was based on the provision of France's law that prohibits "public offense of foreign heads of state, heads of foreign governments, or the foreign ministers of a foreign government." Among other things, the offending book calls the president of Chad "an inveterate assassin," says the president of Gabon is the head of a "predatory elected dictatorship," and accuses the Congo president of crimes against humanity. In April 2001 a Paris judge dismissed the charges, declaring that the French law contravenes Article 10 of the European Convention on Human Rights, which protects the freedom of expression. The court said that the law provides no legal definition of what constitutes "offense" and that the term is too broad to define.

A similar provision of Uruguay's *desacato* law had been invoked some five years earlier in an attempt to vindicate the honor of a foreign head of state. Federico Fasano, editor-in-chief of the Montevideo daily *La Republica*, and his brother Carlos Fasano, managing editor, were charged with insulting Paraguayan President Juan Carlos Wasmosy in a 1996 article that alleged that Wasmosy was involved in mismanagement and corruption in the construction of the Itaipu hydroelectric power plant on the border between Paraguay and Brazil. The brothers were convicted and sentenced to two years in prison, but an appeals court ordered them released a few months later because of an error in the sentencing. When the two were retried in August 1997, they were acquitted. The judge in the latter case based his ruling in part on the fact that while the story had been critical of the Paraguayan president and had undoubtedly irritated him, its publication had not put relations between Paraguay and Uruguay "in danger."

The few cases discussed here are merely the tip of a large iceberg. My study (Walden 2000) identified hundreds of incidents in the past decade involving arrests, charges, prosecutions, and convictions. Yet even those hundreds of cases represent only a small part of the impact of insult and criminal defamation laws on press freedom. Ascertaining how many times such laws are used to threaten and intimidate journalists into backing off from investigations and stories is impossible, as is measuring the self-censorship caused by the mere existence of laws that can send a journalist to jail for investigating official wrongdoing, editorially criticizing official conduct, or even satirizing a president.

Some Good News

Despite the widespread prevalence of insult and criminal defamation laws and their continued use as tools to harass, intimidate, and punish journalists, recognition that such laws are inconsistent with press freedom, and with democracy in general, has been growing. Numerous international organizations and agencies dedicated to human rights in general, and to freedom of expression in particular, have been leading the assault against such laws. In April 2001 at a meeting in Boston nine press freedom and free expression groups—the Committee to Protect Journalists, the Commonwealth Press Union, the Inter American Press Association, the International Association of Broadcasting, the International Federation of the Periodical Press, the International Press Institute, the North American Broadcasters Association, the World Association of Newspapers, and the World Press Freedom Committee—renewed their opposition to such laws and called upon governments throughout the world to repeal them.

For the past two years the U.S. delegation to the Human Dimension Implementation Meeting of the Organization for Security and Cooperation in Europe (OSCE) has emphasized that laws criminalizing political reporting and commentary are inconsistent with democracy and has called for the repeal of such laws in OSCE states. The United Nations special rapporteur on freedom of opinion and expression, the OSCE representative on freedom of the media, and the Organization of American States special rapporteur on freedom of expression have issued a joint statement declaring that "expression should not be criminalized unless it poses a clear risk of serious harm." Their statement called for the repeal of insult and sedition laws, criminal defamation laws, and laws prohibiting the publication of false news.

One of the earliest and strongest denunciations of insult laws came from the Inter-American Commission on Human Rights, which declared in its 1994 annual report: "Desacato laws are incompatible with Article 13 of the American Convention on Human Rights because they suppress the freedom of expression necessary for the proper functioning of a democratic society." Article 13 of the convention states: "Everyone has the right to freedom of thought and expression. This right includes freedom to seek, receive, and impart information and ideas of all kinds, regardless of frontiers, either orally, in writing, in print, in the form of art, or through any other medium of one's choice." Noting that the convention obligates "each signatory country to adapt its legislation to guarantee these rights," the commission called on all member countries of the Organization of American States that have *desacato* laws to "repeal or amend" those laws.

The commission's action came in response to an Argentine case in which journalist Horacio Verbitsky had been convicted of insulting a member of the Supreme Court. In 1993 Argentina repealed its *desacato* law as part of the settlement of the Verbitsky case. Paraguay followed suit, eliminating its *desacato* law in the country's new Penal Code, which went into effect in October 1998, and on May 18, 2001, Chilean President Ricardo Lagos signed into law a provision eliminating a section of the State Security Law that made it a "crime against public order" to insult certain high officials. While that action removed one source of prosecutions for insults in Chile, it left intact the general criminal laws punishing *desacato* and criminal defamation. In March 2002 Costa Rica became the latest Latin American nation to eliminate its *desacato* law.

Efforts to raise awareness of the devastating impact of insult laws on democratic processes and of the need for their elimination have also borne fruit in parts of Europe, but as in Latin America, progress has been slow and often only partial. As mentioned briefly, in 1997 the European Court of Human Rights threw out the conviction of journalist Gerhard Oberschlick for insulting Austrian Freedom Party leader Georg Haider. While not going so far as to call for the repeal of all insult laws, the court declared that Article 10 of the European Convention on Human Rights was applicable to "not only 'information' and 'ideas' that are favorably received or regarded as inoffensive or as a matter of indifference, but also those that offend, shock or disturb." Article 10 declares: "Everyone has the right to freedom of expression. This right shall include freedom to hold opinions and to receive and impart information and ideas without interference by public authority and regardless of frontiers."

As it has in other cases, the European Court stressed that politicians and public officials must tolerate even caustic criticism and commentary.

A few national courts have declared insult laws unconstitutional, or at least severely limited their applicability. For example, in two 1990 cases the German Federal Constitutional Court held that even harsh and satirical attacks on state symbols were constitutionally protected, and in 1976 the court held that public officials must tolerate a greater degree of criticism of their public conduct than private persons. In Hungary in 1994 the Constitutional Law Court declared that the nation's insult law was unconstitutional.

Several nations, including the Czech Republic, the Kyrgyz Republic, Moldova, Sweden, and Uzbekistan, have repealed all or parts of their insult laws; however, in some of these countries government officials continue to bring insult-type charges under defamation laws. In 1995, as part of a revision of its entire Penal Code, Spain repealed its *desacato* or disrespect laws, which had prohibited insulting, offending, or defaming public officials while they were performing their official duties or because of those duties. Nevertheless, Spain still has laws prohibiting defamation and insult of the king and other members of the royal family and prohibiting calumny, insult, and threats against the government in general, certain judicial bodies, and the army. In addition, Spain retains a general insult law under which any person, including a government official, can bring a criminal complaint. The 1995 code, however, provides that if the complainant is a public official, truth is a defense if the insult concerned the exercise of the official's duties or referred to the commission of criminal acts or administrative violations. The problem, of course, is that a truth defense provides absolutely no protection for statements of opinion.

What Needs to Be Done

A number of factors explain why insult laws are regularly and routinely invoked in some countries while in others, even neighboring countries, they have been repealed, struck down by the courts, or remain on the books unused. Two obvious factors affecting the use of insult laws are the structure of the government and the nation's stability. As Siebert observed a half century ago in his landmark study, *Freedom of the Press in England, 1476–1776* (Siebert 1952), the amount of freedom of expression a nation enjoys depends on the relationship between the governed and the government and on the level of stress on the government and society. The more authoritarian the government, the more likely that critics of the government will be silenced or punished. In addition, regardless of the government's basic structure, as threats to a government's security and stability increase—whether because of war, economic pressures, civil unrest, or political opposition—the government tends to clamp down on expression it views as adding to the stress.

A working system of checks and balances within the government, especially the existence of an independent judiciary, seems to significantly reduce the use of insult and criminal defamation laws. So too does the existence of an independent, economically secure, professional press and active nongovernmental organizations dedicated to protecting human rights and exposing governmental abuses.

In some cases the character of a single leader can make a huge difference in the enforcement of insult laws. One of the most striking examples of this is Croatia. Under the late President Franjo Tudjman, the country's insult and criminal libel laws were continually used to punish and intimidate journalists and political opponents. In December 1998 the Committee to Protect Journalists reported that almost 300 criminal cases and more than 600 civil lawsuits were pending against Croatian journalists and newspapers, most brought by government officials and their families, and more than two-thirds targeting four independent newspapers. Since Tudjman's death in 1999 the situation in Croatia has improved dramatically.

Although the reasons insult laws continue to be enforced in some countries while being allowed to lie dormant in others is complex, the solution to the problem is simple. Insult laws, in whatever form they appear, must be repealed. No tinkering with the language or penalties will suffice. As the Inter-American Commission so eloquently said in its 1994 report, a law that protects the honor and dignity of public officials

> unjustifiably grants a right to protection to public officials that is not available to other members of society. This distinction inverts the fundamental principle in a democratic system that holds the Government subject to controls, such as public scrutiny, in order to preclude or control abuse of its coercive powers. . . . A law that targets speech that is considered critical of the public administration . . . . strikes at the very essence and content of freedom of expression.

Likewise, criminal penalties for libel and slander must be abolished. Of course, presidents and prime ministers, as well as government officials at all levels, have the right to legal protection of their reputations, but that protection should come under civil, not criminal, law. The penalty for defaming an individual should be monetary damages paid to the injured party, not prison sentences and fines paid to the state. Damages should be available only to those plaintiffs who can prove the falsity of the defamatory statements. Mere allegations of falsity should not suffice to find a defendant liable nor should unverifiable statements of opinion. As numerous international and national courts have recognized, public officials must tolerate greater criticism and public scrutiny than private individuals, and governmental bodies and institutions should never be permitted to sue for defamation.

The established democracies of the world must lead the way in repealing their own anachronistic statutes. Their continued existence merely invites the filing of charges, such as those brought by the three African rulers in France and by Georg

Haider in Austria. More important, however, the existence of such indisputably undemocratic laws in developed democracies encourages emulation and provides justification for developing nations to retain such laws. The perfect illustration of that occurred in Bulgaria on July 15, 1998, when the Constitutional Court upheld the constitutionality of that country's insult and criminal defamation laws, specifically citing the existence of such laws in Western Europe to support its ruling. The decision came in response to a request from 55 members of the Bulgarian Parliament that the high court review the laws. A year later, Parliament itself amended the Criminal Code to eliminate imprisonment as a penalty for insult and defamation, but established heavy fines for those offenses.

Why do democratic countries such as Austria, France, Italy, and Portugal, which generally respect the value of a free press and its role in self-government, cling to such vestiges of authoritarianism? Perhaps one reason is simple inertia, which ultimately can be overcome by pressure from external forces such as nongovernmental organizations, international bodies, and the media. Undoubtedly, though, some lawmakers and judges in even the most democratic of nations prefer to retain insult and criminal defamation laws "just in case." Authoritarian leaders are not the only ones who resent media exposés of political wrongdoing, critical commentary, and unflattering caricatures and cartoons. Even democratically elected leaders may be loath to give up their sword of Damocles.

Democracy, however, is based on the premise that the people are the sovereigns, the masters of the household of state. Government institutions and officials, from the highest to the lowest ranking, are servants of the people, hired by the people to do their will. No properly run household allows the servants to punish the masters for criticizing the servants' performance of their duties, yet that is exactly what insult laws and criminal libel laws permit. Obviously such laws are inconsistent with both democratic theory and practice. As the late Kalven (1988, p. 63), a leading authority on freedom of expression, explained, laws making it a crime to criticize government are "the hallmark of closed societies throughout the world. . . . political freedom ends when government can use its powers and its courts to silence its critics." A society that penalizes criticism of public officials "is not a free society, no matter what its other characteristics."

Appendix: Sample Insult Laws

France's Law of 1881

Law of July 29, 1881, on Freedom of the Press, modified numerous times during the 20th century. (The title of the 1881 law is misleading in that the bulk of the law comprises press regulations and a criminal code applying to all types public communication.)

Chapter IV, Of Crimes and Misdemeanors Committed by Means of the Press or Any Other Means of Publication, Section 2, Misdemeanors against Public Affairs, Article 26 (Decree of May 6, 1944): "Offense of the President of the Republic" or of "a person who exercises all or part of the prerogatives of the President of the Republic" by one of the means enumerated in Arts. 23 and 28, punishable by three months to one year imprisonment and/or a fine of F 10 to F 10,000. (Article 23, which deals with incitement to a crime or misdemeanor, lists the following means: "By speech, cries or threats made in public places or public meetings, by writings, printed materials, drawings, engravings, paintings, insignia, images or any other medium for writing, words or images, sold or distributed, offered for sale or displayed in public places or public meetings, [and] by bills or posters exposed to public sight.")

Section 3, Misdemeanors against Persons, Article 28 (Decree of May 6, 1944): "Any allegation or imputation of a fact that harms the honor or the reputation of a person or an entity to which the fact is attributed is a defamation. The publication or reproduction by other means of that allegation or that imputation is punishable, even if it is formulated as a question or if it is aimed at a person or an entity that is not explicitly named but whose identification is possible from the terms of the incriminating speech, cries, threats, writings or printed matter, bills or posters. An insult is any insulting expression, term of contempt or invective that does not refer to any fact."

Article 30 (Decree of May 6, 1944): "Defamation by one of the means listed in Article 23 of the courts, the armed forces, established bodies and public administrations," punishable by one week to one year imprisonment and/or a fine of F 10 to F 10,000.

Article 31 (Decree of May 6, 1944): The penalties listed in Article 30 apply to defamation directed at the following individuals because of their functions or positions: "One or more ministers, one or more members of either House of Parliament, a public official, one who holds or exercises public authority, a minister of religion paid by the State, a citizen temporarily or permanently assigned a public service or mandate, a juror or a witness, because of his testimony."

Article 33 (Amendment of April 21, 1939; decrees of November 24, 1943, and May 6, 1944): "Insults committed by the same means to the bodies or persons designated in Arts. 30 and 31," punishable by six days to three months imprisonment and/or a fine of F 5 to F 2,000.

Article 35: "The truth of the defamatory fact, solely if it relates to their functions, can be established by normal means in cases of allegations against established bodies, the armed forces, public administrations and against all of the persons listed in Art. 31. The truth of defamatory or insulting allegations may also be established against directors or administrators of any industrial, commercial or financial enterprise that publicly seeks (investments through) savings and loans."

Decree of May 6, 1944: "The truth of defamatory facts may be proven, except:

a) When the allegation concerns the person's private life;

b) When the allegation refers to facts that are more than 10 years old;

c) When the allegation refers to a fact that constitutes an infraction that has been amnestied or is subject to the statute of limitations, or when the conviction was expunged through rehabilitation or review."

Section 4, Misdemeanors against Foreign Chiefs of State and Diplomats, Article 36 (Amendment of October 30, 1935, Decree of May 6, 1944): "Public offense of foreign heads of state, heads of foreign governments or the foreign ministers of a foreign government," punishable by three months to one year imprisonment and/or a fine of F 10 to F 10,000.

Article 37 (Decree of May 6, 1944): "Public outrage (grave offense) of the ambassadors and ministers plenipotentiary, envoys, acting heads of mission or other diplomats accredited to the government of the Republic," punishable by one week to one year imprisonment and/or a fine of F 10 to F 10,000.

Article 39 (modified by Law number 72-3 of January 3, 1972): "Reporting on defamation trials in the cases provided for in paragraphs a, b, and c of Article 35 of this law is prohibited."

Chapter V, Of Prosecutions and Repression, Section 2, Procedure, Article 48 (Decree of September 13, 1945; Law number 53-184 of March 12, 1953, Article 2): "(1) In case of insult or defamation of the courts and other bodies listed in Art. 30, prosecution shall take place only after they have deliberated in a general assembly and have requested prosecution, or, if the body has no general assembly, upon complaint by the head of the body or of the minister to whom the body is attached. (2) In case of insult or defamation of one or more members of either House of Parliament, prosecution shall take place only upon the complaint of the person or persons concerned. (3) In case of insult or defamation of public officials, those entrusted with public authority or the agents of public authority other than ministers, and of citizens entrusted with a public service or mandate, prosecution shall take place either upon their complaint or automatically upon the complaint of the minister to whom they are attached. (4) In case of defamation of a juror or witness, as provided in Art. 31, prosecution shall take place on the complaint of the juror or witness who claims he was defamed. (5) In case of offense of heads of state, or insult of foreign diplomats, prosecution shall take place after their request to the Minister of Foreign Affairs and its referral by him to the Minister of Justice."

Uganda's Seditious Libel Law

Uganda's seditious libel law is fairly typical of laws in other former British colonies.

Criminal Code, Article 41 (colonial era, amended in 1966): (1) Defines "seditious intention" as the intent "(a) to bring into hatred or contempt or to excite disaffection against the person of the President, the Government as by law established or the Constitution; (b) to excite any person to attempt to procure the alteration, otherwise than by lawful means, of any matter as by law established; (c) to bring into hatred or contempt or to excite disaffection against the administration of justice; (d) to raise discontent or disaffection among any body or group of persons; (e) to promote feelings of ill-will and hostility, religious animosity or communal ill-feeling among any body or group of persons; (f) to raise discontent or disaffection or to promote feelings of ill-will and hostility among any body or group of persons by the use of any symbol connected with or attaching upon, in whatever manner, the name, status, or dignity of the Ruler of a Federal State or the Constitutional Head of a District; (g) to use any symbol connected with or attaching upon, in whatever manner, the name, status or dignity of the Ruler of a Federal State or the Constitutional Head of a District in order to bring that person into hatred or ridicule or contempt or to incite disaffection against the Ruler of a Federal State or the Constitutional Head of a District; (h) to subvert or promote the subversion of the Government, the government of a Federal State or the Administration of a District." (2) Any act, speech, or publication shall not be deemed seditious if it intends only "(a) to show that the Government has been misled or mistaken in any of its measures; (b) to point out errors or defects in the Government or the Constitution, including the constitution of a Federal State as by law established, or in legislation or in the administration of justice with a view to the remedying of such errors or defects; (c) to persuade any person to procure by lawful means the alteration of any matter as by law established; or (d) to point out, with a view to their removal, any matters which are producing or have a tendency to produce feelings of ill-will and enmity among any body or group of persons." (3) For purposes of paragraphs (f) and (g) of subsection (1), "'symbol' includes slogans, titles and any name or other expression which is intended to represent or calculated to represent, or might represent a name." (4) In determining intention, "every person shall be deemed to intend the consequences which would naturally follow from his conduct at the time and in the circumstances in which he was conducting himself."

Article 42: A person who does or conspires to do a seditious act, or "utters any words with a seditious intention," or "prints, publishes, sells, offers for sale, distributes or reproduces any seditious publication," or "imports any seditious publication" shall be punished by up to five years imprisonment and/or a fine of up to U Sh 10,000, with imprisonment increasing to seven years for subsequent offenses. Possession of a seditious publication is punishable by up to three years imprisonment and/or a fine of up to U Sh 6,000, with imprisonment increasing to five years for subsequent offenses.

Article 51: "Any person who, without such justification or excuse as would be sufficient in the case of the defamation of a private person, publishes anything intended to be read, or any sign or visible representation, tending to degrade, revile or expose to hatred or contempt any foreign prince, potentate, ambassador or other foreign dignitary with intent to disturb peace and friendship between Uganda and the country to which such prince, potentate, ambassador or dignitary belongs is guilty of a misdemeanor."

El Salvador's Desacato Law

Criminal Code, Article 339: One who offends, by action or word, the honor or dignity of public officials or threatens them in their presence or in a writing directed at them while they are performing their duties or because of their duties shall be punished with six month to three years in prison. If the offense is aimed at the president or vice president of the republic, a deputy of the Legislative Assembly, the minister or subsecretary of state, a judge of the Supreme Court or Court of Appeals, a trial judge, or a justice of the peace, the punishment may be increased by up to one-third of the maximum.

Kuwait's Insult Laws

Press and Publications Law, March 1961, Article 23: "It is forbidden to insult God, the prophets [and] the disciples of the prophets by allusions or remarks aimed at invalidating them, mockery or denigration. . . . It is forbidden to criticize the person of the Emir. It is also forbidden to attribute words to the Emir without the authorization of the Press and Publications Administration."

Article 24: "It is forbidden to publish anything susceptible of offending the Heads of State or of causing harm to the good relations of Kuwait with Arab or friendly states."

Article 28: "The director of the publication and the author of the article are liable to imprisonment for a period not exceeding six months and/or a fine" for violations of Article 24. For repeated offenses, the penalty increases to not more than a year in prison and/or a fine.

Article 29: "The director of the publication and the author of the publication shall incur the penalty provided in the penal law of defamation if an imputation relative to the activities of a public functionary constitutes a defamation, except in the case of the author proving good faith, a belief in the truth of the alleged facts and that the belief was based on logical reasons after verification. He must also prove that his intention was not only to protect the public interest and that the words were not excessive but also that they were essential to protect the stated interest."

Article 30: "The director of the publication and the author of the article shall incur the penalties provided for such crimes in the penal law if they have published . . . opinions that constitute scoffing at, debasing or diminishing respect for a religion or a religious sect."

Article 31: Violations of Article 29 and 30 can result in suspension of a publication for up to one year, confiscation of the offending issue or cancellation of a publication's license.

Thailand's Insult Laws

Constitution, Chapter II, Section 6: "The King shall be enthroned in a position of revered worship and shall not be violated. No person shall expose the King to any sort of accusation or action."

Criminal Code, Section 118: "Whoever does any act to the flag or any other emblem symbolizing the State with the intent to deride the nation shall be punished with imprisonment not exceeding one year or a fine not exceeding 2,000 bahts, or both."

Section 133: "Whoever defames, insults or threatens the Sovereign, his Queen or her Consort, Heir-apparent or Head of a foreign State shall be punished with imprisonment not exceeding three years or a fine not exceeding 6,000 bahts, or both."

Section 134: "Whoever defames, insults or threatens a foreign representative accredited to the Royal Court shall be punished with imprisonment not exceeding two years or a fine not exceeding 4,000 bahts, or both."

Section 135: "Whoever does any act to the flag or other emblem symbolizing a friendly foreign State with intent to deride such State shall be punished with imprisonment not exceeding one year or a fine not exceeding 2,000 bahts, or both."

Section 135: "Whoever insults any official in the due exercise of his functions or by reason of the due exercise of his functions shall be punished with imprisonment not exceeding six months or a fine not exceeding 1,000 bahts, or both."

Belarus' Insult Laws

Article 129: "Insult, that is, willful humiliation of the honor or dignity of the personality, expressed in a vulgar form and made by a person who has previously been subject to administrative penalties for insult or defamation," punishable by up to two years corrective labor or a fine.

Article 130: Publication of "knowingly false fabrications defaming candidates for the presidency of the Republic of Belarus or the People's Deputies," punishable by up to three years imprisonment, up to two years corrective labor, or a fine. If the accusation is one of committing a crime, punishment shall be up to five years imprisonment.

Article 1862: "Abuse of the state emblem, state flag or state anthem of the Republic of Belarus," punishable by up to two years corrective labor or a fine.

Article 1880: "Insulting a government official in connection with the performance of his duties," punishable by up to one year of corrective labor or a fine.

Article 1881: "Insulting a militiaman, people's guard, serviceman or another person in connection with his performance of official duties or while he is protecting the public order," punishable by up to one year of corrective labor or a fine.

Media Law, Article 5 (1998): For "spreading information that dishonors, defames or libels government officials whose status is established by the Constitution of the Republic of Belarus," a media outlet may be suspended for up to three months.

References

Kalven, Harry Jr. 1988. *A Worthy Tradition*. New York: Harper & Row.

Kolbert, C. F., translator. 1979. *The Digest of Roman Law,* book 47, title 10, *Concerning Insulting Behavior and Scandalous Libels.* New York: Penguin Classics.

Siebert, Frederick. 1952. *Freedom of the Press in England, 1476–1776.* Urbana: University of Illinois Press.

Walden, Ruth. 2000. *An Insult to Press Freedom.* Reston, Virginia: World Press Freedom Committee.

12

Media in Transition: The Hegemony of Economics

Tim Carrington and Mark Nelson

Zofia Bydlinska, an editor at Poland's leading daily, *Gazeta Wyborcza*, did some calculations in early 2000 of the value of the shares she held in the once outlawed newspaper's parent company. The stock she had acquired at preferential prices when the firm went public the previous year had risen as the company moved into radio, television, and the Internet to a value of US$2.3 million, many times what she had paid for it. Twenty years earlier, the beleaguered newspaper ran off hand-operated presses, and the staff was sometimes jailed under the iron-fisted martial law imposed by the communist government in Warsaw.

In January 1999 Anderson Fumulani, an enterprising journalist in Malawi, launched *Business Watch*, an independent quarterly magazine covering business and economic developments in the recently democratized southern African state. He economized by hiring journalists-in-training who expected little if any pay, and he worked tirelessly to attract advertising from Malawi's private sector. However, after four issues—none of which drew more than 500 paying readers—*Business Watch* folded. Rather than unpacking shares to cash in, a year later Fumulani was still sifting through invoices of what he owes. "I still haven't finalized the phone bills," he concedes.

The news media provide an outlet for expression, a source of accountability, a vehicle for civic participation, and a check on official corruption. They are seen as an information lifeline, constitutionally protected in some countries. They can also threaten established power structures. As a result, governments determined to protect themselves from public scrutiny by controlling the flow of news and interpretation work to fence in news organizations they have come to view as adversaries, or failing that, to shut them down.

However, behind the often passionate debates about media rights and responsibilities is a simple fact, too often overlooked by the international organizations that seek to support media development in transition and developing countries: the media are a business. As the two stories at the start of this chapter illustrate, the news business is capable of creating both soaring financial successes and dismal failures. Like any business it is profoundly affected by local economic conditions, but it must do more than ride waves of economic growth and contraction up and down. Rather, media successes arise from strategies for building readership, reputation, and profits in a variety of economic conditions.

Development economists are increasingly recognizing the media as a "development good" capable of contributing to improved accountability, more efficient markets, and more information-rich societies. At the same time, one must recognize that all these beneficial outcomes derive from the media's financial independence. That independence, in turn, is a function both of the local economy and of a particular media company's ability to turn a given economic environment to its advantage.

The Quest for Financial Independence

The quest for financial independence is seldom easy. Often financial pressures push news organizations toward rescuers who assure their solvency, but exact a heavy price in terms of their independence. Financially weak media in fragile democracies are particularly vulnerable to absorption by a narrow set of political or economic interests that are inclined to operate the news organizations not as self-sustaining businesses, but as propaganda units.

Meanwhile, if a country has made, or at least decisively launched, its transition toward open democratic norms, the world is less likely to rush to the aid of failing media concerns than when these organizations perhaps played a heroic part in a struggle to end an oppressive dictatorship. Indeed, virtually all news organizations entering the posteuphoria phase in a society's transition to democracy seem to be beset by economic trials that threaten their viability as much as oppressive political structures did in the past.

In an October 2001 online newsletter (http://www.ijnet.org), the International Center for Journalists reported that

> [P]rint media in Serbia face formidable economic problems and are often looking for financial support. As a result, "they become an easy prey for politicians," Dragan Janjic, editor-in-chief of the Beta News Agency, told a roundtable in mid-October, organized by the Institute for Philosophy and Social Theory.

According to the report, Danjic added that major changes in the media would become visible only when major changes in the economy occur: "Before that, there is nothing we can look forward to. "

As the Serbian editor's testimony underscores, worsening economic pressures often push news organizations to seek a safe harbor, which can mean turning to politicians or special interests for support. They do this, however, at the expense of their editorial independence, because the rescuers, rather than investing in the long-term profitability of the news concerns, look for the short-term gains of owning a propaganda arm that they can commandeer into advancing their political or economic interests. Indeed, the paper or broadcaster might be chalking up losses in its own business, but if it is helping to swing an election or lock in desired legislative or regulatory advantages, the proprietor would likely conclude that the media unit had earned its keep.

Freedom House ranks the environment for media around the world and examines threats and inhibitions to media freedom from several vantage points: political controls, laws and regulations, repressive actions (violence, censorship, arrests), and the economy. International donors, for their part, have increased markedly their assistance to news media in developing and transition countries. The European Commission, through the European Initiative for Human Rights and Democracy, spent €4.3 million on media assistance in 1996, €6 million in 1998, and €9.7 million in 1999. U.S. Agency for International Development funding, particularly in the Balkans, also rose during the same period, while a variety of other organizations, ranging from the World Bank to the World Association of Newspapers, have become more deeply involved in helping news organizations develop strategies to survive in often difficult environments.

However, the bulk of national and multilateral donor programs is oriented toward building reporters' and editors' skills or pressuring reluctant governments to loosen the web of legal and regulatory controls they maintain over local media. Unfortunately, only a handful of international programs deal with the economic environment and the capacity of individual news organizations to craft a business strategy for financial survival, let alone success.

The collapse of the Soviet Union and the Warsaw Pact and some of the other dramatic global economic changes over the past decade have greatly enhanced our understanding of the dynamics of change within news organizations. During the transition from communism to a market economy, some formerly centrally planned economies—at times helped by international organizations and foreign investors—have led the way in creating a viable media and information market. Some of the rapidly changing Asian economies—like India, the Republic of Korea, and Thailand—have begun to create dynamic media sectors that thrive on news and information. These examples have begun to point the way toward successful strategies for creating a working media sector and the building blocks of a knowledge-based economic system.

Nevertheless, our ability to decipher the problems still confronting news businesses in the least developed countries is hampered by the lack of internationally comparable statistics on such areas as profitability, ownership patterns, and local advertising markets. Such statistics, for example, those for the 58 countries published annually by Zenith Media and the World Association of Newspapers, are generally collected as a result of international investor interest in emerging media markets.

While domestic investors can play a major role in transforming a country's media sector, few have managed to do so without some investment from abroad, and few developing countries without major foreign investment have created strong data collection systems that provide a good picture of revenue growth, investment patterns, or changing fortunes of different sectors of the media.

Thus while many of the conclusions that can be drawn are biased toward the more promising and open markets, some general observations are possible. One of the reasons that media markets in the least developed countries tend to receive less attention from investors is that they generally suffer from greater restrictions on press freedom. In its annual survey of press freedom in more than 180 countries around the world, Freedom House (see Freedom House 2000) has consistently found the lowest levels of perceived press freedom in the poorest countries of the South, particularly the Middle East, Africa, and parts of Asia (figure 12.1). These restrictions not only dissuade international investors from considering these markets, but they also discourage domestic investors who might otherwise see the promise of the media business.

Another factor seems to be the development of the advertising business, which is a key source of revenue for most independent news organizations. Among industrial countries spending on advertising varies widely, from 0.68 percent of gross domestic product (GDP) in France to 1.48 percent in the United States. Among developing and transition countries, a growing percentage of spending on advertising is a fairly reliable indicator of a country's improving economy and progression toward having independent media (figure 12.2). One problem is that developing countries often

Figure 12.1. Free Press and Income Levels, 2000

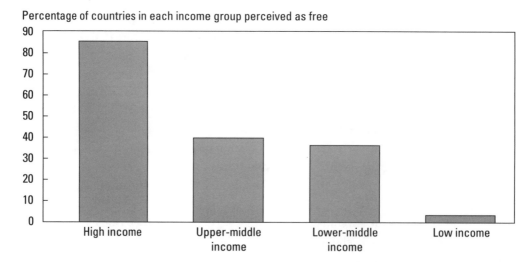

Percentage of countries in each income group perceived as free

Source: Freedom House indicators matched against income groups as defined by World Bank (2001b).

Figure 12.2. Advertising and GDP per Capita, 29 Developing and Transition Countries, 2000

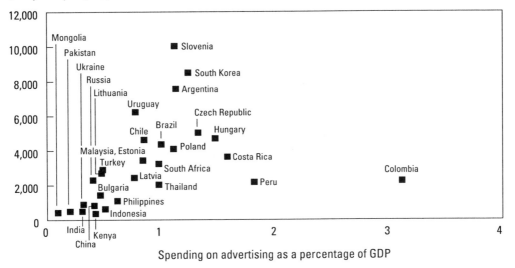

Source: World Association of Newspapers (2001).

offer a highly restricted advertising market, with the bulk of advertising coming from the state.

The incidence of low literacy levels in countries where incomes are also low puts nascent media companies in a double bind. Low incomes inhibit readership and audiences for all media, while low literacy limits the demand for print media and holds back people's capacity to absorb and interpret information, regardless of how it is delivered. While analysts disagree on whether functional and independent media are a product of a flourishing economy or one of its causes, the two seem to go hand in hand.

The media's strength generally parallels the strength of the local economy (figure 12.3). The strength of the media, represented on the vertical axis, reflects a number of measures that track the reach of newspapers and the electronic media and the media's relative independence. Economic health, represented on the horizontal axis, reflects a mix of 21 variables including GDP per capita, debt levels, and trade. The figures are derived from the Wealth of Nations Triangle Index. Updated twice a year since 1996, the index ranks 70 developing countries on 63 variables.

At the turn of the millennium countries such as Belarus and Zimbabwe experienced economic decline combined with a renewed series of political constraints on the media and free expression. Indeed, Zimbabwe's weakening economy and the

Figure 12.3. Media Strength and Economic Health, Selected Countries, 2000–01

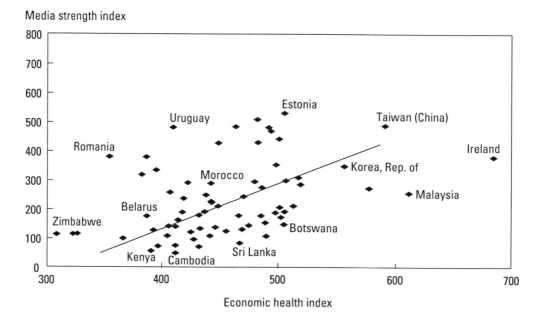

Source: Money Matters Institute data.

resulting political fallout for the Mugabe government has increased the financial pressures on independent news organizations, alongside ever harsher state repression. Estonia and Taiwan, China, achieve higher ratings for both the media and the economy. Under such a virtuous cycle a more robust economy provides more sources for advertising revenue, along with the basis for less political paranoia, providing more opportunities for media companies to expand into new markets and/or formats.

As concern about the world's "digital divide" intensify, note that high-tech connectivity generally tracks low-tech media capacities. According to Norris (2001, p. 51):

> Info-rich countries like Sweden, the United States, and Australia are not just ahead in terms of the Internet but also in the distribution of other media such as newspaper readership, radio and television sets, personal computers, and mainline and mobile cell telephones. Correlation revealed that access to all these media fell into a single consistent dimension. There was little distinction between use of old and new media; the proportion of those online in each country was most strongly related to the distribution of hosts, telephones and PCs, but it was also significantly and strongly related to the distribution of radios, TV sets, and newspaper readership in each nation. This means that people living in poorer societies excluded from the world's flow of communications such as Burkina Faso,

Yemen, and Vietnam were largely cut off from all forms of info-tech, including traditional mass media like radios and newspapers as well as modern ones such as mobile phones and personal computers.

Divergences in Internet use can follow income differences, but in some measures exaggerate them. In the United Kingdom, according to Norris, the most affluent households were five times more likely to be online than the poorest. Similar patterns exist between richer and poor countries. In affluent countries faster connection speeds, better reliability, and declining access costs have accelerated Internet use, while high costs and poor service in developing economies function as persistent constraints.

As countries move into a more information-based, market-oriented economic system, often it is the traditional media companies that lead the way (figure 12.4). *Maeil Business Newspaper* of Seoul, for example, has been one of the leaders in pushing Korea toward a knowledge-based economy. Drawing on the newspaper's strengths as an information source and using the company's staff of trained news gathers, Dae-Whan Chang, president and publisher, created one of Korea's leading Internet portals. Internet subscribers in Korea are now growing at one of the fastest rates in the world, with more than 20 percent of the population having access to the Internet—

Figure 12.4. Prevalence of Traditional and New Media, Selected Regions

Percentage of population using each medium

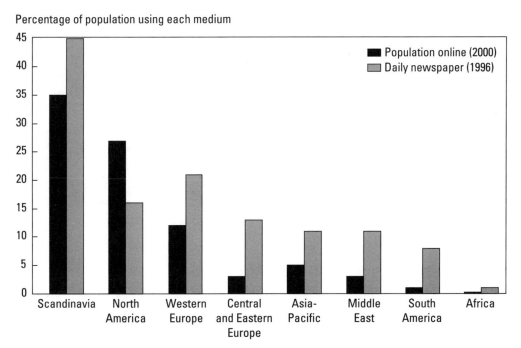

Source: Norris (2001, p.52).

higher than in most European countries (World Bank 2001a, p. 113). Chang argues that building his media company's reputation as a source of analysis, knowledge sharing, and quality information has been a leading factor in its profitability.

The Central European Laboratory

Central Europe provides a useful laboratory for studying the relationship between the news media and the economic environment in which they operate. In the most precocious reformers in Central Europe the news media can both profit from and contribute to far-reaching economic change and reform. The economic transformation has often been reflected directly in the news media environment, leading to sometimes rapid changes in media ownership, investment patterns, and competition. Central Europe is also the one place that in the course of a decade has undergone a shift from heavily censored, government controlled and sponsored media to media that have developed themselves as businesses, financing their operations from producing high-quality newspapers, magazines, and broadcast programs and selling these media products and advertising as a way of financing their growth and development.

While many Central European governments have kept a hand in parts of the television business, the print media and radio have been largely privatized and weaned from financial support by the state. In the Czech Republic, Hungary, and Poland, for example, the transition is virtually complete, with ownership and investment patterns, legal structures, and journalistic practices mirroring those of their Western European neighbors. The quality of Central Europe's media has also improved, with more professional coverage of economics, local business activity, government spending, and corruption.

This transition, 10 years of often rapid and deep change, is instructive for other countries in the south and east of Europe—and indeed across the world—that share many of the same characteristics and face many of the same problems that the Central Europeans faced in enhancing the quality and economic survivability of their media companies. To be sure, Central Europe had some advantages that are absent elsewhere. Public sector and legal reforms, economic restructuring, and mass privatization played important roles in the outcome throughout Central Europe. Most of the countries also benefited from determinedly democratic political leadership that was committed to European integration.

However, close examination of the history of the news media in Central Europe suggests that the news media themselves—their managers, owners, and enterprising editors and journalists—played at least as important a part in this story as did the public authorities. Indeed, high-quality daily newspapers like *Gazeta Wyborcza* and *Rzeczpospolita* in Poland, *Népszabadság* in Hungary, and *Mlada fronta DNES* in the Czech Republic underwent a major process of internal change and re-invention. Each of these papers received help from foreign investors, and each of these newspapers illustrates the importance of good management and independent sources of finance as a key component of the process of creating independent media.

The importance of good management and business skills to this transition has become one of the mantras of the people who lived through it. Tatiana Repkova, who established and ran a business weekly in the early years of Slovakia's transition and is now editor and publisher of *Pravda*, a major Slovak daily, saw that the skills she learned were in demand in Russia, Ukraine, and points beyond. Between publishing assignments she agreed to share her knowledge through seminars managed by the World Bank Institute, the World Association of Newspapers, the Reuters Foundation, and other organizations. As she witnessed the hunger for this knowledge, she decided to record it in a massive bible for newspaper managers in emerging democracies. As she says in the introduction to this 468-page blow-by-blow manual (Repkova 2001, p. xii): "Leadership and self-determination cannot be imported. Know-how can."

One of the key lessons that managers have to learn is how to function in the context of the sometimes volatile economies of developing and transition countries. The year 2000 was the first in the past decade when all the former Warsaw Pact countries experienced positive growth. During the first decade of the transition all the countries in the region experienced traumatic changes and dislocations. While Poland's economy made the fastest turnaround and returned to a growth path in 1992, the Czech Republic and Hungary suffered double-digit declines in 1991 and took two years longer to begin their recovery.

During this period of change many companies in the news business failed, and those that survived endured long periods of decline. The collapse of newspaper readership was particularly dramatic, and resulted from a relative increase in newspaper prices, a decline in readers' purchasing power, and a shift toward television. The increased prices of newspapers—once a virtually free commodity in centrally planned economies where people had little else to buy—accounts for much of this decline. Newspapers, in particular, relied heavily on newsstand and subscription sales. The absence of developed advertising markets meant they had few alternatives to raising cover prices for producing revenue. In Poland, one of the stars of the transition, newspaper readership has dropped steadily and fell 73 percent between 1996 and 2000 (figure 12.5).

Individuals who managed to hang on as employees in the news business and those who joined it endured many personal hardships before finding their footing in the new environment. Yet the handful of success stories in some of the more prodigious reformers was enough to convince both local and international investors that the media business had a future. In much of the region foreign investors were a major element in the turnaround and in helping the news media reform their operations, develop strong management structures, and stabilize their independence from

Figure 12.5. Percentage Change in Daily Newspaper Circulation, Selected Central European Countries, 1996–2000

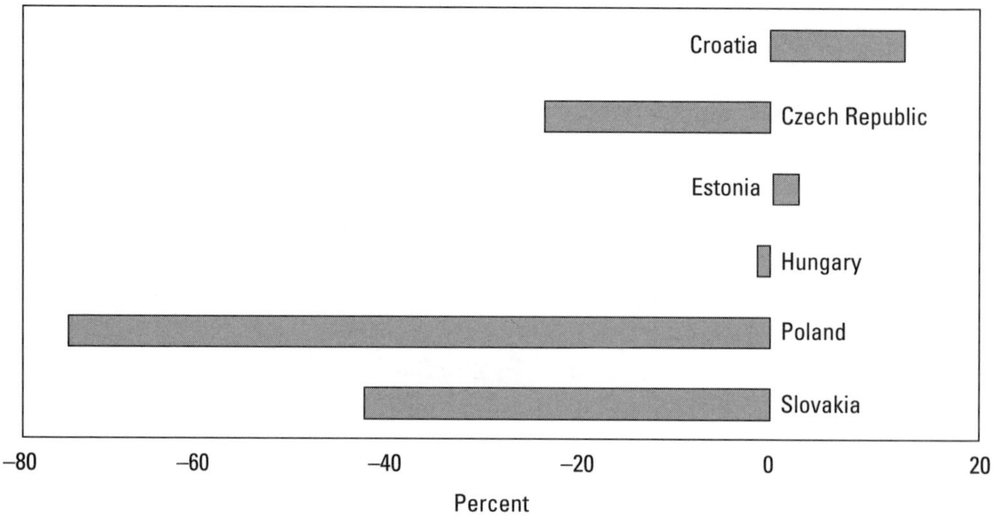

Source: World Association of Newspapers (2001).

their previous masters. According to Repkova (2001, p. 9): "In formerly communist countries media censorship as the main constraint to freedom of speech has been replaced, largely, by economic pressure. . . . For independence, this is a good thing, although it is not always understood that way."

Foreign investors came to believe that Central Europe would soon offer the same kind of returns on investment that they can find in Western Europe. Throughout the 1990s Sweden's Bonnier Group invested in a variety of dailies and periodicals in Estonia, Latvia, Lithuania, and Poland. Schibsted ASA of Norway bought properties in Estonia, and Ringier AG of Switzerland invested in a number of business and economics weeklies and monthlies such as *Profit* and *T´yden* (The Week) in the Czech Republic, *Capital and Success* in Romania, and *Profit* in Slovakia. Bertelsmann AG also made forays into the region, taking interests in daily newspapers and magazines in Hungary, Poland, Romania, and Slovakia. In 1996 the publisher of *Westdeutsche Allgemeine Zeitung,* the large German daily, created controversy by buying out close to 80 percent of the total print circulation in Bulgaria, including the country's two best-selling tabloids, *Trud* (Labor) and 24 *Chasa* (24 Hours).

While foreign investors are important, Tarmu Tammerk, managing director of the Estonian Newspaper Association, worries about the possibility that the media will end up in too few hands to create healthy competition. "Plurality, which was so hard won, is still very fragile," he said in an interview. "In Estonia, we have markets where radio, television, the weekly paper, the morning paper and the evening paper are all from the same group. It's very easy to manipulate the political agenda in such a situation." Yet he still thinks the overall effect has been positive. When the Bonnier Group's *Äripäev* (Business Day) started practicing a code of ethics that forbade its journalists from taking payments in exchange for positive coverage of business groups, it created a new model for the rest of the industry to follow, and the newspaper association adopted similar rules in 1999. "Self-regulation is starting to happen," says Tammerk, "and these foreigners have played a role in helping people realize that this self-regulation is different from self-censorship."

Poland's 1991 decision to grant the government newspaper *Rzeczpospolita* its editorial, and eventually financial, independence is an example of how decisions made at a political level can launch a process of positive change that benefits both the media industry and society at large. The newspaper, which was founded in the 1920s and was passed around among political parties and regimes throughout its history, ended the 1980s as the newspaper of Poland's embattled martial law government. Like newspapers throughout the communist world it depended heavily on the regime's financial and political support. While some figures in the new Solidarity government that came into power in September 1989 would have been quite happy to have a mouthpiece to spout the government line, Prime Minister Tadeusz Mazowiecki had another vision: an independent press that would usher Poland into the modern world.

The first months of that new regime proved brutal for *Rzeczpospolita*. Deprived of its government budget line and thrust into a failing economy, the newspaper's management had to scramble to save the paper from collapse. For a while journalists were given part of their salaries in newspapers, which some sold after work at the central station and other high-traffic areas of Warsaw. Soon, however, the tide began to turn. Within months of the paper's official independence in 1991 a foreign investor, France's Hersant newspaper group, bought 49 percent of the company and helped it upgrade its technology and printing plants.

Recognizing that Poland's new economy would create a demand for information about stock markets, banking reforms, and new legislation, *Rzeczpospolita's* new managers got themselves trained and set out to create a high-quality, fact-based newspaper financed through circulation sales and advertising. The paper expanded and improved its business and economics coverage, creating the now famous "green pages" chronicling Poland's economic transformation. The paper helped explain the mass privatization program to regular Poles, millions of whom suddenly found themselves as shareholders. It reached for Poland's new decisionmakers, making the paper a must-read for the richest and most educated in Poland. This also happened to be just the audience that the country's fledgling advertisers were trying to reach. By the end of 1990s, according to newspaper managers, the paper's business pages and large, high-quality business audience generated more than half its advertising income.

Figure 12.6. Advertising Expenditure Growth, Selected Central European Countries, 1994–2000
(index, 1994 = 100)

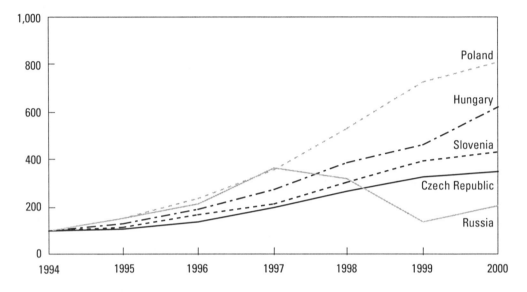

Source: World Association of Newspapers (2001).

Even though newspaper circulation declined dramatically during the transition, the birth of an advertising industry and market helped offset this decline (figure 12.6), and news media companies played an important role in stimulating demand for advertising among the new private sector players in the economy. Those managers of news media companies who learned how to exploit this new source of revenue were the ones who managed to survive the transition.

Russia: A Flowering and a Downturn

Nowhere has this link to the surrounding economic conditions—and the ups and downs of a rocky economic transition process—been more starkly illustrated than in Russia. While Russia experienced an extraordinary flowering of media freedom and openness in the first two years of the 1990s after the fall of the Soviet Union, much of this new media culture was to encounter the bleak realities of the economic downturn that was to follow. That downturn—per capita income fell by more than 50 percent over a decade—led to conditions under which much of the media fell into the hands of new highly politicized sponsors, both public and private, who have used the media for their own narrow ends.

Russia's economic transition, traumatic as it was, was not the most turbulent in the region. Civil war in the Balkans, the Caucasus, and Central Asia created economic conditions immeasurably worse in those corners of the former Soviet empire. Between 1990 and 1999 Russia experienced an average annual decline in GDP of 6.1 percent, with growing inequalities between rich and poor and large regional pockets of abject poverty (World Bank 2001b). Georgia and Ukraine experienced an even more severe deterioration: by the end of 1994 Georgia's economy had fallen to a mere 20 percent of what it had been worth five years earlier.

The Russian story, however, had a major influence on the development of the media in other former centrally planned economies, and shows the importance not only of the legal and institutional framework in which the media operate, but of the business skills and management acumen of the people who run media organizations. Instead of seeking or being forced to survive in the open market, most Russian media sought both to become highly independent editorially, yet continued to survive through payments from public authorities or business sponsors. This was a formula for failure. Not only have the payments from government authorities been too small to assure the creation of modern media companies, but the media's continued dependence on partisan sponsors has done little to create high-quality journalism or to convince readers of the value of the media in the new post-Soviet environment. One analyst of Russian media patterns, Ellen Mickiewicz, Director of the DeWitt Wallace Center at Duke University, found that typical readers have adjusted permanently to these distortions. Russian readers, she said in an interview in August 2002, have little hierarchy of accuracy and reliability, and hold to an understanding that "information isn't in and of itself a stable commodity." From this vantage point, they look at media output as a multiplicity of slanted reports, offering in combination a mosaic that consumers can sort out for themselves.

The problems in Russia have their origins in the old Soviet system, where newspapers were the gears of a well-oiled propaganda machine. The national dailies' circulations were huge—*Trud* printed 11 million copies a day—and the media companies were provided with their every wish, from offices to printing plants. When the Soviet Union collapsed, Russian media companies—reluctant to endure the kind of decline and uncertainty that many of their Central European neighbors had seen—continued to seek support from public authorities and never weaned themselves from these handouts.

Today regional governments still allocate a significant slice of their budgets to mass media, often showered on those broadcasters or newspapers that toe the line for local government bigwigs. These subsidies, while not enormous in monetary terms, can cause major problems for independent competitors, who have to survive without the financial or political collaboration of the local government. Such competitors also find it hard to compete for advertisers against subsidized rivals who are able to cover part of their costs with government funds, and can thus offer lower rates to advertisers.

Russia's first generation of independent media companies provides a memorable lesson about the difficulties of maintaining financial and political independence. Indeed, media companies that did not become dependent on political authorities fell into the hands of the vast financial and business empires that emerged in Russia in the 1990s. By the mid-1990s media ownership was concentrated in the hands of a group of influential industrialists who, rather than trying to run high-quality media companies that survived on media activities, sought to influence Russia's politics. Chief among these were Boris Berezovsky and Vladimir Gusinsky, both of whom later drew the wrath of the Kremlin and faced a barrage of criminal charges related to their business activities and practices.

The persecution of these two most famous oligarchs has done little to reassure media analysts or international press organizations that Russia is on the path to building independent media. Indeed, the uneven application of the law against certain individuals only deepens fears that Russia's media market is still up for grabs by the most well-connected bidder.

"It is no exaggeration to say that virtually every Moscow newspaper survives on cash 'infusions' from shareholders or covert sponsors," writes Belin, an expert on Russian media issues at Oxford University (Belin 2001). In reference to a recent decision to liquidate TV-6, which ran into trouble with its part owner, the big energy conglomerate LUKoil, she notes that laws are being used to go after those media that do not conform to the ruling elite's political views (see also Zassoursky 2001).

Building a successful news media company in Russia's tumultuous economic and legal environment would test the management skills of even the most brilliant entrepreneurs, but Russian media managers say they were woefully unprepared for the challenges that confronted them. Newspaper executives in Russia are usually former journalists, and few have commercial experience. The publisher, which in most successful media companies is a chief operating officer who makes the major business decisions and oversees the major strategic directions of the newspaper, in Russia is often involved in day-to-day editorial management. Strategic planning, budget management, and the development of revenue-raising activities often take a back seat to deciding what will be on page one.

Russia's economic ups and downs have made the process of establishing a steady revenue flow all the more difficult, and the severe downturn of the advertising market after the 1998 financial crisis only made things worse. Other distortions in the market include bogus tax inspections, artificial limits on the amount of newspaper space or air time that can be devoted to advertising, libel actions, and subsidies to government favorites.

Yet many Russian media managers say the country is slowly emerging from the most difficult phase of its transition and will soon be more like Poland or the former Democratic Republic of Germany. Establishing a steadier economy will be crucial, along with a new capacity to build a financial base derived from private advertising rather than government largesse or subsidies from business moguls with political aspirations.

When Economic Problems Are Political

In Bratislava, the newspaper SME faced what was perhaps a more circuitous route to financial independence, but it arrived nonetheless. Like other start-up news companies it faced a host of economic challenges, but a hostile government had engineered many of these. The newspaper's ability to survive these ordeals only underscores the need for managers to have the business acumen to succeed in an environment that may harbor a mix of threats ranging from currency devaluation to political bullying.

Launched in 1948, the paper was charged "to fulfill the tasks drafted in the resolutions of the party and state organs"—hardly a promising charter for a newspaper that would eventually become a popular and truly independent voice in Slovakia. In 1989 the *Smena*, as it was then called (the name translates loosely to "The Shift") was subject to the unstoppable pressures for change that were sweeping through the communist state of Czechoslovakia. Young, relatively open journalists staffed the paper, and its appeal to young people in Bratislava reflected this emphasis. It carried an unexpected variety of features, not necessarily opposition stories, but articles that widened the lens of readers well beyond the confines of Communist Party dogma and information, for example, stories on Sigmund Freud or the Slovak Pen Club.

As Czechoslovakia's Velvet Revolution unfolded, the paper published more stories on pressures for reforms and the prospect that these would eventually succeed. Its readership grew, with circulation swelling to 170,000 copies a day in 1990 from about 100,000 the year before. Meanwhile, economic liberalization laid the foundation for a viable advertising sector.

The divorce of the Czech and Slovak republics in 1992 left the paper in a thorny relationship with the head of the newborn nation, whom the paper had often criticized. A registration problem provided the pretext for shutting down the paper and declaring the company that ran it "nonexistent." A new paper was then hatched, playing off the move against *Smena*. It's name, SME, means, "We exist, we are."

The Juventus Company established the new paper with a controlling investment from the First Slovak Investment Company. High enthusiasm and a level of improvisation that bordered on chaos marked its early days. Losses mounted, and for a time were covered by the Slovak Investment Company. *Smena*, meanwhile, continued to publish under increasing financial pressures, and eventually SME took over the paper.

Meanwhile, the government continued to aim its sights at the SME organization, and succeeded in disrupting its arrangement with a local printing press. The government's dislike of the group may well have provided the fledgling paper with a good part of its marketing strategy. People were naturally quite interested in a news organization that had kindled such robust disapproval in the statehouse. Readership tended to rise whenever the repressive regime sallied forth with a new series of actions against it. At the same time the paper began negotiating with the Media Development Loan Fund, a Soros-backed entity helping independent newspapers out of financial emergencies that were often politically induced, and thus did not reflect the news organization's actual economic prospects.

The Media Development Loan Fund always insisted that borrowers draw up a credible business plan, which a SME editor later said "was almost as valuable as the loan itself." Following the loan agreement, finalized in 1996, the company negotiated the purchase of a second-hand press from a German firm for the equivalent of US$270,000.

The company's ownership of a printing press was the foundation for its expansion. The government, meanwhile, barred state companies and agencies from advertising in SME. Alexej Fulmek, SME's editor, wrote about what turned out to be the basis of the paper's survival as an independent new organ (Fulmek 2001, p. 74). "Fortunately a sufficiently strong private sector existed in Slovakia which advertised for commercial purposes rather than political interests," he said. "This meant that the government could not paralyze the financial vitality of SME by denying it official advertising."

The government's heavy-handed policies not only stirred readership interest, but also provided SME with the opportunity to hire talented, young journalists frustrated by working conditions at publications the government had managed to stifle and control. This, in turn, laid the basis for expanding readership, as well as for pushing into other regions and new media.

Color printing and special section formats proved effective in attracting readers and advertisers alike. A twice weekly career insert offered a wealth of job advertisements, along with opportunities for advanced education and training. An automotive section was equally popular.

Critical to the organization's ability to weather an environment of ceaseless political pressure was an adequate economic base deriving from a flow of advertising revenues from private businesses. In places where the private sector is undeveloped or heavily influenced by the state, this formula for survival breaks down.

Replication Problems

Central Europe's success stories are not easily replicated in other parts of the world. African media proprietors can suffer similar levels of political interference, but unlike their counterparts in Central Europe, they have often lacked an adequate base of private advertising flows to attain financial independence. In Malawi, Fumulani launched *Business Watch* and was determined to steer clear of the political rivalries that periodically gripped the country in its early democratic transition. He planned that his publication would focus on business and economic trends, not politics, in principle insulating its revenues from political reprisals that could damage its prospects. However, the first issue, which was based on a study by one of the international financial institutions, made an unflattering comparison between certain economic conditions under the current democratically elected government and those under their president-for-life. Government officials were displeased.

A major bank, then controlled by the state, called to cancel a series of advertisements, Fumulani recalled in an interview. According to Fumulani, "The decision-makers in the bank were scared they'd lose their jobs." While no newspaper wants to depend on state-run companies for its advertising base, *Business Watch* had little choice. A tobacco firm had closed down, along with the country's largest clothing manufacturer. "The biggest advertiser here is the government," Fumulani concluded, and without that, his publication did not have much of a future.

Unlike SME in Slovakia, the independent publication in Malawi also faced constraints outside the politically motivated economic pressures. Malawi's adult illiteracy rate of 41 percent put much of the population beyond the magazine's reach; deteriorating roads hampered distribution outside Blantyre, the commercial and publishing center; and a per capita annual income of US$170 made even a modest newsstand price exorbitant. "It was considered very expensive at fifty kwacha," said Fumulani. "People in the street could not buy it."

Other African editors say that a less active civil society can also impede growth. Iraki Kibiriti, founder of Nairobi-based *Enterprise Africa*, an English-language, pan-African magazine on business, complains of a "civic disengagement" afflicting many African audiences. "When people feel that what is happening outside their door is none of their business," publishers find themselves working in a difficult environment, said Kibiriti in an interview.

Exploiting a New Media Opening

Yet some media under the watchful eye of the state in developing countries do manage to find ways to conduct their business. One of the world's more interesting media evolutions has occurred in Malaysia, an Asian tiger economy still facing some challenges related to the 1997 financial crisis in the region, and still operating under sweeping state controls on the media. The government enforces a law barring "malicious" news and permitting the government to shutter "subversive" publications. All news publications must be licensed annually. The country's Sedition Act and Internal Security Act further restrict the news media's criticism of government policies.

Contrasted against these various impediments to a free and functional press, the new media platforms of online services and the Internet enjoy a highly protected status in Malaysia, which sees itself emerging as a high-tech power in the coming decade, and therefore wants to avoid ensnaring the emerging information technology sector in the same tangle of constraints that surround the mainstream news media.

Steven Gan, a pioneering journalist who often found himself at loggerheads with the government, launched *Malaysiakini,* an Internet newspaper, in late 1999, and has succeeded in keeping it afloat since then with a readership of between 120,000 and 150,000. Bringing in some seed money from the Southeast Asian Press Alliance, Gan found that *Malaysiakini* had attracted 100,000 readers after 18 months of operation, five times the 20,000 he had hoped to draw. Meanwhile the paper lined up private advertising covering 50 percent of its operating costs.

Malaysiakini's business strategy is tailored to the economic and political realities in Malaysia, where a comparatively vibrant advertising base exists, and where audiences were curious to read online what was missing in the mainstream media. Most crucial was the opening created by the government's divergent policies governing old media and new media. "The government has promised not to censure the Internet while keeping tight controls over the traditional media," Gan said in an interview. "We're exploiting that loophole."

By late 2001 other economic difficulties were in evidence, however. A tumbling Internet economy worldwide, plus a dragging economy in the United States, cut deeply into advertising, which covered only 20 percent of *Malaysiakini's* operating costs. The upshot was a revised business plan that envisions a diversity of revenue sources. High-tech wizards at the company offered software writing services to other companies; analytically-minded journalists began to offer political consulting services; and rather than offer all material in the newspaper for free, *Malaysiakini* has devised a formula for providing news stories for free, while requiring a subscription for opinion columns and archives. A survey showed that 70 percent of the readers were willing to pay for the service. "To survive you have to turn *Malaysiakini* into a proper business entity," Gan added.

Accessing Information and Creating Information Markets

The experiences of developing and transition countries suggest that failure to stabilize the economic standing of the news media is at the root of many of the media's problems that international organizations and bilateral donors say they want to address. The record in some countries suggests that too much time and effort is being spent in training journalists while ignoring the skills of the people who ensure that journalists are paid decent salaries and operate in an environment free of political meddling or corrupt business practices. At the same time, the experience of Central Europe suggests that an aggressive agenda of public sector and economic reform—fully mindful of the needs and demands of the news media—is just as important to the business prospects of the media as direct aid.

Those countries that have made the fastest progress—such as the rapid reformers in Central and Eastern Europe—have made the creation of an information market and effective news media an integral part of the public sector and economic reform agenda. Not only have these countries insisted that the media be privatized and taken off the budgets of national and regional authorities, they have pursued economic and regulatory policies that have tried to create a environment in which the media business—and an information-based economic system—can take hold. They have also learned to live with criticism against public authorities, recognizing that such criticism is in itself one of the ways that governments adjust their policies and correct their mistakes. By helping to create barriers to corruption and expose the misuse of public funds, the media can have an important impact on a country's development process (see, for example, Sen 1999). "In the anti-corruption fight, the press has been more successful than the judicial system," says Dumitry Sandu, a sociologist at the University of Bucharest, speaking about Romania's reform process and attempts to improve its governance systems (interview with Mark Nelson, Bucharest, June 26, 1999).

The media's inability to survive economically often has its roots in overly regulated or inefficient information policies of governments and other public authorities. Journalists who are competing for access to news demand quick, open access to information. The information market develops rapidly in countries where there is easy access to public records, where regulations require disclosure without delay, and where public access to a wide range of records is both guaranteed by the constitution and reiterated in individual laws and regulations. Laws that allow public officials to delay the release of information "for review" or for other bureaucratic purposes not only reduce the benefits of a more open and honest conduct of public business, but impede the ability of the media to survive as enterprises. Countries that restrict access to information increase its costs, not only to the media by forcing them to spend more time and energy to collect it, but also to the economy as a whole, resulting in an inefficient allocation of resources and delaying the countries' development of a modern, knowledge-based economic system. (For a discussion of the media's role in fighting corruption and the costs of corruption in developing economies see Kaufmann, Kray, and Zoido-Lobatán 1999).

Countries are often quite ready to address the obvious problems they see in the media, assuming that errors, distortions, and exaggerations are due to their poorly trained journalists. Few are willing to delve deeper into the problem to examine the distorted legal and economic environment that produces weak media companies and unprofessional journalism.

Open access to information helps create competition in the information economy and a culture of truth in reporting, making it harder for journalists or others to make false or inflammatory charges and harder for criminals or cheats to deny their misdeeds. When information is not readily available and is difficult to verify, journalists are virtually free to make unsubstantiated claims. Such information is close to worthless and drives down the value of all information in the economy. When information can be easily verified, however, readers and employers can sanction journalists who make mistakes or who fail in their professional duties. In such an environment editors start to demand that their journalists produce records rather than rumors, details rather than opinions. Such information becomes highly valuable, and the trade in that information forms one of the cornerstones of the information and knowledge economy.

Many media professionals have linked the strength and profitability of news organizations—and the quality of journalism—to the quality of information laws that assure access by news professionals. In Florida, for example, robust legislation known as the sunshine laws guarantees journalists and members of the public broad-ranging access to almost all state and local government documents, databases, and meetings of public officials. These laws have helped to create one of the most vigorous, professional, and profitable journalistic cultures in the United States. In addition, many Florida newspapers, such as the *St. Petersburg Times,* the *Miami Herald,* and the *Orlando Sentinel,* have a low tolerance of errors by their staff, publishing corrections prominently and quickly firing journalists for repeated mistakes or lapses of judgment.

Countries and international organizations can play a role in laying the groundwork for this sort of information culture that will in turn strengthen the ability of the media to develop themselves as businesses. A working information economy requires multiple layers of professionals in various types of news media who collect, make sense of, and quickly repackage information in ways that the people who need it can use it. Nearly every law and regulation that comes into the public domain needs to be viewed in the context of such an economy. Indeed, public information needs to be part of the process of discussing laws and regulations before they are put into law, a process that will help prevent secrecy from creeping into the picture and crimping the media's ability to develop themselves as major brokers of news and timely information.

In addition to helping countries understand and implement such policies of openness and transparency, the industrial countries and the international donor community can also help stabilize the news media by focusing on programs to improve the management skills of news media executives, financial managers, and others involved in securing the financial sustainability of the media. Many countries have little infrastructure for such training: most journalism schools in the developing world focus on journalistic skills, that is, reporting and writing. Few developing countries have media business consultants who can advise media companies on their media strategies. A program now being implemented by the World Bank Institute in Russia, supported by the Canadian International Development Agency, seeks to create a network of media business consultants to work with newspapers in the major regions of Russia outside Moscow. Other organizations, such as Media Development Loan Fund, help news organizations develop viable business plans and finance these plans in a normal, business-oriented way.

Such approaches lie at the heart of the work of the World Association of Newspapers, which tries to use its worldwide network of newspaper executives as a resource for training programs in developing and transition countries. The U.S.-supported Internews organization has likewise had a major impact on improving the management skills of executives in the television industry, in particular, in the Russian regions. Such programs need to focus on the nuts and bolts of running high-quality, information-based businesses, recognizing the particular role that independent media play in countries' economic and political systems.

Finally, countries from Albania to Zambia are beginning to recognize the importance to their economic future of developing more knowledge-based economic systems. They want to find ways to develop the incentives, the policies, the education systems, and the technical expertise that will allow them to take advantage of the enormous changes wrought by the rapid spread of communications and information technologies. Such countries need to understand that focusing on creating free and professional media—and learning to live with criticism—is a good place to start.

References

Belin, Laura. 2001. "Verdict against TV-6 Is Latest Warning to Opposition Media." *Russian Political Weekly* 1(25), October 15. Available online: http://www.rferl.org/rpw/2002/10/25-151001.html.

Freedom House. 2000. *Censor Dot com: The Internet and Press Freedom: 2000.* New York.

Fulmek, Alexej. 2001. "A Manual for Survival: A Case Study of the Slovak Opposition Newspaper SME." Media Manual Series. Prague: Media Development Loan Fund.

Kaufmann, Daniel, Aart Kray, and Pablo Zoido-Lobatán. 1999. "Governance Matters." Policy Research Working Paper. World Bank, Washington, D.C.

Norris, Pippa. 2001. *Digital Divide: Civic Engagement, Information Poverty, and the Internet Worldwide.* Cambridge, U.K.: Cambridge University Press.

Repkova, Tatiana. 2001. *New Times: Making a Professional Newspaper in an Emerging Democracy.* Paris: World Association of Newspapers.

Sen, Amartya. 1999. *Development as Freedom.* New York: Alfred A. Knopf.

World Association of Newspapers. 2001. *World Press Trends 2001.* Paris.

World Bank. 2001a. *Global Economic Prospects.* Washington, D.C.

———. 2001b. *World Development Indicators.* Washington, D.C.

Zassoursky, Ivan. 2001. "Russia Media in the Nineties: Driving Factors of Change, Actors, Strategies and the Results." Available online: http://www.geocities.com/zassoursky/artic.htm.

Part III

WHAT THE MEDIA SAY ABOUT THE MEDIA

13

The Best Profession in the World

Gabriel García Márquez

A Colombian university was asked what aptitude and vocational tests are administered to persons wishing to study journalism. The response was categorical: "Journalists are not artists." These views are, however, fueled precisely by the conviction that print journalism is a literary genre.

Fifty years ago journalism schools were not fashionable. This craft was learned in newsrooms, print shops, run-down corner cafés, and at Friday night parties. Newspapers were produced in a factory-like setting, where the right training and information were provided, and views were generated in a collaborative atmosphere in which integrity was preserved. Journalists formed a tight-knit group. We shared a common life and were so fanatical about the profession that we talked of nothing else. The work itself fostered a group friendship that left little time for one's private life. Although there were no editorial boards in a formal sense, at five o'clock in the afternoon, the entire staff gathered spontaneously to take a break from the tension of the day and to have coffee in any place where there was editorial activity. It was a kind of loose gathering at which there was heated discussion of the topics of each section and where the finishing touches were added to the next morning's edition. Persons who did not learn in these 24-hour roving academies of fervent debate or those who became bored with all the talking that took place there were those who wanted or believed themselves to be journalists, but in reality were not.

At that time, journalism fell into three broad categories: news, feature stories, and editorials. The section requiring the greatest finesse and carrying the greatest prestige

Extract from remarks by Colombian journalist and writer, Gabriel García Márquez, winner of the Nobel Prize for Literature and president of the Foundation for a New Approach to Journalism in Ibero-America (Fundación para un Nuevo Periodismo Iberoamericano), to the 52nd Assembly of the Inter-American Press Association in Los Angeles, October 7, 1996. Reprinted with permission of the Foundation for a New Approach to Journalism in Ibero-America.

was the editorial section. The reporter's job was the one that was the most undervalued, since it implied that the person doing it was a novice who had been relegated to menial tasks. Both time and the profession have demonstrated that the nervous system of journalism operates in a counterclockwise fashion; to wit: at age 19 I was the worst student in law school and began my career as a member of the editorial staff. Gradually, by dint of hard work, I made my way up, working in different sections, until I became a plain old reporter.

The practice of this profession required a broad cultural background, which was provided by the work environment itself. Reading was a supplementary job requirement. Persons who are self-taught are usually avid and quick learners. This is particularly true of persons of my era, inasmuch as we wanted to continue to pave the way for the advancement of the best profession in the world, as we ourselves called it. Alberto Lleras Camargo, a perennial journalist who was, on two occasions, president of Colombia, was not even a high school graduate.

The establishment of schools of journalism later on was the result of a reaction in academic circles to the fact that the profession lacked scholastic backing. At the moment, this does not apply to the print media only, but to all areas of the media that have been or will be invented.

However, in a bid to expand, even the humble name assigned to the profession since its beginnings in the 15th century has been abandoned. It is no longer called journalism, but rather communication sciences or mass communications. Generally speaking, the results have not been encouraging. Students who graduate from academic institutions with unrealistically high expectations, with their lives ahead of them, seem to be out of touch with reality and the main problems of life in the real world, and attach greater importance to self-promotion than to the profession and innate ability. This is particularly true with respect to two key attributes: creativity and experience.

The majority of students enter the profession with obvious deficiencies: they have serious problems with grammar and spelling and do not have an instinctive grasp of the material they read. Some take pride in the fact that they can read a secret document upside down on the desk of a minister, that they can tape casual conversations without informing the speaker, or that they can publicize a conversation that they agreed beforehand to treat as confidential. What is most disturbing is that these ethical breaches are based on a *risqué* view of the profession, one that has been consciously adopted and is proudly rooted in the sacrosanct importance attached to being the first to know something at any price and above all else. The notion that the best news is not always the news that is obtained first, but very often is the news that is best presented, means nothing to them. Some of these persons, aware of their deficiencies, feel that they have been cheated by their universities and do not mince words when blaming their teachers for failing to instill in them the virtues that are now demanded of them, particularly curiosity regarding life itself.

Clearly, this is a criticism that can be leveled at education in general, which has been corrupted by the plethora of schools that persist in the perverted practice of providing information rather than training. However, in the specific case of journalism, this seems to be compounded by the inability of the profession to evolve at the same pace as the tools of the trade, and by the fact that journalists are getting mired in the labyrinth created by technology as it hurtles forward. In other words, there is fierce competition among companies to acquire modern tools while they have been slow to train their staff and adopt the mechanisms that fostered team spirit in the past. Newsrooms have become aseptic laboratories where people toil in isolation, places where it seems easier to communicate via cyberspace than by touching the hearts of readers. Dehumanization is spreading at an alarming pace.

It is not easy to understand how technology, in all its glory, and communications, which takes place at lightning speed, things that we all hankered after in our time, have managed to hasten and exacerbate the agony associated with closing time. Beginners complain that editors give them three hours to complete a task that really cannot be done in fewer than six, that they ask them for material for two columns and then at the last minute give them only half a column, and that in the chaos of closing time no one has the time or the inclination to provide them with an explanation, let alone a word of consolation. "They don't even scold us," said a novice reporter who was anxious to receive direct feedback from his bosses. Silence reigns: the editor who was a compassionate sage in times gone by barely has the energy or the time to keep up with the punishing pace imposed by technology.

In my view, it is the haste and restriction in terms of space that have reduced the stature of reporting, which we always considered to be the most prestigious genre, but also the one that requires more time, more research, more reflection, and superb writing skills. Reporting is, in reality, a meticulous and accurate reconstruction of facts. In other words, it is the news in its entirety, as events actually occurred, presented in a way to make the reader feel as though he actually witnessed them.

Before the invention of teletypewriters and telexes, someone in the field of radiocommunications with a fanatical devotion to the profession quickly captured the world news amidst the cacophony of the air waves, and a scholarly editor prepared it complete with details and background information, in a manner akin to the reconstruction of the entire skeleton of a dinosaur from a single vertebra. Only the interpretation of the news was off-limits, since this was considered to be the sacred preserve of the editor-in-chief, whose editorials were presumed to have been written by him, although this was not the case. In addition, the penmanship was almost always famous for its flourish. Renowned editors-in-chief had personal linotypists whose job was to decipher this handwriting.

One significant improvement made in the past 50 years is that the news and reports are now accompanied by comments and opinions, and background information is used to enrich editorials. However, this does not seem to have achieved the best results, since this profession has never seemed more dangerous than it does now. The excessive use of quotation marks in statements, either false or true, provides an opening for innocent or deliberate mistakes, malicious distortions, and venomous misrepresentations, which give the news the force of a deadly weapon. Quotations from sources that are entirely credible, from persons who are generally well-informed, from senior officials who request anonymity, or from observers who know everything but are never seen, make it possible for all kinds of offenses to go unpunished. The culprit erects a fortress around himself by citing his right to withhold his source, without asking himself whether he is not allowing himself to be easily exploited by that source who, in transmitting the information to him, packaged it in the manner that best suited him. I think that a bad journalist believes that he depends on his source for his livelihood, especially if it is official, and for this reason considers it to be sacrosanct, agrees with it, protects it, and ends up entering into a perilous relationship of complicity with it, which even leads him to look askance at other sources.

Perhaps this may sound too anecdotal, but I think that there is another major culprit in this process: the recorder. Before its invention, the profession managed quite well with three tools of the trade, which, in truth and in fact, were really one: a notebook, uncompromising integrity, and a pair of ears that we, as reporters, still used to hear what was being said to us. The professional and ethical use of a recorder did not yet exist. People should teach their young colleagues that a cassette is not a substitute for one's memory, but rather, a sophisticated version of the humble notebook that provided very reliable service during the early years of the profession. The recorder hears but does not listen, and, like an electronic parrot, repeats but does not think. It can be depended upon but does not have a heart, and, in the final analysis, its literal rendition is not as reliable as that of the person who pays attention to the live words of his speaker, uses his intelligence to assess them, and judges them based on his ethical standards. While it does, in terms of the radio, offer the enormous advantage of providing an immediate and literal rendition of words, many interviewers do not listen to the responses provided because they are thinking about the next question.

Because of the recorder, excessive and misguided importance is attached to interviews. Radio and television, by their very nature, have transformed them into the supreme genre. However, the print media also seem to share the mistaken view that the voice of the truth is not so much that of the journalist who witnessed an event but of the interviewee who provided a statement. In the case of many newspaper editors, transcription serves as the acid test. They confuse the sound of words, stumble on semantics, trip up on spelling, and become ensnarled in syntax. Perhaps the solution is to return to the modest notebook, so that journalists will use their intellect to edit as they listen and let the recorder occupy its rightful place as an invaluable witness. In any case, the assumption that many ethical and a host of other lapses that debase and bring shame to modern journalism do not always stem from a lack of morality, but also from a lack of professional skill, is a comforting one.

Perhaps the shortcoming of mass communications academic programs is that they teach many things that are useful for the profession, but very little about the profession itself. Clearly, humanities programs should be retained, although they should be made less ambitious and rigid, in order to provide students with the cultural background that they do not receive in high school. However, any kind of education should focus on three key areas: assigning priority to aptitude and vocation; establishing categorically that research is not a specialty of the profession, but rather that all journalists must, by definition, be research oriented; and building awareness that ethical standards cannot be a product of happenstance; like the drone of a bee, they must be the constant companion of every journalist.

The ultimate objective ought to be a return to the basic level of education by offering small group workshops, which provide a critical appreciation of historical experiences, within the original context of public service. In other words, insofar as learning is concerned, the spirit of the 5 p.m. get-togethers should be revived.

I belong to a group of independent journalists, based in Cartagena de Indias, that is trying to achieve this throughout Latin America through a system of experimental, itinerant workshops bearing a rather lofty-sounding name: Foundation for a New Approach to Journalism in Ibero-America (Fundación para un Nuevo Periodismo Iberomericano). This is a pilot program geared toward journalists who are just beginning their careers. They work in one specific area—reporting, editing, radio and television interviews, and a host of others—under the guidance of a veteran of the profession.

In response to a public announcement of the foundation, candidates are proposed by the media organization with which they are working, and that organization covers travel, accommodation, and registration expenses. Persons must be under the age of 30, have a minimum of three years of experience, and demonstrate their aptitude and level of skill in their area of specialty by providing samples of what they consider to be their best and worst work.

The duration of each workshop depends on the availability of the guest instructor, who rarely can spend longer than one week. During workshops, the instructor does not attempt to provide participants with theoretical dogma and academic biases; instead he seeks, during the round table, to strengthen their skills using practical exercises, with a view to sharing with them his experience gained in practicing the profession. The goal is not to teach people how to be journalists, but rather to hone the skills of those who already are, through practical exercises. No final exams or evaluations, diplomas, or certificates of any kind are given. The sifting process will take place through the practical application of their skills.

It is not easy to assess the benefits reaped thus far from a pedagogical standpoint. However, we are heartened by the growing enthusiasm of persons attending the workshops, a phenomenon that is already providing fertile ground for nonconformism and creative rebellion within the media circles of these persons, an approach that is supported, in many instances, by their boards of directors. The mere fact that 20 journalists from different countries met, over a five-day period, to discuss the profession is already a sign of their progress and of the progress of journalism. In the final analysis, we are not proposing a new way of teaching journalism; rather, we are seeking to revive the old way of learning it.

The media would do well to support this rescue mission, either in their newsrooms or through scenarios created for that express purpose, in a manner akin to the air simulators who recreate every incident that can occur in flight so that students can learn how to avoid disaster before they actually encounter it in real life. Journalism is an unappeasable passion that can be assimilated and humanized only through stark confrontation with reality. No one who does not have this in his blood can comprehend its magnetic hold, which is fueled by the unpredictability of life. No one who has not had this experience can begin to grasp the extraordinary excitement stirred by the news, the sheer elation created by the first fruits of an endeavor, and the moral devastation wreaked by failure. No one who was not born for this and is not prepared to live for this and this only can cling to a profession that is so incomprehensible and consuming, where work ends after each news run, with seeming finality, only to start afresh with even greater intensity the very next moment, not granting a moment of peace.

14

The Media and Access to Information in Thailand

Kavi Chongkittavorn

In 1835 Christian missionaries introduced the first printing press to Thailand. At that time interest in publishing was confined mostly to the royal court and foreign missionaries and traders. At least seven English-language newspapers began and ceased publication between 1844 and 1877. One royal publication, *Ratchakitja* (the Royal Gazette*), founded in 1858 by King Mongkut (Rama IV), still exists as the official medium for acts, decrees, ministerial proclamations, and public announcements of newly promulgated laws. Daily newspapers came into their own during King Vajiravudh's reign (Rama VI) in the early 1910s, when 20 dailies, including one Chinese- and two English-language publications, were printed. King Vajiravudh, himself a prolific writer, used several pen names to write newspaper articles commenting on issues of the day.

Today the Thai media are among the freest in Asia, although criticizing the monarchy is taboo. Freedom House's latest survey of the press around the world rated Thailand as one of the six freest countries for the news media in Asia, along with Japan, the Republic of Korea, Mongolia, the Philippines, and Taiwan (China). Freedom House's annual report for 1999 (Freedom House 2000, pp. 31–32) described the condition of the press in Thailand as follows:

> The year started badly with one journalist shot to death after refusing a bribe offer. Yet Thai news media exhibited new openness during the financial chaos in Asia. Because the Asian media had failed to warn of the crisis, the press, particularly in Thailand, was regarded as a necessary element in improving the country's financial position. The new national information act promotes transparency within the government. Lively political and economic news has become routine fare in many newspapers and magazines whose content had traditionally been entertainment news and fiction. The papers have also been investigating the social implications of the economic crisis. Most radio and television are run by the government or the military, and are less apt to follow quickly the print media's new openness.

The Thai case illustrates how changes in laws can begin to change how people act even in societies that are traditionally closed. While an economic crisis was necessary to create the demand for greater openness, the law ensured that once the crisis had abated, people's behavior would change.

Print Media

Thailand's print media are in private hands and are highly competitive. Thailand currently has 21 national dailies in three languages (12 in Thai, 6 in Chinese, and 3 in English), with a combined circulation of 2 million copies per day. After a three-year lull resulting from the 1997 financial crisis, the publishing industry is on the road to recovery assisted by booms in the publishing business. Leading national Thai-language dailies, including *Matichon* and *Krungthep Thurakij,* are popular among well-educated Thais, as are the *Bangkok Post* and *The Nation.* The mass circulation *Thai Rath, Khao Sod,* and *Daily News* have a broader appeal. *Sin Sian Yit Pao* and the *Universal Daily* are the two leading Chinese-language newspapers. Outside Bangkok 320 provincial newspapers are published; however, only three or four provinces sell newspapers every day. In addition to domestic dailies, Thais have access to foreign newspapers that are sold at newsstands and bookstores

More than 14 business newspapers and newsmagazines are on sale every three days or fortnightly. Throughout Thailand more than 200 magazine titles come out weekly, biweekly, monthly, bimonthly, or trimonthly. The period before the 1997 economic crisis is considered the golden days of the Thai media: the number of daily newspapers was double the number in circulation in 2001.

About 3,000 journalists and other media personnel have been laid off since 1997. Twelve newspapers have been forced to shut down for financial reasons, including two English-language papers, the *Asia Times* and the *Thailand Times.* Those who could weather the economic crisis, either because of new investors, new owners, or downsizing, have had to make their newspapers more attractive to readers, who are more choosy than in the past because they can no longer afford to subscribe to more than one newspaper. In addition, with fewer pages to work with because of the high cost of imported newsprint, editors and reporters have had to change their style of writing to maximize the use of space. Journalists have to be retrained as they can no longer follow one particular beat or specialize on a single issue. With few advertising revenues because of the economic crunch, each newspaper has to be creative to ensure its own niche in a tight market.

New media owners and investors are not like their predecessors, who were former journalists, but tend to be politicians or business people. A famous gambler who used to operate a series of illegal gambling dens took over the country's oldest Thai-language newspaper, *Siam Rath.* Before 1997 almost all Thai papers were hostile to the government because publishers, editors, and journalists had had to fight antipress measures and oppression for more than half a century; however, all these papers have now become mainstream papers. Both pro- and antigovernment papers have appeared on the newsstands.

About 300 foreign correspondents, camera operators, and photographers representing 128 news organizations are based in Bangkok. These include representatives of all the major wire agencies, such as Reuters, Agence France Press, and Associated Press, as well as of many other publishers, such as *Asiaweek*, the *Asian Wall Street Journal, Business Asia*, the *Far Eastern Economic Review*, the *Financial Times, The Straits Times*, and *Yomiuri Shimbun*. Apart from print media, the world's broadcasting media organizations are also well represented in Thailand, including the British Broadcasting Corporation, CNN, and Nippon/Hoso/Hykai.

Radio and Television

In 1955 a government enterprise launched Thailand's first television station in Bangkok. Thailand became the first country in Southeast Asia to begin regular television transmissions. Bangkok now has six television stations, all of them government owned and with their own affiliated stations in the provinces; however, the government permits the private sector to run channels 3, 7, and iTV. The government's Public Relations Department runs the National Broadcasting Services of Thailand, which operates Channel 11, whose programs emphasize education and public services. Channel 11 serves as the parent station of eight television station networks in the provinces.

Thailand also has one major cable television network in Bangkok that operates round the clock: the United Broadcasting Company. At the end of last year, iTV started offering 24-hour news. The United Broadcasting Company features popular Western programs, such as HBO, Cinemax, and CNN.

Thai television is mostly commercialized and generally appeals to popular tastes. Each free television channel produces its own programs ranging from news to soap operas. Entertainment broadcasts may be Chinese, Japanese, British, or American, but are usually broadcast with a Thai soundtrack dubbed in.

Thailand has 523 radio stations nationwide, 212 AM stations (38 in Bangkok and 174 in the provinces) and 311 FM stations (40 in Bangkok and 271 in the provinces). The largest operators are the government's Public Relations Department with 145 radio stations, followed by the Royal Thai Army with 128 stations and the Mass Communication Organization of Thailand with 62 stations. AM radio tends to appeal to popular tastes, especially among rural listeners, while FM radio offers more popular music, as well as jazz and classical music, English-language newscasts, and original soundtracks from foreign films shown on local television.

The new 1997 Constitution mandated that all airwaves belong to the public and must be managed by an independent body, the National Broadcasting Commission.

The commission is one of several new bodies created to monitor and regulate the performance of the government to ensure transparency and accountability.

As a whole, Thai journalists and broadcasters view themselves as public watch-dogs; however, two-thirds of the estimated 3,400 journalists and broadcasters still lack media skills and tend to learn their profession on-the-job. Better training in basic reporting, interviewing, and writing is essential to promote press professionalism. Journalists also need to understand and follow a code of ethics. As few receive good salaries, most journalists are not wealthy.

Access to Information

The 1997 Constitution is comprehensive in its approach to protecting freedom of the media, freedom of expression, and access to information (see the appendix for ex-cerpts from various pertinent sections of the Constitution). However, 27 antipress laws that were enacted prior to the adoption of the new Constitution and restrict media freedom are still on the books. These conflict with the new Constitution and must be abolished, but the procedure to get rid of these laws has proceeded at a snail's pace because of bureaucratic red tape and recalcitrance by conservative law-makers, who still think that the media should not be too free. Nevertheless, the gov-ernment must keep some of these laws so that it can monitor the media. In July 1997 the publishers and editors of all the national newspapers decided to set up the Na-tional Press Council, a self-regulating body to enforce press ethics and professional-ism. The public has filed more than 100 complaints with the council in the past three years about such issues as indecent photographs, inflammatory publications, and distortion of the news.

The campaign to enact an information access law started when Anand Panyarachun, a veteran diplomat, was appointed prime minister in 1991. He said the public should have access to government-held information to assess the performance of the government and of government officials. Ironically, his call was based on his own experience, as he had been wrongly accused of being a communist sympathizer because of his role in establishing diplomatic relations between Thailand and Viet-nam in the mid 1970s. He maintained that if the public had access to the Foreign Ministry's records they would learn the truth about his work and performance. De-spite earlier resistance, politicians and officials supported an information act as po-litical reforms gained steam. Public support for the law was high following the bloodshed in May 1992 caused by a military coup, when the state-owned media sanitized news broadcasts about the events. After lengthy public hearings and con-sultations, a compromise draft was agreed on and subsequently passed by Parlia-ment under the government of General Chavalit Yongchaiyudh.

Since the promulgation of the Official Information Act in 1997, more than half a million Thais have made use of it. For the first two years the public was unaware of the new law's existence, what it allowed, and what kind of impact it could have on society, but then several scandals helped publicize it. For example, Sumalee Limpa-ovart spent two-and-a-half years struggling with the administrators of the Kasetsart Experimental School, an experimental school, to find out why her daughter had been denied admission to the school's first grade class. She discovered that the school gave priority to children of privileged families and of donors. After several court battles with the school the Council of Ministers ruled in Sumalee's favor and determined that the school had acted unconstitutionally and in bad faith. The council ordered the school to abolish its discriminatory system. As a result, other state-run demonstrative schools have also done so.

Another example is the 1999 Ministry of Public Health scandal, which involved the procurement of medical supplies worth US$35 million (B 1.4 billion) and led to the resignation of Deputy Public Health Minister Rakkiart Sukthana and two senior officials. Relying on informal tips and information provided by an alliance of nongovernmental organizations and grassroots groups, including rural doctors, the National Counter Corruption Commission was able to investigate illegal procurement networks that jacked up the prices of medical supplies provided to rural health stations. By means of the Official Information Act, advocacy groups and journalists successfully obtained the records of the commission's investigation after several appeals; however, the names of eyewitnesses were blacked out to protect their identities.

With Sumalee's victory, the public began to appreciate the act and increasing numbers of people know that they have the right to access government information. In the past, all official information was considered confidential and not for disclosure except in exceptional circumstances. Now the pendulum has swung the other way and all official information, with minimal exceptions, is considered to be public information. Not only has this eroded the former culture of secrecy, but it also has a number of wider implications, namely:

- It supports all citizens' rights to participate effectively in the government's decisionmaking processes
- It increases government efficiency by allowing public scrutiny of government agencies
- It reduces government corruption by enhancing transparency
- It weakens the long tradition of patron-client relationships that rely on connections and nepotism
- It reduces the possibility of social conflict between citizen groups and government agencies
- It empowers ordinary citizens, especially those in rural areas, because unlike the situation in the past, they will have access to information.

According to the Information Act, some information is not subject to disclosure, especially that pertaining to the monarchy or information that could jeopardize national security, international relations, or the country's economic and financial well-being. Those who want to access information related to the royal family can do so under the category of historical data, which take 75 years to be declassified, with an additional but final extension of 75 years if deemed necessary.

Any citizen can request official information by submitting a simple form. In theory, all requests must be fulfilled within a "reasonable period of time." Failure to do so can result in jail time and fines. This vague time frame has allowed the authorities to stall on responding to requests and has become one of the biggest loopholes in the law. For instance, a business newspaper made a request in October 1998 in relation to paper procurement by the Tobacco Bureau of the Ministry of Finance. The official response took two-and-a-half months. In another case a request to examine an agreement made by the Bank of Thailand in relation to the sale of a state-owned bank took three months to process.

Generally, requests for information are free of charge, even though they can involve thousands of pages of documents, like the recent request by a Ph.D. student researching Thailand's economic crisis who wanted to scrutinize the minutes of Bank of Thailand discussions going back some three decades.

During January–October 2000 a total of 144 complaints and 64 appeals were submitted to the Office of Information Commission (OIC), compared with 124 complaints and 81 appeals in 1999. Approximately 21 percent of the complaints were directed at local government agencies, 13 percent were directed at the Ministry of Education, and 11 percent were directed at the Ministry of Finance. In the case of appeals, 22 percent were filed against the Ministry of Agriculture, 16 percent against the Prime Minister's Office, and 13 percent against the Ministry of Education.

Most complaints concerned officials who refused to respond to requests or provide services. Of the appeals, 56 percent concerned disciplinary investigation documents; 23 percent involved information about current affairs, such as the probe of corruption in the Ministry of Public Heath and asset sales by the Financial Sector Restructuring Authority; and 21 percent concerned information related to concessions, contracts, and meeting reports.

Most cases were filed in Bangkok. Ten cases were filed against the Bangkok Metropolitan Administration and 18 involved municipalities and other local government bodies nationwide. Private citizens were the most frequent users of the access law, followed by government officials and by journalists. Only two politicians made use of the law.

Five of six cases relating to economic and financial matters in 1998-2000 were brought by the *Prachachart Thurajit* newspaper and involved the details of a purchasing contract related to a bid for sales of financial sector debts. The local information disclosure tribunal (one of five such tribunals) ruled that all details had to be disclosed. The tribunal rejected the requests related to the sixth case, which concerned the disclosure of a series of confidential letters written by the Bank of Thailand to the International Monetary Fund.

Barriers to Implementation of the Information Act

The following are some of the problems related to implementation of the Information Act:

- Most people neither understand key elements of the law nor realize their rights. They do not know how to use the law and the procedures to follow to satisfy their demand for access to state information, therefore they cannot exercise their rights.
- Senior officials in government agencies do not understand the act or know how to implement it. They do not consider fulfilling public requests for information to be part of the government's services and view the Information Act as a burden.
- There is a lack of coordination among various ministries, making cross-references almost impossible.
- Members of disclosure tribunals serve on a voluntary basis. This could bias their decisions because they also have other jobs and responsibilities.
- Penalties for noncompliance are insufficient. While those who fail to respond to requests for information face imprisonment for one year and a fine of B 5,000 (US$116), those who disclose information by mistake face the same prison term and a fine of B 20,000 (US$465). This contradiction has discouraged the authorities from taking prompt action, and they prefer to pass requests on to the OIC for further deliberation.
- The 19-member OIC lacks sufficient resources to handle cases submitted by 8,775 state and local agencies.
- No administrative structure is available to support the Information Act.
- The OIC is not independent, but falls under the auspices of the Prime Minister's Office. Responsibility for the OIC should be transferred to Parliament to eliminate opportunities for political interference.

To improve implementation the OIC has prepared a set of guidelines as follows: all state agencies must speed up strict enforcement of the Information Act, all pertinent agencies should allocate enough funds to employ sufficient staff and provide them with the training they need to work with the OIC, ministry representatives to the OIC must work there continuously for at least two years, management of information and document administration must be more systematic and should be consistent nationwide, and promotions of senior officials and the recruitment of new staff should be based on OIC criteria.

This is easier said than done. Despite the guidelines, almost half the state agencies were unable to comply, citing a lack of funds and personnel as the main impediments.

Universities and colleges throughout Thailand are now teaching courses on the Information Act. Workshops are also geared toward Thai journalists to improve their reporting and investigative skills. Most of the articles that won the top journalism prizes awarded by the Thai Journalists Association in the past four decades focused on scandals and corruption revealed by political opponents or whistle-blowers; however, since the Information Act was put in place, investigative reports have gained the top prizes three years in a row (1998-2000). The article that exposed Prime Minister Thaksin Shinawatra's fraudulent asset declaration, which led to his indictment in 2000, won the award for the best report that year. The paper uncovered evidence that Thaksin had illegally hidden US$53 million worth of shares in his telecommunications company through a false stock transfer to one of his maids and a family driver.

Access to Information in the Region

Thailand is the only country in Southeast Asia that has separate legislation on access to information. While the Philippine Constitution guarantees public access to government-held information, discussions among lawmakers, civil society leaders, and journalists about whether a separate information law is needed to promote open and accountable government are ongoing. Indonesia is currently drafting a similar law that Parliament plans to consider in the near future. The Indonesian version is more liberal than the Thai version as it has few limitations, for example, it is applicable to foreigners. Outside Southeast Asia, India promulgated an information law in 2000 and Japan's national information law became effective in April 2001. The Republic of Korea enacted a similar law, the Act on Information Disclosure of and by Public Agencies, in 1996. Nepal has its own draft ready for review by lawmakers. As Nepal and Thailand are both constitutional monarchies, their access laws have many similar features.

The Philippine Center for Investigative Journalism (2001) carried out a comparative study of access to information in eight countries (Cambodia, Indonesia, Malaysia, Myanmar, the Philippines, Singapore, Thailand, and Vietnam). The definition of access to information used in this project is citizens' ability to obtain information in possession of the state. The study surveyed the availability of more than 40 types of public records, such as macroeconomic data, social data (literacy, poverty, infant mortality rates), data on government budgets and contracts, information about parliamentary meetings and inquiries, court proceedings, official investigations, and financial disclosures by officials and companies. Table 14.1 presents the results of the survey.

These preliminary findings indicate that the level of development and access to information are not correlated. The main determinants of access appear to be a democratic and pluralistic polity; a plurality of media ownership; and a culture of

Table 14.1. Availability of Selected Government Records to the Public

Country	Percentage of information not made available to the public
Philippines	11
Cambodia	43
Thailand	18
Singapore	56
Malaysia	38
Vietnam	49
Indonesia	36
Myanmar	56

Source: Philippines Center for Investigative Journalism (2001).

discussion, inquiry, and political participation. For instance, even though Singapore is considered an open society, access to certain information is extremely difficult. Records concerning government officials and military personnel and information on nonresidents and noncitizens are difficult to obtain, because such data are deemed confidential. Myanmar ranks the lowest in the region in all categories, while the Philippines ranks the highest, followed by Thailand. Quite a few Thai newspapers, including *Prachachart Thurakit* and *Krungthep Thurakit*, have set up investigative reporting desks. These follow new topics and review old stories to uncover further information. These desks also take the necessary actions for using the Information Act.

Conclusion

While Thailand and the region still have much to do in terms of improving press freedom, Thailand's recent experience gives reason for hope. The people now recognize the importance of freedom of expression and of information for achieving good economic, political, and social outcomes.

Appendix:
Excerpts from Selected Sections of the 1997 Thai Constitution Pertaining to the Rights and Liberties of the People and the Media

Section 37: "A person shall enjoy the liberty of communication by lawful means. The censorship, detention or disclosure of communication between persons including any other act disclosing a statement in the communication between persons shall not be made except by virtue of the provisions of the law specifically enacted for security of the State or maintaining public order or good morals."

Section 38: "A person shall enjoy full liberty to profess a religion, a religious sect or creed, and observe religious precepts or exercise a form of worship in accordance with his or her belief, provided that it is not contrary to his or her civic duties, public order or good morals. In exercising the liberty referred to in paragraph one, a person is protected from any act of the State, which is derogatory to his and her rights or detrimental to his or her due benefits on the grounds of professing a religion, a religious sect or creed or observing religious precepts or exercising a form of worship in accordance with his or her different belief from that of others."

Section 39: "A person shall enjoy the liberty to express his or her opinion, make speeches, write, print, publicize, and make expression by other names. The restriction on liberty under paragraph one shall not be imposed except by virtue of the provisions of the law specifically enacted for the purpose of maintaining the security of the State, safeguarding the rights, liberties, dignity, reputation, family or privacy rights of other person, maintaining public order or good morals or preventing the deterioration of the mind or health of the public. The closure of a publishing house or a radio or television station in deprivation of the liberty under this section shall not be made. The censorship by a competent official of news or articles before their publication in a newspapers, printed matter or radio or televisions broadcasting shall not be made except during the time when the country is in a state of war or armed conflict; provided that it must be made by virtue of the law enacted under the provisions of paragraph two. The owner of a newspaper or other mass media business shall be a Thai national as provided by law. The States as subsidies shall make no grant of money or other properties to private newspapers or the mass media."

Section 40: "Transmission frequencies for radio or television broadcasting and radio telecommunication are national communication resources for public interest. There shall be an independent regulatory body having the duty to distribute the frequencies under paragraph one and supervise radio or television broadcasting and telecommunication business as provided by law. In carrying out the act under paragraph two, regard shall be had to the utmost public benefit at national and local levels in education, culture, State security, and other public interest interests including fair and free competition."

Section 41: "Officials or employees in a private sector undertaking newspaper or radio or television broadcasting businesses shall enjoy their liberties to present news and express their opinions under the constitutional restrictions without the mandate of any State agency, State enterprise or the owners of such businesses, provided that it is not contrary to their profession ethics. Government officials, officials or employees of a State agency or State enterprise engaging in the radio or television broadcasting business enjoy the same liberties as those enjoyed by officials or employees under paragraph one."

Section 58: "A person has the right to access data and public information under the control of governmental organizations, state enterprises or provincial authorities except in the case that the disclosure will affect the security of the state, safety of people or the interest that associates with lose of protection of other persons as states in the law."

References

Freedom House. 2000. *Annual Report*. New York. Available on: http://freedomhouse.org/pfs99/reports.htm.

Philippine Center for Investigative Journalism. 2001. "The Right to Know: Access to Information in Southeast Asia." Philippine Center for Investigative Journalism and the Southeast Asian Press Alliance, Manila.

15

The Media and Development in Bangladesh

Mahfuz Anam

Bangladesh became an independent state only 30 years ago. Following a bitter war of independence from Pakistan in 1971, during which hundreds of thousands of innocent people died, the country adopted a democratic government. A liberal constitution was adopted in 1972 and a general election was held the following year. However, a reversal toward authoritarianism started soon afterwards. One-party rule with complete nationalization of the media was introduced in January 1975, just three years after independence. Further tragedy befell the nation when the founder of the state was brutally murdered along with 22 members of his family. Thus began 16 years of military rule that ended when the government was toppled by civil unrest in December 1991. It is at this time, when democracy was restored and the media were at last given freedom to operate, that Bangladesh's journey toward development began.

Bangladesh's formation and subsequent development highlights some important issues. First, democracy and free media are symbiotic. Democracy promotes freedom of expression, but free media further develop nascent democracies. Thus while some democratization was necessary to liberate the media, over time the media have become stronger, more vibrant, and more of a voice for the people, promoting a more transparent democracy and a government that makes informed choices. Second, Bangladesh is a poor, mostly rural country, while the print media currently focus mostly on urban areas. A large percentage of the population, 48 percent, is illiterate, and illiteracy among women reaches 71 percent (World Bank 2001). While urban areas can support several newspapers, rural areas cannot. Furthermore, the advertising market is nonexistent in rural areas. Notwithstanding a modest circulation, the media play an important role in rural areas. Third, the prevalence of state involvement in business activities has, until recently, affected the role of the media even in urban markets. Fourth, the media can have a stronger impact on economic and political outcomes when they form alliances with other institutions, such as nongovernmental groups or academics.

The restoration of democracy in Bangladesh saw the immediate growth of the media, both in quantitative and qualitative terms. Today about 83 dailies are published, at least officially, in the capital alone. Granted not all of them are of an equal or acceptable standard, nevertheless, about 10 Bengali and five good English-language daily newspapers are regularly published in Dhaka. Several reasonably good dailies are also published in other major cities, including Chittagong, Khulna, Rajshahi, and Sylhet. Officially more than 200 daily newspapers and nearly 500 weeklies are published in Bangladesh; however, whether all these publications still exist and how regularly they are published is unknown. Nevertheless, we can say that following the restoration of democracy newspapers generally grew in number and in quality, significantly improving the standards of print media in Bangladesh.

The most heartening development that Bangladesh has enjoyed since the restoration of democracy is the growth of independence and freedom of the print media. The boldness, the depth, and the frequency with which some of the leading newspapers write about corruption in government and in the private sector, abuse of political power, nepotism, and irregularities in general is something previously unknown in Bangladesh. While investigative journalism has yet to reach the level and maturity of that in older democracies, Bangladesh can take satisfaction in the knowledge that it is firmly moving in the right direction.

Directly related to the greater freedom enjoyed by the print media is the growth of the private advertising market in the last decade and the liberalization of the economy. Even though it has far to go to reach its potential, the break away of advertising from the government's stranglehold has been perhaps the most significant contributory factor to media independence. In the past more than 80 percent of advertisements consisted of government tender notices and related matters. With the nationalization of the economy in the early days of Bangladesh, private advertising was scarce. The media were thus extremely dependent on the government for their survival. All this has changed for urban media. Today most leading newspapers derive 70 to 90 percent of their advertising revenues from the private sector. In addition, another way in which the government controlled newspapers—supplying subsidized, locally produced newsprint—has disappeared, because imports of high-quality imported newsprint, which most of the leading newspapers use, have been liberalized. High-quality newsprint is also now produced domestically in limited quantities. By contrast, rural newspapers are still almost totally dependent on government advertisements, as the private sector is still underdeveloped in rural areas. However these newspapers, mostly weeklies, do not rate highly either in terms of credibility or of impact.

Another recent positive development is the opening of a private satellite television channel (ETV) and two private cable television channels (Channel i and ATN Bangla). A private radio channel is also currently operating in Dhaka. This is the first time that the private sector has been allowed to own electronic media. During the last 30 years government-run television—the BTV channel—had a complete monopoly and provided nothing but undiluted government propaganda. Of the three private channels only ETV has nearly as large a reach as BTV. It is also the only channel permitted to provide its own news service, although it is legally obliged to carry one of the two news bulletins of the government channel free of charge. The two cable channels are not permitted to provide any news service and offer only entertainment programs.

The Media's Role in Exposing Corruption and Upholding Human Rights

The media have helped Bangladesh on the road to good governance by exposing corruption. The first example concerns fraud in the financial sector. In 1991, following the restoration of democracy and the election of a new government, the media started probing the huge financial mess that the previous autocratic regime, in power for nine years, had left behind. Soon after taking office the new government discovered that more than 40 percent of the banking system's total portfolio of loans were "classified," a term used to indicate bad loans. Thus the banks were undisciplined in granting loans, which they did mostly as a result of political and other influence peddling. Corruption flourished. The authorities initiated some disciplinary measures in response to media coverage. As a result, by December 2000 the proportion of nonperforming loans had fallen to 34 percent. By any standard this is still excessive, and the fight against corruption in the financial sector is by no means over.

A significant success of the media was exposing bank directors withdrawing money from their own banks under false names. Until 1985 all banks were government owned, but in 1985, with the aim of promoting the private sector, the previous government started granting permission to set up private banks. In the early 1990s the central bank discovered that some of the leading business houses that came forward to set up banks appeared to have done so to enable the bank directors to take "insider" loans. Investigations of two banks revealed more than 200 false accounts, and the central bank found that bank directors were taking illegal loans under false names. The end result was that 134 bank directors were found to be involved, of which 57 were removed from their posts, 19 went to court and overturned their removal orders, and 58 regularized their loans and were allowed to continue as directors. Investigative journalism by newspapers helped the central bank carry out its investigations and build the requisite public pressure to institute punitive measures and initiate the necessary reforms. Thus the print media can claim to have helped stop the illegal business of insider lending. Eventually the banking law was reformed so that bank directors can borrow only up to 50 percent of the amount they have actually invested.

Another area where relentless media exposure led to necessary reforms was internal corruption in the bank sector. Bribery played havoc in the lending process, and corruption among bank officials was widespread. Media exposure led to a strengthening of the central bank's supervisory role, and oversight teams whose members have been sent abroad for training now visit bank branches across the country to supervise and monitor their work.

Another area where the media unearthed a major financial irregularity was illegal dealing in foreign exchange. This is an informal system of foreign exchange transfers that avoids official channels and deprives the exchequer of much-needed foreign currency.

Over the years the banks' trade unions became influential players in the banking business. They influenced banks' decisionmaking process forcing their management to take particular loan decisions. They also exerted undue influence on bank officials' assignments and promotions, leading to bank officials appeasing union leaders so as to advance their careers. Union leaders occupied large portions of banks' office space and sometimes operated as alternative management. The media played a significant role in curbing the trade unions' influence and bringing some discipline to their behavior.

Overall the media have significantly helped strengthen governance in the financial sector. Without the media's active support and efforts to build public opinion, the central bank could not have carried out the reforms that it did.

The second example of the media's influence concerns the illegal allocation of residential plots. A newspaper report revealed that municipal governments had given out more than 300 residential plots to favorites of the ruling party by flouting all procedures and regulations. The story, first published in a Bangla daily, was later picked up by other newspapers. This resulted in direct intervention by the prime minister, who canceled the allocations in response to media stories. Similarly, stories about the Dhaka City Corporation, the municipal government of the capital city, focused on how parks, children's playgrounds, and city center parking lots were being sold to private developers to build shopping centers. Most of these actions violated the city's master plan and zoning laws, and were being carried out in exchange for bribes or because of political pressure. Photo stories about children's playgrounds being converted to shopping centers in congested parts of old Dhaka halted the construction.

The media have also made an important contribution to environmental issues. The authorities have consistently and deliberately neglected Bangladesh's rivers, especially around Dhaka, the capital. Over time influential people have acquired property along the riverbanks, and through landfills have narrowed the width of rivers. Eventually this problem became so acute that the flow of water became constricted, resulting in Dhaka's main river, the Buriganga, almost drying up. The river was also threatened by huge inflows of untreated waste. The newspapers launched a campaign to save the Buriganga and exposed how corrupt practices had allowed riverbank property to be "sold" to various private companies for commercial construction. In one case the newspapers found that a major government body had encroached about 90 feet into the river to build storage facilities for itself. Legal actions followed the newspaper reports, and the work was temporarily halted. The final outcome has not yet been determined. While continuous coverage of the discharge of polluting effluent into the river has led to greater public awareness about how negligence could lead to an environmental disaster, this has not yet led to any serious efforts to initiate widespread mitigating measures.

Five years ago the *Daily Star* teamed up with the Bangladesh University of Engineering and Technology and the Bangladesh Scouts and launched a program called Urban Agenda as part of their Save Dhaka, Clean Dhaka initiative. The Scouts mobilized the activists, the university got experts involved, and the *Daily Star* provided media support. It all started with a rally of Boy Scouts, Girl Guides, and citizens, who paraded through the city's streets demanding a cleaner city. Each day, under the leadership of the Scouts and local community groups, people started physically cleaning up dirty areas of the city. The media covered their activity. Soon the municipality, which was responsible for this task, started feeling public pressure and approached the group to ask how it could cooperate. As a result, the garbage collection system improved dramatically and citizens became more demanding and were no longer willing to accept shoddy performance by the municipality.

The same group also organized a series of workshops on waste management, public toilets in cities, traffic management, public awareness and prevention of dengue fever, and zoning law enforcement in Dhaka. For each workshop the group brought together experts and representatives of citizen forums active in civic undertakings. Retired university professors, former bureaucrats, specialists, and senior citizens joined the Scouts to build public opinion on these topics.

City traffic was another area that received a great deal of attention from this group, which brought together traffic experts, representatives of all the government agencies involved, civic activists, and members of the business community, whose activities were being hampered by increasing congestion. Alternative plans were drawn up and published in the newspapers to mobilize public opinion behind them. Similar actions followed in the other areas.

The case of arsenic contamination of water in Bangladesh, a concern in both rural and urban areas, provides an example of the broad impact that the media can have. In a stunning and tragic discovery, researchers found that in large areas of Bangladesh the groundwater is contaminated by arsenic. The story first broke in West Bengal, India, in the 1980s. Reports started to filter into Bangladesh that patients from bordering areas were going to Calcutta for treatment. Bangladeshi experts looked into the matter, and in the mid-1990s a group of doctors from Dhaka Community Hospital ascertained that arsenic contamination was indeed widespread. These doctors approached the media, who took up the issue. Estimates indicate that 60 to 75 million people in Bangladesh run the risk of being affected by this contamination.

The print media were the first to draw attention to this issue and to make it into a major cause. Because of the media coverage, both the national government and the international community, including the multilateral agencies, began to pay attention to the issue. Media coverage sensitized policymakers, who initially accused the media of sensationalizing the issue, but later admitted its seriousness and referred to it as a national emergency. The United Nations Children's Fund, the World Health Organization, and the World Bank all responded to the media stories and sent fact-finding missions to Bangladesh. The *Daily Star* was the first newspaper to provide extensive coverage that included maps of the affected areas to highlight the gravity of the situation. In cooperation with the Dhaka Community Hospital, the *Daily Star* organized a media roundtable and brought out a special supplement on the issue. This supplement was a huge help in bringing together all the national and international partners to mitigate the crisis.

The role of the media in safeguarding human rights is noteworthy. Ever since the restoration of democracy the media have recognized human rights as a fundamental issue. They have popularized the notion of people's rights to information and have created opposition to all forms of secrecy and immunity of government officials. Because of the work of the print media, Bangladeshi citizens are far more aware than in the past about their fundamental human rights and the constitutional protection of their rights. Through constant vigilance and reports on cases of infringement of these rights, and by exposing police brutality and repression, the media have caused a significant rise in public awareness of these issues. Of particular importance has been the media focus on police behavior and deaths of those in police custody. They have also supported judicial activism and increased public awareness of the concept of litigation.

The media have supported nongovernmental organizations working to strengthen human rights and waging a campaign against gender discrimination and religious extremism, and have opposed violence against women and children. The media's coverage of trafficking in children and women has been significant. In several cases journalists worked closely with nongovernment organizations and helped recover or resettle victims of trafficking. Generally speaking, awareness of gender issues is greater than in the past.

Most international reports about the human rights situation in Bangladesh are based on facts reported in the media, for example, those of Amnesty International and Transparency International and the recent U.S. State Department Report on Human Rights in Bangladesh. Thus the media have contributed significantly to raising national and international awareness of human rights issues.

Nevertheless, despite the widespread media focus, human rights abuses remain rampant in Bangladesh, in the media's opinion largely because of the absence of quick and exemplary punishment of offenders once caught. The legal process is far too slow, inefficient, and corrupt for justice to be meted out quickly. A case in point is the abhorrent practice of male suitors throwing acid on young women who have rejected their marriage proposals. We believe that rapid disposition of these cases and severe penalties for those who indulge in this barbaric practice would have helped to decrease the number of cases of acid throwing. We can take limited satisfaction in the fact that media coverage has decreased it somewhat.

Constraints and Challenges

Even though the print media have played an important role in promoting good governance and in changing the way people in Bangladesh interact with each other and with government, the media's role would be greatly enhanced if their reach were broader. The combined circulation of all the newspapers does not exceed 1 million in a country of 130 million people. Even given the high level of illiteracy and the limited purchasing ability of a large proportion of the population, the circulation base is still smaller than might be expected for such a large population. The reality is that journalism has not yet become relevant to the real needs of ordinary people. The issues the newspapers deal with do not touch their everyday lives. This brings us to the question of urban versus rural readership and media coverage. As most newspaper readers are urban based, rural issues are only dealt with peripherally. However, this still does not adequately explain the limited circulation, because Bangladesh's urban population is large enough to support a far larger readership.

In addition, the low level of industrialization, the small size of the private sector, and the limited range of consumer choices do not support a vibrant advertising market. This makes most newspapers outside Dhaka, where the advertising market is virtually nonexistent, extremely dependent on government advertisements. A single noncompetitive source of financing and that source being the state has two potentially adverse consequences: little diversity in the news and a risk of capture by government propaganda. Both these factors would also reduce the demand for print media.

A small market for advertising also means that most of the newspapers are starved of the investment funds necessary for the staff and technology needed to run high-quality newspapers. Inadequate training for journalists is a reality of Bangladeshi journalism. Most reporters are still overly dependent on official handouts and figures as they are neither trained nor given the resources to carry out their own investigations. A widespread political divide within the journalist community is another severe constraint. Too often journalists are divided along political lines, which inadvertently affects their professional output. I believe that but for this political divide Bangladesh would have had a far more vigorous and effective print media than is the case today.

With private ownership of electronic media now being allowed, Bangladesh is beginning to see the birth of a new trend whose ultimate impact is as yet unknown. For the first time these powerful media are no longer functioning as extensions of the government's propaganda mechanism and are showing signs of independence. Further liberalization is desirable. However, this initiative is still in its infancy. Thus for the time being the onus for highlighting the social, political, and economic issues that lie at the core of the development challenge and for acting as advocates of social change falls clearly on the print media, which have existed for longer, and except for a few months in 1975 have never been in government hands.

For all the media the most important challenge in the years ahead is to consolidate democracy and institute an accountable government. Only then will sustainable development be possible. Bangladesh's democratic journey has been bumpy. The media's biggest challenge is to help establish a functioning democracy, which is central to the achievement of all other developmental goals.

References

World Bank. 2001. *World Development Indicators.* Washington, D.C.

16

How the *Cairo Times* Came to Be Published out of Cyprus

Hisham Kassem

The press in Egypt has a long history of state dominance and control ever since Viceroy Muhammad Ali (1805–48) established an official gazette. Since then Egyptian journalism has had to deal with the government as a major protagonist licensing, prohibiting, and controlling the fate of the fourth estate. The outlook for a free press in Egypt is less bleak today than it was 20 years ago, but the practice of journalism is still tainted by deep-rooted political and historical legacies.

In 1996 I paid a visit to the offices of the Higher Press Council, the body responsible for licensing publications in Egypt. Given its notorious reputation I had no hope that I would be granted a license, but rather viewed this as a courtesy call, or as a knock on the door before I made my entrance onto the Egyptian press scene. A polite bureaucrat met me and explained the licensing procedures. I needed nine other partners holding equal shares to be listed on the license application. We would need to deposit LE 100,000 (approximately US$25,000) for a monthly publication, LE 250,000 for a weekly, and LE 1 million for a daily. The money would be set aside in a designated account and no interest would be paid on it while the application was being processed. Applicants could withdraw the money at any time, but in that case the application would immediately be nullified. The sum of money seemed reasonable, as starting up a publication with any less capital would be impossible. The problem was, as I explained to the polite bureaucrat, that I did not know nine other people who might be interested in investing in a startup press business with me. He told me I was lucky, because a recent amendment had reduced the total of founding members from 200 to 10. I asked him about the time frame for processing the application and he replied that he had not the slightest clue. I tried to corner him, but it was no use, and finally I asked, "When was the last time a publication was granted a license?" He said he could not remember. I asked when the Higher Press Council had last convened. "Two years ago," he said. Had I gone through official channels to set up the *Cairo Times*, a weekly news magazine, it would still be in the realm of something you consulted a palm reader about.

I then had to resort to the usual way of setting up a publishing company. This weird situation, where a publication is oriented toward Egypt, is sold on the street only in Egypt, and generates advertising almost solely from Egypt, but is registered abroad, is not exclusive to the *Cairo Times*, but extends to about 80 percent of Egypt's press.

In the early 1970s, when a new president won the power struggle against his erstwhile colleagues in the previous establishment, he termed his success a victory for democracy and political plurality, and as a result found himself forced to make some democratic concessions to shore up his legitimacy. He lifted press censorship and reinstituted political parties, which his predecessor had banned in 1953. Political parties were spared the harsh licensing laws governing the press and were allowed to set up newspapers. While this helped embellish Egypt's political image as a country with a multiparty system, in reality it led to a situation where political entities controlled the press. However, on the free flow of information front, the situation was a significant improvement. Now at least not all Egyptian newspapers sang the praises of the government in their headlines every morning. Nevertheless, these were not newspapers whose main loyalty was to their readers, but rather, they served the interests of political parties and their political agendas.

On the industry front, the disaster was not as great as with the offshore press, because party funds were available to support the papers and helped curb payoffs and corruption, although they did not prevent it completely. As for the existing press, at the time it was not only exclusively government owned, but every publishing house had a government-appointed censor to censor its papers. Sadat's lifting of censorship amounted to nothing in terms of the free flow of information, because in practice state-appointed editors doubled as censors.

Also the private sector did not yet exist due to harsh, socialist-era licensing laws. This changed when a number of journalists started setting up publishing houses abroad, mainly as offshore businesses in nearby Cyprus. The editorial content was prepared in Cairo and flown to Cyprus, printed there and flown back. A costly, exhausting, and absurd business, it was the only available option. The government realized the danger of this loophole and within a few weeks set up the infamous Office for Censorship of Foreign Publications. The rationale behind the newly established office was that it would safeguard national security and defend society's morals and ethics. In practice, it was a way to keep what could eventually have become an alternative press under control. Today this office monitors and censors 80 percent of Egypt's press. At the time it seemed like a convenient solution. It took the pressure off the government to loosen up on the strict licensing laws and gave publishers an easy alternative to lengthy confrontations with the government, even though a number of these publishers were not politically oriented, but were interested in publishing trade magazines, and therefore were not significantly harmed by censorship. On the surface this seemed to be a convenient solution, but it had many unforeseen effects that would only surface years later.

The first and most serious of these was that in practice, the arrangement was such that the government gave up the right to regulate and monitor the industry in return for controlling content. As the region is ruled either by monarchies or military dictatorships that have huge budgets they can use to embellish their image in the media, the sector became a prime target for corruption. Within a few years, at least 90 percent of the "independent" press had the backing of one or more of these regimes. Sales and marketing managers began to disappear and were replaced by pushy publishers trying to curry favor with the regimes' embassies. As these publications were considered fringe press their distribution figures were not audited. This killed the incentive for competition. Who needs high circulation figures when the picture of a colonel who usurped power in his country or of His Majesty (depending on whether the publisher was conservative or progressive) could do the same trick? In this context note that the government press had its own auditing bureau that always falsified the circulation figures. Thus a situation was created whereby Egypt had no independent auditing bureau overseeing the press.

Another effect of this arrangement was on the press syndicate or union. By law journalists were not entitled to become members of the syndicate unless they were full-time employees of a government or "national" paper or had worked for an opposition party paper for five years. This left roughly 80 percent of Egyptian journalists without any form of collective bargaining or social or medical insurance, and violated the syndicate's own by-laws, which prohibited anyone who was not a syndicate member from the practice of journalism. It also left the members of the Egyptian press syndicate at the mercy of the carefully selected state editors. If the wrong syndicate board was elected, this reflected on journalists' promotions and benefits for the duration of that board's term. To avoid the embarrassment of this situation an informal tradition was established that the chairman of the syndicate would come from the government press while the rest of the board would be composed of representatives of the different political parties and other groups. While this would give the appearance of a democratically elected and balanced board, in practice, most board members were employed by the government regardless of their political persuasion. Thus their service was an extension of their political associations, and the board did not consist of unionists working for the betterment of their profession.

When in 1995 a new press law punished libel with imprisonment of up to 10 years, it took the syndicate a year to reduce the prison term to two years. In 2001 a syndicate board member and the head of its Press Freedom Committee served two-year prison terms for libel. Al Ahram, Egypt's biggest publishing house, chaired by the head of the press syndicate, reported the incident in its flagship paper, the *Al Ahram* daily, on the crime pages. Imagine opening the crime pages and reading stories about a brutal murder, the arrest of a drug trafficker, and the imprisonment of a board member of the syndicate for libel. Egypt is one of the few countries in the world today that penalizes journalists for libel with prison terms.

In the past 10 years four political weeklies and one monthly have been granted licenses. The founders of the four weeklies are figures with strong government connections who never cross what has become known in Egyptian press jargon as "the red line." When one of them passed away and his heirs sold the license to the independent publisher Essam Fahmy, the government revoked the paper's license, even though the sale had been conducted through the stock exchange in a perfectly legitimate deal. It took more than two years of litigation and several court rulings, as well as the ousting of an editor in what was seen as a political deal, to get back the license to print. Ibrahim Al Moalem, who is the head of both the Egyptian Publishers Union and the Arab Publishers Union, founded the monthly. It took him 14 months of persistence to get his license. Other trade publications have been licensed in the medical, interior design, and sports fields, but the licenses have so many restrictions that if a publication changes printing houses or any of its staff without notifying the Higher Press Council, its license is immediately revoked.

Today Egypt has a total of seven locally registered dailies for a population of 65 million. By comparison, nearby Malta has a population of 370,000 and four dailies. By law broadcasting is still restricted to government ownership. The government insists that this is actually public ownership and relies on articles from the constitution such as the following to back its argument:

> Article 30: Public ownership is the ownership of the people and it is confirmed by the continuous support of the public sector. The public sector shall be the vanguard of progress in all spheres and shall assume the main responsibility in the development plan.
>
> Article 33: Public ownership shall have its sanctity. Its protection and support shall be the duty of every citizen in accordance with the law as it is considered the mainstay of the strength of the homeland, a basis for the socialist system and a source of prosperity for the people.

The situation shows no signs of improving. The same mindset still prevails. The director of the Bureau of Censorship has long overstayed his retirement age: he is 75 and was due to retire 15 years ago. Even though the Internet and satellite broadcasting stations have made censorship redundant, there is still no sign of any legislative amendments to correct the situation.

When I first set up the *Cairo Times* I submitted a draft to the Bureau of Censorship before printing. The censors would remove whatever they thought was unfit for publication, though I do not recall any of the censored material as being damaging to national security or corrupting the morals and values of Egyptian citizens (see www.cairotimes.com/the forbidden file). Once we ran a story about some citizens who had contracted HIV through the use of a dialysis machine in a government-owned hospital. The reviewer alerted the censor to the story in a section of the *Cairo Times* called *7days*. I was asked to take out the reference to the story on the grounds that it could create a panic and unnecessary turmoil. After the reviewer left I told the censor that she had asked me to take out the reference to the story, but not the story itself, to which he sternly replied, "Take out the whole story."

Given the situation and my fear of having the entire issue banned, the only argument I had was, "Please don't take out the full story."

"All right, but don't ever do it again," was his reply.

Censorship has become a pointless apparatus with no clear guidelines, rather like the Japanese soldier found 40 years after the end of World War II still guarding his post. Since April 1998 we have stopped giving drafts to the censor and the cost was eight banned issues. In all fairness I must admit that the magazine, while still maintaining its independent editorial line, has not been banned since August 1999, but the fact of having to go through a censor week after week is disturbing.

The most significant international support Egypt has received for its press was a donation from the European Union for LE 300 million (US$750,000) to help pay for a LE 600 million printing machine that one of the government-owned printing houses bought. The printing machine is designed to operate at least 23 hours a day, yet it is used for only 1 hour and remains idle for the rest the day, a big white elephant and a total misuse of European taxpayers' money. Egypt simply does not have enough publications to make full use of that machine. Had that sum been invested in capacity building programs for the press industry, it would have had a significant impact on the country's development.

The mistake I fear the international community will make is that it will focus on training journalists. I am being approached more and more often by international donors and development agencies that want to set up training programs for journalists. However, without press management training programs, those highly trained journalists will have nowhere to write. Publishing houses cannot be independent unless they are managed competently to be self-supporting and self-sustaining. Egypt is currently far from such a situation, with both the government and opposition press under political control and void of any competent management, the offshore or unofficial sector rife with corruption and unaccountable to almost anybody except for its editorial content, and a few nominally independent publications that operate in a circle dominated by all these elements.

Thus the biggest threat to the future of Egypt's information industry is not censorship, but the lack of a solid, established industry. Two things need to happen so that Egypt can improve its free flow of information and have accountability and transparency pave the way for development. First, it must pass legislative amendments to its press laws to permit the free establishment of publications, coupled with clear regulations assuring the transparency of financial records. Second, capacity building programs are needed in all branches of the industry, starting with distribution, advertising sales, financial management, and so on, and concluding with journalism. Then and only then will Egypt's press, long under state tutelage, have new life breathed into it and begin the task of building independent and financially viable institutions that serve the reader above all else and help reconstruct the hobbled fourth estate.

17

The Role of the Media in Zimbabwe

Mark G. Chavunduka

More than any other country on the African continent, with the possible exception of South Africa, which became independent in 1994, Zimbabwe has had a unique history since it gained independence from British rule in 1980. Events have been influenced by a number of inter-related factors that have remained the subject of ongoing academic debate, including a strong and stable economy, notwithstanding 15 years of international sanctions against Rhodesia; a high level of literacy; a politically aware citizenry; and a well-developed transport network.

Zimbabwe's war of liberation (1964–79) was spearheaded by two main groups: the Zimbabwe People's Liberation Army, which was the military wing of the Zimbabwe African People's Union, and the Zimbabwe African National Liberation Army, the armed wing of the Zimbabwe African National Union. The two groups were supported mainly by the Eastern bloc countries, but also received substantial support from the Scandinavian countries.

Both liberation movements argued that their aim was to establish a just, democratic society in which all Zimbabweans would be able to live and work without racial or other forms of discrimination. One of the goals often espoused was for a free and unfettered press. Zimbabwe's independent press had operated under difficult circumstances over the years, with a host of restrictive laws that were carried over from the colonial era, and which the liberation movements promised to repeal once they came to power. Until independence in 1980, the minority government of Ian Smith passed several pieces of legislation aimed at stifling newspaper and television coverage and restricting the flow of information, especially information pertaining to national security and the war effort. This legislation included the Defense Act; the Official Secrets Act; the Powers, Privileges, and Immunities of Parliament Act; the Prisons Act; and the Law and Order Maintenance Act (LOMA), promulgated in 1960, which took pride of place in the state's legal armory.

The colonial government was suffering heavy losses in the conflict with the liberation movements, and laws were put into place to effect a blackout on the reporting of casualties suffered on the Rhodesian Front side. This was coupled with an extensive campaign in the electronic media describing how liberation forces were being killed and retreating to bases in Zambia and Mozambique. The cumulative effect of these laws was so restrictive that newspapers resorted to putting blank spaces in their publications to make readers aware that information had been censored. That practice was also made illegal. The system as it operated then was that officials from the Department of Information and from the Criminal Investigation Department would visit the daily paper close to the time the paper went to bed and review it page by page, removing information they considered sensitive.

The Official Secrets Act made it a crime to give or receive information that the state deemed classified. The Prisons Act made it illegal to divulge details of prisoners and their welfare in the country's prisons. The Powers, Privileges, and Immunities of Parliament Act made it illegal to publish the deliberations of a parliamentary committee until it had made an official report to Parliament. The most notorious piece of legislation was the dreaded LOMA, an all-embracing omnibus law that could cater to every conceivable possibility where the state wanted to take action against individuals. Its penalties could go as high as a fine of US$50 000, 20 years' imprisonment, or both.

Despite their promise to remove these pieces of legislation from the statute books once they took power, the liberation movements soon realized that these laws came in handy, so not only have they remained in effect, but additional repressive legislation has been introduced. Thus with the exception of minor amendments to the Powers, Privileges, and Immunities of Parliament Act, which now allows the reporting of committee deliberations, all these repressive pieces of legislation remain intact 40 years after their introduction. The only other major change was the replacement of the LOMA in December 2001 with an even more restrictive law, the Public Order and Security Act, brought to Parliament for approval in January 2002, but later amended following public outcry over its more drastic provisions. It was finally signed into law in March 2002. This year has also seen the introduction of the grossly-misnamed Freedom of Information and Right to Privacy Act.

Relative Instability in the 1990s

The relative stability of the 1980s was followed by a deterioration in the country's economic situation characterized by high unemployment and high inflation, accompanied by a serious decline in the government's popularity in the second half of the 1990s. This period also saw the emergence of a small but vibrant class of independently-owned newspapers, which became increasingly outspoken against various policies of the new government. Among these were the Catholic owned *Moto* magazine, *Parade*, the *Financial Gazette*, the *Independent*, *The Standard*, and the *Daily News*. The independent press, although with less national reach, competed with the government media, which consisted of the mammoth state-owned Zimbabwe Newspapers Group, which published titles in every province of the country and had a well-established distribution network, and the Zimbabwe Broadcasting Corporation and Television, which even today, supported by the Broadcasting Act, is the country's sole radio and television network.

During this time a concerted effort led by civic groups, the independent press, church organizations, opposition parties, and student bodies forced the government to officially abandon the ideology of a one-party state and to grudgingly allow a multiparty political system. However, the ruling party made a fundamental amendment to the Constitution to create an executive presidency to replace the previous system of government agreed on at the Lancaster House conference in 1979. Prior to the amendment, the Constitution provided for a titular or ceremonial president and a prime minister. With the creation of the executive presidency, the president was given immense powers to govern the country virtually without being accountable to anybody, and was vested with powers to deal with the growing political upheavals that the private press played a large part in championing. Several new laws and regulations concerning government policies have been introduced since then, but these have also been aimed at ensuring that the ruling party ultimately remained in power.

Relations between the government and the independent press became increasingly hostile, and the situation was not helped by the number of exposés of government leaders' private and business activities by the independent press.

The Legal Environment

As the relationship between the media and the government weakened, the straw that broke the camel's back was a story published in January 1999 by me and my chief reporter, Ray Choto, which gave details of an attempted coup by officers of the Zimbabwe National Army. The military arrested me and tortured me for nine days, not because the story was untrue, but because they wanted to learn my sources within the army. I refused to tell them, despite savage beatings and the application of live electric wires to my body.

I was arrested based on the LOMA, under which I was charged with "publishing information likely to cause public alarm and despondency." According to this law, I faced a penalty of US$20,000 plus seven years' imprisonment. Ray and I took the unprecedented step of challenging the constitutionality of the LOMA Section 50(2) in the Supreme Court of Zimbabwe. The full bench heard the case in May 2000, and we succeeded in arguing that Section 50(2) infringed upon other sections of the constitution that guaranteed the freedom of speech. We thus set a judicial precedent, and a number of prominent opposition politicians and others charged under the LOMA have since successfully challenged other sections of the same act.

The government, however, has not taken these important defeats quietly. It has introduced a host of new and more vicious laws, including the Public Order and Security Act, and—specifically for troublesome journalists who had been gloating over the scrapping of the LOMA—the grossly misnamed Access to Information and Protection of Privacy Act, passed by Parliament on January 12, 2002. In addition to these pieces of legislation, several new negative developments aimed at restricting the flow of information have undermined the role of the press. These include the Broadcasting Act, passed last year, which has the effect of increasing state control of radio and television, over which the government already has a monopoly through the Zimbabwe Broadcasting Corporation. The government ignored a court judgment obtained in 2001 by the private Capital Radio to enable it to establish a private broadcasting network.

The most worrisome development for the media has been two pieces of legislation recently passed by Parliament. The first is the Public Order and Security Act, passed on January 10, 2002, which is a clear violation of the freedom of speech, expression, and the rights of journalists and Zimbabweans in general. Among its provisions, Clause 15 makes publishing or communicating information that the government deems is prejudicial to the state a criminal offense. A person may be fined or imprisoned for up to five years for publishing a statement "likely to promote public disorder, or undermining public confidence in the police, armed forces, or prison officers."

Clause 16 of the same act makes it an offense to make a public statement "with the intention or knowing that there is a risk of undermining the authority of, or insulting the President. This includes statements likely to engender feelings of hostility, hatred, contempt or ridicule" of the president, or any "abusive, indecent, or false" statement about him personally or his office.

Additional clauses (23-31) regulate the organization and conduct of public gatherings. A senior police officer is designated to be the regulating authority and has the power to disperse people, ban meetings, and use "reasonable" force if necessary to achieve his or her goals. This new law gives the police a great deal of power. They can now effectively determine when people can and cannot meet for personal business, even when no crime is being committed. The independent press maintains that special laws to protect the president, his honor, or his dignity are unnecessary. The new law gives protection to public figures that is not available to the Zimbabwean people. An implication is that public figures now have protection even when undertaking illegal activities. The law makes it a crime to report leaders' shortcomings, and journalists can be arrested for reporting on any kind of wrongdoing by a public official.

Even more pernicious is the so-called Freedom of Information and Right to Privacy Act, which requires all journalists to apply for a one-year renewable license to be able to work. The license is only awarded if the journalist meets a stringent set of criteria, and inevitably the government reserves the right to revoke such licenses at any time. Any journalist found guilty of any offense faces a fine of up to US$100,000 or two years' imprisonment. This act has since been slightly amended following protests from local journalists and international press organizations and a highly adverse report from Zimbabwe's parliamentary Legal Affairs Committee.

Furthermore, the act states that all journalists must be Zimbabwean citizens, which bars all foreign nationals from reporting in the country; that Zimbabwean citizens must apply to the minister of information for special permission to work for the foreign media; and that journalists are barred from publishing "unauthorized" reports of Cabinet deliberations as well as information that could be harmful to the law enforcement process and national security. Public bodies are also barred from releasing information that relates to intergovernmental relations or their financial or economic interests. The repressive nature of the legislation means that the media are under government control and that journalists are allowed to work only at the whim of government. Along with the Public Order and Security Bill, this gives the government unprecedented powers similar to apartheid-era legislation in South Africa.

Harassment of Journalists to Influence Media Content

Since 1999 harassment of the independent press has assumed proportions that, as the *World Press Freedom Review 2000* puts it (International Press Institute 2000), tell the depressing story of how freedom of the press has been sacrificed at the altar of a government's desire to retain power. There have been several instances of harassment of journalists in the last three years, the first being my and Ray Choto's brutal abduction and torture in January 1999 by the Zimbabwe military. Note that the reason we were detained and tortured for nine days was not because the story we published was false, but because, as the military emphasized, they wanted us to identify our sources. They said that the story contained one or two inaccuracies, but they were not concerned with these. All they wanted was the source within the Zimbabwe military who had leaked the story to us. My refusal to cooperate in this regard is what caused my prolonged detention, despite a total of five High and Supreme Court orders for my release, all of which the state ignored.

Soon after this episode, three journalists from *The Standard* were charged with criminal defamation over a story about the government's defeat in a referendum held in February 2000 concerning a new constitution. The three argued that the charge against them was not valid because the story had not defamed any particular individual, but they were nevertheless found guilty of defamation. On April 7, 2000, a *Daily News* crew was detained for two hours by the Zimbabwe African National

Union (Patriotic Front) youths outside Harare and threatened with death for allegedly supporting the opposition Movement for Democratic Change and sympathizing with commercial farmers. The youths confiscated the journalists' cameras, national identity cards, and government-issued press cards. All four members of the *Daily News* team were then marched to a farmhouse where youth leaders took turns questioning them about their reasons for being in the area.

On April 16, 2000, a number of journalists with CNN, the BBC, and the South African Broadcasting Corporation were assaulted by ruling party militants, who carried placards reading "That's enough." Prior to these assaults, in a farmhouse north of Harare, Alexander Joe and Rose-Marie Bouballa, a photographer and journalist with Agence France Press and a cameraman with Reuters, respectively, were threatened by a group of 50 men armed with machetes and iron bars. On April 22 a homemade bomb exploded on the first floor of Trustee House, which houses the offices of the *Daily News*. Although no one was injured in the blast, it partially destroyed a nearby gallery and the distribution offices of the paper. Then in January 2001, the Z$100 million printing press of the *Daily News* was reduced to ashes in a powerful blast in the early hours of the morning, a day after the minister of information had promised to deal with the paper "once and for all." These are just a few of the many instances of harassment that Zimbabwe's independent journalists have faced, but that many of us have come to regard as an occupational hazard.

The government has also adopted another highly effective method of harassing journalists and media organizations: encumbering them with heavy legal bills. The strategy simply involves charging journalists under various laws and securing long periods of remand or postponement of the cases, even when the charges are obviously completely spurious and have no chance of succeeding. Each time the journalists have to appear in court, and throughout the remand period legal charges continue piling up on the journalists or their publications.

Legal fees are extremely high in Zimbabwe. In the case of Ray and myself, our legal bill as of mid-2000 was close to US$2 million, and were it not for the local and international financial support that we received, *The Standard* would have collapsed under the weight of its legal bills. Frustrated at the international support we received, the government has now moved a step further and made it illegal for local media organizations to receive financial or other material support from foreign individuals or organizations.

Another newer dimension to the harassment has been beating up vendors selling independent newspapers and banning newspapers such as the *Daily News*, *The Standard*, and *The Independent* in certain areas. We have now stopped deliveries to certain trouble spots, including Bindura, Kwekwe, Rusape and Ruwa. People traveling in buses have also been beaten for reading independent newspapers, and many of these incidents have taken place at illegal roadblocks set up by Zimbabwe African National Union (Patriotic Front) militia.

The Media's Contributions to Development

Despite the difficult environment in which the media operate in Zimbabwe, they have still managed to contribute a great deal to improved governance. Probably more than any other single civil society institution, the media have played a prominent role in bringing to the forefront certain decisions taken by the state and in exposing corruption and graft within the government and in the private sector. Furthermore, the media's role in championing causes has led to official changes in state policy.

The first major contribution that comes to mind for me, as a fresh reporter barely out of college in 1987 and working for the weekly *Financial Gazette* newspaper, was an article we investigated and wrote concerning a little-known disease called AIDS that was reported to be taking its toll on members of the Zimbabwe National Army. The details were sketchy, but we were able to put together an article that the epidemic had been brought to the attention of the authorities, but that the Cabinet had decided not to publicize the outbreak because of its possible adverse effects on the country's fledging tourist industry. Amid continued personal threats from the minister of health and from the Zimbabwe National Army, we published the article. It ignited concern nationwide and seemed to be the start of serious coverage of the AIDS epidemic by the media in Zimbabwe. Surprisingly, after lengthy Cabinet deliberations and the appointment of a new health minister, the government's reaction was to facilitate maximum publicity and education about the disease and to warn people about the dangers of promiscuous behavior. That was to be the start of massive donor-funded AIDS projects in Zimbabwe, which persist to this day. We continued to write about the disease, which now claims at least 4,000 lives per week.

At about this time on the political front, the government party was vigorously pursuing the concept of a one-party state based on its long association with communist states dating back to the days of the liberation struggle. Again it was the independent media, which at that time consisted of *The Financial Gazette*, the Catholic *Moto* magazine, and the widely read *Parade* magazine, that spiritedly launched an unrelenting campaign against this type of political system. Students, the churches, opposition politicians, and ordinary members of the public joined the campaign, which eventually led to the president announcing in 1988 that the concept had been officially abandoned, and that the country would continue under a multiparty system of government.

In 1989 the media exposed what was to become known as the Willowgate scandal. At that time Zimbabwe was facing an acute shortage of foreign currency, which was seriously disrupting the operations of commerce and industry. One of the hardest hit sectors was the transport industry, because new vehicle kits for both passenger and commercial use could not be imported. It came to light that the few cars and trucks that were trickling through the assembly lines were being hijacked at source by top government ministers and officials and being sold to desperate individuals and companies at highly inflated prices. So serious was the fraud that one vehicle could change owners four times even before it left the assembly line. The media coverage led to the dismissal of six government officials, one of whom committed suicide over the issue. It also led to some sort of order being restored to the transport sector.

In the mid-1990s two other major exposés by the media led to national outrage and to the government taking corrective action. The first was what became known as the Housing Scandal. This involved a government fund of millions of dollars that had been set up to provide building finance to low-income civil servants. The media revealed that on numerous occasions top government, army, police, and other officials had raided the fund and acquired several properties around the country at highly concessionary rates. The fund did not benefit the poor at all. The saga caused an outcry in Parliament, with the minister of national housing being forced to publish the complete list of individuals who had benefited from the fund and their repayment schedules in the national press.

Similarly, the War Veterans Fund was looted in the late 1990s. This fund had been set up to pay compensation to fighters who had participated in Zimbabwe's liberation struggle and had been disabled. Again, top officials raided this fund in differing amounts. For example the commissioner of police claimed 98 percent disability even though he showed no outward signs of any disability and has been performing his functions without any problem for more than nine years. He received a huge payout. Note that civil service regulations state that anyone who claims more than 20 percent disability must retire on medical grounds.

The media also exposed massive irregularities in what was supposed to be a national land redistribution exercise intended to correct the historical imbalances between huge tracts of prime farming land in the hands of a few whites and blacks who had been settled in marginal farming areas. The media revealed how top officials had allocated several pieces of prime land to themselves, much of which was reduced from productive commercial farming to virtual wasteland. The government was forced to take corrective action, although not all the culprits were punished.

The media also highlighted the looting of diamonds in the Democratic Republic of Congo by members of the Zimbabwe National Army who ostensibly were on peacekeeping duties in that country. This led to an international investigation that confirmed the massive looting of the Congo's natural resources.

Needed Changes to the Policy Environment

In discussing what policy environment is required for effective investigative reporting in Zimbabwe, note that the media are not seeking a situation whereby they operate in a legal vacuum. The press does not seek to become a law unto itself, unaccountable to any legal authority, neither does it seek to be allowed to ride roughshod over people's privacy or over matters sensitive to state interests. What the media seek is a level playing field where the rules and regulations are clearly stated; where those laws are fair; and where they do not impose unnecessary restrictions on the media's ability to report on matters of national interest, whether they concern events in public institutions or the private lives of public officials. This situation clearly does not exist in Zimbabwe at present, as the wide array of repressive legal instruments promulgated at a time when the country was embroiled in a war of liberation is still in effect.

The state has constantly sought to move the goal posts as far as the media's operating environment is concerned. The media would like to see a number of changes to the policy environment that would enable effective investigative reporting. The first change would be to scrap all the colonial laws that unnecessarily infringe upon the operations of the press and that no longer have any place in a modern, democratic society.

Second, all the more recent pieces of legislation, such as the Public Order and Security Act and the Freedom of Information and Right to Privacy Act, must also be abolished. In my opinion the law already makes sufficient provision for dealing with cases of defamation when individuals, private or public, believe that their reputations have been unjustly tarnished by the press. Further legislation that exclusively protects public figures and is not available to ordinary citizens is not called for.

Third, because of the nature of the media's work, a law is needed that allows the media access to certain information and documents, especially state documents, on reasonable grounds. The media are fully aware that revelations of certain issues might affect state security, but this should not be a reason for a blanket denial of access. We would like to see legislation along the lines of the Sunshine Act in the United States that would enable the press to obtain court orders for information whose release is in the public interest.

Current laws are overwhelmingly skewed against the press, to the extent that even the most spurious claims against newspapers can succeed. The legal system must be revised to place the onus of proof on the plaintiff rather than on the media organization to prove or disprove claims against an individual or institution. However, while legislative changes are a major and important first step, they are not enough. Zimbabwe's judiciary has often upheld the rights of the press, but sometimes to no avail. Court orders, not only those affecting the media, but also individuals and other sections of society, have been routinely ignored by the government, which needs to be put under increased international pressure to uphold the rule of law and restore a credible legal system.

Mechanisms also need to be established whereby government departments and other public institutions respond to inquiries from the media in a timely manner. When questions are put to government officials, they often ignore them completely, respond some weeks later, or respond by way of a public denial once the newspaper has decided to go ahead with the article despite the absence of a comment from the department concerned. Sometimes journalists are then arrested and charged, even though they had made every effort to seek official comment. For example, the coup story that led to my arrest and torture was one we could have published 10 days earlier. We held that story while we sought comment from the military authorities, and despite several assurances that the minister of defense would be responding, he never did. Satisfied with the substance of our information, we decided to publish. The following day the minister was on national radio and television vigorously denying the story and promising that I would be dealt with. In conclusion, the environment that the Zimbabwean media operate in is clearly one that is largely determined by the political and personal interests of those in authority. Laws are constantly changed to suit the whims of those in power, while media practitioners can never be certain whether or not they are on firm legal ground. Despite these severe limitations, the private press has maintained its vibrancy and determination, has contributed immensely to the country's development, and has forced a reluctant government into being more transparent and open. This endeavor has entailed many casualties and more are likely, but the determination and resolve of Zimbabwe's private media means that they will continue to strive for better governance and accountability.

References

International Press Institute. 2000. *World Press Freedom Review 2000*. Vienna.

18

Journalism after Communism:
Ten Commandments for a Decent Journalist

Adam Michnik

One hundred years ago Emile Zola, an outstanding French novelist, made his mark upon the 20th century by defending Alfred Dreyfus, the Jewish French army officer falsely accused of espionage. In his famous letter "J'accuse" (1898) Zola wrote to the president of the French Republic:

> What a spot of mud on your name—this disgraceful Dreyfus case! . . . I shall tell the truth, since I made an oath that I would publicize it, if the justice authorized to deal with this case does not reveal the whole truth. It is my duty to speak, since I do not want to be one of those who are guilty of this crime. The phantom of an innocent man, suffering in dreadful tortures for the crime he did not commit, would haunt me at night.

Zola stood for a man who had suffered a wrong; for enduring truths; for the idea of a tolerant state; and for the good name of his homeland, France. He made the Dreyfus Affair a benchmark for public opinion. The France of yesterday spoke in its attitudes toward the case: conservative, traditionalist, monarchist, Catholic, and closed to strangers. But in the struggle to pronounce Dreyfus innocent, the France of tomorrow was heard: democratic, secular, republican, and tolerant. It was Zola who made this latter France win.

Zola formulated the standards and morals for writers and intellectuals for the whole century. This is why any writer, critic, or journalist must see Zola's face if he is to understand his profession as something more than just a way of earning money.

Reprinted with the permission of the *Media Studies Journal* (Spring/Summer 1998, pp. 104–13.)

Thanks to Zola, for the next century an intellectual journalist felt morally obliged to be involved in politics as an indication of concern for the common good and not as a struggle for power. And it remained this way for good and for bad. Zola's success became a source of courage for writers, but it also became a source of conceit. It fixed the image of an intellectual being, the defender of human rights, but also as a preacher who states what is good and what is bad in public life. This is why during the whole of the 20th century one saw intellectuals not only on the front lines of struggles against totalitarian systems, but also among those praising these regimes. Following Zola, intellectuals took pride in their belief that they were charged with ripping the mask from society. The conceit bred from this pride, however, led to a blind fascination with fascism or communism, which promised to eliminate all evil from this world. An intellectual's glory and defeat in the 20th century had its source in the same great gesture by Emile Zola.

After the collapse of the communist regime when the free press was new in Poland, I often thought of Zola, because I had to think about the experience of the 20th century journalists who had become a powerful and integral element in modern democracy. However, I also thought about the experience of those journalists who, at the same time, became components in the corruption of modern democracy.

June 1992 shall be remembered in Polish history as the "Night of the Long Dossiers," which is a Polish paraphrase and allusion to the notorious "Night of the Long Knives," when Adolf Hitler did away with his political opponents. Fortunately, in Poland events took a gentler course. The government that lost the parliamentary majority charged that during the period of dictatorship the president, the speaker of the Parliament, the minister of foreign affairs, the minister of finance, and many Parliament members, among others, had been communist secret police agents. The state was on the verge of self-destruction. This was also a moment of trial for the media. And it became obvious to journalists that we are bound by civic responsibility. This is why we almost unanimously refused to publish the list of names of those alleged agents, which the minister of the interior in the falling government had constructed based on dossiers kept by communist secret police agencies.

We decided that a dossier prepared by mortal enemies in order to annihilate a person in a moral or physical sense cannot be a reliable source of knowledge about an activist in a democratic opposition movement. I learned from this scandal, for the first time, that it is very easy to become an instrument in somebody else's hands, and that resistance to secret manipulations must be an issue of dignity in journalism. This resistance is a concern about the ecology of our profession and the cleanliness of the environment of public debate.

I thought about this again when in November 1995 another minister of the interior accused the prime minister of the crime of spying for Soviet intelligence. The prime minister was a former functionary in the Communist Party during the period of dictatorship. The minister of the interior was an outstanding Solidarity activist, later a political prisoner, and then one of the leaders of the underground structures of the democratic opposition. Whom was I to believe? The postcommunist prime minister, who stated that he had never been a spy, or the minister of the interior whom I had known since the time of the underground struggle against dictatorship?

In this most spectacular political scandal of recent years the media were divided in a very characteristic way. Some—almost blindly—trusted the word of the minister of the interior. Others—also blindly—trusted the word of the prime minister. And then the leaks from the government's secret services began. The postcommunist media received information that pointed to the prime minister's innocence. The post-anti-communist media received information that confirmed the minister of the interior's accusations. The whole scandal, which fortunately did not shake Polish democracy too badly, was a great trial for the media. It also became a lesson in the distrust of governmental secret services that get involved in a political struggle. It turned out that the charge of espionage directed against the prime minister were based on totally unconvincing evidence.

Since then I have been certain that the main enemy of free media is the domination of ideological conviction over informative reliability. Another enemy is blindness, which leaves one able to make only trite observations. And there is one more lesson to learn from this scandal: in a democratic country the media are tempted to use exclusive information leaked from such secret services, but these leaks are just an attempt to steer the media from the outside, to manipulate public opinion.

In light of such episodes, people ask me: "Which side are you on? Which party or alliance do you support?" We do not see a place for ourselves in divisions understood in such a way. We are for Poland being a sovereign and lawful state, a state of parliamentary democracy, and a market economy; a state that is consistent in its efforts to join the structures of European-Atlantic civilization and faithful to its historical identity. Only such a Republic of Poland shall be able to oppose all kinds of extreme attitudes, regardless of the name we apply to them: "black" or "red" fascism, "red" or "white" bolshevism. This is why we do not identify ourselves with any political party, whereas we are willing to treat each of them as a normal component of Polish pluralism, provided it implements the goals of Polish democracy. We want to be a component of Polish democracy, one of its institutions. This is how we perceive our role in Polish public life. We also want to stick to our basic principles. Here they are: the 10 commandments (plus 1) of a decent journalist after communism.

Commandment 1: "And God spoke all these words, saying: 'I am the Lord your God, who brought you out of the land of Egypt, out of the house of bondage. You shall have no other gods before me.'"

Our God, who led us out from bondage, has two names: Freedom and Truth. To this God we must subordinate ourselves completely. This God is jealous. He demands absolute loyalty. If we bow to other gods—the state, the nation, the family, public security—at the expense of freedom and truth, we shall be punished with the loss of reliability. Without reliability, one cannot be a journalist.

Freedom means equal liberties for everybody, not only for me, but also for my antagonist, for everyone who thinks differently. We must defend freedom for all, because this is the essence of our profession and vocation. The only limitation to our freedom is the truth. We are allowed to publish everything we write, but we are forbidden to lie. A journalist's lie is not only a sin against the principles of our profession, it is also a blasphemy against our God. A lie always leads to enslavement. Only the truth has liberating power.

Nevertheless, this does not mean that we can feel superior, that we are the repositories of the ultimate truth, and that we are allowed, in the name of this truth, to silence others. Simply put, we are not allowed to lie, even if it is convenient to us or to our friends.

Commandment 2: "You shall not take the name of the Lord your God in vain; for the Lord will not hold him guiltless who takes his name in vain."

Freedom and truth are valuable and celebrated words. One must use them cautiously and seriously. The abuse of sacred words makes them cheap and banal. We see it all the time in Poland. Under the slogan "God-Honor-Homeland" political parties run in parliamentary elections, strikes are staged, and roads are blocked by farmers who demand tax allowances. To squander these great words in electoral struggles or political smear campaigns is, in fact, to sneer at them. When we listen to these great words being transformed into political platitudes we feel, almost physically, that, in the phrase of the revered 19th century Polish poet Adam Mickiewicz, "A word lies to the voice, and the voice lies to thoughts." We also feel that the words lose their meaning. Language ceases to be a means of human communication and becomes a method of blackmail. If servility can be called courage, conformity called common sense, fanaticism called faithfulness to principles, and moral nihilism called tolerance, then a word becomes a means of falsifying reality. This is how "newspeak" is created. Using newspeak is like paying with forged money. We are not allowed to do this.

Commandment 3: "Remember the Sabbath day, to keep it holy. Six days you shall labor; and do all your work; but the seventh day is a Sabbath to the Lord your God. On it you shall not do any work."

Your work is a continuous mess, performed in a state of haste and hustle. You know that a newspaper must be delivered to the kiosks early in the morning, that you must edit the news, commentary, features, and photos and have it all set in columns. You do all this in a rush, under strain. It is often a routine and mechanical activity. You often forget the meaning of your work. This is why you should remember the Sabbath, the day on which you have time for thinking. Put some distance between yourself and the world. Relax and think about the most important things.

Think: as we are all sinful, maybe you should be more moderate in throwing stones at sinners. Think: maybe there is some truth, albeit partial, in the reasoning of your adversaries. Maybe they are driven by reasons, emotions, or interests that you do not understand.

Get some distance from your professional perspective. You are not only a journalist; you are also your parents' child, a parent to your children, a friend to your friends, a neighbor to your neighbors. Look at the world in a different way: from below, from above, from the side. And then look at yourself, at your pigheadedness and phobias, your easy patterns and hidden grudges. Self-examination is necessary, and you will not be able to do an honest self-examination without this.

Commandment 4: "Honor your father and your mother; that your days may be long in the land which the Lord your God gives you."

Respect your heritage. You do not work on a virgin land or a wasteland. Others worked here before you, and you are their descendant, heir, and pupil. This does not mean you should not be critical, but it means that respect and knowledge are necessary so that you can make fair judgments about the history of your nation, your town, your environment, your family.

What was this history like anyway? It was full of nobility and cunning, compromise and revolution, heroism and banality, tragedy and hope, conspiracy and collaboration, orthodoxy and heresy. Select individual threads from this history and construct your own tradition, a chain of people, ideas, deeds that you want to continue. But if you do not want to become a victim of self-idealization you must remember the whole of this heritage. Your adversaries also stick to the commandment to honor their fathers. Try to understand them.

Self-idealization leads directly to self-delusion; to stupidity; and to ideological, ethnic, or religious intolerance. The foundation of human community is memory and respect for one's own mother and father, for their faith, love, and hope, but also for other people's mothers and fathers. Otherwise human thought falls into the trap of lies and narcissism, or into the trap of amnesia, which makes one believe that the past is not worthy of moral judgment. Czeslaw Milosz wrote about a world in which nothing really exists and nothing is true, nothing is final, nothing is worthy of love or worthy of opposition. But what meaning do life or work have then?

> With not quite truth
> And not quite art.
> And not quite law
> And not quite science,
> Under not quite heaven,
> On the not quite earth
> The not quite guiltless
> And the not quite degraded.

Commandment 5: "Jesus said: Love your brother as you love yourself."

Love yourself. Value your dignity; cultivate it. Cultivate your conscience. Ask yourself difficult questions and answer them honestly. See yourself as a subject and not as an object. You should understand your responsibility for your fellow man. This fellow man may be a stranger; he may come from another family, another nation; still you should treat him the same as you treat yourself.

Reject nationalism. George Orwell wrote:

By "nationalism" I mean first of all the habit of assuming that human beings can be classified like insects and that whole blocks of millions or tens of millions of people can be confidently labeled "good" or "bad." But secondly—and this is much more important—I mean the habit of identifying oneself with a single nation or other unit, placing it beyond good and evil and recognizing no other duty than that of advancing its interests. Nationalism is not to be confused with patriotism. ... Patriotism is of its nature defensive, both militarily and culturally. Nationalism, on the other hand, is inseparable from the desire for power. The abiding purpose of every nationalist is to secure more power and more prestige, not for himself but for the nation or other unit in which he has chosen to sink his own individuality.

Orwell was a wise man. And Father Janusz Pasierb, the late art historian, priest, writer, and poet, when he spoke about love for a fellow man and explained to this fellow man: "It is good that you exist," and then added, "It is good that you are different." Because a fellow man is different. He has a different biography, nationality, religion. Quite often he is in conflict with your biography, nation, and faith. But in spite of this, love him as you love yourself. Respect his right to be different, to have another culture, another memory, even if he was your enemy. In other words, do not generalize. Differentiate the sin from the sinner. Try to see in an adversary a partner with whom you must communicate, not an enemy whom you must destroy.

Commandment 6: "You shall not kill."

You can kill with words; this is the poisonous charm of a journalist's work. But one can also do good with words: one can disenchant totalitarian enchantment, one can reach tolerance, one can given testimony to truth and freedom. One can analyze words. This is what the classics of Polish journalism did. Michal Glowinski, Stanislaw Baranczak, Jakub Karpinski, and Teresa Bogucka were the pioneers of thorough analyses of newspeak, of the speech of killers of words, of the speech of hatred.

Struggle with your pen, but struggle in a decent way, without hatred. Do not hit more than is needed. Do not think that you have a prescription for being just. And, especially, do not think that you can be "God's arm" when you strike a deadly blow at your adversary. When you accuse him of the lack of patriotism, of corruption, of treason, always remember that you are killing him. And the truth will be revealed anyway, and then you shall pay for your rascality, even if it shall be only before your conscience. Do not kill. Do not do to others what you do not like others to do to you.

Commandment 7: "You shall not commit adultery."

Be faithful, at least to the few principles that you consider valuable and to at least a few people to whom you owe loyalty. Do not be a hireling. Do not degrade your profession for power, for money, for "I couldn't care less." Only freedom allows you to be faithful. Moreover, the ability to be faithful—to principles, values, people—is proof of the ability to be free. Treason and hatred are the symptoms of internal emptiness that precede capitulation and enslavement. Nothing is more disgraceful than treason.

Commandment 8: "You shall not steal."

Nothing is more compromising for a journalist than plagiarism. It is not only a blow to another man—it strikes the collective sense of justice and rightness.

Plagiarism permits corruption in public life; it is an act of unfairness applied as a method. Plagiarism destroys the ethos of journalism. Manipulating truth, stupefying people—these are specific symptoms of theft, of corruption of the journalist's profession. We read great words: God, honor, homeland. If they are uttered by a corrupt journalist, he steals these words and deprives them of their initial meaning. Values that are turned into emblems die. This is why journalists should tell themselves: do not steal. In other words, do not copy more than is absolutely needed.

Commandment 9: "You shall not bear false witness against your neighbor."

Conflict is normal in a democratic society and state. That is why the style of this conflict, its culture and its language, are so important. We journalists are responsible, to a great degree, for this style. It is worthwhile to realize once again certain obvious things. The commandment to reject lies ("false witness") does not mean that you should be a free-spoken person. Not every truth must be uttered immediately, every day, regardless of the pretext. The poet Mickiewicz wrote:

There are truths which a sage tells all men,
There are some which he whispers to his nation,
There are those which he entrusts to his friends,
And there are those which he cannot disclose to anyone.

What are these truths that cannot be disclosed? They are those that relate to the deepest secrets of conscience, truths uttered during confession, known to God and a priest, and not to the reading audience. These are truths about human intimacy, whose disclosure is a wound inflicted upon a fellow man.

At the same time, revealing only a part of truth about a fellow man can be a perfidious lie about his life, like writing a biography of St. Paul and taking into account only the period when he was Caesar's servant and persecuted Christians. The ability to bear true witness to one's fellowman, especially when this fellow man is our adversary, is a basic test of our professionalism and humanity.

A person who fears to meet others in truth and freedom uses falsehood. False witness is always a symptom of weakness and lack of faith in one's own reasoning. Just as freedom results from truth, violence results from falsehood. Bearing false witness has its murderous logic: it leads from democratic debate to a cold civil war; it turns a partner into an adversary and an adversary into a deadly enemy. The language of false witness is a way of dehumanizing an adversary. If you are against abortion you become similar to the perpetrators of homicide from Auschwitz and the gulag. If you are for the separation of church and state you become an enemy of God, goodness, and the truth of the Gospel. If you refuse to discriminate against people who have different biographies you become a traitor to your nation.

False witness may harm or even kill a victim, but the one who utters it is, at least, injured. False witness is a sin against a fellow man and a blasphemy against God. It is also a capital sin against the standards of our profession.

Commandment 10: "You shall not covet your neighbors house, you shall not covet your neighbors wife. "

You shall not covet anything, including respect and popularity. If your ambition is to be popular and respected, achieve it yourself with your own work, talent, and courage and not by destroying the other person. Ambition is a wonderful and enriching feature, whereas envy is self-destructive. Envy stupefies and degrades; it kills nobility and the ability to experience higher feelings.

Envy of other people's property leads to cowardice, to flattering the powerful and condemning the weak, to flattering crowds and participating in campaigns against the lonely. Envy infringes on the code of normal professional decency, on normal loyalty toward other people.

Commandment 11: Do not mix.

I heard this additional, 11th commandment from people who like to drink alcohol (even in moderate doses). They said: do not mix drinks. Do not mix wine with vodka, cognac with beer, plum brandy with champagne. Such mixing results in an awful hangover. I have tried not to mix genres. Journalism is neither politics nor religious service; it is not trading in flowers or giving a university lecture; it is not a compilation of the telephone directory or a football match, even though it is a bit of each of these things. Each area of life has its own peculiarities, its own rules, its own ethical codes. A politician should not pretend to be a priest, a journalist should not pretend to be a politician. A businessman must seek a decent profit, and a journalist must stick to truth and freedom.

Corruption can infect all areas of public life. We know politicians who get rich when they should not get rich, we know priests who incite hatred, we know businessmen who steal and give bribes. We also know corrupt journalists who use propaganda instead of information, pseudo-advertisements instead of reliable descriptions, noisy smear campaigns instead of sensible discussions.

Am I, therefore, naive in presenting this wishful thinking addressed to myself and to my colleagues from the brotherhood of journalists? Probably I am. But when I lose this naiveté I will change my profession. As of yet, though, I do not know which profession I will choose.

19

The Survival of a Provincial Television Station in an Era of Enormous Changes

Viktor Muchnik and Yulia Muchnik

In 1990, during the wave of democratization in Russia, a new law broke the state's monopoly on the airwaves and legalized private ownership of the media. Across the vast expanses of the country, dozens of local journalists, entrepreneurs, and technicians, working in complete ignorance of each other, found ways to start tiny, private television broadcast operations to serve their local communities. One of these early pioneers was the independent station TV-2 in Tomsk, a university city of about 700,000 people in eastern Siberia.

Like most other television stations in the early years, TV-2 was essentially built from nothing. It survived because the demand for the new service was great and it was the first in Tomsk to address it. However TV-2 was different from some of the other early stations in its obsession with journalistic quality, something that became clear much later, as their local media professionals began to meet their colleagues from around the country and compare notes. This difference was eventually recognized and rewarded with national awards. Today Russia has well over 600 private, local television stations, and the country's economic conditions have changed dramatically. TV-2 continues to thrive, even as it faces new challenges. The authors of this article, who have been participants in this venture since its inception, are working there still.

The Story Starts

The story starts in 1990. At that time a successful young journalist at the local state television station in Tomsk, Arkadii Maiofis, suddenly quit his job and started telling

Translated from the Russian by Persephone Miel, Internews Network's regional director for Russia.

his friends that he was going to start a new kind of television station, a nongovernmental, independent television station. To understand the extravagance of this claim, we need to remember the times. *Perestroika* and *glasnost* were clearly already coming to an end; the authorities were loudly, and progressively more so, talking about the need to enforce order; people were morosely trading food rationing coupons; and nobody was expecting much good to come of any of it. Maiofis's project seemed like a utopian dream, all the more so because other than Maiofis, practically, none of the future participants in this adventure had any practical experience in television. Nevertheless, the idea was attractive. One couldn't help thinking: "Yes, of course, this regime will eventually crash. In the end perhaps we'll be able to speak our minds."

At the time we began this venture there were practically no discussions of money or ownership. Of course we knew that we'd have to buy some kind of equipment, and we did, on credit. The guarantor of our loan was, at the time, the chair of the Tomsk City Council (at that time we did not yet have mayors) who knew Maiofis as a journalist. Having connections clearly helped us. The actual loan came from a commercial bank (these banks had just been created in Tomsk) with the name Finist (Phoenix), a name clearly chosen to refer to the bank's ability to come back to life no matter what difficulty it faced, just like a phoenix, which continually burns up and is reborn from the ashes. Since giving us that loan the bank has gone out of business. It went up in flames, but unlike a phoenix, permanently. With that first fortuitous loan of about US$15,000 the television station bought its first equipment: two videotape players, a couple of televisions, and a video camera (all meant for home use, of course).

Maiofis planned to repay the loan by publicizing the possibility of subscribing to decoders. A decoder was an instrument used to unscramble the signal sent by the new independent television company. He assumed that people who wanted to watch the new programs would buy the decoders from TV-2. Arkadii, who was not very technically oriented, apparently sincerely believed in the possibility of encoding the signal with the help of a small, black box with two cables sticking out of it, and the city believed it too. People stood in line for the decoders, and they sold out in a flash. To understand why, one needs to comprehend the buying habits of those years. In the Soviet economy, where scarcity was the norm, a key term was "it's appeared." Everyone assumed that the item in question—cooking oil, pantyhose, plumbing fixtures, whatever it might be—had appeared in limited quantities, and that by the next day, the next 2 hours, or the next 15 minutes it would all be gone. In 1991 everyone was sure that small portions of goods were being dumped in stores for the last time, and that soon nothing at all would be available. The decoders were clearly perceived as being among these ephemeral goods; people were convinced that in a day or two they too would be sold out like everything else.

The entire population of Tomsk may not have been as entranced by the idea of independence as those who began the television station, but beginning on May 15,

1991, the day of TV-2's first broadcast, every day the channel showed new American movies, sometimes as soon as two weeks after their Hollywood premieres. Needless to say, these were pirated video copies. At that time no one in Russia was thinking much about intellectual property law. So city residents were buying decoders to watch pirated movies on the new channel and the television company was paying back its loan bit by bit. During this time, everyone was told that the final tests for encoding the signal were under way, and that soon they would need the decoder to keep watching these programs. This stimulated demand for the decoders. Only later did it become clear that the decoders, no matter how you attached them to a television set, could not decode anything. At the same time, given its limited technical expertise, TV-2 had no ability whatsoever to scramble its signal. One might have expected the whole affair to lead to a certain loss of enthusiasm for the idea of independent television among the population. But then August 1991 happened.

In Moscow a coup was in progress, tanks were in the streets, state television was showing only "Swan Lake," and the provinces had no information about what was happening. In Tomsk, from the very first day of the coup, the only place people could find out what was going on in Moscow was on TV-2. From its first broadcast, and even before the coup, the company had been a locus of zealous anticommunism. The very first original program on TV-2, which aired on May 15, was the first in a series called "Great Scoundrels from History." The program was dedicated to the first Chinese emperor Tsin Shi Huandi, and emphasized that eventually all empires inevitably collapse under their own weight, and that their destruction is a good thing. In a word, TV-2 was "positioning" itself (at the time, of course, none of us knew that pseudo-scientific term) as an opposition television station. The mascot we chose for TV-2 was Rudyard Kipling's black cat from the *Just So Stories*, the wildest and most independent of the animals who "walked by himself." In August 1991 the cat naturally clambered up onto the barricades with the democrats and strolled proudly beneath the new Russian flag.

During the August coup TV-2 had a crew shooting in Moscow and sending the tapes back to Tomsk on Aeroflot's daily flights. It was a passionate time, almost unreal when we look back on it now. But we were sincere when we said things like, "They will not prevail, victory will be ours." In Tomsk for those three days every single person seemed to be watching TV-2. Afghan war veterans came to the station and offered to guard the premises from any attempts to interfere with our broadcasts. The company, at that time, was crowded into a few rented rooms. People who were listening to foreign radio broadcasts would call the station and share information, which would immediately be announced live on the air. And most touching of all, people brought us food and, if memory serves us right beer, as a demonstration of solidarity. There was a moving unity of journalists and citizens. The coup, as we all know, failed; however, the city came to trust the journalists of TV-2.

Learning How Television Really Works

During all this, how to produce real television and how to make money on it remained quite hazy concepts. There really was no one to teach us. In those years both the Tomsk University Journalism Department and Tomsk State Television were entirely Soviet entities, and they provided negative examples. "We want to make different TV," everyone at TV-2 was saying, but what did different mean? In those first couple of years TV-2 produced dozens of programs. There were programs for children and for gardeners, for automobile lovers and for dog fanciers, for fans of alternative cinema and for heavy metal music devotees. In a word, the content was varied and whimsical. The first editing suite that appeared was a place for fearless experimentation, where we were intuitively mastering the rules of film editing.

We had no money, either for technical development or for salaries. Meanwhile, we came up with plan after plan, each more grandiose than the previous one. In one newspaper interview Maiofis announced that TV-2 had already established a bureau in Germany, and that soon we would have them in Moscow, in the United States, and in other Siberian cities too. With these burgeoning plans and lack of financial management, a financial crisis should have been inevitable. It was only two or three years after this that the first financial manager appeared at TV-2. Even at this time comparing income, which by then we had, and expenses, he was in the habit of telling the management that by all economic laws the company could not exist and that its economic collapse was inevitable in a matter of months. Unable to bear this economic absurdity, he quit, missing his chance to see more optimistic numbers.

It's hard not to believe that if the people who launched TV-2 had had more knowledge of what television really involved, the story of TV-2 would never have begun. Ignorance of how professional, commercial television was supposed to work, or even of the basic rules of market economics, among the staff as well as among the advertisers and audience, freed the company from the need to follow them. The station courageously constructed its own know-how, repeatedly going into debt, gradually paying back the loans, and once not managing to pay one back before the creditor himself managed to go bankrupt and forgot about us. Back then we did not know that a company needed to have a "mission"; we'd never heard the word, but the reality is that if there is one thing that TV-2 did have in those years it was a mission; people were united by an idea. As we didn't know of the existence of lots of "don'ts," it seemed to us that there lots of "we cans."

Over time, bit by bit, we nonetheless did learn some of the business rules of the television profession. TV-2 did have advertisers. In the beginning they were tiny stores, the little kiosks that at that time were sprouting up in Russia like mushrooms after a rain shower. For a while we even had advertisements from an escort agency (that part of the market was experiencing explosive growth at the time). We also had many private announcements, the equivalent of classified advertising. People were selling sewing machines, buying bathroom tiles, exchanging apartments. Our very first advertiser was an Uzbek gentleman from the Fergana Valley who had brought a number of sacks of walnuts to Tomsk and wanted to sell them in a hurry. His little announcement of walnuts for sale was our first commercial.

Thanks to Internews, which had appeared in Russia at the beginning of the 1990s, American consultants began to come to Tomsk. Robert Campbell helped establish TV-2's news program "Chas Pik" ("Rush Hour"). Meg Gaydosik explained the basic principles of how advertising sales work. We are grateful to both of them. Our consultants probably had lots of problems working with us that they tactfully concealed. The gulf of knowledge between us and these professionals was huge, but it always seemed that the notorious "cultural differences" didn't exist. Our consultants also had a mission: they liked building independent television from nothing. And so did we.

It was during those years that the persistent myth started circulating in Tomsk that TV-2 was living on American money. This belief had no basis in reality. We were living off advertising revenues, and living very modestly, not on dollars but on homegrown rubles. This myth, however, turned out to be useful. People thought we were strong, and that perhaps it was better not to interfere with our operations. Otherwise, who knew, perhaps the American Sixth Fleet might have sailed down the Ushaika River.

Television Tomsk Style

Over the years we learned many useful things, for example, how to do reporters' stand-ups and how to use natural sound in our stories. We also learned how not to "cross the line" when shooting videos and how it's preferable, when editing, not to put one medium shot right next to another. We learned how to obtain information, how to structure a news program, how to plan a budget, how to talk to advertisers, and what a "brand" is and how to build one. We also learned how to maintain our distance from all branches of government and political parties. Overall, we apparently learned how to do television more or less professionally. We gave up on dozens of unprofitable programs and concentrated on projects that received good ratings and could bring in money. We built our own building, opened two radio stations, created an advertising agency, and are now getting a handle on the Internet. Since the end of the 1990s, TV-2 programs and individual journalists working for TV-2 have won prizes at prestigious national television competitions ("News—Local Time," "All Russia," "Lazurnaya Star") several times. In 2000 TV-2's news program won a national television award, the TEFI, Russia's equivalent of the Emmy. In general, it's not a bad record.

Throughout the years we held on to some of our ideas. First, provincial television should have its own flavor. Tomsk television should not be like Moscow television, or even like television in Ekaterinburg. Only we could tell our residents what was happening at home or around the corner. We could tell them in a language that they understand, without agitation or melancholy, and with a bit of irony, because a lightly ironic tone is useful for talking about the multifaceted Russian reality in an epoch of such huge changes.

Second, having learned to keep ourselves at an appropriate distance from politicians, we have never concealed that just as before, in the beginning of the 1990s, we are devoted to the idea of free television, not dependent on anyone. The "commissioned" (by political interests) journalism that has become so commonplace in Russia thankfully never took root at TV-2. We must admit that we did not learn how to keep our distance from politicians right away. Like all the free press in Russia at the beginning of the 1990s we were against the communists and for the "democrats." We actively participated in politics and it took some time for us to learn that being dedicated to ideas was one thing, but forming political alliances with specific people was quite different.

Third, in an economic sense we were all always devotees of the idea of Juche (a philosophy of self-reliance from the Democratic People's Republic of Korea): when you strike, you must rely on your own strength alone. We learned to spend only what we earned on the local advertising market and not to put our hopes on massive infusions of money from somewhere outside. In May 2001 we celebrated TV-2's 10th anniversary. By Tomsk standards we celebrated rather extravagantly. By then, we could afford to.

Today

In 2001, not long after those celebrations, a controlling interest in TV-2 was sold to the Moscow oligarch Mikhail Khodorkovsky, the richest man in Russia and the owner of the Yukos oil company. At that time Yukos had already been pumping Tomsk oil for several years and was responsible for nearly half the city's budget. During the preparations for this sale, serious disagreements arose within the group of like-minded friends who had founded TV-2. Those who had initiated the sale maintained that television is a business, and from this point of view the sale of shares was an excellent deal. They argued that the investment package we would get would give us the opportunity to make a serious technological leap, and that nobody would ever again offer us the kind of money that Khodorkovsky was offering. At the same time we were witnessing the high-profile closing of NTV. NTV's predicament led everyone to question whether independent television could exist in Russia without a political "roof," that is, a protector.

Those who were against the deal said that it would turn TV-2 into a political instrument, that it contradicted all the original ideas on which the company was founded. However, the people opposing the sale had enough common sense not to go to extremes, not to step over a line that would have forced TV-2 to split up. One of the important lessons of the NTV story for the Tomsk station was the sad and permanent destruction of a once unified and talented group of colleagues. We wanted to avoid that. When it became clear that the deal with Yukos was unavoidable, TV-2 ratified editorial by-laws that made direct interference in editorial policy by the owners difficult, and elected a chief editor, as stipulated in Russia's media law. Khodorkovsky himself met with the staff of TV-2 in an effort to convince them that he didn't intend to interfere with existing editorial policy in any way, and that he was as devoted to liberal values as the station's journalists. So eventually the deal was completed and the station entered a new stage of its history. What it will be like, as inexperienced journalists love to write in their signoffs, only time will tell.

Index